BIBLIOGRAPHY AND
TEXTUAL CRITICISM

PATTERNS OF LITERARY CRITICISM

General Editors

MARSHALL MCLUHAN
R. J. SCHOECK
ERNEST SIRLUCK

BIBLIOGRAPHY AND TEXTUAL CRITICISM

English and American Literature,
1700 to the Present

Edited by
O M BRACK, JR.
and
WARNER BARNES

With an Introduction by
O M BRACK, JR.

The University of Chicago Press
Chicago & London

Standard Book Number: 226–06984–2 (clothbound)
226–06984–0 (paperbound)
Library of Congress Catalog Card Number: ~~74~~ *92463*

THE UNIVERSITY OF CHICAGO PRESS, CHICAGO 60637
THE UNIVERSITY OF CHICAGO PRESS, LTD., LONDON
PUBLISHED IN CANADA BY
THE UNIVERSITY OF TORONTO PRESS, TORONTO 5, CANADA

For

WILLIAM B. TODD

CONTENTS

CONTENTS

PREFACE

The present collection is an introduction for graduate students in bibliography and textual criticism and a handbook for literary scholars who, often without training, find themselves editing the texts of English and American writers. In this volume, the subject specifically is post-Renaissance literature. (Another volume in the Patterns of Literary Criticism series will deal with Renaissance literature.) Although English textual scholarship concerned with the transmission of post-Renaissance texts has grown up primarily since World War II, it is heavily indebted to previous work on Renaissance texts. The introductory essay briefly traces this development.

Our selections include some half-dozen essays by W. W. Greg, Fredson Bowers, William B. Todd, and Bruce Harkness which are considered classics in the field. Beyond these there are several hundred articles from which the remaining dozen could be chosen. Certainly studies on Faulkner rather than Hemingway, Blake and Keats rather than Hawthorne and Twain, and Eliot rather than Yeats could easily have been substituted. For this reason we have compiled a selective bibliography of articles and books for further reading. (The footnotes to the introductory essay are not mere reference citations but are intended to direct the student to further reading.) Although certain aspects of bibliography, such as descriptive bibliography, typography, paper manufacturing, copyright, literary forgeries, and authenticity and attribution, are obviously related areas, our principle has been to limit our choice of articles for inclusion to certain basic theoretical problems and to those studies of eighteenth-, nineteenth-, and twentieth-century authors which provide representative examples of the application of bibliography to literary study. *Bibliography*, as used in the following essays, will usually mean analytical bibliography, the empirical investigation of a book as material object to determine the process of its manufacture, or textual bibliography, the application of the methods of analytical bibliography to specific textual problems, for example, the study of the transmission of the text.

The editors should like to express their gratitude to the authors and publishers who have kindly permitted them to use the copyrighted essays which appear in this volume. Special thanks are due to Professor Richard J. Schoeck and Professor Ernest Sirluck, general editors of this series, for encouragement and much invaluable advice. Professor Paul Baender and Professor Oliver Steele have also made many useful suggestions and have given liberal moral support. Work on this volume could not have been completed without the excellent assistance of Sharon Graves of the University of Iowa Center for Textual Studies. Finally, in gratitude for continued advice, encouragement and patience, this book is dedicated to Professor William B. Todd.

O M BRACK, JR.
WARNER BARNES

BIBLIOGRAPHY AND TEXTUAL CRITICISM

INTRODUCTION

For English literature, modern critical bibliography (or, as it was to be called, "New Bibliography") began about the turn of the century and was largely concerned with Shakespearean texts.[1] The central problem of the nature and authority of the Shakespeare Quartos and their relation to the First Folio, which has occupied textual scholars for the last seventy years, had scarcely received attention from earlier editors. This neglect was largely the result of textual pessimism based on a mistaken interpretation of a passage from Heminge and Condell's address "To the great Variety of Readers": that "where [before] you were abus'd with diuerse stolne, and surreptitious copyes, maimed, and deformed by the frauds and stealthes of iniurious imposters, that expos'd them: euen those, are now offer'd to your view cur'd, and perfect of their limbes; and all the rest, absolute in their numbers, as he conceiued them." As a number of the plays in the folio were discovered to be printed from the quartos Heminge and Condell had described as "maimed and deformed" they were assumed to be imposters and hence no confidence could be placed in their texts. The most articulate example of this pessimism is Samuel Johnson's:

> To have a text corrupt in many places, and in many doubtful, is, among the authours that have written since the use of types,

[1] I am primarily concerned here with analytical and textual bibliography of printed texts. Although there has for some years been a measure of agreement on general procedures for textual criticism of manuscripts sufficient to give the editor of classical and medieval texts confidence in his methodology, the editor of printed texts has not been so fortunate. Even such provisional agreement as has been reached on procedures for editing printed texts is of relatively recent development. See Paul Maas, *Textual Criticism*, translated by Barbara Flowers (Oxford, 1958) for a convenient summary of the principles for dealing with manuscript texts. The problems of textual criticism applied to printed books, particularly early dramatic texts, and the way these problems differ from those found in manuscripts are discussed in Fredson Bowers's *Bibliography and Textual Criticism* (Oxford, 1964). For a summary of Shakespearean textual scholarship from the late nineteenth century to 1942, see F. P. Wilson, "Shakespeare and the New Bibliography," in *The Bibliographical Society 1892–1942: Studies in Retrospect*, ed. F. C. Francis (London, 1945), pp. 76–135. See also J. Dover Wilson, "The New Way with Shakespeare's Text," *Shakespeare Survey* 7 (1954): 48–56; 9 (1956): 69–80; 10 (1957): 78–88.

almost peculiar to Shakespeare. Most writers, by publishing their
own works, prevent all various readings, and preclude all conjectural criticism . . . .

But of the works of Shakespeare the condition has been far
different: he sold them, not to be printed, but to be played.
They were immediately copied for the actors, and multiplied by
transcript after transcript, vitiated by the blunders of the pen-
man, or changed by the affectation of the player; perhaps
enlarged to introduce a jest, or mutilated to shorten the representation; and printed at last without the concurrence of the
authour, without the consent of the proprietor, from compilations made by chance or by stealth out of the separate parts
written for the theatre: and thus thrust into the world surreptitiously and hastily, they suffered another depravation from the
ignorance and negligence of the printers, as every man who
knows the state of the press in that age will readily conceive.

It is not easy for invention to bring together so many causes
concurring to vitiate a text. No other authour ever gave up his
works to fortune and time with so little care . . . no other editions were made from fragments so minutely broken, and so
fortuitously reunited; and in no other age was the art of printing in such unskilful hands.[2]

With this view of the printed texts of Shakespeare and the
resulting conclusion that all the early texts of Shakespeare had
equal authority, "it therefore became proper and necessary to
look into other old editions, and to select from thence whatever
improves the Author, or contributes to his advancement in
perfectness . . .: that they do improve him was . . . an argument
in their favour."[3] This tradition established by eighteenth-cen-

[2] *Proposals for printing, by subscription, the Dramatick Works of
William Shakespeare*, pp. 3–4, quoted by W. W. Greg, *The Shakespeare
First Folio* (Oxford, 1955), pp. 83–84. Chapter 3 is a summary of this
editorial tradition. For a summary of this tradition and its relationship to
recent textual studies in classical literature, medieval literature and the
New Testament see G. M. Story, "Some Recent Theories of Textual
Criticism," in *Thought from the Learned Societies of Canada* (Toronto,
1962), pp. 25–37.

[3] Edward Capell's Introduction to his edition of Shakespeare (1768),
quoted in Alfred W. Pollard, *Shakespeare's Fight with the Pirates* (London, 1917), p. 89. As late as 1877, H. H. Furness wrote in the Preface to
his *Variorum Hamlet* that he had "availed himself of the liberty to form
his own text" (vol. 1, p. vii) and could remark in the *Variorum King
Lear* (1880) concerning the order of the two quartos: "So much for the
Quartos, with their puzzling, interlaced texts. It is comforting to reflect
that to decide upon precedence, in point of time, of these editions, or in

tury editors governed editorial practice throughout the nineteenth century.

The early editors were seriously handicapped by their ignorance of printing and book production in Shakespeare's day and
by their assumption that the texts of Shakespeare should be edited
in the same manner as the manuscripts of Greek and Roman
authors. Frequently, classical texts exist in a *polygenous* group,
that is, texts which fall into two or more lines of descent from a
common ancestor (nonextant), with the earliest extant members
unrelated to one another as either ancestor or descendant. Printed
texts usually exist in a *monogenous* series of texts, all of which go
back to a single extant ancestor.[4] "The heart of the matter lies
in this difference, for the bibliographical method depends upon
such direct and contiguous derivation from a preserved common
ancestor. If a continuously touching line of direct descent can
be worked out, and if no outside influence can be established as
entering at any point, then only one document, the first printed
edition, can be authoritative. An editor, therefore, cannot pick
and choose among variants in such monogenous series of texts
according to his preference, since the only ground for preference
is the tacit assumption that independently derived pure readings
are being selected from multiple sources. This assumption a
monogenous series denies."[5] The early editors of Shakespeare,
failing to understand this, collated the extant texts and con-

---

other words, which is Q1 and which is Q2, belongs wholly to the province
of Bibliography; it has no bearing whatever on the elucidation of the
text" (p. 359). Quite the contrary: it has considerable bearing, since the
independent readings of the 1619 Jaggard quarto are totally without
authority. See W. W. Greg, "On Certain False Dates in Shakespearean
Quartos," *The Library*, 2d ser. 9 (1908): 113–31, 381–409; and W. J.
Neidig, "The Shakespeare Quartos of 1619," *Modern Philology* 8 (1910):
145–63.

[4] Ronald B. McKerrow, *Prolegomena for the Oxford Shakespeare*
(Oxford, 1939), p. 36.

[5] Fredson Bowers, *On Editing Shakespeare* (Charlottesville, 1966), p.
85. Alice Walker has argued that "collateral substantive prints stand
broadly in the same relationship to the 'true original' as collateral manuscripts at the head of a series to the archetype. Consequently, Housman's
principles for the editing of Juvenal and Manilius hold good for the
editing of those plays of Shakespeare for which we have two or more
substantive prints" ("Collateral Substantive Texts," *Studies in Bibliography* 7 [1955]: 51). For further discussion see Bowers, *Shakespeare*,
pp. 91–96 and note 42.

structed a synthesis by incorporating the 'best' readings. To improve this situation, obviously it was necessary to develop bibliographical techniques which could reconstruct the printing process of Shakespeare's day and establish relationships among the various texts.

The textual revolution in Shakespeare was brought about by three great English scholars, Alfred W. Pollard, Ronald B. McKerrow, and W. W. Greg. The first real manifesto of the new bibliography was Pollard's *Shakespeare's Folios and Quartos*. Although a number of Pollard's views have since been supplanted, his distinction between good and bad quartos and their relationship to the folio has become part of the fundamental knowledge of Shakespearean textual criticism.[6]

This distinction between good and bad quartos not only restored textual authority to certain of the quartos but reclaimed credit for the folio as well. Once authority for these texts had been established, it was necessary for an editor to determine the relative authority of different editions of a play before establishing the text. Only with this knowledge of the history of his text could the editor proceed with "acceptable emendation."[7]

But the consequence of Pollard's book is far greater than any single theory could make it: "it established critical bibliography for good and all as a valuable aid to literary scholarship, and especially to editors of printed texts."[8] Coupled with increased knowledge of Shakespeare's stage, spelling and punctuation, and of the printing-house practices of the day, bibliographical pessimism of two centuries was replaced by healthy optimism. J. Dover Wilson recalls the optimism of the period: "It looked as if editors had only to decide, in regard to any particular original text, whether it was printed from Shakespeare's manuscript or from a prompt-book, and then proceed to edit it in light of

[6] Hardin Craig has attempted to reopen this issue in *The Bad Quartos Reconsidered* (Stanford, 1961).

[7] "By an acceptable emendation I mean, of course, one that strikes a trained intelligence as supplying exactly the sense required by the context, and which at the same time reveals to the critic the manner in which the corruption arose" (W. W. Greg, "Principles of Emendation in Shakespeare," *Proceedings of the British Academy* 14 [1928]: 5). "No emendation can, or ought to be, considered *in vacuo*, but that criticism must always proceed in relation to what we know, or what we surmise, respecting the history of the text" (p. 8).

[8] J. Dover Wilson, "New Way," 7: 53.

the newly acquired knowledge of how Shakespeare wrote, how he spelt, how he punctuated, and how at times he revised portions. of the dialogue by making additions in the margin." But, he adds, "the situation turned out to be far more complicated than was, or could be, realized at that stage."[9] Although subsequent discoveries were to disclose more complications, the hope that what Shakespeare had written could be recovered was not destroyed. The New Bibliographers went a long way toward determining which texts were printed from what kind of copy. They formulated principles of emendation and, in general, carried out a systematic study of the transmission of Shakespeare's text:

> The most important contribution that critical bibliography has made to the textual criticism of Shakespeare is its insistence upon the importance of discovering all that can be known or inferred about the manuscript from which the printer set up his copy, and all that can be known or inferred about what happened to the manuscript in the printing-house, and upon the corollary that once it has been established that one text is more authoritative than another that text shall be chosen as the copy-text and no alterations admitted into it without consideration of the bibliographical evidence.[10]

The theories and techniques in bibliography and textual criticism worked out by Pollard, McKerrow, and Greg to solve the problems of Shakespeare's text proved to be adaptable, with certain essential modifications, to the study of more modern books.

Looking back, it seems almost inevitable that the earliest scholarly interest would focus on the origin and early history of printing. The Bibliographical Society alone, in its first decade of existence, published a considerable amount of information on all aspects of early printed books. Early in the twentieth century Pollard, McKerrow, Greg, and their associates, by application of

9 J. Dover Wilson, "New Way," 11: 79.

10 F. P. Wilson, *Retrospect*, p. 124. In recent years Shakespearean textual studies have shifted from a preoccupation with the manuscripts, now lost, which underlie the first printed editions of the play to a concern with compositor identification and the various modifications of the copy during the printing process itself. This new emphasis has been styled the "Newer Bibliography." See, for example, Fredson Bowers, *Textual and Literary Criticism* (Cambridge, 1959), pp. 77–116; "Established Texts and Definitive Editions," *Philological Quarterly* 41 (1962): 1–17; and Charlton Hinman, "Shakespeare's Text—Then, Now and Tomorrow," *Shakespeare Survey* 18 (1965): 23–33.

the knowledge and techniques gained from these early studies, demonstrated the value of analytical bibliography to the textual criticism of Shakespeare and the early dramatists. Their work brought about a considerable shift of interest from the earlier period to the Renaissance.

The Renaissance continues to be a fruitful area for bibliographical and textual studies. Several multivolume editions of Shakespeare are in progress; the works of other dramatists of the period as well are being made available in authoritative editions, both individually (e.g., R. A. Foakes's *Revenger's Tragedy*) and in complete works (e.g., Fredson Bowers's *The Dramatic Works of Thomas Dekker*).[11] The Yale edition of the works of Saint Thomas More will include all of More's extant English and Latin writings and is undoubtedly "our century's most ambitious editorial enterprise in the non-dramatic, sixteenth-century field." Because More wrote during a period when manuscript and printed book overlapped, the textual problems presented by the various versions and editions embrace "almost every kind of problem that an editor of sixteenth-century material is likely to encounter."[12]

Brief mention should also be made of current work in the Restoration. In addition to the editing of individual plays and poems, several multivolume projects are under way. The California Dryden, for example, has provided scholars with not only a great deal of knowledge concerning textual matters of this period, but also a number of new techniques and mechanical devices useful for textual work in any period.[13] One of the most ambitious editorial projects in the Restoration is the Yale *Poems*

[11] Cyril Tourneur, *The Revenger's Tragedy*, ed. R. A. Foakes (Cambridge, Mass., 1966); Fredson Bowers, ed., *The Dramatic Works of Thomas Dekker*, 4 vols. (Cambridge, 1953–61). For a discussion of these editions see S. Schoenbaum, "Editing English Dramatic Texts," in *Editing Sixteenth-Century Texts*, ed. R. J. Schoeck (Toronto, 1966), pp. 12–24; and Clifford Leech, "A Note from a General Editor," ibid., pp. 24–26.

[12] Quotations are taken from R. J. Schoeck's comments on Professor Richard S. Sylvester's address to the University of Toronto Conference on Editorial Problems, 15 Oct. 1965 (*Editing Sixteenth-Century Texts*, pp. 7–10). An example of the complex problems facing the editor of a text of Saint Thomas More can be seen in Sylvester's edition of *The History of King Richard III* (New Haven, 1963).

[13] *The Works of John Dryden* (Berkeley, 1956–). A number of the techniques and devices are discussed by Vinton A. Dearing in the essay included in this volume.

on Affairs of State: "Most of these poems were issued anonymously or pseudonymously; the innumerable scribes who made copies of them are unknown; the proprietors of the unlicensed presses which printed some of them are in all but a few cases untraceable." Thus editors have been forced to use innovative editorial procedures which enable them to deal with texts of indeterminate authority, many of which exist in an extraordinarily large number of copies.[14]

II

Interest in the application of new bibliographical methods to the printed books of the eighteenth century in the postwar period has been greatly sparked by the work of William B. Todd. Perhaps his foremost discovery was the significance of press figures. These are small symbols at the foot of some pages in certain books printed between the late seventeenth and early nineteenth centuries, and can serve as aids in distinguishing different impressions and editions.[15] In numerous articles Todd has used press figures and other largely neglected evidence to solve bibliographical problems.

The willingness to exploit the evidence gathered from the study of the book as artifact (that is, the examination of the book in order to recover the details of the process of its manufacture) has characterized much of the work done on printed books of the eighteenth century. In addition to information about book production deduced from books themselves, new light has been cast on printing-house practices of the day by the study of surviving printing-house records.[16] Important work has also been done on

[14] George de F. Lord, ed., *Poems on Affairs of State,* vol. 1, *1660–1678* (New Haven, 1963), pp. 441–43.

[15] William B. Todd, *The Identity and Order of Certain XVIII Century Editions* (University of Chicago Microfilm Editions, 433, 1949); "Observations on the Incidence and Interpretation of Press Figures," *Studies in Bibliography* 3 (1951): 171–205. See also G. Thomas Tanselle, "Press Figures in America: Some Preliminary Observations," *Studies in Bibliography* 19 (1966): 123–60.

[16] Important records are William Bowyer's Paper Stock Ledger, an account of the paper allotted for Bowyer's printing jobs from 1717 to 1765, and the recently discovered record of Bowyer's printing house over the years 1730–39 which gives details of compositors' and pressmen's work, and the Printing Ledgers of William Strahan, an account of Strahan's printing activities from the establishment of his business in 1738 until his death in 1785. For Bowyer see Herbert Davis, "Bowyer's Paper

paper and the use of type, initials, factota, and ornaments as a means of identifying the printer of a book.[17] In addition to this work in analytical bibliography, there has been significant work in textual bibliography, for example, Donald F. Bond's edition of *The Spectator*, Arthur Friedman's edition of the *Collected Works of Oliver Goldsmith*, the Yale Johnson, the Wesleyan Fielding, and the Iowa Smollett.[18] But many of the uncertainties in eighteenth-century bibliography discussed by Todd in his *New Adventures Among Old Books* still exist.[19] Much remains to be done.

Todd's alarming representations of the state of eighteenth-century bibliography and his conclusion that "we go on preparing catalogues of what we think are first editions, publishing reprints of what we believe to be the authoritative text, and uttering opinions on what we suppose are the final statements of our authors, all in ignorance of evidence which, some time, may require that we do everything over again"[20] are equally applicable to the state of nineteenth- and twentieth-century bibliography. For as late as 1959 Matthew J. Bruccoli, in an article entitled "Twentieth-Century Books," argued that:

Stock Ledger," *The Library*, 5th ser. 6 (1951): 73–87; and J. D. Fleeman's report in the *Times Literary Supplement* 19 Dec. 1963, p. 1056. The Bowyer material is currently being prepared for publication by Keith I. D. Maslen. For a description of the Strahan ledgers and a rationale for their publications, see O M Brack, Jr., "The Ledgers of William Strahan," *Editing Eighteenth-Century Texts*, ed. D. I. B. Smith (Toronto, 1968), pp. 59–77. Mr. Brack, Patricia Hernlund, and William B. Todd are currently preparing a compilation of the information in these ledgers for publication. See also D. F. McKenzie, *The Cambridge University Press, 1696–1712: A Bibliographical Study*, 2 vols. (Cambridge, 1966).

[17] See, for example, W. M. Sale, Jr., *Samuel Richardson, Master Printer* (Ithaca, N. Y., 1950).

[18] Donald F. Bond, ed., *The Spectator*, 5 vols. (Oxford, 1965); Arthur Friedman, ed., *Collected Works of Oliver Goldsmith*, 5 vols. (Oxford, 1966); only one volume of the Wesleyan Fielding has appeared, Martin Battestin, ed., *The History of the Adventures of Joseph Andrews* (Middletown, Conn., 1967). The problems of preparing a reasonably complete edition of Johnson are discussed by Donald Greene in "No Dull Duty: The Yale Edition of the Works of Samuel Johnson," *Editing Eighteenth-Century Texts*, pp. 92–123.

[19] (Lawrence, Kans., 1958).

[20] *New Adventures*, p. 33.

In a way, the title of this article is misleading. The bibliographical study of twentieth-century books is not a self-contained entity bounded by the year 1900; rather it is an extension of the methods applicable to nineteenth-century books. The period of machine printing was born when stereotyping was introduced at about 1825, and achieved its majority when linotype was invented in 1884–1885. But the bibliographer of twentieth-century books cannot find aid or comfort in this. He cannot draw upon a solid body of work on nineteenth-century books because the nineteenth century has not yet received bibliographical attention.[21]

Numerous explanations have been offered for the dearth of scholarly bibliographical examination of books in the nineteenth and twentieth centuries.[22] One explanation for this is the faith placed in the modern mechanical means of producing books that are 'perfect', or so nearly perfect that a careful examination of them would be fruitless. Another is the belief that the "standardization of book-production, the technological developments in printing and binding, the changes in distribution methods and in reading habits" have created problems so complex as to be beyond comprehension.[23]

That machine-printed books produce textual problems rivaling any of those found in hand-printed books has been amply demonstrated.[24] The nineteenth century alone produced more radical changes in book production than the previous 350 years of printing. These changes affected not only the manufacture of the book but the distributive trades as well. While the theories

[21] *Library Trends* 7 (1959): 567. There are, of course, exceptions. See, for example, the excellent bibliographical techniques displayed by John Carter and Graham Pollard in *An Enquiry into the Nature of Certain Nineteenth Century Pamphlets* (London, 1934).

[22] Michael Sadleir in "The Development during the last Fifty Years of Bibliographical Study of Books of the XIXth Century," *Studies in Retrospect*, pp. 146–58, suggests nineteenth-century bibliography has suffered because it has not attracted sufficient scholarly interest. Additional reasons are suggested by Fredson Bowers in his description of the state of nineteenth- and twentieth-century bibliography in *Principles of Bibliographical Description* (Princeton, 1949), pp. 356–66.

[23] John Carter, "Some Bibliographical Agenda," *Nineteenth-Century Books* (Urbana, 1952), p. 78.

[24] See pp. 23–40. See also R. C. Bald, "Editorial Problems—A Preliminary Survey," *Studies in Bibliography* 3 (1951): 3–17; Carl J. Weber, "American Editions of English Authors," in *Nineteenth-Century Books*, pp. 27–50; Fredson Bowers, *Textual and Literary Criticism*, pp. 1–34.

governing the interpretation of bibliographical evidence and the general principles of editorial procedure have remained the same, new printing methods and the mass production of books, accompanied by the standardization of spelling and uniformity of type face, paper, and ink, have forced the bibliographer of modern books to devise new techniques for the solution of his problems[25]—techniques, for example, such as that devised to discover concealed printings in plated books by comparing multiple copies on the Hinman Collating Machine and by measuring gutter margins.[26] Differentiation of impressions is extremely complicated for modern books. Publishers cast duplicate plates for a promising title and store the second set until the originals wear out. In some cases the duplicate plates do not contain revisions made in the originals and, when used late in the printing history of the book, introduce an earlier or new textual state.[27]

In the twentieth century photo-offset printing has created special difficulties. A book may be reprinted by photo-offset by the photographing of two copies, which may or may not be identical; this may introduce an earlier or new state of the text by the photographing of an early impression. Resetting a book by monotype tape, more common in Europe than in the United States, presents other difficulties, but little is known about these problems.[28] Much more work must be done on imposition before these problems can be solved with any degree of certainty.[29]

In recent years nineteenth-century literature in particular has been receiving a great deal of editorial attention. In addition to the textual work on individual titles, the editing of complete editions with full and accurate texts of major nineteenth-century

[25] Hereafter *modern books* will be used to refer to machine-printed books of the nineteenth and twentieth centuries. The problems related to the mass production of books become important in the last half of the eighteenth century. See p. 142 and William B. Todd, "Recurrent Printing," *Studies in Bibliography* 12 (1959): 189–98.

[26] See pp. 235–43.

[27] Matthew J. Bruccoli, "A Mirror for Bibliographers: Duplicate Plates in Modern Printing," *Papers of the Bibliographical Society of America* 54 (1960): 83–88.

[28] Bruccoli, "Twentieth-Century Books," p. 572.

[29] Oliver L. Steele has done important work on this problem. See, for example, "Half-Sheet Imposition of Eight-Leaf Quires in Formes of Thirty-two and Sixty-four Pages," *Studies in Bibliography* 15 (1962): 274–78.

American authors has received impetus from the Center for Editions of American Authors of the Modern Language Association of America, and numerous editions are now underway. Work is being done on English authors as well; editions of Mill, Arnold, and Dickens, now in progress, are representative.[30]

Some interesting work has been done in publishing history, particularly on individual authors and their works,[31] but fundamental questions remain unanswered: When did it become ordinary for the publisher, rather than the printer, to style an author's manuscript? When did publishing and printing become separate functions and how?[32] Many such questions will be answered by future research, for there is an abundance of research materials: volumes of reminiscences, commemorative volumes issued by various publishers to celebrate their anniversaries and, in some cases, the archives of publishers.[33]

Clearly, bibliographical study is in no position to recline on its laurels—nor by its very nature is it ever likely to be. But the essays in this volume indicate a gratifying measure of progress in accommodating these and other raw materials to the ends of textual criticism and editing.

III

The opening essay, Bruce Harkness's "Bibliography and the Novelistic Fallacy," is a plea for the application of bibliographical techniques to the novel. Although Harkness is concerned particularly with what he calls the novelistic fallacy—the failure of scholars to apply the same rigorous standards of textual study to novels that they apply to poems and plays—the implications are far-reaching and concern most post-Renaissance literature

[30] The editions of Hawthorne, Twain, and Mill are discussed in the essays below.

[31] See the essays on Yeats and Hemingway below.

[32] Fredson Bowers, "Old Wine in New Bottles: Problems of Machine Printing," *Editing Nineteenth-Century Texts*, ed. John M. Robson (Toronto, 1967), pp. 9–36.

[33] "At any rate, the problem for the post–1870 period is evaluating so much evidence and cutting through so many documents, in order to build up, slowly and carefully, a history of each firm and its influence book by book." G. Thomas Tanselle, "The Historiography of American Literary Publishing," *Studies in Bibliography* 18 (1965): 36–37. This essay surveys past work on the history of American literary publishing and suggests many future lines of investigation.

and approaches to it. The essay asks that critics in general pay more attention to bibliography, and bibliographers to criticism, for the importance of sound texts should make their efforts coordinate.[34]

The earliest essay in the collection, upon which many editorial procedures have been based, is W. W. Greg's "The Rationale of Copy-Text," delivered before the English Institute in 1949 and published the next year in *Studies in Bibliography*. In this essay Greg draws his famous distinction between substantive and accidental variants—substantives being those readings "that affect the author's meaning or the essence of his expression," and accidentals being those readings "such in general as spelling, punctuation, word-division, and the like; affecting mainly its formal presentation . . . ."[35] He argues that the earliest authoritative text should serve as copy-text and control the accidentals and that the copy-text readings may be emended with substantive variants from later editions. Underlying this argument is his theory that the earliest printed text based on an authoritative manuscript will most nearly represent the author's own accidentals and that the accidentals of later editions more often than not represent corruption. Greg's theory was restated and codified the following year by Fredson Bowers in "Current Theories of Copy-Text, with an Illustration from Dryden."

Greg's theory of copy-text was based on Renaissance texts for which no prepublication form survived. His theory often needs modification before it can be applied to modern texts.[36]

---

[34] To the reasons given in this article for the lack of bibliographical work in novels Professor Harkness adds a new one in "Bibliography and Modern Studies," *Approaches to the Study of Twentieth-Century Literature* (East Lansing, 1963), pp. 3–24 and the discussion of the paper pp. 25–46. He suggests "that the critical climate today is such that the critic considers the work to be entirely self-contained, and to have nothing to do with the author or his intentions, and it follows from this that you use any text that you happen to have to hand" (p. 25). The paper is concerned in large part with the practical problems, rather than the principles, of producing good texts for undergraduate and graduate study.

[35] See p. 43.

[36] "As editors approach the present day with its extreme uniformity in typesetting and the common contractual practice of imposing a rigid house-style on an author's manuscript at the publisher's before copy is sent to the press, the dwindling authority of the accidentals may make Greg's distinction of little account." Fredson Bowers, "Textual Criticism," *The Aims and Methods of Scholarship in Modern Languages and Literature*, ed. James Thorpe (New York, 1963), p. 41.

On the basis of his experience with Hawthorne texts, Fredson Bowers argues in "Some Principles for Scholarly Editions of Nineteenth-Century Authors," that "when an author's manuscript is preserved, this has paramount authority."[37] Bowers points out that there are thousands of accidental variants between the manuscript and first printing of *The House of the Seven Gables*, *The Blithedale Romance* and *The Marble Faun*, and that though Hawthorne approved the variants, punctuation in the manuscripts must be restored because "the real flavor of Hawthorne, cumulatively developing in several thousand small distinctions, can be found only in manuscript." Yet in "Problems in Editing Mark Twain," William B. Todd argues for using the first printed form as basic text because "unlike Hawthorne's carefully fashioned manuscripts, Twain's essentially are drafts, more often than not hurriedly written with ampersands, dashes, abbreviations, and other kinds of shorthand, then in this form amended, cancelled, extended, and then again as all evidence indicates, gradually refined to the form perfected in print."[38]

Greg's theory of copy-text has been challenged on other grounds by John M. Robson, textual editor of *The Collected Works of John Stuart Mill*. In most instances Robson chooses as copy-text "the last edition known, or reasonably assumed, to have been revised by Mill." Although aware of Greg's condemnation of "some eccentric editors who [take] as copy-text for a work the latest edition printed in the author's lifetime, on the assumption, presumably, that he revised each edition as it appeared," he defends his position on three grounds:

> First, the pejorative words, "on the assumption, presumably," in Greg's statement do not apply in our case, and without them much of the force of the condemnation fails of application. Second, the differences between printing and publishing practices in the Renaissance on the one hand, and the nineteenth century on the other, suggest a proper divergence as justified as that between procedures in editing classical and Renaissance texts. Third, the nature of Mill's corpus suggests a procedure different from that which is obviously proper in some imaginative works, and might be proper in most.[39]

[37] See p. 199.

[38] See p. 207.

[39] John M. Robson, "Principles and Methods in the Collected Works of John Stuart Mill," *Editing Nineteenth-Century Texts*, p. 114. See also pp. 209–43 below.

The views expressed by Bowers, Todd, and Robson make up only a small portion of the continuing debate on the question of copy-text.[40]

A general introduction to textual editing is provided by Vinton A. Dearing's "Methods of Textual Editing."[41] Dearing describes in some detail what he considers the eight essential processes the textual editor must pass through to produce a critical edition. He discusses not only the decisions and procedures involved in editing a text, such as determining the basic text, emending, and writing the textual notes, but also the kinds of questions that ought to be asked and satisfactorily answered before an edition can even be undertaken: What kind of edition will it be? A reprint of a selected text or a 'critical' edition which admits editorial correction and emendation?[42] Will it be edited with contemporary spelling ('old-spelling') or modernized?[43]

[40] This fragmentation in the theory of copy-text and the failure of textual critics to agree on a meaning of the term is discussed in Paul Baender's "The Meaning of Copy-Text," read on 3 Nov. 1967 at the Bibliography section of the Midwest Modern Language Association and published in *Studies in Bibliography* 22 (1969): 311–18. After outlining the confusions in the use of the term "copy-text," Baender argues that it should mean "that version and physical form of text an editor chose to send his printer" and concludes that the "major advantage of copy-text as printer's copy is that it precludes no principles for the establishment of text because it is a function of none. Thus an editor would have to establish his text through principles relevant to his situation, and he would have to describe their bearing in detail: he could not rely upon a naming of copy-text to support doctrinaire procedures or to suggest a rationale he did not provide" (pp. 317–18).

[41] See also Fredson Bowers's useful introduction, "Textual Criticism," *The Aims and Methods of Scholarship in Modern Languages and Literatures*, pp. 23–42.

[42] For discussions of this problem see Bowers, "Principles and Practice in the Editing of Early Dramatic Texts," in *Textual and Literary Criticism*, pp. 117–50; "The Method for a Critical Edition," in *Shakespeare*, pp. 67–101; and "Established Texts and Definitive Editions." There has been a lively, current discussion of this and other editorial procedures in the *New York Review of Books*. See Edmund Wilson, "The Fruits of the MLA: I. *Their Wedding Journey*," 16 Sept. 1968, pp. 7–10; "The Fruits of the MLA: II. Mark Twain," 10 Oct. 1968, pp. 6–14; and replies from various correspondents, 19 Dec. 1968, pp. 36–38.

[43] Currently, the opinion seems to be that texts intended for scholarly use should retain the contemporary spelling whereas texts intended for general reading should be modernized. The matter remains controversial, with much of the argument centering on whether or not one can have a 'critical' edition without 'old-spelling.' For a discussion of the problem

Will there be funds for research and publication? How long will it take to complete the project? etc. Included briefly in his discussion also are the various uses of the computer in textual studies.

In "The Aesthetics of Textual Criticism" James Thorpe draws a distinction between the "potential" work of art—the various forms of the work as it exists before the author is ready to release it to his usual public—and the "actual" work of art—the "version in which the author feels that his intentions have been sufficiently fulfilled to communicate it to the public, as his response to whatever kinds of pressure bear on him, from within or without, to release his work into a public domain." The textual critic, Thorpe argues, is therefore limited to the intentions of the author because the work of art "can only have such integrity, or completeness, as the author chooses to give it, and the only reasonable test of when the work has achieved integrity is his willingness to release it to his usual public," and "the task of the textual critic [is] to recover and preserve its integrity at that point where the authorial intentions seem to have been fulfilled." When a literary work exists in several versions, the author has in fact written separate works, and "there is no simple way to choose the best."[44]

---

see John Russell Brown's argument for modernized texts in "The Rationale of Old-Spelling Editions of the Plays of Shakespeare and his Contemporaries," *Studies in Bibliography* 13 (1960): 54–68, and Arthur Brown's argument for old-spelling texts in "The Rationale of Old-Spelling Editions of the Plays of Shakespeare and his Contemporaries: A Rejoinder," ibid., pp. 69–76. See also S. Schoenbaum, "Editing English Dramatic Texts," and Clifford Leech, "A Note from a General Editor," in *Editing Sixteenth-Century Texts*, pp. 12–26.

[44] See p. 129. Thorpe offers this as "a practical (rather than idealistic) way of separating the potential from the actual" work of art. Lester A. Beaurline in "The Director, the Script, and Author's Revisions: A Critical Dilemma," read on 6 April 1967 at the University of Iowa Conference on Dramatic Theory and Criticism and published in *Papers on Dramatic Theory and Criticism*, ed. David M. Knauf (Iowa City, 1969), pp. 78–91, has raised some objections to this view of the work of art. Beaurline feels that this view puts too much faith in the printed work and fails to take into account that writers, especially the young, poor, or inexperienced, will give way before pressures to alter their work in order to have it published or produced. (A good recent example is John Barth's revision of the ending of his first novel, *The Floating Opera*. In order to get the novel published Barth had to oblige his publisher by rewriting the ending. Fortunately, in this case, after achieving success with *The Sot-Weed*

O M BRACK, JR.

William B. Todd's "Bibliography and the Editorial Problem in the Eighteenth-Century"[45] surveys problems an editor of eighteenth-century English texts must face in discriminating and ordering multiple editions. Another of Todd's essays, "On the Use of Advertisements in Bibliographical Studies," shows how advertisements from eighteenth-century newspapers and magazines can often date the publications of books and in some cases aid in establishing the priority of issue. Often this information is much more reliable than that available in biographies, memoirs, correspondence, or an occasional publisher's ledger. The same author's "Early Editions of *The Tatler*" presents another discovery, the recurrent printing of periodicals. To meet demands of later subscribers the publishers of certain eighteenth-century periodicals, such as *The Tatler*, reprinted their earliest numbers in undifferentiated editions and in doing so introduced alterations in the text. An editor preparing a critical edition of the 271 numbers of this periodical must examine 1,162 settings or run the risk of reprinting unauthorized readings.[46]

In "The Problem of Indifferent Readings in the Eighteenth Century, with a Solution from *The Deserted Village*," Arthur Friedman provides a way for distinguishing whether the author or the compositor is responsible for a given textual variant when

---

Factor and *Giles Goat-Boy*, he was in a position to restore the original ending to the novel.) Beaurline concludes that "an editor's duty is to be as faithful as possible to the author's artistic intention, and if there were different intentions at different times, the editor must choose an intention that existed at one time." (p. 90). Each literary work must be examined upon its own merits and the textual scholar must apply his critical intelligence to produce the best version that was written. Maqbool Aziz, "'Four Meetings': A Caveat for James Critics," *Essays in Criticism* 18 (1968): 258–74, argues that "two versions of a novel cannot be regarded as being separate unless the difference between them extends to the work's main carriers of meaning: plot, action, point-of-view, characterization. If these elements are identical, and the versions differ only in points of emphasis, then the two should be treated as a single work; one version, not necessarily the revised one, sometimes having greater richness of meaning than the other" (p. 270). For a discussion of the importance of variant readings in a text to the critic see Geoffrey Tillotson, "The Critic and the Dated Text," *Sewanee Review* 68 (1960): 595–602.

[45] For a broader discussion of the relationship of bibliography to textual editing, see Fredson Bowers, "Some Relations of Bibliography to Editorial Problems," *Studies in Bibliography* 3 (1951): 37–62.

[46] See also Todd, "Recurrent Printing."

one of a given pair of readings is not manifestly superior to the other. "If we believe that the excellence of an author depends in some degree on small points of style, we cannot," he observes, "consider these readings truly indifferent."[47]

Three of the present essays will be particularly useful to the editors of nineteenth-century texts. In "Some Principles for Scholarly Editions of Nineteenth-Century Authors," Fredson Bowers, using examples from Hawthorne texts, outlines the basic procedures for editing critical editions of this period.[48] Within the framework of Bowers's principles, William B. Todd's "Problems in Editing Mark Twain" discusses the particular difficulties in editing an author for whom exist multitudinous and diverse anterior and posterior texts.[49] In addition to presenting the particular problems in editing Mill's *Principles of Political Economy*, John M. Robson's "Textual Introduction" also considers certain modifications in editorial theory for nonliterary texts. This essay serves as a representative example of the textual introduction.[50]

An important discovery in analytical bibliography, presented by Matthew J. Bruccoli in "Concealed Printings in Hawthorne," has made it possible for editors of nineteenth- and twentieth-century literature to produce more accurate texts. Books printed from stereotype or electrotype plates are likely to have several impressions within a given edition, and there is always the possibility that significant emendations or corruptions may be concealed in them. Methods of determining reimpressions include measurements of the gutter margins, discovery of resetting by machine collation, and analysis of progressive type batter. "Although the researcher engaged in work on concealed printings runs the risk of becoming involved in a kind of biblio-

[47] See p. 190.

[48] For a more detailed discussion of the problems in Hawthorne's texts see the prefaces to the individual volumes of the Centenary Edition of the Works of Nathaniel Hawthorne published by Ohio State University Press.

[49] Methods for handling these problems are presented in the University of Iowa's *Rules and Procedures for the Mark Twain Edition* (1965), and *Procedures for Collating Twain's Minor Works* (1965).

[50] For a discussion of the problems in editing a nineteenth-century English literary text, see John Butt, "Editing a Nineteenth-Century Novelist (Proposals for an Edition of Dickens)," in *English Studies Today*, 2d ser., ed. G. A. Bonnard (Bern, 1961), pp. 187–95.

graphical solitaire—that is, he may find himself playing a game in which there are no textual stakes,"[51] he may discover a variant such as that found in *The Marble Faun* where the first printing of the line "very cold heart to which he had devoted himself" is corrected to a "very cold art."[52]

Bruccoli's "Some Transatlantic Texts: West to East" serves as a transition from the nineteenth century to the twentieth. Bruccoli argues that, in spite of the awareness of the general problems in Anglo-American books of the nineteenth century,[53] there is a good deal of complacency about transatlantic texts of modern novels. Many British editions of modern American novels differ markedly from the American editions. In some cases the changes in the British edition are authoritative, and in other cases not, but the wary critic and textual editor will do well to examine the printings of both American and British editions in order to have the complete textual history.

The last three essays in this volume deal with particular textual problems in three modern authors. First, David Hayman shows how Joyce revised a sentence in *Finnegans Wake* through thirteen stages over a period of fourteen years. In each draft a fresh insight is gained into Joyce's artistic method and into the meaning of the work. Second, Russell K. Alspach points out that because Yeats was an inveterate revisor no edition, printing, impression, or reissue can be ignored in a textual study of his poems. There are curious exceptions, for example, to the assertion that Yeats was "always cutting out the dead wood," and that one has the latest version of the poem if he has the latest-dated volume. A critical edition of Yeats should include not only the substantive variants, but all the accidental variants as well, because these too significantly affect the interpretation of his poems.[54] Last, James B. Meriwether's "The Text of Ernest

[51] See p. 235.

[52] See p. 240.

[53] See, for example, Weber, "American Editions of English Authors," pp. 27–50.

[54] This essay is based on the *Variorium Edition of the Poems of W. B. Yeats* (New York, 1957) and is confined to textual problems appearing in the printed texts. The *Variorium* is not a 'critical' edition; it contains neither editorial correction nor emendation. Using as a basic text *The Poems of W. B. Yeats* (London, 1949) the editors collated the other printed versions against it and recorded all revisions, even those in punctuation, at the bottom of the page. As Yeats revised the poems and cor-

Hemingway" is one of the clearest statements of the problems to be considered in preparing a critical edition of a modern author. The editor must compare the various printings of the author's works; he may also have to concern himself with questions of bowdlerization and censorship, the relation between author and publisher, the printing of books in English in non-English speaking countries, and the intentions in authorial revisions.[55]

This collection does not add up to a panacea. It will not automatically make a reader an editor or textual critic for, although the work done in the bibliography and textual criticism of post-Renaissance literature since World War II is impressive, it is not definitive.[56] The editor of almost any complex book will be faced with problems requiring him to modify old methods of bibliographical and editorial procedure or to devise new ones. It is hoped, however, that the collection will serve as an introduction and reference to some of the theories and problems in bibliography and textual criticism of post-Renaissance literature. A few of the essays here reprinted have become classics in the field, others are representative of the work currently being done. Many of the essays are essentially reports of work in progress, but even these in their provisional quality point up the problems the editor must face in the process of producing a sound text.

Although textual criticism has been emphasized in this volume, literary criticism is not to be ignored, for the two are necessarily

---

rected the proofs for the edition which finally appeared in 1949, only the readings in this edition represent the author's final intention. The rejected readings from the earlier printings are primarily important only insofar as they show the development in Yeats's concept of the poem. Since no manuscript readings are included in this edition, the necessary materials for a study of this development are incomplete.

[55] See also Meriwether's "The Dashes in Hemingway's *A Farewell to Arms*," *Papers of the Bibliographical Society of America* 58 (1964): 449–57.

[56] In an important recent essay "Printers of the Mind: Some Notes on Bibliographical Theories and Printing-House Practices," *Studies in Bibliography* 22 (1969): 1–75, D. F. McKenzie has on the basis of a variety of fresh evidence, reexamined the nature of bibliographical knowledge and has suggested that a number of assumptions about printing-house practices are not viable. This essay appeared too late for detailed discussion, but it should be read in conjunction with the statements on problems in analytical bibliography included in this volume. William B. Todd plans an assessment of the developments in bibliography and textual criticism of post-Renaissance literature in his forthcoming Lyell Lectures.

related. No degree of bibliographical training will prepare one, for example, to choose the best version of T. S. Eliot's *Murder in the Cathedral*.[57] As A. E. Housman concluded long ago, "To *be* a textual critic requires aptitude for thinking and willingness to think; and though it also requires other things, those things are supplements and cannot be substitutes. Knowledge is good, method is good, but one thing beyond all others is necessary; and that is to have a head, not a pumpkin, on your shoulders, and brains, not pudding, in your head."[58]

[57] Robert L. Beare, "Notes on the Text of T. S. Eliot," *Studies in Bibliography* 9 (1957): 47.

[58] "The Application of Thought to Textual Criticism," *Selected Prose*, ed. John Carter (Cambridge, 1961), p. 130. F. P. Wilson described the ideal editor as "at once bibliographer and critic, historian and antiquary, paleographer, philologist and philosopher," *Studies in Retrospect*, p. 134.

I

BRUCE HARKNESS

Bibliography and the Novelistic Fallacy

It is a truth universally acknowledged, that a critic intent upon analysis and interpretation, must be in want of a good text. It is also universally acknowledged that we live in an age of criticism, indeed of "new criticism"—which means that we as critics are dedicated to a very close reading of the text. Sometimes, it is true, that critical principle leads to abuses. The symbol-hunting, the ambiguity-spinning become wonders to behold. As one objector has put it, "nose to nose, the critic confronts writer and, astonished, discovers himself."[1] Nonetheless, the principle of close reading is held central by us all. Immediately that one contemplates novel criticism, however, an oddity appears: the last thing we find in a discussion by a new critic is some analysis of the actual text.

The modern critic is apt to be entirely indifferent to the textual problems of a novel. He is all too prone to examine rigorously a faulty text. As Gordon Ray and others have pointed out, even the Great Cham of British Criticism errs in this respect. F. R. Leavis defends the early Henry James in *The Great Tradition*: "Let me insist, then, at once, . . . that his [James's] 'first attempt at a novel,' *Roderick Hudson* (1874), in spite of its reputation, is a very distinguished book that deserves permanent currency—much more so than many novels passing as classics." Professor Ray adds that "Mr. Leavis goes on to quote three long paragraphs to illustrate the novel's 'sustained maturity of theme and treatment. . . .' These remarks are amply warranted by the passage that Mr. Leavis cites. But unhappily he has quoted, not

This article represents an expanded form of a paper read at the Bibliography Section of the 1957 Modern Language Association meetings. Reprinted with slight changes from *Studies in Bibliography*, XII (1959), 59–73, by permission of the author and the Bibliographical Society of the University of Virginia.

[1] Marvin Mudrick, "Conrad and the Terms of Modern Criticism," *Hudson Review*, VI (1954), 421.

the text of the first edition of 1877 [while carefully dating it from the time of composition to make it appear all the more precocious], which is simple enough, but that of the New York edition of 1907, revised in James's intricate later manner. This leaves him," concludes Leavis's critic, "in the position of having proved at length what nobody would think of denying, that James's writing at the age of sixty-four has all the characteristics of maturity."[2]

Unhappily, few of us can afford to laugh at the poor new critic. We all know the truth that we must have a good text, but most of us do not act upon it. A commonplace? Yes, and unfortunately, I have only that commonplace to urge; but I claim good company. Jane Austen, with whom I started, recognized that *Pride and Prejudice* had no profoundly new meaning. She ironically developed upon commonplaces: don't act on first impressions; don't interfere in your best friend's love affair; don't ignore your younger daughters. My point is that, ironically, everyone ignores the bibliographical study of the novel. People who would consider it terribly bad form to slight the textual study of a play or poem—or even doggerel—commit bibliographical nonsense when handed a novel. It seems that the novel just doesn't count. A key error in many studies of the novel is simply this, that the novel is unconsciously considered a different order of thing from poetry—a poem's text must be approached seriously. I shall illustrate by mentioning the sins of editors, reprinters, publishers, scholars, and, alas, bibliographers. Then, after discussing a few of the many reasons for this bibliographical heresy, I shall turn to my main illustration of the need for textual bibliography, *The Great Gatsby*.

II

A list of representative errors, by no means exhaustive, by sound men whom I admire in all other respects will make clear how faulty the texts of novels are, and how little we care. A good editor has put *The Nigger of the "Narcissus"* in *The Portable Conrad*, an excellent volume the introductions to which contain some of the best Conrad criticism. But what, one may

[2] Gordon N. Ray, "The Importance of Original Editions," in *Nineteenth-Century English Books*, by Gordon N. Ray, Carl Weber, and John Carter (1952), p. 22. See also "Henry James Reprints," *TLS* 5 Feb. 1949, p. 96.

wonder, is the copy-text for *The Nigger*? A search through the
book discloses two references, the less vague of which reads as
follows: "It is from the editions published and copyrighted by
the latter [Doubleday and Company] that the texts reproduced
in this volume have been drawn" (p. 758).

After a spot of searching the reader can discover for himself
that the copy-text for *The Nigger of the "Narcissus"* is not the
collected English edition, which as is well known was Conrad's
major concern. The copy-text was an early American publication, which Conrad habitually did not supervise. The new
critic immediately asks, does it make any difference?

The collected English edition was, as one might suspect with
an author who was constantly revising, changed in many ways.
This final version cuts down Conrad's intrusive "philosophizing,"
and corrects Donkin's cockney accent, among other shifts.[3] I
yield to no man in my admiration for Conrad, but if he has a
fault, it lies in that adjectival "philosophy" which is admired by
some, charitably overlooked by others, and condemned by a few
as pipe-sucking old seadog-talk. Surely the following, from the
early part of Chapter Four, is inappropriate in the mouth of the
sailor-narrator: "Through the perfect wisdom of its grace [the
sea's] they [seamen] are not permitted to meditate at ease upon
the complicated and acrid savour of existence, lest they should
remember and, perchance, regret the reward of a cup of inspir-
ing bitterness, tasted so often, and so often withdrawn before
their stiffening but reluctant lips. They must without pause
justify their life. . . ." Most of this passage, and much similar
sententiousness, were cut by Conrad from the collected English
text; but they all stand in *The Portable Conrad*.

As for the class of books known loosely as "reprints," I suppose that no one expects a good text for twenty-five or thirty-
five cents. These books I am not concerned with, but the more
serious paperbacks, obviously intended for use in colleges, are
sometimes faulty. For example, Rinehart Editions' copy of *Pride*

---

[3] C. S. Evans of the editorial department of Heinemann wrote Conrad
on 2 Sept. 1920 about Donkin's inconsistent dialect: "I have queried the
spelling of 'Hymposed,'" and so on. (See *Life and Letters* [London:
Heinemann, 1927], II, 247–48, for the exchange with Evans.) J. D. Gordan
in *Joseph Conrad: The Making of a Novelist* (1940), p. 139 and passim,
discusses many of the revisions of the text.

It might be possible to defend the use of an early text for *The
Nigger*, but no reason is given in *The Portable Conrad*.

and Prejudice reprints Chapman's excellent text—but suppresses the indication of three volume construction by numbering the chapters serially throughout.[4] Though three volumes are mentioned in the introduction, this misprinting of such a tightly constructed novel can only be regretted, for the effect on the college reader must be odd.

What of the publisher of more expensive novels? It can easily be seen that errors are not limited to the paperback field. Consider, for example, the one-volume Scribner edition of James's *The Wings of the Dove,* dated 1945 or 1946. Here is no scrimping for paperback costs, but the book is not what one would think. It is not a reprint of the famous New York edition; it is another, unacknowledged impression of the 1902 first American edition, dressed up with a new-set New York preface—an odd procedure the reason for which is not apparent. The publisher nowhere tells the reader that this is like some wines—an old text with a new preface. Yet one line of print would have made the matter clear. It is only by his own efforts of collation of the preface and the text itself that the reader knows where he is.[5]

To turn to the errors of scholarship, take F. O. Matthiessen's lengthy appreciation of Melville's phrase "soiled fish of the sea" in *White-Jacket.* Melville's narrator says of himself, after he had fallen into the sea, "I wondered whether I was yet dead or still dying. But of a sudden some fashionless form brushed my side— some inert, soiled fish of the sea; the thrill of being alive again tingled. . . ." This section Matthiessen acclaims as being imagery of the "sort that was to become peculiarly Melville's . . . hardly anyone but Melville could have created the shudder that results from calling this frightening vagueness some '*soiled* fish of the sea'!" Then follows a discussion of the metaphysical conceit and its moral and psychological implications.

[4] Though I cannot pretend to have examined them all, I know of only one independently produced paperback novel with good textual apparatus. This is Rinehart Editions' *Lord Jim,* which contains a collation of the four main texts. Riverside's *Pride and Prejudice* has a good text, but again Chapman's edition lies behind it. There must be, I am sure, many more good texts beside *Lord Jim* in the higher class of paperbacks, and even in the cheaper ones. But what publishers draw them to our attention, and what publisher doesn't (apparently) feel that a properly edited paperback novel will frighten away the common reader by its appearance?

[5] Furthermore, it would be difficult to defend the choice of first-edition text, as one might for *The Nigger of the "Narcissus,"* or *Roderick Hudson,* since James was writing in his intricate manner by 1902.

As has been pointed out, the genius in this shuddering case of imagery is not Melville, who wrote *coiled* fish, not *soiled* fish. "Coiled fish" stands in the first editions of *White-Jacket*, and to an unknown Constable printer should go the laurels for soiling the page with a typographical error.[6]

Matthiessen's error does not concern me now, but it does concern me that the scholar who first caught the mistake has a strange but perhaps understandable attitude toward textual matters. Recognizing that such an error "in the proper context" might have promulgated a "false conception," the scholar feels that the slip does not actually matter in Melville's case. Furthermore, he feels that Matthiessen's position is essentially sound—he was merely the victim of "an unlucky error." While sympathizing with common sense and professional etiquette, one may still wonder, however, how many such slips in illustration are allowable. Could the critic, if challenged, produce as many sound illustrations as one would like? Does not Matthiessen, in his categorizing of conceits, virtually admit that this particular kind is rare in *White-Jacket*?

When we look at the texts of novels from the other way, how many good editions of novelists do we have? How do they compare with the poets? We know a good bit about the bibliographies of Scott, Trollope, Meredith, but those of Dickens, Thackeray, Conrad, Hawthorne, and many more are completely out of date.[7] How many collected editions can be put on the same shelf with Chapman's 1923 Jane Austen? "We have virtually no edited texts of Victorian novelists," says Mrs. Tillotson in the introduction of *Novels of the Eighteen-Forties* (1954). How slowly we move, if at all.

Take Hardy for example. In 1946 Carl Weber said that "many scholars have apparently made no attempt to gain access to Hardy's definitive texts." In March, 1957, a scholar can complain that "As late as November 1956, sixty full years after the publication of the book, the only edition of *Jude* printed in the United States took no account of either of the two revisions which Hardy gave the novel. . . . The New Harper's Modern Classics edition . . . [however] is *almost* identical with that of the defini-

---

[6] See J. W. Nichol, "Melville's 'Soiled Fish of the Sea,'" *AL*, XXI (1949), 338–39.

[7] See John Carter, *op. cit.*, p. 53 and passim; reasons for the lack of bibliographical study are also discussed.

tive 1912 'Wessex Edition.' "[8] One is hardly surprised that Professor Weber is the editor.

Sixty years is a long time, but American literature is no better off. *Moby-Dick*, our greatest novel, presents no problem of copy-text. Yet more than 100 years went by after publication before we had what a recent scholar called the "first serious reprint," by Hendricks House. Before that, the careful reader did not even know, for example, the punctuation of the famous "Know ye, now, Bulkington?" passage. But how good is this reprint? The same scholar—not the editor—asks us to consider it a definitive edition. His reasons? It contains only 108 compositor's errors and twenty silent emendations.[9] Would anyone make such a claim for a volume of poems?

So much for editors, publishers, scholars. The sins of the bibliographer are mainly those of omission. For well-known reasons he tends to slight 19th- and 20th-century books in general, and in consequence most novels.[10]

The critic therefore needs convincing that novels should be approached bibliographically. The critic appreciates the sullied-solid-sallied argument about Shakespeare, but not that of 108 typos for *Moby-Dick*. A false word in a sonnet may change a fifth of its meaning; the punctuation at the end of the "Ode on a Grecian Urn" can be considered crucial to the meaning of the whole poem; but who, the critic argues from bulk, can stand the prospect of collating 700 pages of Dickens to find a few dozen misplaced commas? Like the "soiled fish" reading of *White-Jacket*, a few mistakes seriously damage neither novel nor criticism. They are swallowed up in the vast bulk of the novel, which by and large (and excepting a few well-known oddities such as *Tender is the Night* in which case one must be sure

[8] Robert C. Slack, "The Text of Hardy's *Jude the Obscure*," *N-CF*, XI (1957), 275. Italics added.

[9] William T. Hutchinson, "A Definitive Edition of *Moby-Dick*," *AL*, XXV (1954), 472–78.

[10] See Fredson Bowers, *Principles of Bibliographical Description* (1949), p. 356 ff, for a discussion of these reasons on the part of the bibliographer. One should admit, furthermore, that the non-professional bibliographers, the scholarly readers and editors, may have reasons which are indefensible, but are nevertheless *reasons*. I daresay one would be shocked to know how many trained men feel today that novels aren't really "literature"; or that modern printing is either perfect or too complicated ever to be fathomed.

which text one is attacking) is decently printed and generally trustworthy. The critic feels that a mistake here or there in the text is immaterial. "It doesn't *really* alter my interpretation," is the standard phrase.

This attitude has long since been defeated by bibliographers for all genres except the novel. One wonders indeed, if the critic would be willing to make his plea more logical. Could not the attitude be extended to some formula for trustworthiness versus error? It ought not to be difficult to arrive at a proportion expressing the number of errors per page, exceeding which a novel could be condemned as poorly printed.

Amid bad reasoning, there is some truth to the critic's defence against bibliography. The argument can be shifted from the ground of a novel's size and a reader's energy to the aesthetic nature of the novel. The critic is certainly right in maintaining that novels are more loosely constructed, even the best of them, than poems or short stories. The effects of a novel are built through countless small touches, and the loss of one or two— whether by error in text or inattention in reading—is immaterial. Putting aside the counter claim that this truth is damaging to the critical and crucial premise of close reading, surely all is a matter of degree. And what is more, the theory applies mainly to character portrayal. If we fail to recognize Collins as a fawning ass on one page, we will certainly see him aright on another.

That much must be granted the critic. In other concerns, however, the novel may not be repetitive. To give just one illustration: F. Scott Fitzgerald's *Last Tycoon* as published in unfinished form contains a boy whom the reader should compare to the "villain" of the piece, Brady (or Bradogue as he was called in an earlier draft). In Fitzgerald's directions to himself left in his MSS, he says "Dan [the boy] bears, in some form of speech, a faint resemblance to Bradogue. This must be subtly done and not look too much like a parable or moral lesson, still the impression must be conveyed, but be careful to convey it *once* and not rub it in. If the reader misses it, let it go—don't repeat."[11]

My last and painful reason why virtually no one is concerned with the texts of novels is this: most bibliographers are also university teachers and many of them suffer from schizophrenia. I do not refer to that familiar disease which makes us scholars by

[11] F. Scott Fitzgerald, *The Last Tycoon*, in *Three Novels* (1953), p. 157. Italics added.

day and diaper washers by night, but that split in the man between Graduate Seminar number 520 in Bibliography and Fresh-
man "Intro. to Fic.," 109. How many of us make bibliographical
truths part of our daily lives or attempt to inspire our graduate
students so to do? In this respect many bibliographers are like
socialists and Christians: walking arguments for the weakness of
the cause.

Let me give one or two illustrations from experience. Not very
long ago I sat in a staff meeting while we worried over a sentence
of Conrad's introduction to *Victory* in the Modern Library
edition. The sentence contained the odd phrase "adaptable
cloth," used about mankind. It made no sense until it was finally
pointed out that "adap-table" was divided at the end of the line
in both American collected edition and reprint—a domestically
minded compositor was talking about a table cloth, while Conrad was saying that Man is "wonderfully adaptable both by his
power of endurance and in his capacity for detachment." And
our silly discussion had gone on despite long teaching, and one's
natural suspicion of the cheaper reprints that perforce must be
used in college classes.

More seriously, consider Dickens' *Great Expectations*, taught
to freshmen at many universities, by staffs composed of men
nearly all of whom have been required to "take" bibliography.
Yet how many of these teachers have turned to the facts of serial
publication to explain the figure of Orlick, extremely puzzling
by critical standards alone? One immediately sees that Orlick's
attack on Mrs. Joe, which ultimately causes her death, is used by
Dickens to pep up a three instalment sequence the main purpose
of which is simply to let Pip age. This sequence would have been
too dull, too insistent on domestic scenes round the hearth while
Pip gradually withdraws from Joe, were it not for the Orlick
subplot.[12] The novel apparently had to have thirty-six weekly

[12] See instalments 8, 9, 10 (Chapters XII and XIII, XIV and XV, XVI
and XVII). The Pip-Magwitch strand is early developed as much as can
be without giving away the plot. Pip loves Estella early, but is apprenticed
back to Joe by the beginning of Chapter XIII. The glad tidings of Great
Expectations don't come until instalment 11. Without Orlick, more than
four chapters would have to deal with domestic bliss and withdrawal.
Orlick is introduced and attacks Mrs. Joe, all in the ninth instalment.

At the other end of the book a similar situation obtains. The reconcilia-
tion with Miss Havisham comes in instalment 30; that with Joe is brief
enough not to be needed until after instalment 33. Estella is not brought
in until the end. Instalments 31, 32, 33 are needed, therefore, to make the

units, and Dickens therefore could not simply skip this period of Pip's life. The figure of Orlick may not be critically acceptable, but he is at least understandable when one views him in the light of publishing history.

I am also indicting myself for not understanding this point; for it was not many months ago that I looked up the weekly issues of *All the Year Round* and now have far more detail than, as the saying goes, "the short space of this article will permit the discussion of." I was derelict in my duty partly because life is short and bibliography is long, but also partly because I unconsciously resented the editor of my paperback *Great Expectations* whose job I was having to do.

For I am more familiar with the schizophrenia than most people, though mine takes a different form. With critics I am apt to claim to be a bibliographer; among bibliographers, I proclaim myself a critic.

The critic, one must recognize, can argue on aesthetic grounds against working on the texts of novels. He can produce the *tu quoque* argument. And he can say that the bibliographer neglects *what* he is working on. Of 244 articles on textual bibliography in the *Studies in Bibliography* list for 1954, only three were related to novels.[13] "What has the bibliographer been doing?" asks the new critic.

---

36 weekly unit structure complete—but they cannot all contain the secret plan to get Magwitch downstream. The reader cannot go boating with Pip, Startop, and Herbert for two entire instalments before the disastrous attempt to get Magwitch out of the country; so instalment 32 is devoted to Orlick's attempt to kill Pip.

In other words, serial publication took Dickens to melodrama, but not quite in the crude form that one's unsubstantiated suspicions would indicate.

[13] There are, it is encouraging to note, signs of change. In the last year or two, one has the feeling that perhaps six or eight articles appeared on the texts of 19th- or 20th-century novels. For example, see Linton Massey, "Notes on the Unrevised Galleys of Faulkner's *Sanctuary*," *SB*, VIII (1956), 195–208; or Matthew J. Bruccoli, "A Collation of F. Scott Fitzgerald's *This Side of Paradise*," *SB*, IX (1957): 263–65. The latter article is especially interesting in pointing out changes between impressions of editions.

Having mentioned Dickens, I must add that Mrs. Tillotson has followed up her remark (*Novels of the Eighteen-Forties*) that we have no Victorian texts, and "no means, short of doing the work ourselves, of discovering how (and why) the original edition differed from the text we read." I refer of course to John Butt and Kathleen Tillotson, *Dickens at Work*

It may be that under the aspect of eternity George Sandys' *Ovid* is more important than Conrad's *Nostromo* or Melville's *Moby-Dick*, but it would be hard to convince the novel critic of that.

III

For these reasons I have chosen F. Scott Fitzgerald's *The Great Gatsby* as my main illustration. It brings out nearly all my points: inconsistent editing, an unknown or unidentified text, a publisher who is good but vague, important errors in an important book, schizophrenia in the bibliographer-teacher. Not only is *Gatsby* a fine novel, but it is taught so often because it contains many of the basic themes of American literature: West versus East; the search for value; the American dream; crime and society; and in young Jim Gatz's "General Resolves," it even reaches back to Ben Franklin and Poor Richard.

How many know, however, what they have been teaching?

The Great Gatsby exists in print in three main versions: the first edition, beginning in April, 1925; a new edition in the volume with *The Last Tycoon* and certain stories, beginning in 1941; and a sub-edition of the latter text in the Modern Standard Authors series (*Three Novels*) together with *Tender is the Night* and *The Last Tycoon*, beginning in 1953.[14] Though

---

(1957); on the importance of part publication, it deals mainly with novels other than *Great Expectations*. While it also illustrates how long it takes for a general appreciation of the importance of bibliographical facts to culminate in a specific study, the book makes my comments on Dickens, so to speak, unspeakable.

[14] The first edition has had three impressions: April, 1925, August, 1925, and August, 1942. I have collated three copies of the first impression, including Fitzgerald's personally corrected volume now located at Princeton. The August, 1942, impression I have not examined. I would like to record here my special thanks to Lawrence D. Stewart of Beverly Hills, California, for most kindly checking my collation against his copy of the rare second impression.

The second edition of *Gatsby* is that printed with *The Last Tycoon* and certain stories, as supervized by Edmund Wilson. It uses as copy-text the August, 1925, first edition. I have collated three impressions, 1941, 1945, 1948.

The sub-edition of *Gatsby*, as printed with *Tender is the Night* and *The Last Tycoon*, in the *Three Novels* volume, has been collated in three impressions, 1953, 1956, 1957.

The parent company, Scribner's, has permitted several reprints, which I have not examined thoroughly. There is also a recent (1957), third

Gatsby in the *Three Novels* version is another impression of *The Last Tycoon* plates I call it a sub-edition because *Gatsby*'s position is different, coming first in the volume, and there are many changes in the text.[15]

So far as I know, the only available information about the text of *Gatsby* is buried in the notes to Arthur Mizener's *The Far Side of Paradise*. Mizener says that Fitzgerald found a misprint in the first edition: the future Nick Carraway speaks of at the end of the novel should be "orgiastic," not "orgastic":[16]

> It was one of the few proof errors in the book [adds Mizener], perhaps because Scribner's worked harder over *Gatsby* than over Fitzgerald's earlier books, perhaps because [Ring] Lardner read the final proofs. The only other proof error Fitzgerald found was the reading of "eternal" for "external" on p. 58 [of the first edition] . . . . Edmund Wilson's reprint in his edition of *The Last Tycoon* corrects all it could without access to Fitzgerald's personally corrected copy.[17]

---

edition of *Gatsby*, by Scribner's, a paperback, called "Student's Edition." I shall refer to these editions of *Gatsby* by the short but obvious forms of *First*, *Last Tycoon* or *LT*, *Three Novels* or *TN*, Student's Edition or *SE*. For convenience I shall give the line in a page reference by a simple decimal; as *TN* 31.30, for *Three Novels*, p. 31, line 30.

[Professor Matthew J. Bruccoli in "A Further Note on the First Printing of *The Great Gatsby*," *SB*, XVI (1963), 244, reports that a collation of his privately owned copy of the August, 1942, printing "reveals that there are no fresh corrections or revisions in the third printing. . . . However, this collation did turn up a second-printing correction Prof. Harkness missed: 211.7–8 Union Street station] Union Station." B.H.]

15 My thanks are due to Princeton University Library for permitting me to examine both Fitzgerald's own copy of *Gatsby* and the surviving manuscripts. Doubtless I should add that since my special concern is the printed texts, I did not rigorously collate the mass of MS, TS, and galleys.

I would like also to thank Wallace O. Meyer of Scribner's, Harold Ober, Edmund Wilson, Malcolm Cowley, and Dan C. Piper for their advice and for patiently answering my queries about the changes in the texts.

16 The comment is a trifle misleading, because the reading "orgastic" stands in MS, galleys, and first edition. Perhaps this is another example of Fitzgerald's well-known weakness in matters of spelling, grammar, and so on; at any rate, it can hardly be called a "proof error."

17 Arthur Mizener, *The Far Side of Paradise* (1951), p. 336, n. 22. Mizener points up the generally sad fate of Fitzgerald's texts by mentioning that the reprints of The Modern Library, New Directions, Bantam (first version), and Grosset and Dunlap all have the word "orgastic." One therefore assumes they reprint the first edition, though at least the Mod-

Let us couple these comments with Matthew Bruccoli's interesting article on Fitzgerald's *This Side of Paradise*. Bruccoli is surprised that thirty-one errors are corrected in later impressions of the novel. He concludes that "the first printing was an inexcusably sloppy job," although Fitzgerald was himself in part responsible for the difficulty. We might infer two things, therefore: far fewer errors in *Gatsby*'s first edition, and a correction of the word "eternal," in *The Last Tycoon*.

Not so. The correction to "external" is not made in the second impression of the first edition, nor in any impression of *Last Tycoon* (202.2,TN 38.2). Though there are only four changes from the first to second impression of the first edition, there are no less than twenty-seven changes between *First* and *Last Tycoon*. Between *First* and the 1953 *Three Novels*, there are more than 125 changes. Of these changes about fifty are quite meaningless. They change "to-morrow" with a hyphen to "tomorrow," for example. Or they change "Beale Street Blues" to *Beale Street Blues*. This class of change will not be commented upon nor included in statistics, except to add that the publisher was not at all consistent in making such alterations.[18]

There are, in other words, 75 changes of moment between the first edition and *Three Novels*—forty-four more than in *This Side of Paradise*. Many of them are more important. Of the changes the August, 1925, first edition brought, the most important was the substitution of the word "echolalia" for "chatter" in the phrase "the chatter of the garden" (*First* 60 line 16). [19]

---

ern Library reprints the second impression. The later Bantam edition and *The Portable Fitzgerald* both use the faulty *Last Tycoon* as copy-text.

[18] See, for example, the word "today," in LT, p. 280 line 36 and TN, p. 116 line 36; but "to-day" (as in *First*, p. 184 lines 7 and 10) is kept three lines later—LT p. 281.1, TN p. 117.1. In addition to forty-two such changes, there are six more which are nearly as minor: the word "sombre" is changed to "somber"; "armistice" to "Armistice," as examples. All these, and the change in the spelling of a name (Wolfshiem to Wolfsheim) which was usually but not always wrong in the first edition, are not included in my statistics.

[19] See LT 203.4 and TN 39.4. The other changes in the August, 1925, *First* are as follows:
April, 1925: it's driver (p. 165.16) August, 1925: its driver. April: some distance away (p. 165.29) August: some distance away. April: sick in tired (p. 205.9 & 10) August: sickantired. All four are, presumably, authorial.

But we must remember that *Last Tycoon* and *Three Novels* are both posthumous, and that of the twenty-seven changes from *First* to LT, twelve are clearly errors, seven are dubious improvements, and only eight are clearly better readings. Of them all, the word "orgiastic," apparently, alone has the author's authority. What's more, the sub-edition *Three Novels* retains all but two of these bad changes. An example of an error begun in LT and continued in TN occurs on page 209.6 of *First* (296.8 of LT and 132.8 of TN). The sentence of Nick's, "It just shows you." is dropped from the text, thereby making the punctuation wrong and leading the reader to confuse speakers.

Between *First* and *Three Novels* the changes are of several kinds. In addition to the fifty or so "meaningless" changes, there are (*a*) fifteen changes of spelling, including six that change the meaning of a word and others that affect dialect; (*b*) seventeen changes in punctuation, including quotation marks, paragraph indication, and so on; (*c*) six incorrect omissions of a word or sentence or other details; (*d*) six proper deletions of a word or more; (*e*) thirty-one substantive changes—the substitution of a word or the addition of a phrase or sentence. For instance, Gatsby is transferred from the Sixteenth to the Seventh Infantry during the war. (See *First* 57.17, LT 201.12, TN 37.12.)

For when we turn to *Three Novels* we must move out of the camp of strict bibliography into the field of its important ally, publishing history. Fitzgerald's own copy of the first impression, with pencilled notes in the margins, is now located at the Princeton University Library and was used to make the sub-edition.

Of the seventy-five changes between *First* and TN, thirty-eight are with Fitzgerald's sanction and thirty-seven are without. Most of the thirty-seven changes not recommended by Fitzgerald are "corrections" made by a publisher's staff editor or by Malcolm Cowley, who supervised the sub-edition. However, some of this group are clearly errors, many of them having crept into the text by way of the *Last Tycoon* version. The noteworthy thing is that no reader knows the authority for *any* of the changes. The sub-edition itself does not even announce that it takes into account Fitzgerald's marginal comments—which, one would have supposed, would have been good business as well as good scholarship.

Furthermore, some of the thirty-eight "sanctioned" changes were only queried by Fitzgerald: no actual rewording was directed. An example is the phrase "lyric again in." Fitzgerald questioned "again" and the editor dropped it. But in five instances of Fitzgerald's questioning a word, no change was made— as, for example, Fitzgerald was unhappy to note that he had used the word "turbulent" twice in the first chapter.[20] There is also one instance in which Fitzgerald expressly asked for a change that was not made. At *First*, 50.1, Fitzgerald corrected "an amusement park" to "amusement parks," but the later version does not record the request (TN 32.32).

On the whole, one can say this, therefore: that about sixty of the changes from *First* to *Three Novels* are proper. That is, they either have the author's authority or are stylistic or grammatical improvements or are immaterial. I speak just now as a devil's advocate—a critic with a jaundiced eye toward bibliography. He would call the deletion of a comma from a short compound sentence "immaterial," though it was not done by the author.[21] I am trying, in other words, to make the text sound as good as I can. Problems arise, however, from the fact that awkward readings sometimes come from purely typographical errors, sometimes from editor's decision, and sometimes from Fitzgerald's own notes. Everyone would accept such changes as "an Adam study" for "an Adam's study," (*First* 110.26, LT 233.30, TN 69.30); but by the same token few critics will be pleased by a Fitzgerald marginal correction reading "common knowledge to the turgid sub or suppressed journalism of 1902," instead of "common property of the turgid journalism of 1902" (*First* 120.11, TN 76.5).

We are left then with fifteen or sixteen errors begun or continued in *Three Novels*, errors which I trust even the newest of new critics would accept as having some degree of importance. That degree of course varies. The dedication "Once again, to Zelda," is left off, for example. Dialectical words are falsely made standard English, or half-doctored-up, as in this sentence where the word in *First* was "appendicitus": "You'd of thought she had

---

[20] See "lyric again in," *First* 62.17, LT 204.12; "lyric in," TN 40.12. Cf. "turbulent," *First* 20.17, LT 178.25, TN 14.25; "turbulence," *First* 7.28, LT 171.3, TN 7.3

[21] See *First*, 35.21: Her eyebrows had been plucked and then drawn on again at a more rakish angle, but the efforts of nature. . . . LT 188.7 and TN 24.7 remove the comma.

my appendicitis out" (*First* 37.4, LT 188.37, TN 24.37). Sentences start without a capital[22] or end without a period[23] or are dropped altogether.[24] Quotation marks appear or disappear[25] and awkward readings come from nowhere. To illustrate that last: on page 149.10 of *First* Nick says that "the giant eyes of Doctor T. J. Eckleburg kept their vigil, but I perceived, after a moment, that other eyes were regarding us with peculiar intensity from less than twenty feet away." The eyes are Myrtle Wilson's but in *Three Novels* 95.1 (and LT 259.1) the sentence is confused when "the" is added without any reference and "from" and "with peculiar intensity" are dropped: "the giant eyes of Doctor T. J. Eckleburg kept their vigil, but I perceived, after a moment that *the* other eyes were regarding us less than twenty feet away" (italics added). Another dubious change is this: a joking slip or drunken mistake by Daisy is corrected—"Biloxi, Tennessee" becomes academically placed in its proper governmental locality.[26] One hardly needs to add that none of these changes have Fitzgerald's sanction.

The biggest errors, critically speaking, are ones that also occur in *Last Tycoon*. The principle of order in *The Great Gatsby* is a simple one: Nick Carraway, the narrator, tells his story wildly out of chronological order, but *in* the order that he learned it—

[22] *First* 111.14 and LT 234.5 When I try . . . TN 70.6 when I try . . .

[23] *First* 115.25 generating on the air. So LT 236.33. TN 72.33 generating on the air

[24] The sentence "It just shows you," mentioned above as an error begun in LT.

[25] *First* 141.6, LT 253.38, TN 89.38. Tom Buchanan is speaking, and by closing a paragraph with quote marks, LT and TN give the reader the momentary impression that the next sentence and paragraph beginning "Come outside . . ." is by someone else.
First 139.26, LT 253.7, TN 89.7 represent the obverse. "The bles-sed pre-cious. . . . spoken by Daisy loses the quotation mark in LT and TN.

[26] See *First* 153.8, LT 261.14, TN 97.14. TN alone reads "Biloxi, Mississippi." I realize that the line can be interpreted in other ways, that for example, Fitzgerald wished an obviously fictional town. But I cannot agree that Fitzgerald was so ignorant of Southern geography as to put the city in the wrong state. I am all the more certain that Fitzgerald meant it as a joke because there is other geographical wordplay in the same scene, and it is only four pages earlier that Tom snorts that Gatsby must have been an Oxford man—"Oxford, New Mexico."

with one exception.[27] The first half of the book is concerned with the development of the outsiders' illusions about Jay Gatsby—he is "nephew to Von Hindenburg," and so on (TN 47). The second half is a penetration in depth of Gatsby's illusion itself. The shift in the theme of the book is marked by the one major sequence which Nick gives the reader out of the order in which he himself learned it. I refer to the Dan Cody episode from Gatsby's early days.[28]

Now the most important structural unit in the book below the chapter is the intra-chapter break signified by a white space left on the page.[29] In *Last Tycoon* and *Three Novels* four of these important indications of structure are suppressed.[30] Oddly enough, it is the one following the Dan Cody story that is the first one missing. The detail that divides the book into its two structural elements is botched.

In the *Three Novels* version of *Gatsby*, then, we have a book quite well printed—surprisingly so when we look at the galley proofs. They are filled with changes—with page after page added in longhand, with whole galleys deleted or rearranged. (I would estimate that one-fifth of the book was written after the galley

[27] The statement is not quite accurate: there are one or two other violations of this order, minor ones very late in the book. For example, the giving of Michaelis's testimony, p. 124 of TN is apparently after the scene on pp. 119 ff.

[28] The scene was, in the manuscript, at the place where it is referred to in the chapter now numbered VIII, p. 112 of TN. Fitzgerald then changed it to its present position, ending at TN 76, LT 241, *First* 121—Chapter VI.

[29] Since I have mentioned Conrad so often, it might not be amiss to add Conrad's name to the list of influences mentioned by Cowley in the introduction to *Three Novels*. (See Fitzgerald's introduction to the Modern Library *Gatsby* and *The Crack-Up* for his interest in Conrad.) The time scheme of *Gatsby* is, of course, Conradian, as well as the narrator. And there are quite a few passages that echo Conrad—the closing section on the old Dutch sailors' feelings in New York might be a twist on parts of "Heart of Darkness." "In the abortive sorrows and short-winded elations of men," p. 4 of TN's *Gatsby*, is just one of the verbal echoes of Conrad. More pertinently, the intra-chapter break was a device very much used by the older author. For a detailed examination of this relationship, see R. W. Stallman, "Conrad and *The Great Gatsby*," *TCL*, I (1955), 5-12.

[30] See *First* 121.26, LT 240 foot, TN 76 foot; *First* 163.26, LT 267 foot, TN 103 foot; *First* 192.16, LT 285 foot, TN 121 foot; *First* 214.21, LT 299.21, TN 135.21. In all but the last of these the break in the page comes at the turn-over of the page and, unfortunately, no space was left for it.

stage.) And we have a book that tries to take into account the author's latest stylistic revisions. Unfortunately, it is also a book that has far too many errors.

Perhaps this is the place to mention the third Scribner edition of *Gatsby*, the paperback Student's Edition, which uses TN as copy-text. Have matters been improved? Some have, but more errors have been added. There are twelve changes from TN to SE: it makes two distinct improvements, including the replacement of the dedication; but it adds three places in which intra-chapter breaks are suppressed.[31] The other changes are "immaterial" typographical errors such as "turned to be," instead of "turned to me" (SE 71.17 and TN 54.20) and "*police*," instead of "pol*i*ce" (SE 27.27 and TN 22.19).

I hope it is clear, then, that *Three Novels* represents the best present text of *Gatsby*. No doubt it and the Student's Edition will be the ones most used in colleges for some time. It should also be clear that in *Three Novels*, we have this kind of book:

1. A book which nowhere gives the reader the authority for seventy-five changes, all of them posthumously printed.

2. One which fails to make use of all of Fitzgerald's corrections.

3. One which contains thirty-seven changes which Fitzgerald did not authorize—some of which are of most dubious value.

4. A book which contains at least fifteen quite bad readings, one of which is of the highest structural importance.

So, armed with this mixed blessing, or with the worse one of *Last Tycoon*, or worst of all, with a reprint by another publisher which has none of Fitzgerald's corrections and additions, many students unwittingly face the next semester with their prairie squints. Only a nonexistent, eclectic text, combining the best of the August, 1925, first edition and the *Three Novels* text of *The Great Gatsby* would be proper.[32]

---

[31] For the suppressed intra-chapter breaks, see TN 126.31 and SE 167.26; TN 132.24 and SE 175.19; TN 136.24 and SE 181.7. The other improvement is at TN 89.7 and SE 117.3, where SE returns to *First* to get the quotation marks of "The bles-sed . . ." as spoken by Daisy, correctly once more. SE 175.1 does not restore Nick's sentence "It just shows you." but it does "correct" the quotation marks that were wrong in the preceding sentence in TN 132.9.

[32] I should add that the collation of these three editions has of course not been reproduced in full here—and there are several places in the text that call for emendation though there are no changes between editions.

Could we not as critics pay more attention to Bibliography, and we as Bibliographers to criticism? Can not we somehow insist that editing actually be done—instead of the practice of putting a fancy introduction on a poor text? Can not we have sound texts reproduced and publisher's history stated by the editor? Can not we know *what it is* we have in our hands? For it is simply a fallacy that the novel does not count.

For example, Tom brings the car to a dusty spot under Wilson's sign. (So in *First* 147 and TN 93.23 and SE 123.7). Should it be a dusty stop?

[The discussions of the readings "orgastic/orgiastic" above illustrate another common difficulty, but one not developed in this article: the problem of conflicting authorial evidence. The change of "orgiastic" in the Princeton copy is the only revision there made not by rewriting but by printer's mark. One is puzzled to account for the difference.

On January 24, 1925, furthermore, Fitzgerald wrote Maxwell Perkins: "It's deliberate. 'Orgastic' is the adjective for 'orgasm' and it expresses exactly the intended ecstasy." See *The Letters of F. Scott Fitzgerald*, ed. Andrew Turnbull (1963), p. 175.

In short, the making of a "proper" text would be enormously complicated, requiring not only thorough examination of all editions and printings, but of proofs and manuscripts—and even these would not lead to certainty. Emendation and resolution of conflicting authorial evidence would be necessary. B. H.]

II

W. W. GREG

The Rationale of Copy-Text

When, in his edition of Nashe, McKerrow invented the term
"copy-text," he was merely giving a name to a conception already familiar, and he used it in a general sense to indicate that
early text of a work which an editor selected as the basis of his
own. Later, as we shall see, he gave it a somewhat different and
more restricted meaning. It is this change in conception and its
implications that I wish to consider.

The idea of treating some one text, usually of course a manuscript, as possessing over-riding authority originated among classical scholars, though something similar may no doubt be traced
in the work of biblical critics. So long as purely eclectic methods
prevailed, any preference for one manuscript over another, if it
showed itself, was of course arbitrary; but when, towards the
middle of last century, Lachmann and others introduced the
genealogical classification of manuscripts as a principle of textual
criticism, this appeared to provide at least some scientific basis for
the conception of the most authoritative text. The genealogical
method was the greatest advance ever made in this field, but its
introduction was not unaccompanied by error. For lack of logical analysis, it led, at the hands of its less discriminating expo-
nents, to an attempt to reduce textual criticism to a code of
mechanical rules. There was just this much excuse, that the
method did make it possible to sweep away mechanically a great
deal of rubbish. What its more hasty devotees failed to understand, or at any rate sufficiently to bear in mind, was that authority is never absolute, but only relative. Thus a school arose,
mainly in Germany, that taught that if a manuscript could be
shown to be generally more correct than any other and to have
descended from the archetype independently of other lines of

Read before the English Institute on September 8, 1949, by Dr. J. M.
Osborn for W. W. Greg. Reprinted from *Studies in Bibliography*, III
(1950), 19–36, by permission of the Bibliographical Society of the University of Virginia.

transmission, it was "scientific" to follow its readings whenever they were not manifestly impossible. It was this fallacy that Housman exposed with devastating sarcasm. He had only to point out that "Chance and the common course of nature will not bring it to pass that the readings of a MS are right wherever they are possible and impossible wherever they are wrong."[1] That if a scribe makes a mistake he will inevitably produce nonsense is the tacit and wholly unwarranted assumption of the school in question,[2] and it is one that naturally commends itself to those who believe themselves capable of distinguishing between sense and nonsense, but who know themselves incapable of distinguishing between right and wrong. Unfortunately the attractions of a mechanical method misled many who were capable of better things.

There is one important respect in which the editing of classical texts differs from that of English. In the former it is the common practice, for fairly obvious reasons, to normalize the spelling, so that (apart from emendation) the function of an editor is limited to choosing between those manuscript readings that offer significant variants. In English it is now usual to preserve the spelling of the earliest or it may be some other selected text. Thus it will be seen that the conception of "copy-text" does not present itself to the classical and to the English editor in quite the same way; indeed, if I am right in the view I am about to put forward, the classical theory of the "best" or "most authoritative" manuscript, whether it be held in a reasonable or in an obviously fallacious form, has really nothing to do with the English theory of "copy-text" at all.

I do not wish to argue the case of "old spelling" *versus* "modern spelling"; I accept the view now prevalent among English scholars. But I cannot avoid some reference to the ground on which present practice is based, since it is intimately connected with my own views on copy-text. The former practice of mod-

[1] Introduction to Manilius, 1903, p. xxxii.

[2] The more naive the scribe, the more often will the assumption prove correct; the more sophisticated, the less often. This, no doubt, is why critics of this school tend to reject "the more correct but the less sincere" manuscript in favour of "the more corrupt but the less interpolated," as Housman elsewhere observes ("The Application of Thought to Textual Criticism," *Proceedings of the Classical Association*, XVIII (1921), 75). Still, any reasonable critic will prefer the work of a naive to that of a sophisticated scribe, though he may not regard it as necessarily "better."

ernizing the spelling of English works is no longer popular with editors, since spelling is now recognized as an essential characteristic of an author, or at least of his time and locality. So far as my knowledge goes, the alternative of normalization has not been seriously explored, but its philological difficulties are clearly considerable.[3] Whether, with the advance of linguistic science, it will some day be possible to establish a standard spelling for a particular period or district or author, or whether the historical circumstances in which our language has developed must always forbid any attempt of the sort (at any rate before comparatively recent times) I am not competent to say; but I agree with what appears to be the general opinion that such an attempt would at present only result in confusion and misrepresentation. It is therefore the modern editorial practice to choose whatever extant text may be supposed to represent most nearly what the author wrote and to follow it with the least possible alteration. But here we need to draw a distinction between the significant, or as I shall call them "substantive," readings of the text, those namely that affect the author's meaning or the essence of his expression, and others, such in general as spelling, punctuation, word-division, and the like, affecting mainly its formal presentation, which may be regarded as the accidents, or as I shall call them "accidentals," of the text.[4] The distinction is not arbitrary or theoretical, but has an immediate bearing on textual criticism, for scribes (or compositors) may in general be expected to react, and experience shows that they generally do react, differently to the two categories. As regards substantive readings their aim may be assumed to be to reproduce exactly those of their copy, though they will doubtless sometimes depart from them accidentally and may even, for one reason or another, do so intention-

[3] I believe that an attempt has been made in the case of certain Old and Middle English texts, but how consistently and with what success I cannot judge. In any case I am here concerned chiefly with works of the sixteenth and seventeenth centuries.

[4] It will, no doubt, be objected that punctuation may very seriously "affect" an author's meaning; still it remains properly a matter of presentation, as spelling does in spite of its use in distinguishing homonyms. The distinction I am trying to draw is practical, not philosophic. It is also true that between substantive readings and spellings there is an intermediate class of word-forms about the assignment of which opinions may differ and which may have to be treated differently in dealing with the work of different scribes.

ally: as regards accidentals they will normally follow their own habits or inclination, though they may, for various reasons and to varying degrees, be influenced by their copy. Thus a contemporary manuscript will at least preserve the spelling of the period, and may even retain some of the author's own, while it may at the same time depart frequently from the wording of the original: on the other hand a later transcript of the same original may reproduce the wording with essential accuracy while completely modernizing the spelling. Since, then, it is only on grounds of expediency, and in consequence either of philological ignorance or of linguistic circumstances, that we select a particular original as our copy-text, I suggest that it is only in the matter of accidentals that we are bound (within reason) to follow it, and that in respect of substantive readings we have exactly the same liberty (and obligation) of choice as has a classical editor, or as we should have were it a modernized text that we were preparing.[5]

But the distinction has not been generally recognized, and has never, so far as I am aware, been explicitly drawn.[6] This is not surprising. The battle between "old spelling" and "modern spelling" was fought out over works written for the most part between 1550 and 1650, and for which the original authorities are therefore as a rule printed editions. Now printed editions usually form an ancestral series, in which each is derived from its immediate predecessor; whereas the extant manuscripts of any work have usually only a collateral relationship, each being derived from the original independently, or more or less independently, of the others. Thus in the case of printed books, and in the absence of revision in a later edition, it is normally the first edition alone that can claim authority, and this authority naturally extends to substantive readings and accidentals alike. There

[5] For the sake of clearness in making the distinction I have above stressed the independence of scribes and compositors in the matter of accidentals: at the same time, when he selects his copy-text, an editor will naturally hope that it retains at least something of the character of the original. Experience, however, shows that while the distribution of substantive variants generally agrees with the genetic relation of the texts, that of accidental variants is comparatively arbitrary.

[6] Some discussion bearing on it will be found in the Prolegomena to my lectures on *The Editorial Problem in Shakespeare* (1942), "Note on Accidental Characteristics of the Text" (pp. l-lv), particularly the paragraph on pp. liii-liv, and note 1. But at the time of writing I was still a long way from any consistent theory regarding copy-text.

was, therefore, little to force the distinction upon the notice of editors of works of the sixteenth and seventeenth centuries, and it apparently never occurred to them that some fundamental difference of editorial method might be called for in the rare cases in which a later edition had been revised by the author or in which there existed more than one "substantive" edition of comparable authority.[7] Had they been more familiar with works transmitted in manuscript, they might possibly have reconsidered their methods and been led to draw the distinction I am suggesting. For although the underlying principles of textual criticism are, of course, the same in the case of works transmitted in manuscripts and in print, particular circumstances differ, and certain aspects of the common principles may emerge more clearly in the one case than in the other. However, since the idea of copy-text originated and has generally been applied in connexion with the editing of printed books, it is such that I shall mainly consider, and in what follows reference may be understood as confined to them unless manuscripts are specifically mentioned.

The distinction I am proposing between substantive readings and accidentals, or at any rate its relevance to the question of copy-text, was clearly not present to McKerrow's mind when in 1904 he published the second volume of his edition of the Works of Thomas Nashe, which included *The Unfortunate Traveller*. Collation of the early editions of this romance led him to the conclusion that the second, advertised on the title as "Newly corrected and augmented," had in fact been revised by the author, but at the same time that not all the alterations could with certainty be ascribed to him.[8] He nevertheless proceeded to enunciate the rule that "if an editor has reason to suppose that a certain text embodies later corrections than any other, and at the

[7] A "substantive" edition is McKerrow's term for an edition that is not a reprint of any other. I shall use the term in this sense, since I do not think that there should be any danger of confusion between "substantive editions" and "substantive readings".

I have above ignored the practice of some eccentric editors who took as copy-text for a work the latest edition printed in the author's lifetime, on the assumption, presumably, that he revised each edition as it appeared. The textual results were naturally deplorable.

[8] He believed, or at least strongly suspected, that some were due to the printer's desire to save space, and that others were "the work of some person who had not thoroughly considered the sense of the passage which he was altering" (II, 195).

same time has no ground for disbelieving that these corrections, *or some of them at least*, are the work of the author, he has no choice but to make that text the basis of his reprint."[9] The italics are mine.[10] This is applying with a vengeance the principle that I once approvingly described as "maintaining the integrity of the copy-text." But it must be pointed out that there are in fact two quite distinct principles involved. One, put in more general form, is that if, for whatever reason, a particular authority be on the whole preferred, an editor is bound to accept all its substantive readings (if not manifestly impossible). This is the old fallacy of the "best text," and may be taken to be now generally rejected. The other principle, also put in general form, is that whatever particular authority be preferred, whether as being revised or as generally preserving the substantive readings more faithfully than any other, it must be taken as copy-text, that is to say that it must also be followed in the matter of accidentals. This is the principle that interests us at the moment, and it is one that McKerrow himself came, at least partly, to question.

In 1939 McKerrow published his *Prolegomena for the Oxford Shakespeare,* and he would not have been the critic he was if his views had not undergone some changes in the course of thirty-five years. One was in respect of revision. He had come to the opinion that to take a reprint, even a revised reprint, as copy-text was indefensible. Whatever may be the relation of a particular substantive edition to the author's manuscript (provided that there is any transcriptional link at all) it stands to reason that the relation of a reprint of that edition must be more remote. If then, putting aside all question of revision, a particular substantive edition has an over-riding claim to be taken as copy-text, to displace it in favour of a reprint, whether revised or not, means receding at least one step further from the author's original in so

---

[9] Nashe, II, 197. The word "reprint" really begs the question. If all an "editor" aims at is an exact reprint, then obviously he will choose one early edition, on whatever grounds he considers relevant, and produce it as it stands. But McKerrow does emend his copy-text where necessary. It is symptomatic that he did not distinguish between a critical edition and a reprint.

[10] Without the italicized phrase the statement would appear much more plausible (though I should still regard it as fallacious, and so would McKerrow himself have done later on) but it would not justify the procedure adopted.

far as the general form of the text is concerned.[11] Some such considerations must have been in McKerrow's mind when he wrote (*Prolegomena*, pp. 17–18): "Even if, however, we were to assure ourselves . . . that certain corrections found in a later edition of a play were of Shakespearian authority, it would not by any means follow that that edition should be used as the copy-text of a reprint.[12] It would undoubtedly be necessary to incorporate these corrections in our text, but . . . it seems evident that . . . this later edition will (except for the corrections) deviate more widely than the earliest print from the author's original manuscript. . . . [Thus] the nearest approach to our ideal . . . will be produced by using the earliest 'good' print as copy-text and inserting into it, from the first edition which contains them, such corrections as appear to us to be derived from the author." This is a clear statement of the position, and in it he draws exactly the distinction between substantive readings (in the form of corrections) and accidentals (or general texture) on which I am insisting. He then, however, relapsed into heresy in the matter of the substantive readings. Having spoken, as above, of the need to introduce "such corrections as appear to us to be derived from the author," he seems to have feared conceding too much to eclecticism, and he proceeded: "We are not to regard the 'goodness' of a reading in and by itself, or to consider whether it appeals to our aesthetic sensibilities or not; we are to consider whether a particular edition taken *as a whole* contains variants from the edition from which it was otherwise printed which could not reasonably be attributed to an ordinary press-corrector, but by reason of their style, point, and what we may call inner harmony with the spirit of the play as a whole, seem likely to be the work of the author: and once having decided this to our satisfaction we must accept *all* the alterations of that edition, saving any which seem obvious blunders or misprints." We can see clearly enough what he had in mind, namely that the evidence of correction (under which head he presumably intended to include revision) must be considered *as a whole;* but he failed to add the equally important proviso that the alterations

11 This may, at any rate, be put forward as a general proposition, leaving possible exceptions to be considered later (pp. 55 ff.).

12 Again he speaks of a "reprint" where he evidently had in mind a critical edition on conservative lines.

must also be *of a piece* (and not, as in *The Unfortunate Traveller*, of apparently disparate origin) before we can be called upon to accept them *all*. As he states it his canon is open to exactly the same objections as the "most authoritative manuscript" theory in classical editing.

McKerrow was, therefore, in his later work quite conscious of the distinction between substantive readings and accidentals, in so far as the problem of revision is concerned. But he never applied the conception to cases in which we have more than one substantive text, as in *Hamlet* and perhaps in *2 Henry IV*, *Troilus and Cressida*, and *Othello*. Presumably he would have argued that since faithfulness to the wording of the author was one of the criteria he laid down for determining the choice of the copy-text, it was an editor's duty to follow its substantive readings with a minimum of interference.

We may assume that neither McKerrow nor other editors of the conservative school imagined that such a procedure would always result in establishing the authentic text of the original; what they believed was that from it less harm would result than from opening the door to individual choice among variants, since it substituted an objective for a subjective method of determination. This is, I think, open to question. It is impossible to exclude individual judgement from editorial procedure: it operates of necessity in the all-important matter of the choice of copy-text and in the minor one of deciding what readings are possible and what not; why, therefore, should the choice between possible readings be withdrawn from its competence? Uniformity of result at the hands of different editors is worth little if it means only uniformity in error; and it may not be too optimistic a belief that the judgement of an editor, fallible as it must necessarily be, is likely to bring us closer to what the author wrote than the enforcement of an arbitrary rule.

The true theory is, I contend, that the copy-text should govern (generally) in the matter of accidentals, but that the choice between substantive readings belongs to the general theory of textual criticism and lies altogether beyond the narrow principle of the copy-text. Thus it may happen that in a critical edition the text rightly chosen as copy may not by any means be the one that supplies most substantive readings in cases of variation. The failure to make this distinction and to apply this principle has naturally led to too close and too general a reliance upon the text chosen as basis for an edition, and there has arisen what may be called the tyranny of the copy-text, a tyranny that has, in my opinion, vitiated much of the best editorial work of the past generation.

I will give a couple of examples of the sort of thing I mean that I have lately come across in the course of my own work. They are all the more suitable as illustrations since they occur in texts edited by scholars of recognized authority, neither of whom is particularly subject to the tyranny in question. One is from the edition of Marlowe's *Doctor Faustus* by Professor F. S. Boas (1932). The editor, rightly I think, took the so-called B-text (1616) as the basis of his own, correcting it where necessary by comparison with the A-text (1604).[13] Now a famous line in Faustus's opening soliloquy runs in 1604,

> Bid *Oncaymæon* farewell, *Galen* come

and in 1616,

> Bid *Oeconomy* farewell; and *Galen* come ...

Here *Oncaymæon* is now recognized as standing for *on cay mæ on* or ὅν καὶ μὴ ὄν: but this was not understood at the time, and *Oeconomy* was substituted in reprints of the A-text in 1609 and 1611, and thence taken over by the B-text. The change, however, produced a rather awkward line, and in 1616 the *and* was introduced as a metrical accommodation. In the first half of the line Boas rightly restored the reading implied in A; but in the second half he retained, out of deference to his copy-text, the *and* whose only object was to accommodate the reading he had rejected in the first. One could hardly find a better example of the contradictions to which a mechanical following of the copy-text may lead.[14]

My other instance is from *The Gipsies Metamorphosed* as

---

[13] Boas's text is in fact modernized, so that my theory of copy-text does not strictly apply, but since he definitely accepts the B-text as his authority, the principle is the same.

[14] Or consider the following readings: 1604, 1609 "Consissylogismes," 1611 "subtile sylogismes," 1616 "subtle Sillogismes." Here "subtile," an irresponsible guess by the printer of 1611 for a word he did not understand, was taken over in 1616. The correct reading is, of course, "concise syllogisms." Boas's refusal to take account of the copy used in 1616 led him here and elsewhere to perpetuate some of its manifest errors. In this particular instance he appears to have been unaware of the reading of 1611.

edited by Dr. Percy Simpson among the masques of Ben Jonson in 1941. He took as his copy-text the Huntington manuscript, and I entirely agree with his choice. In this, and in Simpson's edition, a line of the ribald Cock Lorel ballad runs (sirreverence!),

All wch he blewe away with a fart

whereas for *blewe* other authorities have *flirted*. Now, the meaning of *flirted* is not immediately apparent, for no appropriate sense of the word is recorded. There is, however, a rare use of the substantive *flirt* for a sudden gust of wind, and it is impossible to doubt that this is what Jonson had in mind, for no scribe or compositor could have invented the reading *flirted*. It follows that in the manuscript *blewe* is nothing but the conjecture of a scribe who did not understand his original: only the mesmeric influence of the copy-text could obscure so obvious a fact.[15]

I give these examples merely to illustrate the kind of error that, in modern editions of English works, often results from undue deference to the copy-text. This reliance on one particular authority results from the desire for an objective theory of text-construction and a distrust, often no doubt justified, of the operation of individual judgement. The attitude may be explained historically as a natural and largely salutary reaction against the methods of earlier editors. Dissatisfied with the results of eclectic freedom and reliance on personal taste, critics sought to establish some sort of mechanical apparatus for dealing with textual problems that should lead to uniform results independent of the operator. Their efforts were not altogether unattended by success. One result was the recognition of the general worthlessness of reprints. And even in the more difficult field of manuscript transmission it is true that formal rules will carry us part of the way: they can at least effect a preliminary clearing of the ground. This I sought to show in my essay on *The Calculus of Variants* (1927); but in the course of investigation it became clear that there is a definite limit to the field over which formal rules are applicable. Between readings of equal extrinsic authority no rules of the sort can decide, since by their very nature it is

---

[15] At another point two lines appear in an unnatural order in the manuscript. The genetic relation of the texts proves the inversion to be an error. But of this relation Simpson seems to have been ignorant. He was again content to rely on the copy-text.

only to extrinsic relations that they are relevant. The choice is necessarily a matter for editorial judgement, and an editor who declines or is unable to exercise his judgement and falls back on some arbitrary canon, such as the authority of the copy-text, is in fact abdicating his editorial function. Yet this is what has been frequently commended as "scientific"—"streng wissenschaftlich" in the prevalent idiom—and the result is that what many editors have done is to produce, not editions of their authors' works at all, but only editions of particular authorities for those works, a course that may be perfectly legitimate in itself, but was not the one they were professedly pursuing.

This by way, more or less, of digression. At the risk of repetition I should like to recapitulate my view of the position of copy-text in editorial procedure. The thesis I am arguing is that the historical circumstances of the English language make it necessary to adopt in formal matters the guidance of some particular early text. If the several extant texts of a work form an ancestral series, the earliest will naturally be selected, and since this will not only come nearest to the author's original in accidentals, but also (revision apart) most faithfully preserve the correct readings where substantive variants are in question, everything is straightforward, and the conservative treatment of the copy-text is justified. But whenever there is more than one substantive text of comparable authority,[16] then although it will still be necessary to choose one of them as copy-text, and to follow it in accidentals, this copy-text can be allowed no over-riding or even preponderant authority so far as substantive readings are concerned. The choice between these, in cases of variation, will be determined partly by the opinion the editor may form respecting the nature of the copy from which each substantive edition was printed, which is a matter of external authority; partly by the intrinsic authority of the several texts as judged by the relative frequency of manifest errors therein; and partly by the editor's judgement of the intrinsic claims of individual readings to originality—in other words their intrinsic merit, so long as by "merit" we mean the likelihood of their being what the author wrote rather than their appeal to the individual taste of the editor.

Such, as I see it, is the general theory of copy-text. But there

16 The proviso is inserted to meet the case of the so-called "bad quartos" of Shakespearian and other Elizabethan plays and of the whole class of "reported" texts, whose testimony can in general be neglected.

remain a number of subsidiary questions that it may be worth-while to discuss. One is the degree of faithfulness with which the copy-text should be reproduced. Since the adoption of a copy-text is a matter of convenience rather than of principle—being imposed on us either by linguistic circumstances or our own philological ignorance—it follows that there is no reason for treating it as sacrosanct, even apart from the question of substantive variation. Every editor aiming at a critical edition will of course, correct scribal or typographical errors. He will also correct readings in accordance with any errata included in the edition taken as copy-text. I see no reason why he should not alter misleading or eccentric spellings which he is satisfied emanate from the scribe or compositor and not from the author. If the punctuation is persistently erroneous or defective an editor may prefer to discard it altogether to make way for one of his own. He is, I think, at liberty to do so, provided that he gives due weight to the original in deciding on his own, and that he records the alteration whenever the sense is appreciably affected. Much the same applies to the use of capitals and italics. I should favour expanding contractions (except perhaps when dealing with an author's holograph) so long as ambiguities and abnormalities are recorded. A critical edition does not seem to me a suitable place in which to record the graphic peculiarities of particular texts,[17] and in this respect the copy-text is only one among others. These, however, are all matters within the discretion of an editor: I am only concerned to uphold his liberty of judgement.

Some minor points arise when it becomes necessary to replace a reading of the copy-text by one derived from another source. It need not, I think, be copied in the exact form in which it there appears. Suppose that the copy-text follows the earlier convention in the use of *u* and *v*, and the source from which the reading is taken follows the later. Naturally in transferring the reading from the latter to the former it would be made to conform to the earlier convention. I would go further. Suppose that the copy-text reads "hazard," but that we have reason to believe that the correct reading is "venture": suppose further that whenever this word occurs in the copy-text it is in the form "venter": then "venter," I maintain, is the form we should adopt. In like manner

[17] That is, certainly not in the text, and probably not in the general apparatus: they may appropriately form the subject of an appendix.

editorial emendations should be made to conform to the habitual spelling of the copy-text.

In the case of rival substantive editions the choice between substantive variants is, I have explained, generally independent of the copy-text. Perhaps one concession should be made. Suppose that the claims of two readings, one in the copy-text and one in some other authority, appear to be exactly balanced: what then should an editor do? In such a case, while there can be no logical reason for giving preference to the copy-text, in practice, if there is no reason for altering its reading, the obvious thing seems to be to let it stand.[18]

Much more important, and difficult, are the problems that arise in connexion with revision. McKerrow seems only to mention correction, but I think he must have intended to include revision, so long as this falls short of complete rewriting: in any case the principle is the same. I have already considered the practice he advocated (pp. 45–48)—namely that an editor should take the original edition as his copy-text and introduce into it all the substantive variants of the revised reprint, other than manifest errors—and have explained that I regard it as too sweeping and mechanical. The emendation that I proposed (p. 48) is, I think, theoretically sufficient, but from a practical point of view it lacks precision. In a case of revision or correction the normal procedure would be for the author to send the printer either a list of the alterations to be made or else a corrected copy of an earlier edition. In setting up the new edition we may suppose that the printer would incorporate the alterations thus indicated by the

[18] This is the course I recommended in the Prolegomena to *The Editorial Problem in Shakespeare* (p. xxix), adding that it "at least saves the trouble of tossing a coin." What I actually wrote in 1942 was that in such circumstances an editor will naturally retain the reading of the copy-text, this being the text which he has already decided is *prima facie* the more correct." This implies that correctness in respect of substantive readings is one of the criteria in the choice of the copy-text; and indeed I followed McKerrow in laying it down that an editor should select as copy-text the one that "appears likely to have departed least in wording, spelling, and punctuation from the author's manuscript." There is a good deal in my Prolegomena that I should now express differently, and on this particular point I have definitely changed my opinion. I should now say that the choice of the copy-text depends solely on its formal features (accidentals) and that fidelity as regards substantive readings is irrelevant—though fortunately in nine cases out of ten the choice will be the same whichever rule we adopt.

author; but it must be assumed that he would also introduce a normal amount of unauthorized variation of his own.[19] The problem that faces the editor is to distinguish between the two categories. I suggest the following frankly subjective procedure. Granting that the fact of revision (or correction) is established, an editor should in every case of variation ask himself (1) whether the original reading is one that can reasonably be attributed to the author, and (2) whether the later reading is one that the author can reasonably be supposed to have substituted for the former. If the answer to the first question is negative, then the later reading should be accepted as at least possibly an authoritative correction (unless, of course, it is itself incredible). If the answer to (1) is affirmative and the answer to (2) is negative, the original reading should be retained. If the answers to both questions are affirmative, then the later reading should be presumed to be due to revision and admitted into the text, whether the editor himself considers it an improvement or not. It will be observed that one implication of this procedure is that a later variant that is either completely indifferent or manifestly inferior, or for the substitution of which no motive can be suggested, should be treated as fortuitous and refused admission to the text— to the scandal of faithful followers of McKerrow. I do not, of course, pretend that my procedure will lead to consistently correct results, but I think that the results, if less uniform, will be on the whole preferable to those achieved through following any mechanical rule. I am, no doubt, presupposing an editor of reasonable competence; but if an editor is really incompetent, I doubt whether it much matters what procedure he adopts: he may indeed do less harm with some than with others, he will do little good with any. And in any case, I consider that it would be disastrous to curb the liberty of competent editors in the hope of preventing fools from behaving after their kind.

I will give one illustration of the procedure in operation, taken again from Jonson's *Masque of Gipsies*, a work that is known to have been extensively revised for a later performance. At one point the text of the original version runs as follows,

a wise Gypsie .. , is as politicke a piece of Flesh, as most Iustices in the County where he maunds

[19] I mean substantive variations, such as occurs in all but the most faithful reprints.

whereas the texts of the revised version replace *maunds* by *stalkes*. Now, *maund* is a recognized canting term meaning to beg, and there is not the least doubt that it is what Jonson originally wrote. Further, it might well be argued that it is less likely that he should have displaced it in revision by a comparatively commonplace alternative, than that a scribe should have altered a rather unusual word that he failed to understand—just as we know that, in a line already quoted (p. 50), a scribe altered *flirted* to *blewe*. I should myself incline to this view were it not that at another point Jonson in revision added the lines,

> And then ye may stalke
> The *Gypsies* walke

where *stalk*, in the sense of going stealthily, is used almost as a technical term. In view of this I do not think it unreasonable to suppose that Jonson himself substituted *stalkes* for *maunds* from a desire to avoid the implication that his aristocratic Gipsies were beggars, and I conclude that it must be allowed to pass as (at least possibly) a correction, though no reasonable critic would *prefer* it to the original.

With McKerrow's view that in all normal cases of correction or revision the original edition should still be taken as the copy-text, I am in complete agreement. But not all cases are normal, as McKerrow himself recognized. While advocating, in the passage already quoted (p. 47), that the earliest "good" edition should be taken as copy-text and corrections incorporated in it, he added the proviso, "unless we could show that the [revised] edition in question (or the copy from which it had been printed) had been gone over and corrected *throughout* by" the author (my italics). This proviso is not in fact very explicit, but it clearly assumes that there are (or at least may be) cases in which an editor would be justified in taking a revised reprint as his copy-text, and it may be worth inquiring what these supposed cases are. If a work has been entirely rewritten, and is printed from a new manuscript, the question does not arise, since the revised edition will be a substantive one, and as such will presumably be chosen by the editor as his copy-text. But short of this, an author, wishing to make corrections or alterations in his work, may not merely hand the printer a revised copy of an earlier edition, but himself supervise the printing of the new edition and correct the proofs as the sheets go through the press.

In such a case it may be argued that even though the earlier edition, if printed from his own manuscript, will preserve the author's individual peculiarities more faithfully than the revised reprint, he must nevertheless be assumed to have taken responsibility for the latter in respect of accidentals no less than substantive readings, and that it is therefore the revised reprint that should be taken as copy-text.

The classical example is afforded by the plays in the 1616 folio of Ben Jonson's Works. In this it appears that even the largely recast *Every Man in his Humour* was not set up from an independent manuscript but from a much corrected copy of the quarto of 1601. That Jonson revised the proofs of the folio has indeed been disputed, but Simpson is most likely correct in supposing that he did so, and he was almost certainly responsible for the numerous corrections made while the sheets were in process of printing. Simpson's consequent decision to take the folio for his copy-text for the plays it contains will doubtless be approved by most critics. I at least have no wish to dispute his choice.[20] Only I would point out—and here I think Dr. Simpson would agree with me—that even in this case the procedure involves some sacrifice of individuality. For example, I notice that in the text of *Sejanus* as printed by him there are twenty-eight instances of the Jonsonian "Apostrophus" (an apostrophe indicating the elision of a vowel that is nevertheless retained in printing) but of these only half actually appear in the folio, the rest he has introduced from the quarto. This amounts to an admission that in some respects at least the quarto preserves the formal aspect of the author's original more faithfully than the folio.

The fact is that cases of revision differ so greatly in circumstances and character that it seems impossible to lay down any hard and fast rule as to when an editor should take the original edition as his copy-text and when the revised reprint. All that can be said is that if the original be selected, then the author's corrections must be incorporated; and that if the reprint be selected, then the original reading must be restored when that of the reprint is due to unauthorized variation. Thus the editor

[20] Simpson's procedure in taking the 1616 folio as copy-text in the case of most of the masques included, although he admits that in their case Jonson cannot be supposed to have supervised the printing, is much more questionable.

cannot escape the responsibility of distinguishing to the best of his ability between the two categories. No juggling with copy-text will relieve him of the duty and necessity of exercising his own judgement.

In conclusion I should like to examine this problem of revision and copy-text a little closer. In the case of a work like *Sejanus*, in which correction or revision has been slight, it would obviously be possible to take the quarto as the copy-text and introduce into it whatever authoritative alterations the folio may supply; and indeed, were one editing the play independently, this would be the natural course to pursue. But a text like that of *Every Man in his Humour* presents an entirely different problem. In the folio revision and reproduction are so blended that it would seem impossible to disentangle intentional from what may be fortuitous variation, and injudicious to make the attempt. An editor of the revised version has no choice but to take the folio as his copy-text. It would appear therefore that a reprint may in practice be forced upon an editor as copy-text by the nature of the revision itself, quite apart from the question whether or not the author exercized any supervision over its printing.

This has a bearing upon another class of texts, in which a reprint was revised, not by the author, but through comparison with some more authoritative manuscript. Instances are Shakespeare's *Richard III* and *King Lear*. Of both much the best text is supplied by the folio of 1623; but this is not a substantive text, but one set up from a copy of an earlier quarto that had been extensively corrected by collation with a manuscript preserved in the playhouse. So great and so detailed appears to have been the revision that it would be an almost impossible task to distinguish between variation due to the corrector and that due to the compositor,[21] and an editor has no choice but to take the folio as copy-text. Indeed, this would in any case be incumbent upon him for a different reason; for the folio texts are in some parts connected by transcriptional continuity with the author's manuscript, whereas the quartos contain only reported texts, whose accidental characteristics can be of no authority whatever. At the same time, analogy with *Every Man in his Humour* sug-

---

[21] Some variation is certainly due to error on the part of the folio printer, and this it is of course the business of an editor to detect and correct so far as he is able.

gests that even had the quartos of *Richard III* and *King Lear* possessed higher authority than in fact they do, the choice of copy-text must yet have been the same.

I began this discussion in the hope of clearing my own mind as well as others' on a rather obscure though not unimportant matter of editorial practice. I have done something to sort out my own ideas: others must judge for themselves. If they disagree, it is up to them to maintain some different point of view. My desire is rather to provoke discussion than to lay down the law.

III

FREDSON BOWERS

Current Theories of Copy-Text, with an Illustration from Dryden

The choice of the best copy-text is often the most serious problem in an old-spelling critical edition of a text printed in the sixteenth through the eighteenth centuries. The uncritical use of the last edition within an author's lifetime is now, or should be, thoroughly discredited, although it is still occasionally found.[1] Recognition of the corruption inherent in reprints and of the necessity to inquire closely into the authority of any old text chosen as the basis for a critical edition has very properly shifted the emphasis back to that printed text closest to the author's manuscript, that is, to the first authoritative edition. When there is only one edition set from manuscript and when all subsequent editions are mere reprints,[2] the first is now the logical and automatic choice. Difficulty arises, however, when authority is pres-

Reprinted from *Modern Philology*, LXVIII (1950), 19–36, by permission of the author and the editor.

[1] In theory, such an edition was the last which could have undergone authorial revision. Yet the choice of such a final edition was essentially uncritical, in that the editor usually made no attempt to discover if, indeed, alterations were present which could have come from a revising author. In thus declining the responsibility of determining whether or not there was any basis for his choice of copy-text, such an editor invariably saddled himself with a corrupt and unauthoritative reprint. Montague Summers' edition of Dryden's plays is an example.

[2] An authoritative edition is one derived from an author's manuscript directly or through intervening transcription. A later edition derived from this primary edition may, somewhat loosely, also be called "authoritative" when it contains revisions emanating in some manner from the author. However, in this latter case the authority is mixed, since all variants cannot be presumed to be authorial. Properly speaking, only the ascertained revisions are authoritative and not the entire text. A reprint may be taken as an edition derived from an earlier, usually with the sense that no authorial revision is present. Its readings, therefore, even when obvious corrections, have no "authority."

ent in more than one edition. Thus a later edition may be set from an independent manuscript,[3] or, more commonly perhaps, from a revised copy of an earlier printed text marked by the author.[4]

In this latter case the most common editorial practice has been to choose the latest authoritatively revised edition as the copy-text. This popular principle of editing has not gone unchallenged, however, and it is noteworthy that the objection has come from editors who have originally been trained as analytical bibliographers. Thus the conservative McKerrow, reversing his earlier views, laid it down as his rule for the Oxford *Shakespeare* that, under ordinary circumstances, he would select as his copy-text the edition closest to the author's manuscript and would thereupon incorporate in this basic text the substantive alterations from any revised edition.[5] More recently, W. W. Greg has re-examined the question in some detail[6] and has materially clarified the problem by his strict differentiation of the *substantives*, or actual wording of a text, from the *accidentals*, or formal presentation of a text in such matters as spelling, punctuation, and capitalization. In basic form his argument is that an editor should not confuse the authority of substantives with that obtaining for accidentals. Clearly, the accidentals of a text set from manuscript are more authoritative than those of a later edition, even one

[3] This special case is not considered here, since the choice and subsequent treatment of the copy-text usually has no bibliographical basis and lies in the province of pure textual criticism.

[4] For the purposes of this study I exclude all the intermediate possibilities, such as recourse to a manuscript to fill up missing pages of a printed edition used as copy or to incorporate major units of additional material.

[5] R. B. McKerrow, *Prolegomena for the Oxford Shakespeare* (1939), pp. 17–18. Special cases, of course, prevent the application of the rule. For instance, no one but a madman would attempt in an old-spelling text to choose the first quarto of *King Lear* and thereupon to substitute all the Folio revisions. The primary reason here is, obviously, that the quarto was not set from a manuscript which had any transcriptional link with the author's manuscript. As a secondary reason, the activities of "Scribe E," who prepared a copy of the quarto for the Folio printer, were apparently so extensive that it would be very difficult to disentangle his alterations from those of the Folio compositors, although the attempt would be worth while if the quarto had not been set from a memorial reconstruction.

[6] "The Rationale of Copy-Text," to be published in *Studies in Bibliography*, vol. III (1950). This paper was originally delivered, *in absentia*, at the English Institute on September 7, 1949.

containing authoritative substantive revisions. Just as clearly, true revisions are more authoritative than are the original readings for which they substitute. Thus when a critical editor encounters a revised edition, under most circumstances he should choose for the texture, or accidentals, of his old-spelling text the earliest edition set from an authoritative manuscript, and into this he should insert those substantive or other alterations from the revised edition which his editorial judgment passes as authoritative.[7]

It is as yet too early to estimate the effect that Greg's logical argument will have on editorial practice. Nevertheless, one may speculate about the objections which may be brought forward to the practical application of his propositions. One set will certainly come from editors uneasily conscious of their new obligation to distinguish between readings which are authoritative and unauthoritative, since each variant in a revised edition must, in Greg's opinion, be considered on its own merits.[8] The answer to this is clear. If an editor is not simply reprinting some single authority for the text but is engaging himself with a critical edition, which is supposed to present the best detailed text of an author in a form as close to his intentions as can be managed, then editorial responsibility cannot be disengaged from the duty to judge the validity of altered readings in a revised edition. Automatically to accept all the plausible readings in a revision is an unsound bibliographical principle.

A second objection may be anticipated: that Greg's proposals will result in an amalgamated, or bastardized, text—in effect, the

[7] The major difference between McKerrow's and Greg's views lies in the proposed treatment of the revisions. McKerrow's conservatism led him to the position that, once it had been determined that a later edition was authoritatively revised, *all* the substantive alterations (except for obvious misprints and errors) must be incorporated. On the contrary, Greg points out that normal compositor's substantive variants can be expected as readily in a revised edition as in a reprint and that these are by no means always so recognizable as are simple misprints or errors. It is, therefore, an editor's responsibility to select only those variant readings which he estimates are true revisions, while rejecting those which he believes to be unauthoritative.

[8] Since Greg's purpose in his paper was primarily to lay down general principles with major illustrations, all parts were not minutely developed, as in an extensive monograph. In particular, there is perhaps room for a textual critic to enlarge by means of a greater number of typical workaday examples that section of the paper devoted to the distinction of authority or nonauthority in variant readings from a revised edition.

conflation of two or more editions. In so far as it concerns purity in text, this objection has no basis, once the distinction is grasped between a critical edition and a reprint of some single authority.[9] Moreover, the fact that old-spelling texts are in question has no bearing on any difference in principle.[10] Under the circumstances of most revised editions, an amalgamated old-spelling text according to Greg's procedures will actually produce the nearest approach to the author's intentions. A revised edition is usually typeset from a copy of some previous edition suitably marked up by the author, although in some cases the author may, instead, submit a separate list of alterations which are to be made in the new edition. Let us suppose that the author's annotated copy used for a revision had been preserved. Certainly, no editor would print his critical text from the actual revised edition which was set from this marked copy. Without question he would feel obliged to choose the earlier (especially if it were the first edition) and to substitute the author's corrections in the same way that errata lists are incorporated. Thus, when Greg's theory is applied to revisions, it is seen that the preservation of the accidentals of the first edition but the insertion of authoritative substantive alterations from the revised text does, in fact, reproduce as nearly as possible the critical text as it would be made up from a preserved printer's copy for the revision.[11]

[9] Under many circumstances a critical edition cannot help being eclectic; but eclecticism ceases to be a word of fear when suitable safeguards are erected to prevent the unprincipled selection of readings according to personal taste and without consideration of authority or bibliographical probability, which was too often a characteristic of eighteenth- and nineteenth-century editing.

[10] It would seem to reflect a basic misunderstanding of the rationale of the old-spelling text to accept the usual amalgamated reading edition of *Hamlet* in modernized form but to reject it in a rationally contrived old-spelling version. Greg's remarks on old spelling may very profitably be consulted in *The Editorial Problem in Shakespeare* (1942), pp. liii–lv, but especially in his forthcoming "Rationale of Copy-Text."

[11] The respect given by nonbibliographical editors to the accidentals of a derived edition, even though revised, seems to be based on the theory that the author in every respect has approved of this revised edition, whereas, in fact, all he has done is to give general approval to the copy from which the revision was set. Unless he reads the proof himself, the author thereupon has no control over what will be produced from this copy by the printing process. Moreover, at least in the sixteenth and seventeenth centuries, it is unrealistic to believe that a proofreading author ever set himself to restore the texture of the original by altering the usual accidentals of the second compositor unless they were in positive error.

In this line of reasoning, however, there is a possible hitch, and it is here, we may expect, that the strongest resistance will collect. For example, an editor may feel prepared to take the responsibility for deciding between variant substantive readings but at the same time recognize what seems to be the practical impossibility of assigning the variant accidentals in the revised edition to author or compositor. He may then be strongly inclined to argue that, although admittedly the general texture of a revised derived edition is one step further removed from that of the author's manuscript, yet in accepting the later texture he is at least not discarding whatever alterations in spelling, punctuation, and capitalization the author may have made.[12]

This general position has recently been stated, although not with ideal clarity, in Mr. A. Davenport's justification for basing his old-spelling text of Joseph Hall's first six books of *Virgidemiarum* on the revised 1598 rather than on the original 1597 edition:

> The choice of copy-text was clearly between 1597 and 1598. From the facts stated above it is evident that the bulk of 1597 is one stage closer to Hall's manuscript than 1602 or the bulk of 1598. On the other hand, the authoritative readings of 1598 must obviously be adopted, and whether the minor variants in 1598 are compositor's errors or genuine corrections it is usually impossible to decide. The choice therefore was between printing 1597 and correcting from 1598, or printing 1598 although its authority where it differs from 1597 on minor details, is doubtful. It has seemed wiser to take 1598 as the copy-text, and make no alterations in it without due warning, rather than to produce an amalgam of two editions. But since the authority, on minor details, of 1597 is at least as high as that of 1598 it has seemed necessary to record in the textual notes all variants, however trivial, which could suggest the slightest difference of sense, emphasis or intonation.[13]

This is an example of what Greg calls "the tyranny of the copy-text" as it influences abnegation of editorial responsibility. The plausibility of its general position will not, I think, bear strict

[12] One might idly speculate on the unconscious influence on textual criticism of Anglo-American jurisprudence with its initial presumption of innocence. Bibliographers are more inclined to apply to a revised text the theory of certain Continental codes, according to which the accused is required to demonstrate his own innocence.

[13] *The Collected Poems of Joseph Hall*, ed. A. Davenport (1949), pp. lxiv–lxv.

examination.[14] Although his wording is not very specific, Davenport seems to be referring to various minor substantive variants in which a choice appears to be indifferent, as well as to certain classes of accidentals (even including capitalization) which might govern emphasis or intonation. In both of these the specific and limited authority which applies to the recognizable substantive revisions (which were not especially extensive) is allowed to affect the question of the general authority of the texture of the two editions. This is, I think, an anomaly; for Greg's arguments in favor of the separation of the two matters are especially convincing and are buttressed by McKerrow's equally thoughtful consideration. As for the indifferent substantives, it is one of Greg's three criteria for determining the authority of variants that when a choice seems indifferent, the odds are in favor of the specific authority of the original reading. If this is indeed correct, then a text constructed on Davenport's criteria will probably contain more corruptions than authentic revisions among these indifferent readings,[15] and, in addition, the general texture will be almost completely unauthoritative.[16]

It is desirable, however, to narrow the case more closely by setting aside the difficulties in the choice between substantive variants in order to concentrate on the question of the acciden-

[14] Nn. 10, 11, and 12 above, as also various remarks in the text, have already touched on certain weaknesses of this theory of copy-text.

[15] Greg takes exception to the implicit but fallacious assumption in much textual discussion that some mechanical principle can be evolved which will construct an absolutely perfect and correct text. He very pertinently remarks that the procedure which he advocates will not lead to consistently correct results; but in the hands of a competent editor the results, if less uniform, will, on the whole, be preferable to those achieved through following any mechanical rule. We must, I think, consider which method is likely to retain more authoritative readings than it rejects and also whether, in retaining the maximum possible number, such unauthoritative alteration is elsewhere permitted to enter as to make the overall text less pure.

[16] It is interesting to observe that, in the nine brief satires comprising the first book of *Virgidemiarum*, the editor is forced to return to 1597 a round dozen times to correct, chiefly in the accidentals, the forms in 1598. Yet, on the evidence provided in the collation, if 1597 had been chosen as the copy-text, at the maximum only six alterations (four substantives and two accidentals) would have been drawn by an editor from 1598, and of these only three would be positively required. One may well inquire whether more of an amalgamation has not resulted than would have occurred had the text been edited according to Greg's criteria.

tals. Editorial judgment, at least in theory, can select from substantives according to some less rough-and-ready principle than the presumed overriding general authority of a revised text, an authority which will frequently not hold up when specifically applied. On the other hand, implicit in most opposition to the McKerrow-Greg procedure is a sense of helplessness about the possibility of utilizing critical principles to determine an author's revisions of the accidentals. That there is, indeed, greater difficulty in this connection, and sometimes an insuperable one, is not of sufficient importance to justify the adoption of a general system still further removed than the original from whatever characteristics of the author's manuscript have been preserved.[17] Under almost any conditions the successive modernizations, misinterpretations, and rationalizations derived from new typesettings introduce in an early text a score of unauthoritative variants for each legitimate one which might have been introduced by an author. An editor, therefore, is only playing the correct odds when, as a general proposition, he retains the texture of the original edition. Otherwise, in order to preserve a single accidentals variant which *may* have been the author's, he is introducing a very considerable number of other alterations which under no circumstances could possibly have been authorial. This is throwing out the baby with the bath with a vengeance, to destroy, say, nineteen accidentals which *may* be the author's in order to preserve some one unspecified accidental which *may* be a revision.[18]

[17] There is no space here to discuss with proper thoroughness the real interest residing in the accidentals of a critical old-spelling edition. All bibliographical experience indicates that, in general, a compositor imposes a great deal of his own system on a manuscript text but is, to some extent, influenced by his copy. Thus, although no printed early text can be taken as an over-all faithful representation, it is at best of some authority and at worst it is one which is characteristic of the time in which the work is written and therefore usually consonant with the author's style. A later setting, although following printed copy more closely than for manuscript, imposes still further compositorial alteration, most of which cannot stem from authorial markings and, as McKerrow has pointed out, is in effect always a modernization. If one moves away from basic authority, the true purpose of old-spelling editions is vitiated and only "quaintness" remains. For example, one might as well modernize the text as to accept the accidentals of the 1701 Folio or of any of the 1696 quartos of Dryden's *Indian Emperour*, first printed in 1667.

[18] After working carefully through his detailed collations, I feel that this is about the proportion which one finds in Davenport's edition of Hall, referred to above.

Investigation of a most arduous and lengthy nature may be applied in specific cases to assist in the decision,[19] but in the usual text the matter is not, perhaps, of sufficient importance to warrant the considerable effort involved. In such circumstances, Greg's procedure will undoubtedly yield a superior text both for accidentals and for substantives than can be assured by other less scientific methods.

As a matter of fact, to what extent an early author revising an edition would concern himself with altering accidentals which were not distinctly in error has been insufficiently investigated, in part because of the paucity of materials. The usual examples, such as what we know of Ben Jonson's proof corrections in his Folio, are too specialized for wider application.[20] The care which the average author might devote to improving the accidentals is perhaps not a matter for generalization, since authors could well vary widely in their practice. However, general bibliographical experience founded on a close comparison of texts seems to foster the belief that usually, so long as accidentals were not positively wrong or misleading, the author concentrated on substantive revision and was content, as a general rule, to accept the accidentals which normal printing practice had imposed on his work.[21]

[19] If the text is a most important one, very scrupulous bibliographical investigation may perhaps go a considerable distance toward a separation of compositor's and author's accidentals in a revised edition. A minute study of the characteristics of the compositor or compositors of the revised text, once they have been isolated by bibliographical tests, can be made against the control of other books from the same printing-house and typeset by the same identifiable workmen. Up to the latter part of the seventeenth century the characteristics of different compositors can, in fact, be identified with some accuracy, and when their habitual variants are removed from consideration in the text under examination, a more scientific examination may be made of the residue in an attempt to determine possible authorial revisions.

[20] Even after the scrupulous attention which Jonson gave to the proofs of his Folio, Greg is still able to remark a number of cases where an editor, choosing the Folio, must return to the quarto copy to preserve special Jonsonian characteristics modified by the Folio compositors and inconsistently passed over by Jonson in the proofreading.

[21] Observation of manuscripts seems to indicate that the punctuation, for example, was often very sketchy indeed, and not of the kind that an author would wish to appear in print as the result of a faithful following of copy. In earlier times, as in the present, most authors seem to count on the printer to correct and fill out their unsystematic practice.

The lack of very much material to test authorial practice in a revised edition, at least in the sixteenth and seventeenth centuries, leads me to present as a kind of case history a brief example in 1668 from John Dryden. The play is *The Indian Emperour,* first published in 1667, with a revised second edition in 1668 and a revised third edition in 1670.[22] My chief concern is with a part of the second edition; but, before we come to this, there is one matter in the first edition worth notice. Collation of six of the seven recorded American copies of the 1667 edition discloses six press-variant formes in the nine sheets comprising the text. In four of these formes the correction is far from extensive: four variants appear in one, two in another, and only a single one in the other two. The alterations are almost equally divided between substantives and accidentals, but they are corrections, not revisions, and do not seem to be beyond the capacity of an intelligent proofreader giving a final examination to formes already proofed from sheets pulled on a proofing press. Each of these variant formes is in a different sheet, outer B, D, H, and inner E.[23] Sheet I, however, is abnormally variant in both formes. In the outer forme ten alterations were made, only one of them substantive. Two egregious misprints in the original state lead me to believe that this forme had received no proofreading before being placed on the press and that the unusual number of corrections indicates this fact. The majority are concerned with re-punctuating eight lines on sig. I3r (which seem to have been added to the manuscript at a late date), and the one substantive alteration may actually be unauthoritative if, as seems probable, this is printing-house proofreading.

The case is different, however, when we come to inner forme I, for here almost certainly Dryden himself (and I think for the first and only time in this edition) made the revisions. In the stage direction on sig. I4r, for example, the ususual word "Zoty" is substituted for "Balcone," that is, "balcony." A marked characteristic of the revised second edition is Dryden's care in sub-

[22] J. S. Steck, "Dryden's *Indian Emperour:* The Early Editions and Their Relation to the Text," *Studies in Bibliography,* 2 (1949): 139–45.

[23] One of the corrected errors in outer H seems to have been caused by imperfectly raised types, and hence there is also a possibility that this forme, as may be conjectured for outer forme I, was not given a careful proofing before printing began.

stituting "which" or "who" for "that" used as a relative pronoun. On sig. I3v such a revision is made in 1667 to alter the original lines

> He saw not with my Eyes that could refuse:
> He that could prove so much unkind to thee,

to

> He saw not with my Eyes who could refuse:
> Him that could prove so much unkind to
>   thee....[24]

Finally, a few lines down, a necessary "and" is added to a stage direction. In these four pages Dryden made four substantive revisions but not a single alteration in any of the accidentals. In the second edition seven lines in these pages were further revised, chiefly by grammatical correction; but, in addition, we note two spelling, nine capitalization, and five punctuation alterations. If an editor, therefore, chose the 1668 edition as his copy-text, in these four pages he would be incorporating sixteen alterations of the accidentals of the first edition in the belief that they *may* have originated with Dryden, although, on the evidence of the proofreading, Dryden had seemed to express his satisfaction by failing to alter any when given the opportunity in 1667.

But the end is not yet. The third edition, in 1670, was also revised by Dryden from the 1668 copy, although, significantly, no substantive revisions occur after sig. H1r, where he seems to have dropped the project. There is considerable doubt, then, that he ever went over this inner I forme to revise it for 1670. However, in the revised third edition for these four pages we have added to the sixteen 1668 variants three alterations in word division, eleven in capitalization, and one in punctuation, or a total of fifteen extra variants, none of which, in all probability, is authoritative. Interestingly enough, one of the capitalizations and the punctuation restore original forms in 1667 altered in 1668, though passed then by Dryden. As a consequence, if an editor of this play chose the 1670 edition as his copy-text on the theory that it was the last revised, he would reprint in these four pages a minimum of fifteen variants from the accidentals of 1668, none of which is likely to have been marked by Dryden; and if

---

[24] In the 1668 revision the second line finally reads "Him who could...."

we take the more probable view that the 1668 variants are in the same class, this editor would reproduce a total of twenty-nine unauthoritative alterations in the readings of the 1667 first edition, which would be his proper copy-text if for various reasons he decided to reject the 1665 scribal transcript of the text in an early state. Under these conditions one might well query whether any rationale exists for an old-spelling text based on the revised editions.

With this background we may now come to an even more interesting, though perhaps less clear-cut case. Collation of six copies of the 1668 edition reveals that only one forme was press-altered, and, significantly, this was inner forme B, or, as can be demonstrated, the first forme of the text through the press. Seven stop-press alterations were made in this forme, of which one is a substantive revision, three are substantive corrections, and three are concerned with punctuation. The revision shows that the proofreading was authoritative, for it alters relative "that" to "which," a grammatical nicety already started in the author-corrected forme of inner I in 1667 and continued, in combination with other revisions, throughout the 1668 edition.

When we examine the uncorrected state of this forme in 1668, however, we find that it is not wholly a normal reprint of 1667. A speech-heading omitted in 1667 has been inserted, another corrected, and two substantive corrections performed. The first could have occurred to an alert proofreader, since it set right an obvious misprint, but the other would have been recognized only by the author, who in all probability was also responsible for the speech-heading changes. We find, then, this situation. Certain alterations have been made prior to the setting of the original state of the forme, but others, including a grammatical correction which is to be a characteristic of the edition as a whole, have been held over until printing was started. I conjecture that Dryden had sent an errata list covering the correction of various real errors he had observed in 1667 text and had planned on reading proofs to make whatever other revision seemed necessary. However, it would appear that when he read the proof for the first two formes of sheet B he discovered that a more thorough revision for "correctness" of diction and style was necessary than he had envisaged and that this—as the evidence of the rewriting in the whole play indicates—involved more alterations than could be conveniently made in proof. Since in the invariant outer forme of B in 1668 we find a number of substantive revisions, including the correction of a relative "that," it seems a plausible conjecture that Dryden completed reading proof on sheet B by revising the proof for the outer forme (not yet printed) and then marked up the 1667 copy for the rest of the play.

If this reconstruction of the events is roughly accurate, then we have another instance of a control for separating author's and compositor's variants in a revision. The control is perhaps less exact than for inner forme I of the 1667 edition, for the substantive corrections already present in the original state of inner B of 1668 demonstrate some sort of revision before printing. But if this revision, as seems to be indicated, was the result of an errata list for errors, we could reasonably expect that it was confined to substantives, as was inner I of 1667.

The three proof corrections in the accidentals affect the punctuation. In the first, the original state read

> Each downfal of a flood the Mountains pour,
> From their rich bowels, rolls a silver shower.

Dryden removed the comma after "pour" in proof to secure a run-on line slightly affecting the sense.[25]

> Which gather'd all the breath the winds could
> blow.
> And at their roots grew floating Palaces,
> Whose out-blow'd[26] bellies cut the yielding
> Seas.

Dryden changed the period after "blow" to a colon to secure continuity, although the sentence then was increased to six lines.

> Then judge my future service by my past.
> What I shall be by what I was, you know,
> That love took deepest root which first did
> grow.

[25] In 1667 no comma had appeared after "bowels," but the 1668 comma may not derive from a Dryden marking; for, if he had inserted it in copy, he presumably would have removed the comma after "pour" at the same time. On the other hand, the debated medial comma is present in the 1665 scribal transcript.

[26] "out-blow'd" is a misprint for 1667 "out-bow'd," the correct reading being restored in 1670. This is only one of several occasions when Dryden as proofreader or reviser overlooked serious errors on the same page with his corrections.

The light comma after "know" was altered to a colon, perhaps to indicate a stronger pause so that the demonstrative pronoun "That" would not be mistaken for a relative.

Of these three examples, two seem to be concerned with clarifying the meaning to some slight extent. Since they accompany substantive revision, they are clearly authoritative and should ideally be present in any old-spelling edition. However, if collation had not revealed them and an editor had chosen 1668 as his copy-text for just this contingency, what of an apparently unauthoritative nature would also have been taken over in this forme? In the uncorrected state of inner B, and therefore presumably to be isolated as compositor's variants, are two variant spellings, two variant word divisions, three variant capitalizations, and three punctuation alterations. Since with a 1667 copy-text none of the three authoritative punctuational variants would have called for emendation unless their special status as proof-corrections had been determined by a careful collation of 1668 copies, the choice of the 1668 copy-text produces ten unauthoritative alterations to secure three authoritative.

But for this play the further revised 1670 third edition would need to be chosen if popular procedure is to be followed. In the four pages of the inner forme of B the revised 1670 text makes four substantive alterations, one a correction of a 1668 misreading and another a further revision of a line partly touched up in 1668. There is no way to demonstrate that, at the time he marked the copy of 1668 for these, Dryden did not also make various alterations in the accidentals, even though he had passed these once in 1668. Yet it is impossible to believe that all these variants in 1670 have an authoritative source; for, in addition to following the 1668 alterations, the 1670 edition makes three changes in word division, twenty-three in capitalization, and eight in punctuation, at least one of these last being a manifest error. The 1670 edition as copy-text, therefore, would depart from 1667 in a total of forty-four accidentals, of which only three can be demonstrated as authoritative. Similiar rough studies which I have made of the corrections in standing type versus variants in reset pages in Dekker's *Magnificent entertainment* and *Honest whore*, in the first few years of the seventeenth century, produce the same conclusions.

These two specific cases in which evidence is available to act as a control for judging the relative contributions of revising author and resetting compositor serve, in my opinion, to discredit the rationale behind the choice of the latest revised edition as copy-text on the grounds that thus one secures every possible authorial correction or revision in the accidentals. It seems clear that by this procedure in old texts one departs from the author more frequently than one follows him. When only printed texts are available, the odds for retaining the closest possible approximation to the author's own accidentals are predominantly in favor of the first edition set from an authoritative manuscript. If an editor chooses this as his basis, as Greg advises under most conditions, and thereupon incorporates in the texture those substantive revisions which in his judgment are authoritative, together with such conservative alteration of accidentals as seems necessary to avoid misreadings or more than momentary ambiguity, he may miss some few refinements; but he will in the long run produce a text which, more accurately than by any other method, comes as close as possible to the author's original and revised intentions.

IV

VINTON A. DEARING

Methods of Textual Editing

I speak to you today as a representative of a dicipline that produced its first significant work, Zenodotus' critical edition of
Homer, more than twenty-two centuries ago; a discipline that
has numbered among its practitioners Augustine and Erasmus,
Richard Bentley and A. E. Housman, Dr. Samuel Johnson and
Sir Walter Greg; but a discipline that in twenty-two hundred
years failed to free itself from inconsistency and subjectivity.
Zenodotus finished his Homer shortly before 274 B.C., so the
twenty-second century of textual editing was completed by
1926. It is therefore remarkably interesting, although of no
significance whatsover, that in 1927 Walter Greg built the first
unshakable foundation for textual criticism in his *Calculus of
Variants*. Then in 1940 John M. Manley and Edith Rickert
described in their edition of Chaucer's *Canterbury Tales* the first
method for accurate and speedy recording of variant readings,
in which one uses specially prepared cards. Next, after the war,
Charleton Hinman adapted an optical device used for comparing
aerial and sidereal photographs so as to make possible for the
first time speedy and accurate comparisons of books that differ
only in minute resettings of their type. Finally, this spring,
Ronald Bland completed a program for recording variant readings with the IBM 7090 computer, which I shall have the pleasure
of describing publicly for the first time today. Clearly, textual
editing began a new cycle with its twenty-third century, and in
describing to you its present promise, I have no hesitation in
adopting Milton's words in the *Areopagitica*, "Methinks I see
in my mind a noble and puissant [discipline] rousing herself like
a strong man after sleep, and shaking her invincible locks: methinks I see her as an eagle mewing her mighty youth, and

Originally delivered at a seminar on bibliography held at the William
Andrews Clark Library, University of California at Los Angeles, 12 May
1962. Reprinted by permission of the author and the University Librarian.

kindling her undazzled eyes at the full midday beam, purging and unscaling her long abused sight at the fountain itself of heavenly radiance."

As we hear these noble words, do we not all, in spirit, hoist ourselves up and look burly and dominant, as Keats used to do in the flesh? Are we not united in our love of literature? For a textual editor, unless he be a Koheleth or a Carlyle, preaching "whatsoever thy hand findeth to do, do it with thy might," does not suppose the road to salvation leads on through his work considered merely as work. On the other hand, he does see in his tasks a dimension other than the literary. Exploring books and manuscripts is his avocation; his vocation is the pursuit of truth. An adventurer on the wide sea of knowledge, he has abandoned the tactics of Arnold's Tyrian trader, who, you will recall, held on indignantly when he descried another sail, and has adopted instead those of Melville's Captain Ahab, ready to hold a gam with any crew that might have news for him. News today comes to the textual editor from quarters not traditional—I utter the word "automation." There are scholars who regret the invention of the typewriter, so I pile up my allusions to seduce, if it were possible, even the elect to join in admiring the poetry that roused my friend John Harrison—the powerful and contemporary metaphor of Colonel Glenn just before the Friendship 7 lifted from its launch pad, "I am go; all systems are go."

For this is the age of systems, and the textual editor, who is a systems analyst in the field of literature, finds himself surrounded by those who have wrestled successfully with similar problems and are willing to share their methods. The systems the textual editor analyzes are the family trees through which his texts have descended. If the texts circulated at all widely in manuscript, the systems are almost always enormously complicated. Furthermore, collecting the evidence upon which to base an analysis of even a simple system almost always means carefully comparing thousands of words, and sometimes millions. It is not surprising, therefore, that the rules for analysis laid down before Greg's time were mostly rules of thumb for ignoring the evidence. Greg, however, established a set of universal logical principles, a set that may be added to, but may not be ignored if one is to avoid inconsistency and uncontrolled subjectivity. Manley, Rickert, and Hinman made it possible for Greg's successors to give less time to collecting data and more time to enlarging the set of known principles for analysis. The advent of the computer has made it possible for the textual editor to work still faster, and at the same time has made it imperative for him to devote the time saved from routine labor to developing principles, for a computer, being inflexibly consistent and completely objective, shows at once in its output any failures in the logic of its instructions. Whereas in the past, then, textual editors, finding the way rough, got over the stile into By-Path Meadow and, benighted and storm-beaten, were captured by Giant Despair, now the genial pressure of automation, like the sun in the fable, will cause us to throw off what before we hugged about us.

I use automation in the wide sense of systematizing and speeding routine procedures with any mechanical device. By this definition, Hinman automated a part of textual editing with his collating machine, and so did Manley and Rickert with their printed and tabbed cards for recording variant readings. But even if he does not use any mechanical devices at all, the textual editor can profit from the kind of thinking that these devices have stimulated. For instance, machines are often used to determine by the critical path method the best organization of long and complex tasks, but the textual editor can do the same work mentally. Those who employ the critical path method do no more in essence than analyze their tasks into components, and determine which parts of the work may be pursued simultaneously, and which must wait upon the completion of other parts. The longest train of tasks, that is, the one that will take the longest to work through, determines the minimum time that must be allotted to the task, and progress through it is critical. Progress along any parallel paths needs watching, but calls for special effort only when it has fallen so far behind as to hold up work in the critical path. This method is entirely applicable to any of our tasks, academic or not, where ease and dispatch bring comfort or reward, and has therefore been understandably popular wherever foresight will replace pessure and confusion with preparedness and order.

For the textual editor, the critical path that ends in a critical edition will normally pass through the following eight processes:

Exploring the implications of the project
Collecting the texts

Choosing a base text for comparison
Comparing the texts
Determining the archetype or copy text
Emending
Normalizing
Writing the textual notes

If the editor begins early to think through his rules for normalizing and for writing his notes, he may be able to save himself time in comparison, for there is not much sense in recording variants that will be normalized or that will for any other reason not appear in the notes. If he is going to automate the comparison, he must assemble his equipment and staff while he is collecting the texts. If he is going to automate the processes of determining the archetype or copy text and of emending, he must in addition decide among the schools of thought on these subjects and perhaps find someone to write computer programs for him —or learn to write them himself. Programs already exist for systematizing the determination of archetypes, for compiling concordances, and for filling lacunae on the basis of the author's practice, but the editor may be dissatisfied with these or wish to develop, go beyond, or link them in some way. If he wishes to do much programming, he may find that his critical path runs from exploring the implications of the project through programming to determining the archetype or to emending, and I shall therefore devote some consideration to this matter further along. In any case, the initial process is to explore the implications of the project.

This is not so simple a matter as it may seem, and if one conscientiously examines other projects and seeks the advice of others, he may spend a month or two before he is ready to go ahead. Many questions must be answered. First, is the end in view to reproduce a text already accepted as standard or one that owing to wide circulation and influence has its own historical importance, or is the goal rather to embody in a new text the author's best conception of his work? Next, should contemporary spelling be reproduced, or should it be "discreetly modernized," as the cover blurb on the Viking Portable Milton discreetly puts it? Having determined so much, one must ask, like Burr in *The Wild Gallant*, "Where's the money for this, dear heart?" Will there be generous funds for research and publication, so that one may have satisfaction in the work itself and in its product? And satisfaction is not dependent merely upon adequate funds. Is the textual editor alone to determine every detail of the text and the form and extent of the textual annotations? If not, what freedom will the other editors have to choose readings and make emendations, what share will they and the officials of the press have in the design of the text and notes? Even if the textual editor is not to bestride his narrow world like a Colossus, he should be satisfied with the working arrangement he negotiates.

Equally important is investigating whether the edition will ever appear.. Textual editing is a long, exacting, and often monotonous task, whose sole monument, almost, will be the finished edition. What guarantees can the textual editor receive here, and what guarantees can he give? Can he complete his part of the edition in reasonable time? Is he willing to share his task with others if necessary to speed the work? If he should decide to withdraw from the project, would he expect his successor to do the work over, or would he expect the next man to have free use of the materials already collected? These questions answered, what evidence is there that all the associates in the project will answer these questions similarly? If there are any doubts here, it is surely wiser that text and commentary appear in separate volumes; and, if the work has already begun on some other plan, one ought not to enter it.

Finally, if one is to have continuing satisfaction in the project he will need to believe and continue to believe that the project is worth the effort he will be expending on it. Here he must make the most serious examination into his reasons for undertaking the task and the firmness of his literary tastes. The importance of exploring the implications of the project cannot be overestimated, for only upon its successful completion can one say, "I am go."

Now for the second of the eight processes on the critical path, collecting the texts. If an editor is to reproduce a standard or received form of a work, he may yet wish to discover any differences in the texts that have been accepted as equivalents. If he is producing a new text, he will wish to identify all the changes that have been introduced into the work, with a view to separating out any that were not intended by the author, and commonly also with a view to establishing the genealogy of the texts, at least during the author's lifetime. If one does not care to establish the genealogy of the texts after it has ceased to cast light on the author's intentions, he can normally save time and effort.

There are, therefore, two questions to be answered: how many texts are to be examined, and how many copies of each? Only one aspect of the first question needs special comment: British scholars do not take much account of manuscript material unless the author never saw his work in print, but any American editor who agrees with them is only joining them in a silent invitation to some other American to supplement or supersede his edition. In the current slang of Hollywood, Americans have a thing about manuscripts. If *aere perennius* is one's goal, therefore, he will search for manuscripts. For the California Dryden we now examine (1) all printings and manuscripts we can locate, down to the author's death; (2) all manuscripts down to the first printing of posthumous works; and (3) the earliest eighteenth-century collected editions, in the event that they may prove to have drawn upon manuscript material now lost. We also examine the major scholarly editions preceding our own, but here we are looking for useful emendations.

The other question, how many copies of a text ought to be compared, is an extremely interesting and complex problem for the editor who wishes to sort out any changes not introduced by the author. It is now, I believe, common knowledge that no single copy of a printed text can be unhesitatingly accepted as containing no changes introduced without the author's consent. One's goal therefore is the identification of copies that preserve the text as it was before it was tampered with. Unauthorized changes may be introduced at the same time as authorial revisions are introduced, and they may be introduced at more than one stage in the run of the press. Of course, changes are introduced independently on each side of the printed sheet, unless part of it is cut away.

Now, how many copies must one examine to locate all the possible changes? To simplify the calculations, let us say that "success" is locating at least one copy of every sheet in the state that had the fewest copies produced. By this definition of success, the search becomes a binary experiment in probability, and there are tables from which one can answer the question. Supposing a normal edition size of 1500 to 2000 copies, that the copies coming to hand are a representative or random sample, and that within each copy all the sheets were printed about the same place in each run, one must examine 100 copies to be 99 44/100 percent sure that he has located all the changes found in 5 percent or more of the copies, and to have about two chances out of three of having located all changes found in 1 percent or more of the copies.

As Professor James Jackson of our Business School put it to me, this immediately poses the problem of whether the expense of such an examination is justified by the results. Surely it will be seldom that one can answer yes. Most editors would have doubts about the expense of comparing ten copies. What is the probability that a sample of ten copies will include an example of the state found in the least number of copies? It is 98 percent certain to include an example if that state was common to one third of the copies produced, and it has three chances in four of including an example if that state was common to at least one eighth of the copies produced. If the order of the sheets has been mixed in the process of drying them or in any of the other moves from the press to the bindery, the three in four probability will be less in proportion to the length of the volume and amount of mixing. Therefore if one assumes that no change would be peculiar to less than one eighth of the run in printing each side of the sheet, then by comparing ten copies of a book of ten sheets (a play, for instance) that suffered some mixing of the order of those sheets after printing, one might have something like a fifty-fifty chance of having located all the changes.

Under the circumstances, there appear to be three ways of approaching the problem of expense. A first is not to compare multiple copies except in editions printed from independent manuscripts or evidently revised by the author, and so to compare more than would otherwise be possible. A second is to make a random sample of passages from the text in the editions examined, and so to compare more copies than would be possible if each were compared throughout. A third, suggested to me by Professor James Jackson, is to search for passages that either seem to have been corrected or seem to need correction and to examine these passages in a large number of copies. The last proposal is doubly interesting as focusing attention on the probabilities of when and how the text has been altered, which if one uses what is called Bayesian inference have a good deal of effect on his satisfaction with the sample size.

Someday, I hope, a statistician who is also a bibliographer will provide us with special formulas and tables to guide our calculations more surely. The textual editor is like the boy who found nothing at the end of the foggy alley where he expected the omnibus of the Surbiton and Celestial Road Car Company. " 'Give the bus every chance,' he thought cynically, and returned into the alley. But the omnibus was there." Certainty about variants is the textual editor's celestial omnibus, and if he can only determine what constitutes giving it "every chance" he will find it. In the California Dryden, we have normally examined five copies of every edition likely to reflect the author's intentions, three copies of other contemporary editions, and one only of the rest. Professor Bowers normally compares many more. But only Charleton Hinman and Harris Fletcher in their work with Shakespeare and Milton can be said to have found their omnibus by the methods presently in use.

Will you not agree with me that if many texts are to be collected, two years is a normal minimum for the work? One year will be devoted to searching published lists and to securing grants for microfilm and for travel to distant libraries. Since the textual editor can argue that microfilm may not reproduce important characteristics of manuscripts and printed books—Professor William Jackson and others have written and spoken eloquently on this subject, and may be cited in his support—and since there is no great likelihood that grant-making will be automated, it may be that two years will remain a normal minimum. But the time spent in going through printed lists will be significantly reduced as book-finding is automated.

Once I had to search through the catalogues of Thomas Thorpe in the Grolier Club. Considering that I was paid for the work, and was working in the most august surroundings, *forsan et haec olim meminisse juvabit*—but I doubt it. I don't think I have ever minded dust on books at any other time, but those catalogues, grimy volume upon grimy volume, page upon page of fine print, and nothing, nothing, nothing that I wanted—my memory of those catalogues is tactile. I can still feel them, and with the same revulsion. John Livingston Lowes told his Chaucer class when I was a member that he had quested his way through most of the writings in Middle English; he had always some linguistic or folkloristic grail-vision that sustained him when the literary landscape patterned the scene around Childe Roland's tower. Order librarians, like our good Mrs. Davis, no doubt have a similar talisman. But not I, not I. I yearn for the day when all lists and indexes of books and manuscripts will be transferred to film or electronic tape in some central library, and I can receive by return mail photographs or transcripts of the entries that will interest me.

My colleague, Hugh Dick, has long cherished, I know, the project of a universal catalogue of English literary manuscripts. The day will surely come when some center for documentation will be ready to answer inquiries about manuscripts in the libraries of the world. For some time a similar service has been available to members of the American Metals Society from the Center for Documentation at Western Reserve University in Cleveland. The Center is extending its activities into medical and legal literature, and I was questioned, when I studied its operations last summer, as to what I thought would be worthwhile projects in imaginative literature. I sow my seed again here, for while the first certainly did not fall on stony ground, it may have fallen among thorns. Perhaps it will be you, Robert Vosper, who will provide us this much needed help.

What is the present situation? If a Jackson has preceded one with a Pforzheimer catalogue or a revised *STC*, or a Greg or a Bowers with bibliographies and checklists based on minute examination of many copies, one has no great problems. Some of the published catalogues of the great private collections of the recent past or present give fairly full descriptions of many books, and there are briefer but still distinctive descriptions in many other published library catalogues, and in booksellers' and auctioneers' catalogues. Workers in the neoclassical period have also an immensely valuable first-line index to poems in miscellany volumes, compiled by Richard C. Boys and Arthur Mizener and as yet unpublished. With Dryden we are particularly fortunate, for we have Hugh Macdonald's descriptive bibliography of Dryden and James Osborn's report on discoveries made by a group of scholars who at his request compared Macdonald's descriptions with the holdings of major libraries in this country; we have Woodward and MacManaway's *Check List of English Plays 1660–1700*, and Bowers' *Supplement* to it. Even so, we occasionally turn up something new. If one is the first to survey his field, he is quite likely to find something new in the catalogue of every library he visits.

It is harder with manuscripts. All manuscripts known to contain Anglo-Saxon have been catalogued, and almost all those known to contain Middle English verse, but the only extensive guides to other British manuscripts in public collections are the catalogues of the British Museum and of the college and university libraries at Oxford and Cambridge—particularly, of course, the Bodleian. The National Library of Scotland and a few others have published catalogues of most of their holdings. My feeling is that manuscript material in any volume ceases to flow to public collections well within a century of the death of the author in question; therefore workers in the more hallowed fields of English literature need not be particularly concerned that catalogues of recent acquisitions, especially by the Bodleian, have not yet been published. Major acquisitions appear in annual reports and bulletins published by the libraries.

Both the British Museum and the Bodleian have relatively complete first-line indexes to the manuscript poems in their collections. The British Museum's is in volumes and could be microfilmed complete for a relatively small sum (Yale has such a microfilm); the Bodleian's is on cards. The British Museum has a consolidated subject index in volumes, the Bodleian has a consolidated author, title, and subject index on cards. I did not find, myself, that subject indexing provided many leads I did not pick up elsewhere more easily, but I hesitate to set this up as a general rule. The *ASLIB Directory* gives some idea of the holdings of other libraries, and their librarians will answer queries. The editors of the *Poems on Affairs of State* wrote to libraries to inquire if they had any likely holdings and were good enough to share what they had learned with us Drydenians. But manuscript cataloguing at present is incomplete enough in most libraries to warrant a visit by the textual editor to any whose holdings sound promising. In searching for manuscripts of Dryden's works, my greatest proportion of plums to pudding came during a morning at the University of Nottingham among the manuscript miscellanies in the Portland Papers. The name Nottingham conjures up to workers in my period Swift's old enemy, Dismal, the Don Diego of *The History of John Bull*, but, Sir, if you call a dog Nottingham I shall love him.

Workers in American literature now have the Modern Language Association's *American Literary Manuscripts: A Checklist of Holdings in Academic, Historical, and Public Libraries in the United States*, Phillip N. Hamer's *Guide to Archives and*

Manuscripts in the United States, and Crick and Alman's *Guide to Manuscripts Relating to America in Great Britain and Ireland,* all published last year. Before that time they had to rely almost solely upon the bulletins and annual reports of the various libraries. Until the advent of automation there will be no other way of bringing these publications up to date, except by making inquiries among friends. Of course, the milk of human kindness flows freely in the scholarly world, and nothing is more pleasant than to review the letters that accumulate during a textual investigation.

For locating manuscripts in booksellers' and private hands, Osborn's article in the *English Institute Annual* for 1939 is surely the best guide. It is in some ways the counsel of perfection, but all the more useful for being so, and it reflects the experience not only of a scholar but of one of the foremost private collectors of our time.

Whether one is searching for books or manuscripts, he must not forget that music will often include literary texts, and that in many libraries music and books are catalogued separately.

Finally, where his texts are monumental inscriptions, the editor should get in touch with a local historian or the local historical society. The Gloucestershire County Archivist told me by return mail that I should find in Haresfield Church the original of Dryden's epitaph headed in the printed editions "On young Mr. Rogers of Gloucestershire." Wyndham Ketton-Cremer similarly located for me the epitaph "On Mrs. Margaret Paston of Barningham in Norfolk," a member of the famous Paston family about which Ketton-Cremer has written so well, and who is not buried at Barningham. A bank of pews now covers most of this inscription, which is on the floor of the parish church at Blofield, Norfolk, but the rector sent me a copy made by the father of one of his parishioners before the pews were installed.

The third process in the critical series is deciding which text is to be the one with which the others are to be compared. Ideally, this will be the text upon which the edition will principally be based, the copy text, so called, because this will mean a minimum of rewriting of the notes that set forth the variations, notes that are always keyed to the text printed with them. If you open the heart of a textual editor you will find written there, "Beware of the leaven of the scribes," and he is under no illusions as to the difficulties of avoiding scribal error in rewriting his textual notes. But he cannot decide on his copy text until he has completed his comparison. If he does not make his comparisons against some standard form of the text, he may guess that the first apparently authorized edition or the earliest "good" manuscript will turn out to be his copy text and proceed accordingly. If he plans to use Mr. Bland's program for comparing the texts by computer, he will, other things being equal, choose the longest text as the basis for comparison. The choice itself is not time-consuming, but it had better be postponed until the editor has some fairly clear idea of the nature of the texts with which he will be working.

The fourth process, comparing the texts, can then start immediately. One part of the comparison work could begin while the editor is visiting the great libraries, that is, the comparison of copies printed from the same or nearly the same setting of type, which is most conveniently done with Hinman collating machines. These machines can only be used with the books themselves, and only a few great libraries have enough books that might be compared to make it worth while for them to purchase a machine. The only other reason why it might be more efficient to begin comparison before collecting all the texts would be that the editor was doing the work himself at intervals in a life largely given to other things. If he employs students at an hourly rate, and they are not much concerned about a steady income, he can do the same. But if he pays weekly or monthly wages to his assistants, and especially if he rents machines, he will do well to put off the comparison until he can work men and machines without interruption, perhaps even on double shifts, until the work is done.

There are at least five methods of comparing texts, all of which have been used with Dryden. The first is to take an available printed text, correct it to agree with the base text, and note any variations in other texts in its margins. This is the best way in the world to have one's slips show. Any failure to correct the text used will allow a late variant to creep into the text printed. Montague Summers, for example, obviously sent to the press a copy of the folio of 1701 with which he had compared the other texts of Dryden's plays.

The editors of the California Dryden have used typescripts of the copy texts, and will in the future use photographic reproductions as well. Typescripts are more satisfactory when the text must be altered a good deal by the editor, but photographic reproductions are cheaper and more accurate—although they must still be proofread. Typescripts and photographic reproductions on flexible paper allow the editor to juxtapose his texts when comparing them so that he does not need to depend on his memory as he must when he moves his eye from one to the other. He tapes his typescript or photostat round a suitably dimensioned frame made of closely set rods, most of which rotate, but two of which, near the ends, are firmly fixed in the side pieces. He rolls each line in turn to the top of the frame, which he positions just below the corresponding line in the book being compared. He can then see both lines at once. Obviously this method will be most economically used if one compares all the relevant texts with the lines on each typed sheet or photostat before proceeding to the next. One must still watch carefully for additions in the other texts that might fall between the last line on one typed sheet or photostat and the first line on the next.

For our first volume of Dryden's plays, I used this method only when checking and proofreading, for we entered variants between the lines of our typescripts. Only a few texts had to be compared, but even so it became hard to read between the lines, so to speak, in many places, and this resulted in more rechecking than would have otherwise been necessary.

Another way of recording variants is to enter them in columns on separate sheets, one set of sheets for each edition, the readings of the base text on the left, the variants therefrom on the right. The sheets must then be consolidated in a master set, which not only takes extra time in itself but introduces the possibility of error in transcription. The comparisons for the first volume of the poems in the California Dryden were prepared in this way, but as the work was done carefully, and carefully rechecked by a number of people, the results seem to have been very accurate. Mr. Robert Chamberlin, who has been working on the comparisons for our next volume of plays, has introduced in place of the separate sets of sheets the use of multicolumned ledger sheets on which the readings of the base text are entered in the left column and the variants in series in their proper columns to the right. One must estimate how many spaces to skip when entering the first comparisons, since others will be turning up as the work proceeds, but this has not proved to be an insuperable objection.

Having always before the eye the variants previously discovered draws one's attention to some of the errors that creep into the work, and this is a positive advantage. With a base text of approximately 70 pages, Mr. Chamberlin needs about 125 hours to compare seven other texts in minute detail, that is, even as to capitalization.

Manley and Rickert's method of recording variants similarly relieves the memory and has so many other advantages as to make it the most perfect method of comparison, if one has the time to use it. In this method, each line of the base text is typed at the very top of a card, slip, or sheet, on which has been printed, dittoed, or mimeographed, a list of the texts to be compared. The card is proofread by placing it on the base text so that it covers any lines in that text below the one in question. The eye can then see at once whether the typing is correct; no memory work is involved. The cards are then compared with the other texts in the same way and any variants noted are written in their proper place below the typed line, together with the sigla of the texts in which they have been found. As each card is compared with each text, the list of texts on it is marked, so that there will be no question as to whether a text has been examined—as there might otherwise be if it did not vary from the base text.

Having completed his collating, the editor may examine his base text on its cards with all the variants written out beneath the lines in which they occur, decide which, if any, he will take into his own text, write in these, and any other changes he wishes to make, in the typed lines, and turn his packet of cards over to a typist. He can read proof on the text she produces by positioning his cards as before. The typescript is then ready for submission to the press with a minimum of further change. He can read his printed proof in the same way. During all these proofreadings, his list of variants is always at hand for immediate consultation should doubts arise as to the evidence for any of the readings he has printed. Finally, he can compile his textual apparatus easily and accurately, since all the material for each entry is already gathered together on one sheet.

The method is easiest to use with poetry, because the lining is usually the same in every text. It is not much less advantageous for prose, but memory is involved when the line on the card or typescript is partly on one line of the text being checked and partly on another—additions or omissions at the ends or the beginnings of the lines must be specially watched for. One prime advantage, being able to juxtapose the lines compared, will be lost if the typing is not at the very top of the card, if the texts must be examined under glass (Manley and Rickert used photostats of the Chaucer manuscripts), or if the reading room attendant will not let you touch the texts with the card.

Manley and Rickert's cards allow rapid as well as accurate, work once they have been prepared, and we have used them in comparing the texts for our second volume of Dryden's poems. I compared in detail approximately 600 octavo pages in two months. When one is pressed for time, especially if he already has a typescript of his copy text, he has some difficulty in reconciling himself to making another copy on cards or slips. It is probable, however, that even under these circumstances it would be better to take the necessary time. In preparing the text of the first volume of Dryden's plays, for example, we spent so much time in checking and proofreading, time that we should have saved had we used cards or slips, that I believe the additional typing would have been more than justified.

We expect to check our comparisons for the second volume of the plays by using Mr. Bland's program for the IBM 7090, and thereafter to rely on it alone. My friend Charles Hobbs interested Mr. Bland in the work, and helped him somewhat in the planning of it. Both these men have worked on their own time—both were at first employed at System Development Corporation and Mr. Bland is now at Douglas Aircraft Corporation—and neither has received any payment. I do not hesitate to say that the scholarly world's indebtedness to them is incalculable.

This is how we shall proceed using the computer program. Reading from a small microfilm projector, a typist sitting at an IBM card puncher will copy each text, a line on a card, or on two cards if it is a long line. A different typist will take the film and the cards to an IBM card verifier. If her typing as she reads the film does not exactly match the information on the cards, she can go no further until she has corrected her error or twice verified her typing and notched the card where it is wrong. Since both typists work by touch, there is no great opportunity for memory lapses, and such as do occur, together with any misreadings, will not normally exactly match in the work of both. After any necessary corrections, the cards will be sorted by machine so that all cards for line 1 are together, with that for text

1 first, all the cards for line 2 next, and so on. Then these, with the program, will be sent to the 7090 computer, which will produce a complete copy of the first text, and under each line a record of the variants in the rest. In general, where the texts are the same, it will leave a blank; sometimes it will print material that does not vary, but only in the process of printing the variants, and this we have not felt it necessary to refine to the last degree. When the material is in prose, I expect to work with simple sentences and independent clauses instead of lines.

As presently set, the program handles up to 99 texts, and any amount of data; it could be adjusted easily enough to deal with 999 or 9,999 texts. If there is more data than its memory will hold, it feeds in the rest after it has dealt with what it has taken in, retaining the last 10 lines of the earlier material in the new batch.

The machine looks at the beginnings and ends of the lines, matching each new text of each line against the base text of that line. If it finds no differences it reads along the line, left to right until it comes to a difference, then from the end toward the front until it comes to a difference. It prints out any differences it finds, below the words from which they differ, as well as any material between the outermost two differences, if it finds more than one. Poetical rhetoric being what it is, the machine works a considerable way into the beginning of the line before deciding that the lines correspond. If it finds differences near the beginning and at the end of the line, it first searches 10 lines in either direction in the base text to be sure it has not come upon an omission, insertion, and transposition of lines. If it has not, it proceeds as before. It compares transposed lines with those they match in sense, but gives the line numbers as transposed, with a special mark beside the line numbers to draw attention to the fact that a transposition has occurred. Should an eye-skip result in a line composed of parts of two original lines, the variant line is recorded under each of the original lines. Finally, before printing, the machine checks to see if any previously-examined text had the same variant, and if so it merely notes the fact. The printed output is very similar in appearance and usefulness to that found on the Manley and Rickert cards. The increase in speed of comparison is, of course, enormous. Five texts of 56 lines are collated in twelve seconds, 27 texts of 24 lines are collated in 30 seconds.

Further increases in speed are still possible. As you can see, typing and retyping the texts on the card punching machine is a bottleneck, especially as the card punching machines are slower than typewriters. Other users have been perfectly aware of this, and have begun to develop machines that will read printed or typewritten text much more rapidly than a man can. Reasonably flexible machines will in time appear on the market at prices that will make them attractive to universities as well as to businesses and industries, and I believe we may then expect universities to expend the additional money necessary to modify such machines so they will recognize long "s" and other type forms no longer in use. It will then be possible to do textual comparisons in minutes instead of months.

Until such a time comes, Hinman's collating machine remains the speediest and best method for comparing books printed from the same or substantially the same setting of type, but the textual editor will have to use some other method for comparing books that cannot be assembled in one library. It is possible to speed the work with two slide projectors adapted for unperforated roll film and a shutter or shutters for alternately interrupting the images they project. The more sophisticated one can make the devices to interrupt the images and to turn, tilt, elevate, and advance or draw back the projectors, the better. Even with very crude equipment and having given no special instructions to the microfilm photographer, one can normally make the images from the projectors coincide more or less perfectly over an area of a third to a half a page, but the cruder the device the slower the work. Careful instructions as to size, when ordering the film, much diminish the amount of adjustment required, especially of fore and aft displacement of the projectors. Having the images superimposed, one starts to interrupt them alternately. Any difference in the images will result in a jumping about or a blinking on and off of the letters, and punctuation marks, just as with a Hinman machine. With microfilm, however, there will be more or less adventitious jumping about in those parts of the page where the images do not coincide perfectly.

Professor Dick put me on to this method by describing some of Hinman's early experiments. I should warn anyone who wishes to try such a device that, in its cruder forms, the adjustments may become rather tiresome when no variants appear. One should at least provide screws for tilting one projector and elevating the other, a fixed track for fore and aft movement of one projector, and a fixed pivot for the other; and he should start his work with pages where he already knows there are variants, for the thrill of seeing them pop out as the type jumps about will hearten him for the much greater number of pages where he will merely be proving that no variants exist. Our comparisons for the first volume of Dryden's plays were partially made with such a device.

The fifth process in the critical path, determining the archetype and copy text, will normally wait until the completion of the comparison of the texts. If, however, one is not comparing all the texts with each page of a typescript before going to the next page, and is not using a computer, and if he is taking the texts in chronological order, he will discover after a time that he is no longer turning up variants that seem to him preferable to the readings of his base text, and he can then begin his fifth process with small risk of having to do the work over. This process is harder to describe than to perform; a thousand lines a day is not a fast rate.

The first decision the textual editor must now make, if he has not already done so, is what variations are significant. Classical scholars tend to ignore variations where they cannot decide that one reading is the cause of the other or others. This seems to scholars in English and American literature to be ignoring many variations that are not only relevant but perhaps decisive in the analysis. Of course, the inflected languages provide many more variations in which one can decide that one reading is original, the other or others derivative. Still, it hardly seems reasonable to suppose that varying conventions in expression would lead to the same sort of fluctuations in readings that the varying conventions in spelling do. Workers with English texts commonly suppose that scribes and compositors will try to reproduce the exact wording of their copy, together with any punctuation required to make the meaning clear—and it is variations in these details that they analyze. There remains the question of whether variations in title and by-line are of equal significance with those in the text. I think they are.

One other very important set of decisions the textual editor must make concerns the evidence he will accept as distinguishing earlier, and so more authoritative, readings from the later and less authoritative. It is very hard to decide on absolute principles here, and still harder to determine when they shall apply.

Many of the rules in common use are comparatively vague, and others are in dispute. For example, when one text is known to be earlier than another, it usually seems reasonable to attribute to authorial revision any striking and otherwise inexplicable differences between them, but the more differences there are that may reasonably be attributed to non-authorial carelessness or tampering, the more striking must be the differences that are to be attributed to the author. This is a sufficiently vague rule, but one that the textual editor must often resort to.

Even when there are some changes that one can call authorial, he has a problem with the so-called indifferent variations, which, if they do not seem particularly authorial, do not seem particularly non-authorial either. It used to be the practice to accept the indifferent variations as authorial revisions, and this position is today called the conservative one. Then in 1951 Sir Walter Greg, in an influential essay in *Studies in Bibliography*, proposed that indifferent variations be rejected as non-authorial, and this position today is called the liberal one. It was as a representative of the liberal position that Professor Bowers proposed facsimile reprints should reproduce uncorrected states of their texts wherever possible. This distrust of compositor, scribe, and proofreader runs counter to our attitude toward their handling of the other parts of texts: obviously they cannot have consistently deviated from their copy. Perhaps Professor Bowers has felt the force of this contradiction, for if I read his latest discussion of textual editing correctly, he has changed over to the conservative point of view.

Decisions as to how to tell early readings from late are also important because they affect one's understanding of the evidence for conflation when only three texts are in question: conflation or contamination means producing a text by reference to more than one exemplar. Most discussions of this last point seem wrong to me, but each textual editor must make up his own mind.

If the editor is working with printed texts, and it is clear that all but the earliest are reprints at one or more removes of the earliest, then he will normally choose the earliest as his copy text, that is, the text he is to reprint, though he may introduce alterations into it. The theory behind this decision is that (1) there will be no authority in changes introduced into mere reprints, and (2) even revisions introduced by the author into later editions do not certify his approval of every change that may be found in such editions. If the author is discovered to have approved every detail of a certain edition, as Pope approved the quarto edition of his First Moral Essay, then his wishes are to be respected. If he does not express such approval, however, one reasons that the earliest compositor is at least following copy supplied by the author or descended from the author's manuscript and so represents the author's practice better than any reprint into which further changes have crept. It might be argued that an author would wish his work to appear in the latest style, but textual editors today generally prefer to reproduce as much as possible the author's style when he wrote the work.

How does one determine that one printed text is the ancestor of all the rest? Quite simply: such an ancestor will be the earliest text and those subsequent to it will agree with it in details that can best be explained as having been copied from it, or will agree in the same way, but in different details, with editions that agree in this way with the earliest. The appearance in any later text of what seem clearly to be authorial revisions indicate that the author made his changes in a printed copy of his work and sent that to the press.

In the absence of such indications of ancestry, the textual editor may still simply decide that the earliest edition will be his copy text, but if he finds any edition not certainly descended from the first and which includes some readings that seem more like the author than those in the first edition, he will choose as his copy text the edition that seems to him best to represent the author's style in his holograph. If he has only two such texts, he has only to choose between them, but if he has more, he must reconstruct the manuscript to which ultimately they all trace back, called the archetype, and he will then choose as his copy text the edition that best represents the archetype.

When any of his texts are in manuscript, the textual editor will normally conclude that he must reconstruct an archetype, and he will plan to choose as his copy text the manuscript or edition that proves to be the best representative of the archetype. Normally, however, he soon finds himself in a snarl, and not a few editors then resort to taking as their copy text the one they will have to change the least as they introduce into it readings they like in the other texts. This eclectic method, as it is called, can always be justified on human grounds, but editions produced by it are always in danger of being superseded by those constructed on logical principles.

There are two steps in determining an archetype. The first is determining the paths by which likenesses between texts could have travelled from one text to another. The second is deciding where the archetype lies along these paths. Now the textual editor who ignores Greg's rules for determining the paths will fall into illogicality—it is as simple as that. Greg's rules are complete, however, only for variations where there are only two alternate readings (called simple variations), and where the paths do not run in circles (this occurs when there are chance likenesses between texts, or when one or more are conflated). I have worked out rules for variations where there are more than two alternate readings (called complex variations) and have embodied them and Greg's rules for simple variations in a program for the IBM 7090 computer. A great many problems, however, are simple enough to work out with pencil and paper. Various conventions for breaking circular paths have been proposed, and the textual editor must examine the logic of each if he wishes to avail himself of one.

The second step, placing the archetype in the network of paths, depends upon finding enough variations in which one reading is clearly authorial. The archetype is at the only point on the paths to which all the authorial readings can be traced. If there are not enough such readings, and in uninflected languages there commonly are not, one simply cannot tell exactly where to place the archetype. Greg is emphatic and unanswerable on this point. Since the archetype stands at the head of the network of paths, its placement affects the pattern into which the network will fall.

Archibald Hill has proposed that when one cannot locate the archetype, he can by convention accept it as standing at the point that will result in the simplest pattern of paths. I find this a very attractive thesis, in spite of disagreements with Hill as to what the criteria of simplicity should be in this matter. Others, however, maintain that their experience with texts disproves it. Of course, no experience with texts will prove or disprove the thesis, unless it is some kind of a laboratory experience—and we cannot experiment with past occurrences. It occurred to me, however, that with a computer such laboratory experiments were possible.

Since there are no physical laws that determine the form of a textual family tree, except that the second must be copied from the first and that no text can be copied from one that has been destroyed, these family trees in nature grow at random. It would be possible to make a number of copies and copies of copies of a text, choosing the exemplars at random, but it is enough simply to assign relationships at random to numbers representing texts: 2 must be a copy of 1; as for 3, decide at random whether it is to be a copy of 1 or 2; and so on. The principle computer at the Western Data Processing Center can in thirteen seconds generate a hundred random trees of ten text numbers each and then destroy the numbers, according to any general pattern desired, say, that of a Restoration poem with small circulation in manuscript, and can report the probability that the last two extant texts of such a poem will be ancestor and descendant.

Hill and I did agree that with only two extant manuscripts, simplicity demanded the ancestor-descendant pattern. The machine reports that in most situations probability and simplicity are at odds. I am still developing my program for these experiments, but I feel that it can ultimately be extended to determine the most likely pattern of descent for any set of real texts in which the distribution of authorial readings has not already decided the question.

The reconstruction of lost texts is simply a matter of taking a majority vote of their nonconflated independent descendants. When no majority accrues, the reconstruction is doubtful unless one of the readings is clearly original. It may then be hard to determine which of the extant texts is or best represents the archetype and so should be the copy text, but a decision must be made.

The sixth process in the critical path is emending the copy text, for even if it is the archetype, this is no guarantee that it transmits the author's intentions or practice with absolute fidelity. The principles of emendation are simple enough: the copy text is to be changed wherever its readings are not authorial and (1) the authorial readings can be identified in other texts, or (2) they can be reconstructed from the readings in the copy text, or (3) the copy text is unsatisfactory without some sort of change—but some scholars reject this last principle.

Ideally the textual editor should be familiar with the rules for reconstructing readings as they have been established, not without some dispute, by classical scholars, and should know at least Greg's and Bowers' discussions of the evidence for the nature of manuscript copy in the Elizabethan period. He can be familiarizing himself with these matters while he is working on the earlier processes in the critical path. As for readings that the editor recognizes as authorial revisions, it goes without saying that he introduces them into his text. These, however, he today emends in reverse; that is, if they do not agree with the author's practice in the rest of the text in matters where the sense is not affected, the editor adjusts them to harmonize with their surroundings, giving them a spurious appearance of antiquity for aesthetic reasons. As I have not made any literary allusions for some time, you may have forgotten that a textual editor has any aesthetic sensibility, but he does. It may be an antiquarian aesthetic, but it is still an aesthetic, and he treasures it as much as Horace Walpole treasured his.

Well, let us return to business. Emending can be a slow process if the archetype is very corrupt, and therefore computers can be a great help because they can so quickly run through a text, looking for any details one wishes and recording what they find. Missing portions of the Dead Sea Scrolls have been restored by computer. Concordances to the Revised Standard Version of the Bible and to Matthew Arnold's verse have been produced by computer, and no one needs to be told what a help a concordance is to understanding an author's practice. If a textual editor decides to use Mr. Bland's program for comparing his texts, it will be easy for him to run his data through a concordance program and so provide himself with a concordance before he comes to emend. I therefore predict that concordances will be regular adjuncts of critical editions in the near future. Without a computer program for emending, each editor must estimate for himself the time he must give to this process.

We have now passed through all the processes in which the textual editor can at present avail himself of a computer. This seems, then, the proper place to discuss more fully the effect that using computers may have in determining the critical path to his edition, that is, whether it will slow down his work instead of speed it up, or at any rate lighten its burden of routine. The textual editor can sometimes obtain programs from others, sometimes prevail upon an expert to help him, as Mr. Bland helped us with Dryden, or he can learn to write programs for himself.

Programs are nothing more than suites of formulaic instructions for the machines. The instructions belong to languages, as they are called, of which there are a considerable number, each with its special advantages and disadvantages. In the language called FORTRAN, for example, the instruction A = A + B means that A is to have not its former value but the sum of that value and the value of B. In the language called FAP (sounds like Major Hoople, doesn't it?), the same result requires three instructions: CLA A, which selects the value of A; ADD B, which is self-explanatory; and STO A, which means that A is now to have the value of the sum just calculated. Obviously FORTRAN is simpler to learn and use. On the other hand, its formulas will not handle data received as words instead of as numbers. Therefore Mr. Bland's program for comparing texts could not be written in FORTRAN, and is in fact written in FAP. The language to be used depends also upon the installation where the work is to be run through the machines, for machines do not all speak the same languages. On the other hand, if a program can be transferred from one language to another at all, it is not hard to make the change.

There are books that explain how to write programs, but I learned FORTRAN in courses given gratis at the Western Data Processing Center on my campus, and I learned FAP by instructing the machine to translate some programs I had written from FORTRAN into the new language, which I was then able to puzzle out with the help of a manual. While courses do not always fit one's own teaching schedule very well, most institutions offer them at a wide variety of times, and many different institutions offer them; they are not always free, however. It took eight hours in class to learn the elements of FORTRAN, and sixteen more to learn most of its refinements, but of course continued practice was necessary for growth toward mastery. I suppose it required another sixteen hours of intensive study before I recognized most of the parallels between FORTRAN and FAP and saw pretty clearly the advantages of each. Whenever I found that I did not understand something in either language, the staff of the Western Data Processing Center gladly answered my questions. It gives me great pleasure to acknowledge the help given me by the friends I have made at the Center, and to express my gratitude to the IBM Corporation and to my University, which jointly maintain it. Mr. Bland's program and my own have been devised for use with the machines there, and while, as I have suggested, they can be adapted for similar machines, still the fact that this equipment and instruction were made freely available has led to real advances in textual editing.

There are three main sources of wasted time in writing programs. One is not thinking through what one wishes to do before he starts or gets a friend to start on the job. Another is devising a program that will solve a small-scale problem but will not solve a large-scale problem of the same kind without extensive rewriting. And the third is figuring out for oneself what someone else already knows how to do. When in doubt, ask an expert, or be prepared to write off some time as spent in gaining what may prove to be invaluable experience. Even if one avoids waste, however, I think it would be unwise to allow less than an academic year for perfecting a program that breaks new ground, unless one could work at it full time. Even then it may require months to perfect a complex program.

I cannot leave the matter without pointing out that writing a program forces one to work out explicit step-by-step ways for putting his reasoning into practice, and so helps to clarify its logic. Furthermore, if egregious logical errors have escaped him, the machine will point out those that prevent it from following instructions. Lastly, since the machine follows its instructions to the letter, one can give it problems to which he already knows the answer, and then if he gets wrong results, can trace their causes in the instruction and correct them. No greater device for ensuring logical thought has ever been developed than the modern electronic computer.

The machine programs already developed make it highly advisable that institutions with large computers on their campuses establish centers for computation in language and literature, to which their faculties and other scholars may send data for processing by trained personnel; where research staffs, which visiting scholars may be invited to join, will refine and coordinate present programs and develop others in textual editing, linguistics, indexing, and so on, disseminate clear statements of the hypotheses upon which the programs are based, and be prepared to adjust them for users who wish to start from different hypotheses; and where beginners may be trained. As these centers come into being, every textual editor will not only be able to draw upon the best thinking of his time but to ensure the embodiment of that thinking in almost all the details of his edition. Another important result will certainly be a steady increase in the rapid production of sound scholarly editions, and will you not agree with me that this is a consummation we have long devoutly wished? I hope I shall see my own institution lead the way here.

Some of you may be pleased that in the last two processes in the critical path, normalizing the text and writing the textual notes, I have come to the place where an editor need no longer be rigidly logical and consistent. If so, let me remind you that some consistency is desirable in both these processes, and that in normalizing, at least, it is a real problem to attain a respectable standard of consistency. If one sticks to pre-established rules he can work off a thousand lines a day, easily enough, but if he changes or develops rules as he goes along he must go through the text again with the new rules.

Unfortunately, there are no universally recognized rules for normalization. For example, in Dryden's plays, we do not normalize speech headings, where other editors would. Professor Bowers reports in his latest discussion of textual editing that bibliographers no longer believe Elizabethan printers had house styles that they impressed upon an author's work. Why then, say I, impress a style upon speech headings at this date, especially in editions that elsewhere carefully reproduce more minute details of the copy text? It is a different matter, of course, if one is not editing an old-spelling text. I suppose everyone who had edited such a text has had to say "Get thee behind me, Satan," to the suggestion that spelling should be normalized in all critical editions. I always comfort myself at times like these by calling to mind that one reason we can be sure Wordsworth heard "notes" as a perfect rhyme with "thoughts" is because he spelled it *noughts*—a detail one would be sorry not to know of. The theory of copy-text being what it is, however, an editor always is accounted justified in normalizing or modernizing spelling if he is satisfied that his texts do not give a consistent picture of his author's spelling, as they may not, for instance, when they come from a variety of non-authorial manuscripts.

I come then at last to the eighth and final process in the critical path, writing the textual notes. Since these notes are to be understood, not wondered at, a reader ought to be able to see at once the variants from the text printed by the editor and the support among the earlier texts for his text and for the variant readings. A variety of styles in recording variants has been used successfully enough by different editors; but within a single work it no doubt helps the reader's immediate comprehension if the style is generally uniform. At the same time, there will often be variants that can be more neatly expressed by some deviation from the normal practice. Ease of comprehension is the criterion. Writing the textual notes is relatively mechanical, but it is time-consuming because it must be accurate. Five hundred lines of text a day would very likely be a maximum. In all estimates of time, however, and particularly here, the textual editor would not be unwise to double his figures as a safety factor.

As I said at the beginning, the textual editor can have decided long before he comes to this last task how he is to proceed in it. If in addition he has chosen to use Manley and Rickert's method of comparing his texts, or Bland's computer program, he will find it easy to attain accuracy now, where his accuracy will be easiest to criticize. But he cannot write out his notes in the form in which he will send them to the printer until all his other work is complete. And only when he is satisfied with his progress in this last process can he say, "All systems are go."

The form for recording variants used at the Clarendon Press is remarkably attractive for its brevity. Editors of classical texts often use an even briefer form, not citing their own reading when it is clear from the variants what it is they vary from. I myself prefer the fuller form we use in the California Dryden, in which we cite our reading and specify its support, then the variants and their support. For tabulating variations between normally duplicated copies, Professor Bowers, who first made full records of this sort of thing, provides a method in his edition of Dekker. We use a variant of this method in the Dryden, when we feel there is enough material to warrant a table; otherwise we merely call attention to such variations in our explanation of the texts compared. We include all the material again, in either case, in our list of the other variations. In this longer list, some editors put the readings from their own texts in bold-face type, but we do not. I personally prefer the more uniform appearance of our pages, and as we number every variation by its line, I believe the reader finds his way about well enough. I prefer to have the list arranged in paragraph blocks, each representing a natural or artificial block of the text, a scene, say, or a hundred lines, but mistakes discovered after the material is in type are then more expensive to repair, and it is more expensive to make adjustments in any material arranged at the foot of the text pages.

Since I do not read critical editions for pleasure, but study the text in conjunction with the notes, I like to have all the textual variants, in fact all the commentary, on the same page as the text to which it refers—even if this squeezes the text right off some pages. It is my impression, however, that most users prefer to have the text stand by itself, some because they like the look of the pages better, and others because they dislike learned annotations. I have already noted that an edition may have text and notes in separate volumes. In the California Dryden, we provide a list of our variants from the copy text at the foot of the page in a modified columnar arrangement, and a full list of variants with commentary in paragraph blocks at the end of the volume. This latter material is keyed to the text by page or title references in the running heads.

Professor Bowers likes to argue some of his emendations or refusals to emend. I do not. The other editors in our volumes provide explanatory notes, which are sufficient for details, and I set forth my general principles in my textual introductions. I do not at all mind the sort of remark made by a reviewer of our first volume, which was to the effect that I had no doubt explained somewhere certain matters that seemed inconsistent—as in this case I had in fact, in the list of normalizations on the first page of my textual introduction. My colleagues have not spared their exertions in helping me avoid reviews couched in the words of Melissa in *Secret Love*, that "a poor collation awaits you within," and this is my only concern.

Melissa's speech tickled Mr. Chamberlin when he came upon it in comparing the texts of the play for us. It will remind you that the textual editor is far from blind to the rewards of literature. One of my dearest recollections of John Harrington Smith is how he would chuckle over *The Wild Gallant* as he helped us in comparing the texts. My great attachment to *Absalom and Achitophel* was formed when I realized, after comparing fourteen editions straight running, that favorite passages were still enticing me from my word-by-word labor. In addition, textual editing has always granted deep personal satisfactions in the handling of books and manuscripts, and the decipherment and restoration of texts. A subtle flame runs through my body whenever I think of " 'a babled of green fields," even though I know that there is as good evidence for " 'a talkd" or even for the unemended "a table." I have never forgotten how one day in Professor Jackson's course in bibliography I held a little book that had passed through Milton's hands before it reached mine. Milton was present to me then—it made no difference to me that it was only his *Accidence Commenct Grammar* and had been rebound; it had his signature.

Today, however, the textual editor sees a new heaven opening. As he discovers the unvarying principles that govern his work, he lifts his vision from Milton to Milton's fount itself of heavenly radiance. And as he applies these principles in his work, as he approaches the time when he can say, "All systems are go," he experiences rewards almost unutterable. Treasured though my other experiences are, they are as nothing to the insights of this new kind, whether they have come as it were unsolicited or after that mental wrestling that Newton, describing his discovery of his law of gravitation, called "incessantly thinking about it." Seeing at once that pairs of numbers could represent a textual stemma, or winning through to the principles for transmuting complex into simple variations, I knew what Jacob felt at Bethel and at Peniel. Contemplating those insights into principle, I tell you with absolute humility that I hear the morning stars sing together and all the sons of God shout for joy.

V

JAMES THORPE

The Aesthetics of Textual Criticism

Many people on occasion prefer a textual error to an authentic reading. One mistake by a compositor of Melville's *White-Jacket*—setting "soiled fish of the sea" instead of "coiled fish of the sea"—achieved an adventitious fame some years ago. Various readers have since declared themselves in favor of the error, on the grounds that "soiled fish" makes a richer, more interesting passage than the ordinary "coiled fish of the sea." In short, the error seems to them to create a better work.

The preference for one reading over another, the basic decision of textual criticism, is in this case being made on what are called aesthetic grounds. And the decision is made despite demonstrable proof that the preferred reading is a compositorial mistake. Most bibliographers, editors, and textual critics would at this point join in a chorus of denunciation of the person so ill-advised as to make such a preposterous decision.

On what grounds shall we decide which party to join? Does the wretch who hugs the error deserve denunciation because he decided on aesthetic rather than textual grounds? Because he put out the palace fire in Lilliput by improper means? Because we mistrust his taste? Because we fear lest the taste of any individual become the norm? Or because he contumaciously refused to prefer what the author wrote?

On the other hand, suppose we side with the man who chose the error. What is our reason? As a vote for value in a topsy-turvy world in which the worse is so often preferred? As a protest against those vile mechanics, the textual bibliographers, who claim that their findings alone are logical, scientific, and irrefutable because they involve infinite pains? As a forthright preference for the best work of art?

Reprinted from PMLA, LXXX (1965), 465–82, by permission of the author and the Modern Language Association.

Some choose one way and some the other. A recent writer has suggested a rearrangement of Ben Jonson's eulogy on Shakespeare by transferring lines 51–54 to a point ten lines before the place that Jonson chose to put them. The passage "would seem less awkward following the lines just quoted than where it actually occurs." The transposed passage "forms with the lines preceding and succeeding it, a perfectly coherent unit." In short, "I think," the writer says, "a good case can be made that the change is an improvement."[1] The case rests on the greater literary merit of the resulting passage. The first flowering of William Empson's genius as an anatomist of language, his *Seven Types of Ambiguity*, included discussions of several passages in which he found the authorial readings inferior to revisions which he could make. In Rupert Brooke's line about "The keen / Unpassioned beauty of a great machine," he considered "unpassioned" as "prosaic and intellectually shoddy" in comparison with his own word, "impassioned," which provided a daring and successful image. Similarly, his high evaluation of the playful dignity and rhythm of the line "Queenlily June with a rose in her hair" depended on his misreading the first word as "Queen Lily" rather than as an adverb, which made the line (he thought) ebb away "into complacence and monotony."[2]

On the other hand, writers have suggested changes which resulted, they thought, in a text of less literary merit. In his edition of Shakespeare, Samuel Johnson replaced the passage in *Hamlet* which editors had been printing as "In private to inter him" with the original reading "In hugger mugger to inter him," which had apparently been considered inelegant. "That the words now replaced are better," Johnson observed, "I do not undertake to prove it: it is sufficient that they are *Shakespeare's*." He went on to give his rationale for retaining the authorial reading in the face of a possible improvement. "If phraseology is to be changed as words grow uncouth by disuse, or gross by vulgarity, the history of every language will be lost; we shall no longer have the words of any authour; and, as these alterations will be often unskilfully made, we shall in time have very little

[1] Wesley Trimpi, *Ben Jonson's Poems: A Study of the Plain Style* (Stanford, 1962), p. 151.

[2] London, 1930, pp. 260–61, 83; see also p. 34. These examples were retained in the revised edition (London, 1947).

of his meaning."[3] In wanting to conserve the past, his argument is basically historical.

Thus the choice in these cases seems to be between the better word and the words of the author. Such a choice was not likely to arise under an earlier view of textual study which assumed that the authorial version was always the "best" reading. If the power of a divine afflatus enabled the poet to create, he could hardly be improved upon. Shelley, for example, maintained in "A Defence of Poetry" that "poetry is indeed something divine" and that verse is "the echo of the eternal music." George Lyman Kittredge was horrified by the notion "that prompters and proofreaders can (or could) improve Shakespeare."[4] With a less romantic view of the act of artistic creation, one can face this possibility with equanimity: if you happen to believe that the compositor improved on Melville, the Great Chain of Being is not endangered.

Whether our preference lights on the better word or on the words of the author, and whatever reason we give for our decision, we have done more than make one elementary choice. For all textual decisions have an aesthetic basis or are built on an aesthetic assumption, and it is idle to try to dissociate textual grounds from aesthetic grounds as the reason for our choice. Consequently, to make one kind of textual decision is to commit oneself, in principle at least, to a whole series of related decisions. Before we realize what we have done, we may have decided who should be called the author of MacLeish's *J. B.*, whether the eighteenth-century emendations to *Comus* deserve to be incorporated into the text, and which one of the versions of Hardy's *The Return of the Native* is the "real" novel.

Before we make our choice, it might be useful to bring into the open at least the first aesthetic assumption which lies behind textual criticism, and to expose it to scrutiny. The basic questions are no different from those which one confronts in every form of literary study, and in the course of this essay I will discuss three assumptions about the work of art, assumptions which have a controlling effect on the practice of textual criticism. The most fundamental question is this: what is the phenomenon or aesthetic object with which textual criticism properly deals?

[3] Notes to *Hamlet* (IV.iv.84 in modern editions, IV.v in Johnson's edition).

[4] Ed., *The Tragedy of Hamlet* (Boston, 1939), p. viii.

The things which can be called aesthetic objects because they are capable of arousing an aesthetic response in us are (permit me to say) of three kinds: works of chance, works of nature, and works of art. Works of chance are any objects which are formed by random activity: a painting created when a can of paint is tipped over by the vibration of an electric fan and spills onto a canvas; a poem formed by combining an entry (selected by a throw of dice) in each column of a dictionary; a musical composition made by recording the sounds of traffic at a busy intersection; a sculpture consisting of a wastepaper basket into which an office worker has tossed the envelopes which brought the day's mail. Works of nature are any objects or effects which are formed by natural phenomena: a changing pattern of cumulus clouds against a blue sky, the sound of the wind whistling through the boughs of a tree, the smell of the blossoms of Viburnum carlesii. Since language is a human invention and not a natural phenomenon, literary works cannot by definition be works of nature. Works of art are any objects created by human agency for the purpose of arousing an aesthetic response. These are the works which satisfy our conventional ideas of the painting, the sculpture, the symphony, the poem, the play, the novel. Since the work of art is an intended aesthetic object, the idea of either a random or a natural work of art is self-contradictory. Human intelligence was purposefully engaged in the creation of the work of art, but it may not have been successful; the term "work of art" is thus descriptive rather than evaluative, and it includes failures as well as successes. The language of the literary work, whether judged a success or a failure, is a fulfillment of the author's intentions.

Having pushed all aesthetic objects into these three rooms, we cannot, however, very properly slam the doors and go on our way rejoicing. For every thing is an aesthetic object for somebody. The complex organization of human beings will respond in aesthetic experience to the stimulus of any object, particularly if its usual scale is altered or its ordinary context is displaced. Moreover, memory stands ready, on the least hint, to supply the substance for aesthetic response. A classified ad describing a cottage for sale in Florida, with the beach on one side and an orange grove on the other, may create a response which is indistinguishable from that which derives from Marlowe's "Passionate Shepherd to His Love"; for a melancholic reader, however, the ad may be the poor man's "Dover Beach." Likewise, a random pile of beer cans may arouse a response similar to a sculpture, and so forth. These facts make the situation complicated, but we cannot simplify it by saying that people do not or should not have aesthetic experiences from such objects, or that they are all mad if they do; they do in fact have such experiences, and the invocation of madness may in these cases be the last defence of a bewildered man. Moreover, these examples do not represent clear types; there are innumerable objects which may be responded to as sculpture between the pile of beer cans on the one hand and the Pietà of Michelangelo on the other, and there is no convenient line that can be drawn which marks the limit of where the "normal" person "should" make an aesthetic response. It took "the wise men of the society of Salomon's House," in Bacon's *New Atlantis*, to be able "to discern (as far as appertaineth to the generations of men) between divine miracles, works of nature, works of art, and impostures and illusions of all sorts."

The problems of criticism becomes immense, even intolerable, if every object must be taken seriously as a potential source of aesthetic experience, if criticism is invited to preside over all creation. So, in self-defence, we are always on the lookout for ways to cut the area of responsibility but never in search of less authority. In the last generation or two, one tendency in criticism has been to limit attention to the aesthetic object and to move away from the complex problems associated with the artist as unpredictable personality. We have been taught, by the French Symbolists and their followers at second and third hand, that the intentions of the artist are not to be trusted, that the intentions of the work of art are all-important, and that the task of the reader or critic is to understand the intentions of the work of art. Paul Valéry put the case sharply: *"There is no true meaning to a text*—no author's authority. Whatever he may have *wanted to say*, he has written what he has written. Once published, a text is like an apparatus that anyone may use as he will and according to his ability: it is not certain that the one who constructed it can use it better than another. Besides, if he knows well what he meant to do, this knowledge always disturbs his perception of what he has done."[5]

[5] "Concerning *Le Cimetière marin*" (1933), in Paul Valéry, *The Art of Poetry* (New York, 1958), p. 152.

Though one may not like to think of art as gymnastic apparatus on which to exercise, the focus on the work of art seems manifestly sound as a way of trying to understand its intentions and its meaning. However, two secondary effects present themselves. First, we may be suspicious of anything that can be called authorial intention, for fear of committing the "intentional fallacy." Thus the authority of the author over the words which make up the text he wrote is subtly undermined by confusing it with the authority of the author over the meaning of his text. While the author cannot dictate the meaning of the text, he certainly has final authority over which words constitute the text of his literary work.

The other secondary effect is that of overturning the distinction between the aesthetic object (the genus) and the work of art (a species), of thinking that all automobiles are Fords. The fact that it generates an aesthetic response does not mean that it is a work of art. These two effects are interconnected, of course, at least under the definition I have given for the work of art, as an object created by human agency with the intention of arousing an aesthetic response. If the element of intention is minimized, the work of art tends to blend into, and be indistinguishable from, works of chance and works of nature. Indeed, these distinctions seem less important and less useful if commerce is restricted to the aesthetic object and to the general aesthetic response of the individual. The loss of these distinctions, however, leads to confusion and (ultimately) to abandoning conceptual thinking about works of art.

The difficulties which arise from these confusions are not merely visions of theoretical possibilities or of the ineluctable deviations from ideal purity. In every art one can point to aesthetic objects which in fact blend art, chance, and nature to a significant degree. Indeterminate music, for example, combines art and chance. The composer supplies blocks of music for the performers, who are to play the sections in whatever order they fancy on a given occasion; thus the composer incorporates in the work itself a variable governed by random chance. Examples of aesthetic objects which are not primarily works of art can be multiplied: the paintings of Beauty, the chimpanzee at the Cincinnati Zoo, for whose works there has been a ready commercial market; "happenings," or unstructured episodes with characters; self-destroying machines, which are designed to follow an unpredetermined course in destroying themselves. Let me say again that each of these examples will be the occasion for aesthetic response on the part of some people, perhaps a few and perhaps a great many, and no amount of laughing at them, of saying that they are being duped by frauds, will alter the fact that they are responding to aesthetic objects.

In the literary line, there are various current examples of aesthetic objects which depend on chance. The "novel" by Marc Saporta entitled *Composition No. 1*, published by Simon and Schuster in 1963, consists of loose printed pages which are to be shuffled before reading. Many poems have been written by computer. These examples may sound familiar in their resemblance to the language frame described in the Academy of Projectors in *Gulliver's Travels*. That engine was actually a device to insure a random arrangement of words. All of the words in the language had been written on pieces of paper which were pasted on all the sides of bits of wood, which were linked together by wires. This device, twenty feet square, had forty iron handles on the sides which could be used to shake the frame and thus change the words which showed. Any groups of words which made part of a sentence were written into a book, and a rearrangement of those broken sentences was to produce the body of all arts and sciences. Swift's machine was a satire on modern learning; we are taking similar experiments in wise passiveness, perhaps because we are not sure of our grounds for responding otherwise.

The question of importance that these distinctions about aesthetic objects raise is whether criticism can deal with works of chance and nature as well as with works of art. I think that it can, but in very much more limited ways. It can give an account of affective qualities, and these reports may range from crude impressionism to elaborate psychological inquiry. It cannot ordinarily deal with those features on which criticism is most useful, matters of genre, tradition, and convention, without giving vent to a large amount of foolishness. Since textual criticism cannot traffic in works of nature, we need only distinguish between the kinds of authority it can have in dealing with works of chance and works of art. It is of course possible to establish a set of principles by which textual criticism could be applied to works of chance. In view of the random element in all works of chance, however, it is evident that an irrational variable of indefinite importance would always have to be included in the textual principles. Thus the operation of those principles would in the long run be little better than guesswork, and the results of a textual criticism established for works of chance would be about like pinning the tail on the donkey without peeking.

Let us return for a moment to the question of choosing between the "soiled fish of the sea" (the compositorial error) and the "coiled fish of the sea" (the authorial reading). What should our decision now be? Obviously we should choose the one which better fulfills our purposes. If we want to maximize our aesthetic experience by getting the biggest return from our attention, we are free to choose whichever reading satisfies that condition—with the error just as valid a choice as the authorial reading. Those readers who prefer the error—which is a simple example of a work of chance—can thus find perfectly logical grounds for their choice. It is a choice which repudiates the value of differentiating among classes of aesthetic objects, however, and the consistent application of it will, consequently, aid self-gratification on non-intellectual grounds. On the other hand, critics whose prime aesthetic interest is at that moment in works of art must choose the authorial reading whether they think it better or worse. Their main concern is to understand the literary production as a work of art, as an order of words created by the author; they cannot permit their attention to be pre-empted by any auxiliary effects, and they cannot properly set up in business as connoisseurs of all human experience. I certainly do not mean to suggest, however, that people should in general limit their aesthetic experience to works of art; it would be a sadly reduced world if we went about avoiding sunsets and other innocent forms of beauty. Only this: although one person may from time to time enjoy aesthetic experiences from a wide variety of sources, he is not in a position to deal with works of nature and works of chance in his role as a textual critic; he is left, then, with literary works of art as the sole practicable subject for textual criticism.

II

Emily Dickinson's poem "I taste a liquor never brewed" was first printed, in May 1861, in the Springfield *Daily Republican*. The first stanza there reads as follows:

> I taste a liquor never brewed,
>   From tankards scooped in pearl;

109

> Not Frankfort berries yield the sense
> Such a delicious whirl.

That was not, however, precisely what she had written. Her stanza had been more forthright and less delicate:

> I taste a liquor never brewed—
> From Tankards scooped in Pearl—
> Not all the Frankfort Berries
> Yield such an Alcohol!

The editor of the *Daily Republican* apparently thought that the stanza deserved a rhyme; he may well, like any sensible man, have objected to the logic of the third line. The version which he printed was a new stanza, produced under that power reserved by the editor to correct rhymes and alter figures of speech; he thought it (I feel sure) a notable improvement over Emily's crude work. Emily Dickinson was not at the time averse to publication; but she was, in the words of her distinguished modern editor, Thomas H. Johnson, concerned "how one can publish and at the same time preserve the integrity of one's art." [6] This is a topic which can lead into the central question, even paradox, relating to the creation of the work of art: whose intentions are being fulfilled, who can be properly called the author? The obvious answer in the present case—Emily Dickinson—is true enough, and it will serve perfectly for the manuscripts of those poems which she did not communicate to anyone. But once works of art are performed—even in elementary bardic song, or on the stage, or by a reader from copies reproduced from the author's inscription—then complex questions begin in time to arise.

In examining the nature of authorship, I am trying to inquire into what constitutes the integrity of the work of art. Whatever it is, it is apparently something which various classes of persons either do not respect or else define with such latitude that it includes their own efforts. On many magazines, for example, the editorial practice has been to alter the author's text to suit the policy or need of the magazine while retaining the author's name. The author is a tradesman, his work is a commodity which can be made more or less vendible, and the magazine is in a more favored position in the commercial hierarchy than is the author. A multitude of examples of the results can be gleaned from the

[6] *The Poems of Emily Dickinson* (Cambridge, Mass., 1955), I, xxvi.

pages of Frank Luther Mott's study of American magazines. When A. J. H. Duganne refused to furnish further chapters for his serial story, *The Atheist*, the editor of *Holden's* simply wrote the final chapters himself; Emerson's peculiarities were edited out of his contributions to the *Dial*.[7] William Dean Howells acted the part of an "academic taskmaster freely blue-penciling the essays of his unhappy pupils," and he said that his proofreading "sometimes well-nigh took the character of original work, in that liberal *Atlantic* tradition of bettering the authors by editorial transposition and paraphrase, either in the form of suggestion or of absolute correction"; James Russell Lowell (the second president of the Modern Language Association) wrote to a contributor to the *North American Review* that "I shall take the liberty to make a verbal change here and there, such as I am sure you would agree to could we talk the matter over. I think, for example, you speak rather too well of young Lytton, whom I regard as both an imposter and as an antinomian heretic. Swinburne I must modify a little, as you will see, to make the *Review* consistent with itself. But you need not be afraid of not knowing your own child again."[8] Edward Bok, the editor of the *Ladies Home Journal*, once deleted a substantial portion of a story by Mark Twain; and the editor of *Collier's* modified a story by Julian Hawthorne about a seduced maiden by inserting a secret marriage and legitimizing the child.[9] When extracts for *Huckleberry Finn* were printed in the *Century Magazine*, they were carefully altered by Richard Watson Gilder, the editor, with Twain's full consent, even though they had already been pruned both by Mrs. Clemens and by William Dean Howells; Gilder excised about a fifth of the extracts, including descriptive passages and those which (like "to be in a sweat") he thought too coarse or vulgar for his audience.[10] Examples could be multiplied indefinitely. Sometimes the editor is a famous man of letters and the author a hack, and sometimes it is the other way around;

[7] *A History of American Magazines 1741–1850* (New York, 1930), p. 504.

[8] *A History of American Magazines 1865–1885* (Cambridge, Mass., 1938), p. 21.

[9] *A History of American Magazines 1885–1905* (Cambridge, Mass., 1957), p. 37.

[10] Arthur L. Scott, "The *Century Magazine* Edits *Huckleberry Finn*, 1884–1885," *AL*, XXVII (1955), 356–62.

sometimes a change seems to later critics to have been improvement, and sometimes debasement.

The reflection on these facts might be simple were it not that when authors publish their periodical contributions in book form, they very frequently retain the changes which have been introduced by the editors. Thus, by inference, they validate the changes and give them some kind of authority. Nathaniel Hawthorne, for example, retained the changes, despite his objection to editorial meddling; at least, in the case of the four short stories for which the manuscript is extant, he seems not to have restored the original readings when the editors altered his text, in punctuation, spelling, capitalization, and diction.[11] Similarly, when Thomas Nelson Page's stories were collected by Scribner's, he did not re-introduce the omitted passages (about drink, religion, and horror) nor the original Negro dialect; the changes made by the editors of the *Century Magazine* were largely allowed to stand.[12] Charles Reade objected strenuously to the editorial pressure from *Blackwood's* on *The Woman Hater*, but he then used the serial text as copy for the book, with only a few inconsequential changes in phrasing.[13]

On the other hand, occasionally authors have restored their original readings in book publication. When Thomas Hardy's novels were first published in periodicals, the texts were considerably changed at the urging of editors. Sometimes the alterations were verbal, as the change from "lewd" to "gross," "loose" to "wicked," and "bawdy" to "sinful" in *Far from the Madding Crowd;* sometimes they were more substantial, as the omission of the seduction scene from *Tess of the D'Urbervilles* and the substitution of a mock marriage. When Hardy got his manuscripts ready for book publication, however, he restored nearly everything that the magazine editors had made him change.[14] But not always, even with Hardy. Many editorial changes were made in his manuscript for the first serial appearance, in the

[11] Seymour L. Gross and Alfred J. Levy, "Some Remarks on the Extant Manuscripts of Hawthorne's Short Stories," *SB*, XIV (1961), 254–57.

[12] John R. Roberson, "The Manuscript of Page's 'Marse Chan'," *SB*, IX (1957), 259–62.

[13] Royal A. Gettman, "Henry James's Revision of *The American*," *AL*, XVI (1945), 295.

[14] Oscar Maurer, " 'My Squeamish Public': Some Problems of Victorian Magazine Publishers and Editors," *SB*, XII (1958), 21–40.

Atlantic Monthly, of *Two on a Tower*. This edited text then served, with few changes, as copy text for the first London edition, and the edited version has continued in all later editions of Hardy.[15]

In cases of these kinds, there is generally some uncertainty as to the interpretation to be put on the author's actions. Often we cannot be sure whether he makes suggested changes because of a compliant nature, whether he allows editorial alterations to stand in later editions out of laziness, whether he reverts to earlier readings out of pertinacity, or whether there is reasoned conviction in support of his actions. Once another hand helps to prepare a work of art for dissemination, it is usually difficult to distinguish with certainty which part is not by the author.

One of the most common kinds of intervention in the publication of books is made by the publisher's editor—the person whose job it is to read material before publication, to recommend acceptance or rejection, to "house style" the text, to query anything which seems inaccurate, ineffective, or offensive, and to make or suggest any changes which appeal to the editor as desirable. I suppose that almost every writer—even the lowly scholar—has found his deathless prose altered by a publisher's editor, who is sometimes an eminent man of letters and sometimes a mere slip of a girl barely out of college. Some authors blanch at the thought of any alteration, some accept any change gratefully as an improvement. There appears to be a perennial joke among editors of "educational" publishers that they completely re-write the books of some authors, reducing the text to half of its original length, and the authors never realize that any changes have been made.

Probably the most celebrated editor of this century was Maxwell E. Perkins of Charles Scribner's Sons, editor for Fitzgerald, Wolfe, Hemingway, and a dozen other writers of consequence. Perkins was rather reluctant to offer any specific suggestions to authors except about legal or libellous matters. Frequently he sent long letters or memoranda of advice to "his" authors about their manuscripts; but his suggestions were general and undemanding. He was like a kindly parent, proud of his children, always encouraging them to fulfill their potentialities, ready to offer a guiding hand in time of need. It was only when an author called

[15] Carl J. Weber, "The Manuscript of Hardy's *Two on a Tower*," *PBSA*, XL (1946), 1–21.

for help that he would be party to the making of important changes in a manuscript. The most significant revisions he ever made, presumably, were his extensive cuts in Wolfe's first two manuscripts, trying to bring order out of chaos.[16] The cuts were apparently made by Perkins with Wolfe's acquiescence, and they reduced *Look Homeward, Angel* (for example) by thirty percent.[17] To mention only one more of an almost unlimited number of instances, Theodore Dreiser had the advantage—however unlikely it seems—of several editors, notably Louise Campbell. She acted as literary assistant, revised eight of his books while preparing them for publication, and even wrote character sketches for publication under his name in *Esquire*.[18] What is called ghost writing, however, goes a little beyond the usual requirements of editing.[19]

Then there are some books the final form of which (it would be accurate to say) are not so much written as constructed. Mark Twain, for example, left *The Mysterious Stranger* unfinished; Albert Bigelow Paine put it together somewhat arbitrarily and added a last chapter found separately among the author's papers. Bernard de Fallois reconstructed Marcel Proust's *Jean Santeuil*, that first rough version of *Remembrance of Things Past*, by the use of seventy notebooks and several boxes of torn and detached pages made available to him after Proust's death by Madame Gérard Mante-Proust.[20] *More Stately Mansions* was made by Karl Ragner Gierow by shortening Eugene O'Neill's partly revised script.

Editors play an important role in the production of magazines and books, and they are often responsible for changes in the author's text. I am not trying to say whether these changes are or are not improvements, whether they are made willingly or

[16] *Editor to Author: The Letters of Maxwell E. Perkins*, ed. John Hall Wheelock (New York, 1950), pp. 171–74, 175–80, 286–94, 227–30, 98–102.

[17] Francis E. Skipp, "The Editing of *Look Homeward, Angel*," *PBSA*, LVII (1963), 1–13. On the basis of analyzing the material cut, Skipp is of the opinion that the changes improved the work.

[18] Robert H. Elias, rev. of *Letters to Louise: Theodore Dreiser's Letters to Louise Campbell* (Philadelphia, 1959), *AL*, XXXIII (1961), 90–91.

[19] For an interesting account by a noted editor (of O'Neill and Faulkner, for example) who had been a prolific ghost writer, see Saxe Commins, "Confessions of a Ghost," *PULC*, XXII (1960), 26–35.

[20] Marcel Proust, *Jean Santeuil* (London, 1955), pp. ix, xxi–xxii.

reluctantly by the author, whether there should or should not be editors—only that textual changes for which an editor is responsible do in fact take place, frequently and regularly.

This editorial activity results in the embodiment of the editor's intentions in the work of art. In a complex way, the integrity of the work of art is thereby, in some measure, the effect of a juncture of intentions. Another major entanglement, this one mainly accidental in nature, occurs in the translation of the text from authorial to public form—the physical process of turning the author's dictated or typed or handwritten copy into print or (in earlier times) into scribal manuscript form. To speak only of printing, I suppose it is true to say that few if any books of any size have ever been printed without mistakes, even that "No book is completed until *Error* has crept in & affixed his sly Imprimatur." The usual assumption is that every printed book includes many errors, and it is easy to see why this must be: a page of type may contain from one to five thousand characters; there is only one way of getting each of them right, and many ways of getting each one wrong. No matter how experienced the compositor, he will make changes, the proofreader will fail to notice some of them, and every change is an error. The editors of the Centenary Hawthorne have sought to minimize this state of nature by having *all* proofs "read at least five times and by three or more editors."[21]

Proofreading by authors was not usual before the eighteenth century; indeed, early proofreading normally consisted of a reading (by the master printer or his assistant) of one of the first sheets printed off, without recourse to the copy, and marking any apparent errors for correction; in the meantime, of course, a certain number of uncorrected sheets would have aleady been printed. The fact that proof sheets were later run off, and given to the author for correction, is certainly no guarantee that all the mistakes were caught. Careless proofreading is not uncommon, and writers differ in their interest and skill in handling such details. It has been said that F. Scott Fitzgerald's *This Side of Paradise* is an "inexcusably sloppy job, and that the blame must be distributed between author and publisher"; the first edition contained a large number of misspellings, inconsistencies, and other examples of carelessness which neither the author nor the publisher corrected—indeed, some of the errors noted by the re-

[21] *The Scarlet Letter* (Columbus, Ohio, 1962), p. xlvii.

viewers in 1920 have not yet been corrected.[22] Even when the author and publisher both take care, there are still errors. Sinclair Lewis, for example, wrote as follows to his publisher after he had seen a list of errors and inconsistencies observed by Mr. Louis Feipel in the published version of *Babbitt*: "J. Henry! This man Feipel is a wonder—to catch all these after rather unusually careful proofreading not only by myself and my wife but also by two or three professionals!"[23] Sometimes misprints become, in effect, a permanent part of the text.[24]

Sometimes an author prefers the mistakes to his own work. Richard Ellmann has described such a preference on the part of James Joyce. It occurred while Joyce was dictating *Finnegans Wake* to Samuel Beckett. "There was a knock on the door and Joyce said, 'Come in.' Beckett, who hadn't heard the knock, by mistake wrote down 'Come in' as part of the dictated text. Afterwards he read it back to Joyce who said, 'What's that "Come in"?' 'That's what you dictated,' Beckett replied. Joyce thought for a moment, realizing that Beckett hadn't heard the knock; then he said, 'Let it stand'."[25]

Perhaps the play is the form of literary art in which the principles associated with the integrity of the work and the identity of the author are most visible. If the playwright wants his play to find its way onto the stage, he must accommodate his text to the financial claims of the producer, the presentational claims of the director and actors, and the undefined claims of the theatre-going public. William Gibson has given a detailed account of his struggles in revising and re-writing *Two for the Seesaw*. From the time that the first draft was completed until it opened in New York, Gibson re-wrote the entire play several times and re-cast some parts of it as many as five times. These changes were made in trying to meet objections and accommodate the text to the

[22] Matthew J. Bruccoli, "A Collation of F. Scott Fitzgerald's *This Side of Paradise*," *SB*, IX (1957), 263–65.

[23] Matthew J. Bruccoli, "Textual Variants in Sinclair Lewis's *Babbitt*," *SB*, XI (1958), 263–68.

[24] M. R. Ridley, "The Perpetuated Misprint," *TLS*, 28 August 1959, p. 495.

[25] "The Backgrounds of *Ulysses*," *KR*, XVI (1954), 359–60. I have heard it said that Joyce retained some of the printer's errors in *Ulysses* because he preferred them to what he had written, but I have been unable to find any evidence for this claim.

various claims made on it. For example, the male star did not like the character which he was to portray, and the changes made for his benefit covered a wide range: from the deletion of those speeches in which the character talked aloud to himself (since the actor "personally did not talk aloud to himself") all the way to the assurance that he would not "go onstage with one line unrewritten that he felt uncomfortable or untruthful with."

Gibson came to feel that the play as it was produced was not quite his: his collaborators had made a new play. It was a successful play, one which was (he thought) much better and more effective because of the revisions which had been forced on the writer. But not quite his. He told of visiting the studio of a painter and envying her because "she was working in a medium where she alone could ruin it. This seemed to me a definition of art." When Gibson turned over a text to his publisher, he could not bear to put his name to the final version: so he rewrote once more, using much of the stage version, restoring much of what had been surrendered, writing new bits, and ending with a composite of several versions.[26]

The rewriting of plays to meet the demands of performance has for some time been typical of theatrical practice. Oscar Wilde, for example, wrote *The Importance of Being Earnest* as a four-act play, and he did not submit it until it had passed through three stages of composition; when Sir George Alexander (the manager of St. James's Theatre) told him to re-cast it into three acts and to reduce the length in order to allow time for a curtain raiser, Wilde complied. It is only a few writers of strong will, fierce independence, and eminence—such as G. B. Shaw and Eugene O'Neill—who have been able to see their work performed in accordance with their own intentions, and they have had to fight for their convictions.[27] For the most part, Moss Hart's description in *Act One* (New York, 1959) of the birth

[26] William Gibson, *The Seesaw Log: A Chronicle of the Stage Production, with the Text, of "Two for the Seesaw"* (New York, 1959), pp. 32, 37, 101, 43, 140.

[27] "Often the rehearsals of an O'Neill play would degenerate into a series of running battles between the playwright and the producer, the director, and the actors. Invariably, O'Neill was able to stand his ground against them all." Croswell Bowen, "Rehearsing *The Iceman Cometh*," in *O'Neill and His Plays: Four Decades of Criticism*, ed. Oscar Cargill and others (New York, 1961), p. 460.

of *Once in a Lifetime* is more characteristic: throughout rehearsals and try-outs the author is busily engaged in re-writing the text, adjusting it to the realities of performance, trying to make it into a show which will be a public success.

This process is by no means limited to the work of commercial experts. The conversion of Archibald MacLeish's *J. B.* is an instructive—if rather sad—example. MacLeish spent four years writing the play, which was published by Houghton Mifflin in book form in March 1958 and produced in the Yale University Theatre the next month. Alfred de Liagre, Jr., bought the play, engaged Elia Kazan as director, and brought Kazan and Mac-Leish together. Kazan thought the play "needed important changes for professional production," gave detailed directions, and MacLeish enthusiastically agreed. The story of the revision of the play, from July through December 1958, is one filled with demands for changes by Kazan and agreement by MacLeish. "You are right to want something from Nickles at the end of Act I," says MacLeish. "Hell, you are always right. Why should I mention it? Here is what I propose." After the Washington opening, Kazan told MacLeish that the play needed a "recognition scene," and he outlined where and why it should take place. MacLeish agreed, and in two days supplied the scene.[28]

It appears likely that the production of plays has always occasioned considerable modification of the text. Undoubtedly a few dramatists at any given time have been able to stand their ground in the running battle with actors, directors, producers, and public; but usually the writer seems to have thought of his words as variable in the process of converting a text to a finished performance.[29] Thus there are, in theory at least and often in practice, two or more versions of every produced play. In Elizabethan times, the author's foul papers represent a non-pro-

[28] "The Staging of a Play," *Esquire*, LI (May 1959), 144–58.

[29] There is considerable evidence in Shakespeare's plays, for example, of revision for production. "All of the texts of the First Folio of 1623 for which there are documents for comparison show stage alteration in varying degrees, and in that fact there is a proof of the universality of stage influence on acted plays. . . . One may say that stage alteration appears in all plays that have been acted on the stage." Hardin Craig, "Textual Degeneration of Elizabethan and Stuart Plays: An Examination of Plays in Manuscript," *Rice Institute Pamphlets*, Vol. XLVI, No. 4 (1960), p. 74. See also Craig's *A New Look at Shakespeare's Quartos* (Stanford, 1961).

duced version and the prompt book a produced version.[30] For *J. B.*, the Houghton Mifflin edition (1958) is a non-produced version, while a produced version was printed in *Theatre Arts* (February 1960) and by Samuel French, Inc.; the versions are naturally different.

In dramatic performances, collaboration on the text is greater as the non-verbal effects become more important. In a musical, for example, the author is less in control of his text than in a play, while in a musical revue the identical show is not usually repeated for two performances in succession. In the production of movies, the writer ordinarily has little control over his text, must supply changes upon demand, and may be properly listed in the credits among the chief cameraman, electrician, and sound man. In the production of *Cleopatra* (released by Twentieth Century Fox in 1963), the valuable properties were the female star and the assignational publicity, not the text. Three distinguished writers were successively employed to provide a scenario, and most of their work was scrapped.

It can be claimed that nearly every person involved in the transmission of literary works helps, in some sense, to shape the effect that a work will have on a reader. The designer, for example, can in some measure make the experience of reading the book a little more pleasant or easy or irritating by the appropriateness of the format, paper, binding, font and size of type. His work is not usually observed consciously. In order to realize something of the range of his effect, however, one has only to imagine reading *Tom Jones* in black letter throughout, on coated art paper, with the sheets printed alternately in red and black, in a tight binding with no inner margin, with illustrations by Willem de Kooning. On the other hand, influences which shape the intentions of the artist are sometimes advantageous. Few re-

[30] A vast amount of modern Shakespearean scholarship has been concerned with trying to infer which of these was the basis for the first printed edition of a given play. There seems to be a tacit assumption among some scholars that the earliest editors of Shakespeare were most interested in printing the words that he wrote. Alice Walker (with whom one fears to disagree) believes that Heminge and Condell "may have known that the *Lear* prompt-book better represented what Shakespeare wrote than the *Hamlet* prompt-book" (*Textual Problems of the First Folio*, Cambridge, Eng., 1953, p. 136). It seems a more plausible assumption that men of the theatre like Heminge and Condell would (unlike many modern scholars) have preferred the text which better represented the play in a good production.

gret, I suppose, that James T. Fields (the publisher) was successful in persuading Hawthorne to make *The Scarlet Letter* into a full-length novel rather than finishing it (as Hawthorne had planned) as a long story for publication with a half dozen shorter ones.

So far, this discussion about the integrity of the work of art has emphasized its creation and the agents who are then at work in modifying the intentions of the artist. In fact, the work of art is also subject to alteration long afterwards. For nine plays by Euripides, the earliest manuscript—and the only one with any authority—is of the thirteenth-fourteenth centuries; thus any changes made in the text in the course of that transcription, some 1,750 years after the plays were composed, would have definitively altered the intentions of the author so far as the modern reader is concerned.

Emendation may be taken as an example of that range of editorial effort which modifies the works of the past in the hope of purging corrupt readings from them. Boswell tells of Johnson confronting him with a textual problem that required an emendation for its solution. "On the 65 page of the first volume of Sir George Mackenzie's folio edition, Mr. Johnson pointed out a paragraph beginning with *Aristotle*, and told me there was an error in the text which he bid me try to discover. I hit it at once. It stands that the devil answers *even* in *engines*. I corrected it to *ever* in *enigmas*. 'Sir,' said he, 'you're a good critic. This would have been a great thing to do in the text of an ancient author'."[31] Boswell here casts himself in the role of the clever schoolboy responding to the questions of the schoolmaster, who knows all the answers. In real life, however, nobody knows the answers, and it is impossible to say "I hit it at once."

As an expression of editorial preference, emendation is the exercise of textual decision. The corrupted readings in most of the manuscripts of the authors of Greek and Latin antiquity have made their works the happy hunting ground for ingenious editors. Since any plausible reading is preferred to one which is obviously corrupt, and since there is usually no way to validate conjectural emendations beyond the tests of meter and sense, our received texts are peppered with editorial guesses which have

---

[31] *Boswell's Journal of A Tour to the Hebrides With Samuel Johnson, LL.D.*, ed. Frederick A. Pottle and Charles H. Bennett (New York, 1936), p. 173. Entry for Wednesday, 15 September 1773.

silently become indistinguishable from what textual scholars have agreed to consider the author's intentions.

This process of reconstruction by emendation has by no means been limited to writers of classical antiquity. Even such new-comers as English and American authors have also had these benefits conferred on them. The emendations suggested by some eighteenth-century editors and critics to two lines in Milton are instructive. In the 1645 edition of Milton's *Poems*, lines 631–35 of *Comus* (the beginning of the "Haemony" passage) appear as follows:

> The leaf was darkish, and had prickles on it,
> But in another Countrey, as he said,
> Bore a bright golden flowre, but not in this soyl:
> Unknown, and like esteem'd, and the dull swayn
> Treads on it daily with his clouted shoon. . . .

It is the third and fourth of these lines that were thought to require emendation. Hurd said that "the passage before us is certainly corrupt, or, at least, inaccurate; and had better, I think, been given thus . . . 'Bore a bright golden flower, *not* in this soil/Unknown, *though light* esteem'd'." Seward proposed "*but* in this soil/Unknown and *light* esteem'd." Newton suggested that no change be made beyond the omission of either "but" or "not"; thus the reading could be "*but* in this soil/Unknown and like esteem'd" or else "*not* in this soil:/Unknown, and like esteem'd." Fenton printed "*little* esteem'd" rather than "*like* esteem'd," while Warburton proposed "*light* esteem'd" as the only change.[32] No one of these emendations is now accepted. The weight of the testimony in favor of the reading with which we began is apparently so overwhelming that no one now thinks to suggest any alternative. The same reading (minor variants in orthography and punctuation aside) is to be found in the Trinity College Manuscript (in Milton's hand), in the first (1637) edition of *Comus* (which derived from the Trinity College Manuscript), in the corrected copy of the 1637 *Comus* which Milton presented to the Earl of Bridgewater, and in the 1645 *Poems;* moreover, there is no shred of evidence elsewhere that

[32] These various emendations are recorded in the notes to Henry John Todd's edition of Milton's poetical works (London, 1801, and many later editions). The most elaborate and extensive of all unnecessary emendations to Milton were undoubtedly those made by the great classical scholar Richard Bentley in his edition of *Paradise Lost* (1732).

Milton's intentions were not carried out in this passage, which he reviewed so many times while he still had his sight. Each of the editorial emendations was thus (we may conclude) a temporary substitution of the intention of the editor for that of the author.

Very frequently, emendations are made in cases where there is not enough external testimony to confirm or reject them with any feeling of confidence. Sometimes they slide into the text and become the objects of our veneration on the principle that whatever is printed is right.[33] Such is the case in an indefinite number of passages in the works of writers of the past.

Emendation offers the appeal of a puzzle and the release of creation. "The allurements of emendation are scarcely resistible," Samuel Johnson wrote. "Conjecture has all the joy and all the pride of invention, and he that has once started a happy change, is too much delighted to consider what objections may rise against it." Johnson offered a great many emendations to Shakespeare, most of them pure guesses sanctified by the supposition that Shakespeare wrote them. Unlike many critics and readers, however, he came to be aware that his own textual conjectures were likely to be mistaken; and he believed that the best any person can do is produce one of many plausible readings. He trusted conjecture less and less, and he congratulated himself on including none of his own emendations in the plays of Shakespeare that he latterly edited.[34]

Johnson put a high value on the creative aspect of emendation. He described one change by Bishop Warburton as "a noble emendation, which almost sets the critic on a level with the author."[35] One can go further than Johnson: without praising

[33] See, for example, the history of the reading "mid-May" in Keats's "The Fall of Hyperion," l. 92.

[34] "Preface to Shakespeare," *The Works of Samuel Johnson, LL.D.* (Oxford, 1825), V, 151, 150, 149.

[35] This is the "god kissing carrion" passage in *Hamlet:* "For if the sun breed maggots in a dead dog, being a god kissing carrion—Have you a daughter?" (II.ii.181–83). The folios and quartos concur in the reading "good," which Warburton emended (without any external evidence) to "god"—a reading which has been pretty generally accepted, although W. W. Greg objected, a little primly: "It is facile and plausible, but I think unnecessary. Hamlet's fancies are not always as nice as editors would have them" (*Principles of Emendation in Shakespeare*, London, 1928, p. 68). Johnson's observation appears in his edition of Shakespeare at the conclusion of his reprinting of Warburton's note to the passage.

either Warburton or the emendation, one can say that the critic who adopts an emendation of his own creation, without a genuine basis for showing it to be a recovery of what the author intended to write, has indeed become co-author of this portion of the work of art—he has in fact been set on a level with the author.

This brings us to a major point about the nature of authorship and of the integrity of the work of art. The literary work is frequently the result, in a pure sense, of composite authorship. We do not have to meddle with the unconscious, the preconscious, or the race consciousness in order to hold this view. In a quite literal sense, the literary work is often guided or directed or controlled by other people while the author is in the process of trying to make it take shape, and it is subject to a variety of alterations throughout its history. The intentions of the person we call the author thus become entangled with the intentions of all the others who have a stake in the outcome, which is the work of art. And yet we agree to say simply *"Two for the Seesaw,* by William Gibson." Not *"Two for the Seesaw,* by William Gibson, Henry Fonda, Fred Coe, Arthur Penn, Anne Bancroft, the elevator boy, wives, friends, and others." *"Jean Santeuil,* by Marcel Proust," not "by Marcel Proust and Bernard de Fallois." *"Look Homeward, Angel,* by Thomas Wolfe," not "by Wolfe and Perkins." *"J. B.,* by MacLeish," not "by MacLeish and Kazan." Our identification of the author is partly a convention for the sake of simplicity, partly a case of the Boss being given credit, whether he wants it or not, for all the work that the office (including volunteer workers) turns out.

Whatever complexities we agree to ignore in our daily encounters with works of art, it remains a fact that the literary work is a mingling of human intentions about which distinctions should be made. Its status as a work of art is not affected by whether these intentions all belong to the titular author; even collaborative authorship does not alter that status, however much it may endanger friendships. On the other hand, the integrity of the work of art depends very much on the work being limited to those intentions which are the author's, together with those others of which he approves or in which he acquiesces. When these intentions have been fulfilled, the work of art has its final integrity or completeness. It may be aesthetically imperfect or unfinished, and it is altogether possible that an indefinite number of people may be capable of improving it. But in the authorial sense it is already finished, it is already complete, it already has that final integrity which should be the object of the critic's chief attention. This is the final integrity which it is the business of the textual critic to identify as an order of words in fulfillment of the authorial intention, the business of the literary critic to understand as an order of words in the context of all literature.

We commenced this discussion with the question, put in the mouth of Emily Dickinson, as to how one can publish and still preserve the integrity of one's art. In a pure sense it is probably impossible, but anyone who is concerned enough to ask the question will undoubtedly realize that a good deal depends on the exercise of will: one must fulfill one's own intentions rather than the conflicting intentions of others, however valuable and well-meaning. Their desire to help is praiseworthy, and altruism is all the more appealing when it is self-effacing; but the dedication of such help to the improvement of others' works of art dissipates the integrity of those works.

III

In the conclusion to *Great Expectations*, Charles Dickens thought it necessary to have a final confrontation between the hero, Pip, and the greatest of his lost expectations, Estella. They meet casually in London. Estella has married a Shropshire doctor after the death of her first husband, the cruel Drummle. She sees Pip walk by on the street while she is sitting in her carriage. They shake hands, she wrongly assumes that the boy with him is his own child, he perceives that suffering has given her an understanding heart, and the book ends. This is the "unhappy," or at least unromantic ending; in less than three hundred words these ships pass one last time, saluting each other gravely all the while. Bulwer Lytton was dissatisfied with this ending, and at his urging Dickens wrote another. This time Estella is free: she has been a widow for two years and has not remarried. They meet, not in impersonal London, but in memory's lane itself—the site of Miss Havisham's house, where they had first met, which neither has visited for some thirteen years. A silvery mist is rising, the stars are shining, and the first rays of the moon illumine the tears that course from Estella's eyes. They are full of forgiveness for one another, and understanding; they emerge from the ruins holding hands, and there is no shadow of another parting. This is the "happy," the romantic ending, accomplished in a thousand pulsing words. The ending which you read must to some degree affect your understanding of the entire novel. Which is the real *Great Expectations?*

The collection of W. H. Auden's sonnets and verse commentary which he entitled "In Time of War" concludes with these lines:

> Till they construct at last a human justice,
> The contribution of our star, within the shadow
> Of which uplifting, loving, and constraining power
> All other reasons may rejoice and operate.

It is an eloquent plea for men of good will to join together and "construct" a "human justice" for the benefit of all mankind. So the passage appeared in its first publication in 1939, in *Journey to a War*. Within a few years Auden's ideas about the right way to attain human justice—as well as his ideas about many other subjects—had changed markedly. When he came to reprint "In Time of War" in his *Collected Poetry* of 1945, he altered the concluding passage of the commentary as follows:

> Till, as the contribution of our star, we follow
> The clear instructions of that Justice, in the shadow
> Of Whose uplifting, loving, and constraining power
> All human reasons do rejoice and operate.

Instead of constructing human justice, man is now enjoined to follow Divine Justice.[36] Which is the real "In Time of War"?

Thomas Hardy printed four different versions of *The Return of the Native*, from 1878 to 1912. Between the first and second versions he made some 700 changes (of which 40 are major revisions), between the second and third about 350 changes, and between the third and fourth about 115. These changes substantially altered the characterization and plot. In his first manuscript version, Hardy envisioned Eustacia Vye as a literal witch, a demon; by the time he had finished his revisions,

---

[36] For an account of the very numerous revisions, excisions, and eliminations which Auden silently made in preparing his text for the *Collected Poetry* (New York, 1945) and *Collected Shorter Poems* (London, 1950), see Joseph Warren Beach, *The Making of the Auden Canon* (Minneapolis, 1957); his remarks on "In Time of War" are on pp. 5–10. Auden has continued to revise: the unsuspecting reader may be surprised to discover that there is a strong possibility of a significant change in any given poem reprinted in one of the "collected" volumes.

she had become a passionate, unconventional beauty with a surprisingly rigid sense of morality. An example of the change in
plot may be found in Eustacia's plan to run away from her husband, Clym Yeobright. In the early versions, her moral problem
was whether it was right to accept assistance and financial help
from Wildeve since each was married to another; in the later
versions, with Wildeve more forward, her problem was whether
she could avail herself of his services or whether she also had to
accept him as her lover and go away with him.[37] Which is the
real *Return of the Native*?

I have asked this kind of question three different times, partly
because the three situations are somewhat different, partly to
suggest that the problem which I am now to treat is very widespread. That problem is the existence of the work of art in
multiple versions, each created by the author. The principle
which is involved touches the nature of composition: the work
in process, the work in completion, the work in re-completion.
Familiar examples of authorial revision abound in all periods:
there are two distinct versions of *Piers Plowman*, two of
Chaucer's Prologue to *The Legend of Good Women* and two
(possibly three) of *Troilus and Criseyde*, five of Gower's *Con-
fessio Amantis*, two major versions of Sidney's *Arcadia*, two of
Ben Jonson's *Every Man in His Humour*, several versions of
Browne's *Religio Medici* and Walton's *Life of Donne*, two of
Pope's *Rape of the Lock* and of *The Dunciad*, two of Keats's
"La Belle Dame Sans Merci," four of FitzGerald's *Rubáiyát of
Omar Khayyám*, seven of Whitman's *Leaves of Grass*, from two
to five for each of Arnold's major prose works, and so on and
so forth.

These are all familiar instances. To add a few other writers
who have been notable revisers, within the limits (say) of nineteenth-century poetry, one might first mention Wordsworth,
who spent forty-five years in tinkering with *The Prelude*, making the 1850 version in may ways a quite different poem from
the 1805 version.[38] Or Tennyson, who was a devoted, continual,
and minute reviser: he worked over his manuscripts (sometimes

[37] See Otis B. Wheeler, "Four Versions of *The Return of the Native*,"
NCF, XIV (1959), 27–44. See also John Paterson, *The Making of "The
Return of The Native"* (Berkeley, Calif., 1960), particularly for Hardy's
first intentions.

[38] See Helen Darbishire's revision of Ernest de Selincourt's edition (Oxford, 1959), pp. liv–lxxiv.

in as many as six versions), he altered the texts in the proofs for the first and later editions, and he made marginal changes in the printed editions. Sometimes there are as many as fifteen texts, all different, each armed with the poet's authority.[39] Or Emily Dickinson, who had second and third and fourth thoughts about what she wrote, and who sometimes could not decide which was the final form of a poem. For "Blazing in Gold and quenching in Purple," in the three fair copies she sent to friends, each time one line was different in the supposed final version; "the Otter's Window" in one is "the kitchen window" in another, which is "the oriel window" in a third. She wrote them all and meant each of them to be the poem.[40]

Recent scholarly investigations have revealed that authorial revision is embodied in multiple printed versions to an extent which seems to be almost limitless. I can at least hint at the spread of these findings through the mere mention of a sampling of the subjects, naming only those to whom I have not already alluded. For the twentieth century, Joyce, Faulkner, Yeats, Conrad, Lewis, Dos Passos, Lindsay, Cozzens, and West. For the nineteenth century James, Twain, Crane, Pater, Clough, Hawthorne, Poe, Emerson, Thoreau, Longfellow, De Quincey, Blake, and Coleridge. For the eighteenth century, Swift, Fielding, and Johnson. For the seventeenth and latter sixteenth centuries, Shakespeare, Drayton, Daniel, Burton, Crashaw, Lee, Rochester, and Dryden. The prize for revision should probably be awarded to Philip James Bailey. He wrote seven different versions of his poem *Festus*, which was, or were, published in thirteen British (and at least forty American) editions between 1839 and 1903. In the process it grew from a modest 8,103 lines (a little shorter than *Paradise Lost*) to a monstrous 39,159 lines.[41]

The more of these scholarly studies one reads, the more one is

---

[39] See, for example, Edgar F. Shannon, Jr., "The History of A Poem: Tennyson's *Ode on the Death of the Duke of Wellington*," *SB*, XIII (1960), 149–77; or Shannon, "The Proofs of *Gareth and Lynette* in the Widener Collection," *PBSA*, XLI (1947), 321–40; or W. D. Paden, "A Note on the Variants of *In Memoriam* and *Lucretius*," *Library*, 5th ser., VIII (1953), 259–73.

[40] See Thomas H. Johnson, "Emily Dickinson: Creating the Poems," *Harvard Library Bulletin*, VII (1953), 257–70; or, more comprehensively, *The Poems of Emily Dickinson*, ed. Johnson (Cambridge, Mass., 1955), esp. I, xxxiii–xxxviii and 163–65.

[41] Morse Peckham, "English Editions of Philip James Bailey's *Festus*," *PBSA*, XLIV (1950), 55–58.

impressed by the likelihood of authorial revision in any literary work where the writer had an opportunity to alter his work before communicating it to his public yet another time. What the scholar seems to need in order to demonstrate authorial revision in these cases is simply the good fortune to find that the evidence has not been destroyed. It seems logical to assume that revision may have taken place in other cases, wherever there was occasion for it, even though the editions, manuscripts, or letters to prove it are no longer extant.[42]

I am trying to make it clear that the examples with which I began, of works by Dickens, Auden, and Hardy, are by no means instances of authorial revision which can be dismissed because they are rare freaks. On the contrary, they seem to be examples of a fairly common phenomenon. The matters of principle which they raise will have widespread application.

When people write about literary works which exist in multiple versions, the question they commonly address is "Which is the best version?" About *Great Expectations*, for example, J. Hillis Miller writes that "the second ending is, in my opinion, the best. Not only was it, after all, the one Dickens published (would he really have acceded to Mrs. Grundy in the mask of Bulwer-Lytton without reasons of his own?), but, it seems to me, the second ending, in joining Pip and Estella, is much truer to the real direction of the story."[43] On the other hand, Edgar Johnson is somewhat contemptuous of the second ending as a "tacked-on addition of a belated marriage to Estella." "Both as art and as psychology," he informs us, "it was poor counsel that Lytton gave in urging that the shaping of a lifetime in Estella be miraculously undone. Save for this, though, *Great Expectations* is the most perfectly constructed and perfectly written of all Dickens's works." Johnson then proceeds to outline a third ending, of his own imagining, which he prefers to either of those that Dickens wrote. "It should close with that misty moonlight scene in Miss Havisham's ruined garden," but the final action should be that of Pip and Estella "bidding each other a chastened

[42] The consideration of this possibility will, of course, complicate the reasoning of the textual critic. On the whole, it is a possibility which has usually been disregarded unless the evidence to demonstrate the fact of revision has been overwhelming.

[43] *Charles Dickens: The World of His Novels* (Cambridge, Mass., 1958), p. 278.

farewell."[44] Personally, I do not feel greatly assisted by any of these answers. The making of a choice between the versions may seem to be of a high order because it involves the exercise of taste; but it is not the first question to ask, and it turns out to be more of an innocently curious quest than a serious critical inquiry.

The first problem is to identify the work of art. The basic proposition which I submit about works created by authorial revision is that each version is, either potentially or actually, another work of art. It remains a "potential" work of art—it is in process, it is becoming—so long as the author is still giving it shape, in his mind or in successive drafts or interlineations or in whatever manner he suspends those works which he is not yet ready to release to his usual public. On the other hand, the "actual" work of art is a version in which the author feels that his intentions have been sufficiently fulfilled to communicate it to the public, as his response to whatever kinds of pressure bear on him, from within or from without, to release his work into a public domain. The distinction which I am offering is a practical (rather than idealistic) way of separating the potential from the actual, the work of art which is becoming from the work of art which is. The distinction thus turns on the intentions of the artist: the work can have only such integrity, or completeness, as the author chooses to give it, and our only reasonable test of when the work has achieved integrity is his willingness to release it to his usual public. His judgment may not always be good, and he may release it too soon or too late or when (we think) he never should have; but it is his judgment not ours, his intention not ours, his work of art which he makes ours.

The nature of the public differs for different writers. For Dickens—as for most writers since the invention of printing—it was the readers of a periodical or of a book issued by publishers to whom he had turned over a text. For Emily Dickinson, however, her usual public might be her sister-in-law, Susan Dickinson, or Thomas Wentworth Higginson, or Helen Hunt Jackson. If she sent a fair copy of a poem to one of them, this action—as the equivalent of voluntary publication—can be taken as evidence that the work had achieved its integrity. For William Blake, the usual public might be anyone in the small circle of

[44] *Charles Dickens: His Tragedy and Triumph* (New York, 1952), II, 988, 992–93.

friends and kindly benefactors who accepted or purchased a copy of one of his books—written, designed, engraved, colored, and bound by Blake, with the assistance of his wife.

The application of this test is sometimes difficult, mainly when the evidence leaves obscure the question as to whether the artist intended to release the work to his public in the form in which we have it. Books which are published piratically or circulated surreptitiously are examples. Sir Thomas Browne "at leisurable houres composed" *Religio Medici*, as he says in his address "To the Reader," "for my private exercise and satisfaction"; "being communicated unto one, it became common unto many, and was by transcription successively corrupted untill it arrived in a most depraved copy at the presse. He that shall peruse that worke, and shall take notice of sundry particularities and personall expressions therein, will easily discerne *the intention was not publik*." (I use italics to call attention to the key phrase.) There were two unauthorized editions issued anonymously in 1642, but Browne then proceeded to supply—to the same bookseller who had pirated his work—text for an authorized edition; he used a copy of one of the pirated editions, correcting some 650 errors (while overlooking many others), and adding four new sections, a dozen new passages, and many new errors.[45] However hasty and careless his alterations, *Religio Medici* was then a public work. With some writers, pirated (or even manipulated) publication has been used as an excuse to issue works (like Pope's publication of his own letters) which it might otherwise seem immodest to release to the usual public. Sometimes a writer feels that publication puts an end to his freedom to revise. Guillaume De Guileville told, in the prologue to his *Pélerinage de la vie humaine*, of a wonderful dream he had in the year 1330 and of writing it down hastily "that I myht after, by leyser, / Correcte hyt when the day were cler." But before he had finished mending it, it was stolen from him and published abroad, "a-geyn my wyl & my plesaunce." Up to that time, he says, "fredam I hadde / To putte away, and eke to adde, / What that me lyst, lyk as I wende"; but after publication he lost that freedom. It was only after the passage of twenty-five years that he made a new version, by thorough revision, and was ready to send it forth into the world to

---

[45] Jean-Jacques Denonain, ed., *Religio Medici* (Cambridge, Eng., 1953), pp. xxiv–xxviii.

replace the incomplete version which he had not wished published.[46]

The revisions which a writer makes while a work is in process —that is, before it becomes a version which he chooses to make public—constitute an intimate and complex view of that writer at work. "The minute changes made in their compositions by eminent writers are," in Edmond Malone's blunt dictum, "always a matter of both curiosity & instruction to literary men, however trifling and unimportant they may appear to blockheads."[47] The study of revisions can enlighten us, as Paul Valéry says, "about the secret discussion that takes place, at the time when the work is being done, between the temperament, ambition and foresight of the man, and, on the other hand, the excitements and the intellectual means of the moment. The strictness of the revisions, the number of solutions rejected, and possibilities denied, indicate the nature of the scruples, the degree of conscience, the quality of pride, and even the reserves and diverse fears that are felt in regard to the future judgment of the public." With a writer whose mind is reflective and rich in resonances, the work can only emerge "by a kind of accident which ejects it from the mind."[48] The taste for making endless revisions, is according to Valéry, an occupational disease; "in the eyes of these lovers of anxiety and perfection, a work is never *complete*—a word which to them is meaningless—but *abandoned*."[49] Other writers have less difficulty with the creative process, and some find greater satisfaction in the results they obtain.[50]

In any event, the several verbal forms in which the literary work exists while it is being written are in the private province of the writer as part of his interior dialogue with himself. When extant documents preserve these variant forms, we must remem-

[46] EETS (Extra Series), LXXVII (1899), 6–8. (The Lydgate translation.)

[47] Quoted by James M. Osborn, *John Dryden: Some Biographical Facts and Problems* (New York, 1940), p. 131.

[48] "On Mallarmé" in *Selected Writings* (New York, 1950), pp. 217, 216.

[49] "Concerning *Le Cimetière marin*" in *The Art of Poetry* (New York, 1958), pp. 140–41.

[50] For discussion and examples of authorial revision of work in progress, see *Poets at Work*, ed. Charles D. Abbott (New York, 1948), and Robert H. Taylor and H. W. Liebert, *Authors at Work* (New York, 1957).

ber that they provide glimpses into the creative process and not a final form. Dickens never used the first ("unhappy") ending of *Great Expectations;* he wrote it, sent it to the printer, had it set in type, and read the proofs. But he allowed his mind to be changed and wrote the second ending, which he used in the serial and book editions of the novel. The first ending was preserved by his friend and biographer, John Forster; it was never printed as part of the novel until 1937, when it was used in the Limited Editions Club version, which carried the imprimatur of an introduction by George Bernard Shaw. The Rinehart edition prints both endings, as if each reader could choose the one he preferred. As I read the evidence, the first ending never became an integral part of the novel in a public version; only the second ending—no matter whether you think it better or worse—attained that status, and the only "real" *Great Expectations* by Charles Dickens is the one with that ending. Edgar Johnson's "third" ending, being his own construction, could have status only if Johnson were considered a co-author of the novel. The work of art cannot be judged by loading it with hypotheses of what it might have been or of what it could be made to be: the work of art has a radical integrity, and we must take that integrity, once discovered, as it is. The tactic of posing self-made alternatives is one which involves tremendous risks for a doubtful advantage.

When the literary work emerges as a public version it then has the integrity of its unique authorial form. Our suspicions about the sheer decency of contemplating more than one public version of a single literary work may be allayed if we think of the versions as separated in time, with something like five years between the two versions of Auden's "In Time of War," with about thirty-four years for insulation between the first and the last *Return of the Native.*

"I cannot go back over anything I have written," said Valéry, "without thinking that I should now make something quite different of it."[51] If we consider the theory and practice of William Butler Yeats and Henry James, the status of multiple versions of a work of art will perhaps be clearer. Yeats understood, with the ultmost clarity, his drive to revise. When friends objected to his habit of returning again and again to his old poems and altering them each time, he replied with these lines:

[51] "Concerning *Le Cimetière marin*" in *The Art of Poetry*, p. 144.

> The friends that have it I do wrong
> When ever I remake a song,
> Should know what issue is at stake:
> It is myself that I remake.[52]

Yeats was an inveterate reviser because he was, quite simply, always trying to make his poems contemporaneous with his self as a changing human being. "This volume contains what is, I hope, the final text of the poems of my youth," he wrote in the Preface of January 1927 to the thirteenth reprinting and revision of his *Poems* of 1895; "and yet it may not be," he added, "seeing that in it are not only the revisions from my 'Early Poems and Stories,' published last year, but quite new revisions on which my heart is greatly set." To read his prefaces to the various editions of "The Countess Cathleen," for example, is to see more clearly what is involved in the making of a new public version of a literary work.

Yeats was always re-reading his earlier poems, and always making new versions to issue to his public. He did not scruple to keep re-writing any of his previous work. Henry James, on the other hand, approached the revision of his earlier novels with anxiety, as a job that bristled with difficulties.[53] He had been at pains to dismiss his earlier work, to put it behind him, to become unacquainted with it. He was disinclined to exhume it, and very loath to start tidying it up for fear that he would become involved in expensive renovations. He had been accustomed all of his life to revising his work, it is true, to changing the periodical version for book publication, to altering the text from one edition to another; but those revisions were made in warm blood while the original vision of the story was still with him. What has made his revisions of special interest was this task that he approached with such reluctance, for the Definitive New York edition. The

[52] Untitled poem *ss*, in *The Variorum Edition of the Poems of W. B. Yeats*, ed. Peter Allt and Russell K. Alspach (New York, 1957), p. 778. (This poem is not included in the "definitive" edition.)

[53] The Prefaces to *Roderick Hudson* and *The Golden Bowl* (Vols. I and XXIII, respectively, in the New York edition) set forth James's central ideas on revision. In the collection of his Prefaces called *The Art of the Novel*, with an introduction by Richard P. Blackmur (New York, 1934) the passage about revision in the Preface to *Roderick Hudson* is on pp. 10–12 and the one in the Preface to *The Golden Bowl* on pp. 335–40. My exposition of James's views is based mainly on the latter passage and includes close paraphrase of what I take to be the major issues.

gulf of time which separated him from most of the novels to be included made him think of the idea of re-writing them as so difficult, or even so absurd, as to be impossible; it would not be a mere matter of expression, but of somehow harmonizing the man he then was and the man he used to be.

James resolved his dilemma by discarding the idea of re-writing altogether and by taking the task of revision in its etymological sense—to see again, to look over, to re-peruse. Thus he never thought of himself as re-writing a novel, but of seeing it again and recording the results of that re-vision in so many close notes that the pages were made to flower. James respected his novels and their characters as having an independent existence of their own, and he wanted to keep his hands off of them. By his own application of the term "revision," he made himself believe that he had done so. I take his argument to be an innocent but necessary piece of deception to avoid facing the fact of rewriting. However James looked on his job, the revisions for the New York edition resulted in new versions of the works. He made, for example, more than two thousand revisions in *The Reverberator*.[54] Voices rise and fall as to whether James improved or debased his novels by revision, as to whether his later style is more tortuous and labored or clearer and more expressive, even as to whether the revision of a given novel makes a radical or minimal change in the effect of a certain character, like Newman in *The American*. The unarguable fact is that James supplied multiple versions of the novels which he revised.

The literary critic can afford enough detachment to observe the work of art as an historical phenomenon, as a part of the past from the moment of its creation. But few writers are able to take this view; for many of them the work continues, as for a possessive parent, a part of the self, as a child whose hair must be brushed into submission, as an adult who must be nagged into wearing more stylish clothes.

[54] See Sister Mary Brian Durkin, "Henry James's Revisions of the Style of *The Reverberator*," *AL*, XXXIII (1961), 330–49. There has been, I dare say, more extensive scholarly investigation, in books and articles and theses, of the revisions by James for the New York edition than of those by any other writer on any occasion. The three novels in which the revisions have so far been examined the most thoroughly are, probably, *The American*, *The Portrait of a Lady*, and *The Ambassadors*. Such fertile fields are attractive to the husbandman, and we can expect every last one of the twenty-four volumes to be harrowed in each direction.

I suggested that our suspicion of multiple versions of the work of art may be allayed if we think of them as separated by long periods of time. Time is, however, only a practical convenience in envisioning why multiple versions may or must exist. No clock can measure the rate at which a man becomes different, a little, a lot. Enough might happen in a day or even in a flash to require that the man rediscover his self and make a poem over in a new way.

We come back again to the questions with which we began this discussion. The problem of identifying the "real" *Great Expectations*, we found, was simplified when we insisted on respecting the public version to which Dickens gave authorial integrity. The application of this basic test will not select one or the other of Auden's "In Time of War," however, since each is a fulfillment of his intentions, and each was communicated to his usual public. From our review of what takes place in revision for private and public versions, I hope it is clear that the two versions of the Auden collection are equally "real." They stand, side by side, as two separate works, and each has every bit of the dignity and integrity with which an author can endow any work of art. So it is with Hardy, with Yeats, with James, with all multiple versions of works of art where each was given authorial integrity and communicated to the usual public.

This embarrassment of riches may make us restless to distinguish. Hence the critic asks "which is the best?" And the editor asks "which shall I print?" And the student asks "which shall I read?" Usually these three questions are the same, the latter two being applications of the first.

There is a conventional answer, made smooth by constant use. "It is generally accepted that the most authoritative edition is the last published in the author's lifetime." "The book collector may prefer to possess a first edition, however faulty the text, but an author's last revision must, as a rule, claim precedence in literature." This answer can be duplicated from the writings of most of the famous bibliographers and textual authorities, and it is also the password when one is explaining one's terms in a footnote to a textual study: "By 'best text' I mean the text that represents the poet's own final choice among variants of the poem."[55]

[55] The first quotation is from R. W. Chapman, "The Textual Criticism of English Classics," in *English Critical Essays: Twentieth Century*, ed.

It is a bit puzzling to know why this dictum should for so long have passed unchallenged. For it is much like saying that an author's last poem (or novel, or play) is, as a general rule, his best one; it may be, and it may not be. This rule of thumb—whether applied to the choice among multiple versions of a work of art or among works of an author in general—is a desperate substitute for the whole process of critical understanding, which is the only sensible way of trying to arrive at a sound evaluation of anything.

IV

What is the aesthetic object with which textual criticism can deal? What constitutes the integrity of the work of art? When a literary work exists in several authorial versions, which is the real work of art?

These are the three questions which we have been addressing. The first invites us to consider the characteristics of the several types of phenomena which can be called aesthetic objects because they yield an aesthetic response. I have argued that the textual critic must limit himself to works of art: thus aesthetic objects which are the result of chance or nature are beyond his scope, however appealing or meritorious they may be, even if they improve the work of art. In being limited to the work of art, the textual critic is thereby limited to the linguistic intentions of the author. The basic goal of textual criticism is, therefore, the verification or recovery of the words which the author intended to constitute the literary work.

The second question asks us to explore the nature of authorship and of the literary work as an intricate entangling of intentions. Various forces are always at work thwarting or modifying the author's intentions. The process of preparing the work for dissemination to a public (whether that process leads to publication in printed form or production in the theatre or preparation of scribal copies) puts the work in the hands of persons who are professionals in the execution of the process. Similarly, the effort to recover a work of the past puts it in the hands of

---

Phyllis M. Jones (London, 1933), p. 274. The second is from Sir Harold Williams, *The Text of "Gulliver's Travels"* (Cambridge, Eng., 1952), p. 36. The third is from Zahava Karl Dorinson, " 'I Taste a Liquor Never Brewed': A Problem in Editing," *AL*, XXXV (1963), 363, n. 1.

professionals known as textual critics, or editors. In all of these cases, the process must be adapted to the work at hand, and the work to the process. Sometimes through misunderstanding and sometimes through an effort to improve the work, these professionals substitute their own intentions for those of the author, who is frequently ignorant of their craft. Sometimes the author objects and sometimes not, sometimes he is pleased, sometimes he acquiesces, and sometimes he does not notice what has happened. The work of art is thus always tending toward a collaborative status, and the task of the textual critic is always to recover and preserve its integrity at that point where the authorial intentions seem to have been fulfilled.

The third question opens the nature of composition and seeks to define the authoritative quality of each work of art. Works which are in process can be called potential works of art, while the actual work of art is the one which fulfills the author's intentions. Our only practicable way of distinguishing is to observe whether the author does or does not communicate the work to his usual public. When the author provides us with multiple actual versions of what we commonly think of as a single literary work, he has in fact written separate works, among which there is no simple way to choose the best.

Throughout this discussion, the intentions of the artist have occupied a central position. It is his intentions which distinguish the work of art as an order within the class of aesthetic objects, which must be protected in order to preserve the work from becoming a collaborative enterprise, which give the integrity of completeness to the actual work of art. The inference for the textual critic is that the intentions of the artist are of controlling importance over textual work. While the textual critic should not neglect to carry out the more or less mechanical operations which his masters enjoin upon him, he must also undertake to discover all that he can, from whatever source, about the linguistic intentions of the artist. It is his interpretation of this evidence, within a consistent aesthetic, which plays the crucial role in giving his work value.

I would not wish to argue that these inferences simplify the task of the textual critic, nor that they supply him with a ready formula for solving hard cases, nor that they qualify him as a seer. They do, in fact, make his work more difficult. Whenever we deal with human motives and the operation of human intentions, we soon reach the point—if we do not have the advantage of being the omniscient author—beyond which the best we can suggest is probability, then possibility, then uncertainty. Whenever these stages are reached, the incidence of error is necessarily high. The main merit of establishing textual criticism on a consistent set of aesthetic assumptions is (I think) that it brings the real problems into the open and provides a fairer chance of producing results which will be fundamentally sound.

VI

WILLIAM B. TODD

Bibliography and the Editorial Problem in the Eighteenth Century

Of the many problems that harass the bibliographer of eighteenth-century literature, perhaps the most vexing are those involving the proper discrimination and ordering of multiple editions. In this period undenominated reprints are to be suspected everywhere, among elaborate editions running to several volumes, among popular books of any length, even among casual works of lesser size and consequence. Though it would be futile to suggest an occasion for all of this duplication, an explanation for some may be found in a reported conversation between Andrew Millar, a prominent bookseller of the day, and several members of the clergy at St. James. When asked what he thought of David Hume's essays, Millar replied, as he later informed the philosopher, "I said I considered yʳ Works as Classicks; that I never numbered yᵉ Editions as I did in Books We wished to puff."[1] From this we may presume that, for Millar and others of similar intent, multiple editions may appear as the result of a deliberate policy among the booksellers to disguise reprints of standard works. The greater the importance of a book, they must have reasoned, the less the necessity for pushing its sale, and the more the inducement for duplicating the original issue. A close facsimile would be readily accepted by those who wished to buy the first, authoritative printing. A close facsimile was, then, what they oftentimes attempted to produce.

If Millar's statement can be inferred as expressing a general policy, then we have not only been forewarned as to what we may expect in Hume's works and advised as to what actually

Read before the English Institute on September 11, 1950. Reprinted from *Studies in Bibliography*, IV (1951), 41–55, by permission of the author and the Bibliographical Society of the University of Virginia.

[1] *The Letters of David Hume*, ed. J. Y. T. Greig (1932), II, 354.

happened in those of Fielding's which Millar published, but given some reason for the presence of two or three concealed editions in practically every major production in the eighteenth century, and some anticipation of further discoveries and other difficulties in this neglected province of bibliography.[2]

For the presence of other reprints, however, Millar's observation will not suffice, since it excludes all works not considered—in the eighteenth-century view—as classics. But where there are two or three hidden editions of the major works, there seem to be among certain kinds of minor productions as many as four, five, or six, all very much alike and often undiscriminated in bibliographies. The occasion for multiplicity of this order arises, perhaps, from economic rather than literary considerations. For obvious reasons, a publisher would be reluctant to invest in such ephemera as topical poems, plays, and political tracts, and would accordingly prefer to underprint, and print again as necessary, than to overproduce a lot of sheets which would then remain unsold. Paper, in these days, was an expensive item, amounting to forty per cent of the cost of production for small issues, over sixty per cent for larger ones,[3] and therefore not to be squandered on

[2] As this goes to press still another reason is suggested by the recollection that many of the contributors to the 5th and 6th volumes of Dodsley's *Collection of Poems by Several Hands* were much displeased by his production, some insisting that their material was included without their consent, others that what they had entered must be extensively revised in a second edition. Faced with these protests and demands, Dodsley surreptitiously published another uncorrected edition so much like the first as to remain undetected then and thereafter. [See my account forthcoming in *BSA*.] Through this stategem he—and, I would suspect, many others—easily avoided considerable expense, not only in extra pay to the compositors for work from manuscript, but in royalties to the authors, who were generally entitled then, as now, to some of the proceeds from a revised edition.

[3] The ratio of size of issue to cost of paper and printing is illustrated in the following data:

copies	paper cost & percentage			printing cost & percentage		
500	£ 7 8 10½		42.1	£11 0 6		57.9
750	11 15 9		46.2	14 8 0		53.8
1500	72 0 0		63.7	41 2 0		36.3

Data computed from statistics for Gibbon's *Vindication of the History* (1st and 2d eds) and Smollett's *Humphry Clinker* (ed. identified as "B" in this paper), as cited by George K. Boyce in *BSA*, XLIII (1949), 337, and by Charles Welsh in *A Bookseller of the Last Century* (1885), pp. 357–58.

casual effusions of uncertain reception. Hence we may see why Lawton Gilliver printed four limited editions of Bramston's *Art of Politicks* (1729), any one of which might be considered as a "first";[4] why Thomas Cooper, a prolific purveyor of literary trifles, found it necessary to print five editions of Lord Lyttelton's *Court Secret* (1741–42) before a lagging demand required a "puff" with one called the second; and why this same publisher, a year later, printed no less than six editions of Edmund Waller's and Lord Chesterfield's *Case of the Hanover Forces* (1742–43) prior to the publication of a "second."[5] Given the cause in economic necessity, all of this reprinting becomes credible, and should become a matter of record.

In addition to the literary and economic reasons, already presented, another and more significant occasion for reproduction in the eighteenth century is the removal of all legal restrictions upon the size and frequency of issue and the use and reuse of type. With the expiration of the Licensing Act in 1695 and the gradual abrogation of the powers exercised by the Stationers' Company, the esoteric "arte and mysterie" of printing, as it was called in the earlier period, became in this a common trade, subject to few prohibitions, and producing on a scale of greater extent and complexity than anything witnessed before. Despite the laws of copyright, or perhaps because of them, the publishers duplicated their own issues, not infrequently copied those of their competitors, and, with notable exceptions, resorted to the term "edition" for successive issues only as an expedient for moving the book. Thus for one reason or another, or for no reason at all, reprinting became a custom, evident, as I have indicated, among first editions of any sort, and, as well, in several other categories: (1) among subsequent editions properly described, as in the two fourth editions of Gray's *Elegy* (1751), the two second editions of Pope's *Use of Riches* (1733), and, if I may again refer to variants undifferentiated in the present accounts, the three third editions of Pope's *Epistle to Burlington* (1731);[6]

---

[4] Besides these four, I. A. Williams describes two others, one of the same date with a Dublin imprint, and one dated 1731. Cf. *Points in Eighteenth-Century Verse* (1934), pp. 63–67.

[5] For notes on Chesterfield and Lyttelton see *BSA*, XLIV (1950), 224–38, 274–75, and other of my articles forthcoming in the same journal.

[6] Supplementary information on the works by Pope, Johnson, and Goldsmith cited in this paper will be provided in future publications.

(2) among authorized but undesignated reprints, as in the double editions of the 1723 *Hamlet*, the 1724 *Othello*, the 1729 *Macbeth*,[7] and the 1770 versions of Goldsmith's *Traveller*; and (3) in outright piracies, as in the three undiscriminated 1797 editions of Burke's *Letter to Portland*[8] and the four misrepresented 1770 editions of Goldsmith's *Deserted Village*. And so the reprinting continues, to be reported for relatively few books, to be observed in many, to be suspected in all.

If multiple editions in different settings of type represent a problem too often ignored in contemporary accounts, even more of a problem, but one accorded even less recognition, is that of multiple impressions from the same setting of type. Where the seventeenth-century compositor, with a limited amount of type at his disposal, usually had to break down a setting after every sheet in order to recover sorts for further use, the eighteenth-century compositor, with apparently unlimited quantities of type at hand, could on occasion set as many as 350 pages and allow this enormous aggregate of metal to remain intact for innumerable impressions. Some of these are labeled second and third editions, some are not so dignified. Some appear with substantial textual alterations, some without the alteration of a comma. In one printing house no less than 94,900 pieces of type were composed for a certain book and then retained for a series of impressions, all published within seventeen days. The paper which went over the presses in these seventeen days I conservatively estimate at 137,500 sheets.[9]

For such extensive reimpression as this there is no precedent in the sixteenth or seventeenth century, hitherto no exposition of an expedient means for detecting it in the eighteenth, and consequently, no reliable method for interpreting the complexities in printing which have developed over the years. To illustrate the resulting confusion, let us consider the voluminous bibliographical literature on Samuel Johnson, and particularly the commen-

---

[7] It is convenient to list as reprints what Giles E. Dawson has demonstrated to be, in each case, a reprint and a piracy. Cf. "Three Shakespearian Piracies, 1723–1729," *Papers Biblio. Soc. Univ. Virginia*, I (1948), 49–58.

[8] More precisely, these are unauthorized printings of material suppressed by Burke's literary executors.

[9] This is the conclusion to be drawn from the account offered in "The Bibliographical History of Burke's *Reflections on the Revolution in France*," *The Library*, 5th ser., VI (1951–52).

tary on those of his works published by Thomas Cadell. Since Cadell was an apprentice to Andrew Millar, and later his successor, we should expect some irregularity. And something is amiss, both in the bibliographies and in the books. Of four works published between 1770 and 1775 a "second edition," not otherwise described, is recognized from its designation in the books I will call A, C, and D, and presumed from the existence of a "third edition" in B. Actually all, including B, have at least one "second edition," but of a kind quite different from that which the term implies. In A and the unknown B it consists of a partial resetting and a partial reimpression; in C, a complete reimpression; and in D, no less than three distinct reimpressions. With the evidence now at our disposal, and shortly to be divulged, all of this is easily perceived. Without it, the second edition of B remains "suppressed," as we are now informed,[10] the three second editions (*i.e.*, impressions) of D undiscriminated, and the problems inherent in all of these entirely undisclosed.

From this example of misinformation we now turn to bibliographies in which, though more may be expected, occasionally less is fullfilled. In S. L. Gulick's account of Chesterfield—recommended, I might add, by no less an authority than R. W. Chapman as a model of accuracy[11]—an examination of seven works discloses all manner of confusion: two impressions erroneously classified as states, two sets of two editions, each described as one, and a third set entirely overlooked. Similarly, in R. H. Griffith's bibliography of Pope, a survey, again confined to seven works, reveals two states classified as impressions, three sets of two editions, each described as one, and one set of three, likewise represented as a single entity. This production has also been approved in the reviews, including, for instance, those by George Sherburn and A. E. Case,[12] where it is reported in one (and implied in the other) that the copies at Chicago and Yale are identical with the ones described, when, as a matter of fact, they differ from these, from others accessible to the reviewers, and indeed from others in the same collection. If this is the situation in the bibliographies of Johnson, Chesterfield, and Pope, all of which are considered as definitive, what may we expect to

[10] Robert E. Styles, "Doctor Samuel Johnson's 'Taxation No Tyranny' and Its Half Title," *American Book Collector*, I (1932), 155–56.

[11] *The Library*, 4th ser., XVII (1936), 120–21.

[12] *MP*, XXII (1925), 327–36; XXIV (1927), 297–313.

find in those not so recognized? And what, we may inquire, is the status of scholarly commentary based on the premises of these bibliographies? To these questions we may individually provide the answers which seem appropriate.

Having the temerity to proceed thus far in what may be taken as a general indictment, I must go a step further. No one, least of all the present writer, should presume to say what has happened without suggesting the cause and the cure. As any insinuation of incompetence would, of course, be irrelevant for bibliographies regarded as authoritative, this may be discounted and two other reasons advanced. For one, the standards of examination so readily accepted ten or twenty years ago, and so often in evidence today, have been superseded by those which require, among other things, some facility in the interpretation of various technicalities, the comparison of such differentiæ as headlines, the use of control copies or something that will serve as a control, and—whatever the inconvenience to the person concerned—the inspection of numerous copies in addition to the several represented in special collections. For the other, the books to be examined, in the eighteenth century, are, as I have intimated, the products of conditions of greater complexity than those which apply in the earlier periods, and therefore occasionally require supplemental techniques for their analysis. It has not been sufficiently realized that printing, in this century, has progressed beyond the era of the simple handicraft and now represents one of mass production, where not a few but hundreds of pages of type may be retained and repeatedly returned to press, where not one or two individuals but batteries of pressmen and compositors may produce, in a matter of hours, editions running into thousands of copies, where not one but several books may be put to press and worked concurrently by the same personnel. These practices, though extraordinary in the seventeenth century, have become commonplace in the eighteenth, and now demand a consideration frequently evaded or ignored in our present studies.

The only procedure that fully accounts for the altered circumstances of book-production in this period is one that utilizes the evidence peculiar to these circumstances. Evidence of this sort, we may be assured, is usually not to be found in the *materials* of production—in obvious irregularities in type, paper, and ink—all of which tend to be standardized and uniform, but in the actual *process* of production, as this is revealed by the press figures. These little symbols, appearing now and then in the lower margin of the page in many eighteenth-century books, were first reported, I believe, by Griffith in his Pope bibliography, and have since become involved in several suppositions as to their original use to the printer and their present use to the bibliographer. Contrary to McKerrow's prediction that they would prove to be of little importance, recent investigation has shown that they may be interpreted as signs of cancellation, variant states, half- or full-press operation (indicating the employment of one or two men at the machine), type pages arranged within the forme in some irregular pattern, sheets impressed in some abnormal order, an impression of the formes for each sheet by one man working both formes in succession, or two men working both simultaneously, impressions interrupted for one reason or another, reimpressions or resettings of the book, in whole or in part, copy distributed among several shops, overprints involving an increase in the number of sheets machined for certain gatherings in order to meet an unanticipated demand for copies, and underprints consisting of a decrease in the number of sheets in order to reduce the issue and speed its publication.[13] Now that they are displayed in the figures, these various ramifications in composition and presswork may not be overlooked by any editor cognizant of his responsibilities, for here and there in a process so involved he should expect to find an unnoticed reading, an altered passage, or an entirely different edition from that on record.

Since the figures disclose so much of possible textual significance which might otherwise remain unrevealed, they are, notwithstanding McKerrow, of some importance, not only in the discrimination and analysis of concealed or known editions, but in the bibliographical description of the books examined. If the figures are included in the record, any variant unknown to the compiler can be immediately detected and appropriate measures taken to establish its relationship to others in the series. If they are not included, then, of all the variants already mentioned, the most elaborate description will permit the identification of only a few of the editions and none of the impressions.

An interesting example of the relative value of the figures and of the more conventional means of discrimination is afforded by

[13] See my "Observations on the Incidence and Interpretation of Press Figures," *Studies in Bibliography*, III (1950), 171–205.

Burke's *Reflections on the Revolution in France* (1790). According to Gathorne-Hardy's account, which is duly offered on the basis of differentiæ in catchwords, ornaments, the spacing of type, and the length of a rule preceding the text, the first two editions of this book consist of sheets in two settings of type separate or mixed in several combinations.[14] As the figures intimate, however, and as an inspection of the discrepant copies will disclose, the type for this book exists in one to four settings, each occurring in one to four impressions, and all combined in a strange and wonderful manner to produce five distinct variants. Among these we may identify two editions—A, comprising a single impression throughout, and B, comprising four impressions, of which two (B1-B2) are undesignated and two (B3-B4) called a "Second Edition." Now, with all of this decided, unequivocally, the editor can proceed, in the manner that Sir Walter Greg suggests, to select as his copytext what is identified as the first edition, and then to add to this the revisions which Burke introduced in the edition called the "Third," an edition disregarded in the previous commentary, and also, in part, a reimpression. Though this is the required procedure, it has not been followed for the *Reflections* or for numerous other works of a similar nature simply because the problems incident to their manufacture have been ignored or misconstrued.

Even when the variants are known, however, their relationship may be undetermined, again for want of appropriate bibliographical techniques. In some cases, as with the *Reflections*, the several editions and impressions can be ordered on the evidence of the figures alone, without reference to copy. In others, the later edition may be identified by the usual criteria, such as the inclusion of textual matter in the preliminary gathering of the *Deserted Village* piracies—those which are so highly esteemed as "private issues," or the gradation in the size and format of the Bramston, Chesterfield, and Lyttelton pamphlets to which I have referred, or the correction of errata in *Tom Jones* and in Gibbon's *Decline and Fall*, or the absence of cancels in Johnson's edition of Shakespeare, or finally, in watermarks, imprints, and advertisements, all of which materially assist in deciding the priority of the *Monk* editions. Other works not amenable to these several approaches can be subjected to a mechanical demonstra-

[14] Item 28 in *Biblio. Notes and Queries*, I, Nos. 1–3 (January-August, 1935). For a rejoinder cf. n. 8 above.

tion, such as the one Fredson Bowers exemplified for Dryden's *Wild Gallant* in his address before this Institute last year.[15]

Nevertheless, with all of these techniques at our command, we still must contend with many eighteenth-century editions which continue to be bibliographically intransigent. These bugaboos infest what one writer has called "The Bibliographical Jungle"[16] —a wild locale visited by a goodly number of adventurers, all of whom have hacked about in the bushes, but produced nothing to show for their labors except a covey of unappealing conjectures and misconceptions. To produce the results desired, we should, once again, abandon the conventional methods of attack, all of which would seem to be of little avail, and devise for our purpose some unconventional tool.

The one I would propose concerns the use of a third text of known date and provenance, deriving independently from and therefore identifying the first of several editions under consideration, yet, paradoxically, extraneous to these editions, to their printer, and to the author, and thus, in a strict sence, of no editorial or bibliographical significance whatever. This anomalous text is that provided by the literary reviews which, beginning with those to be found in the early numbers of the *Gentleman's Magazine*,[17] usually appear shortly after the publication of the first edition and occasionally cite passages of considerable length "for the interest of their readers," and now, we may say, for our interest too. When the readings in the abstracts are collated with those in the indeterminate editions they will, of course, collate only with those in the text from which they were copied, and thus establish the priority of that edition in the sequence. It is rather surprising that evidence so abundantly available in the

[15] More fully discussed by him in *The Library*, 5th ser., V (1950–51), 51–54.

[16] *Times Literary Supplement*, August 5, 1949, p. 512.

[17] Mr. John Cook Wyllie reminds me that the periodicals, especially this one, were also frequently reprinted, sometimes as many as twenty-five years after the date assigned. Just recently I discovered, in what appeared to be a first edition of the *Magazine*, a reference in the February 1733 number to a citation in a number issued in the following year. When the alteration involves nothing more than this, the reprint may still be used as an index to the *princeps* of a book, since new errors would derive independently of the texts. But when the reprint substitutes one passage for another —one perhaps in greater esteem than the one originally printed—the replacement may originate in a text later than the first edition. The periodicals should therefore be used with some discretion.

periodicals should be so rarely employed. In fact, so far as I can recall, only one scholar, Austin Dodson, has ever resorted to the reviews for the purpose I recommend, and on that occasion—some thirty years before the discovery of the printer's ledger confirmed his decision—he was able to demonstrate by a simple collation that, contrary to normal expectation, the expurgated version of Fielding's *Voyage to Lisbon* (1755) was issued prior to the one with the original text.[18]

Of the many books which can be ordered through reference to the journal readings, several may be mentioned here. The first, Smollett's *Humphrey Clinker* (1771), has long confounded every attempt at analysis. For the last twenty-five years a succession of bibliographers have undertaken the disheartening task of collating the 800 pages in this novel, amassed reams of worthless notes, and eventually confessed their failure to establish the precedence of the editions.[19] For this, as for numerous other works, a mixture of corrupted and corrected readings precludes a demonstration of priority.

Undoubtedly, any approach to a solution in the case of *Humphrey Clinker* has been somewhat impeded by an uncertainty as to the number of existing variants. Once the true editions are disengaged from sophisticated copies, variant states, and "ghosts," all of which have crept into the discussion of this riddle, it will be noted that there are, essentially, four distinct settings:

Volume I

Edition	Title-page		Press figures[20]
A	1671		Throughout
B	1671 or 1771		Only in gathering M
C	1772	2d ed	None
D	1771	2d ed	None

[18] Henry Fielding, *The Journal of a Voyage to Lisbon*, ed. Austin Dobson (1892), pp. v–xii. J. Paul de Castro, "The Printing of Fielding's Works," *The Library*, 4th ser., I (1920–21), 268–69.

[19] See A. Edward Newton, *This Book-Collecting Game* (1928), p. 26; David Randall's notes in John T. Winterich, *A Primer of Book-Collecting* (1946), p. 152; and notes by various contributors in *Biblio. Notes and Queries*, II, No. 1 (January, 1936), 7; II, No. 3 (April, 1936), 3; II, Nos. 4–5 (May, 1936), 3.

[20] At the time of this address I chose not to amplify my commentary on *Humphry Clinker* though a matter of record in my dissertation on *The Number and Order of Certain Eighteenth-Century Editions* [University of Chicago Microfilm Edition 433 (1949), pp. 48–50, 131–35], in the

Now between June 18, 1771, the date of original publication, either for A or for B, and September 1, the approximate date that work was completed on the alternate "first edition," a total of seventy-four pages from the novel were reprinted in four journals, *The London Magazine*, *The Gentleman's Magazine*, *The Critical Review*, and *The Weekly Magazine, or Edinburgh Amusement*.[21] As these reprinted pages represent 138 readings, all differing from those in B, and all agreeing with those in A, the conclusion follows that A is unmistakably the first of the two editions. With the order of these determined, the relationship of all texts, complete and abstracted, may be represented in the stemma:

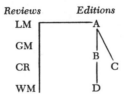

Thus after years of misdirected activity, a little effort, very little, has here provided a certain decision.

No less certain are the results to be obtained by the use of figures and reviews, independently or together, in the reconsideration of problems already known and decided. Two instances may be cited, one reported within the past several months, one on record for the last twenty years, both entertaining versions of the kind, number, and order of variants, and both entirely contrary to fact. The first, appearing in the latest catalogue issued by Peter Murray Hill, is a brief notice of *The Life*

---

expectation that a full account would appear in a study then in preparation by Franklin B. Newman. Since Dr. Newman preferred to undertake this investigation without assistance and to disregard the findings incorporated in my thesis, his analysis, now published in *BSA*, XLIV (1950), 340–71, fails to supply all that the bibliographer should know concerning the location of copies, discrepancies in the make-up of the title-pages for the three volumes of each edition, variant states, an occasional reimpression, collateral evidence for the priority of variants, and the case for a pirated edition (D in the above stemma, corresponding to C in Dr. Newman's account). Thus the question, in some of its particulars, remains unresolved.

[21] *London Magazine*, XL (1771), 317–19, 368–70; *Gentleman's Magazine*, XLI (1771), 317–21; *Critical Review*, XXXII (1771), 81–87; *Weekly Magazine*, XIII (1771), 39–40, 76–79, 105–7, 225–27, 272–73.

of David Hume, Esq. (1777)—a book about which Millar has given us ample warning. Concerning this, Hill reports two "issues," with the first containing a reading "himself" and the second containing the reading supposedly corrected to "myself." Actually these are not "issues," as they are called, or states, as we might infer from the description, but separate editions, of which the figures indicate different settings of type and the reviews a different order of publication.[22]

For the second instance, Edward Moore's periodical, *The World* (1753-56), the current explanation is as simple as the one I have just refuted, but the circumstances of printing somewhat more complex. In J. H. Caskey's account we are informed that there were, apparently, two simultaneous "issues" of every one of the 209 numbers.[23] First, it would seem, came the issue bearing a vignette, and then, set from proof-sheets of this, the one containing a headpiece of printers' ornaments. Though the reasons for this facile hypothesis are not made explicit, they seem to rest on a reference to the fact that 2500 copies were required of some numbers. Perhaps it was thought that Robert Dodsley, the publisher, needed to have two settings for an impression running over the limit established by regulation, or that two were necessary in order to shorten the time at press. From the point of view of those dealing with the literature of the sixteenth or seventeenth centuries, either explanation would appear to be plausible. From our vantage ground in the eighteenth, both must be considered irrelevant.

The size of an impression was certainly not determined, at this time, by directives of the Stationers' Company. That these had long since become inoperative is attested by the printers' own accounts: William Woodfall cast off 4500 copies of *Edward and Eleanora* (1739); Samuel Richardson, 2500 of *The Centaur Not Fabulous*, third edition (1755); William Strahan, 3000 of *Tom Jones*, third edition (1749), 3500 of the fourth edition

[22] Hill, Catalogue 34 (March, 1950), item 220. Further discussed in my "First Printing of Hume's *Life* (1777)," *The Library*, 5th ser., VI (1951–52).

[23] "Two Issues of The World," *MLN*, XLV (1930), 29–30. For this periodical the notes offered here and in my dissertation (*The Number and Order of Certain Eighteenth-Century Editions*, pp. 50–53, 140–41) are to be viewed as a casual summary of what will be more thoroughly considered in George P. Winship's forthcoming edition.

(1750), 5000 of Amelia (1752);[24] and each of these editions, I am satisfied, is of a single impression. Nor can it be argued that there was insufficient time to produce an issue of *The World* from one setting of type. If two presses were used for the full sheet, one for printing, the other for perfecting, and a third press for the half-sheet, even as many as 2500 copies could be easily completed within three days, well within the schedule for a weekly paper. With the liberty and the time to do what he pleased, the publisher would hardly put himself to the expense of a second, unnecessary setting at the time of publication. The only reasonable explanation therefore seems to be that the variant "issue" was set at some time after publication to meet an unexpected demand for certain numbers.

If the variants are, thus, nothing more than occasional reprints, they should occur irregularly in the sequence of numbers and not, as the previous hypothesis would require, in every number. What, then, is the situation, and to what extent may it be explained by the usual method of analysis? Examination discloses that, among the copies I have examined, the variants are not precisely two to a number, nor can they be considered as "issues," nor were they printed in the sequence described. From the 19th to the 209th and last, all numbers bear the vignette. Among the first eighteen numbers one encounters the usual disorder in what is assumed to be entirely regular: three editions of the first and second numbers, two from the fourth through the eleventh, one from the twelfth to the seventeenth, and two of the eighteenth. A distinguishing characteristic of some of these editions is the headpiece, of which there are, not two, but three variants:

A   Five rows of ornaments
B   Vignette of author at his desk
C   The same vignette, broken diagonally
    across the center of the block

Whenever one copy differs from another in any of these respects it also differs in setting. And whenever the settings B and C are found for the same number of the periodical, we may assume from the evidence of the fractured block that C was printed at

[24] *Notes and Queries*, 1st ser., XII (1855), 218; Ralph Straus, *Robert Dodsley, Poet, Publisher & Playwright* (1910), p. 355; de Castro, "Printing of Fielding's Works," pp. 263–64, 266.

a later date than B. This date is fixed by the progressive deterioration of the vignette in the numbers which exist as a single edition. From the 19th to the 23rd number the block is sound; from the 24th to the 87th it is broken in one place, as in variant C; and beginning with some copies of the 88th number a second break appears. Thus the C edition of the earlier numbers, though dated January, 1753, must have been printed after June 7 of that year, the date of the 23rd number, and before September 5, 1754, the date of the 88th.

Whereas B and C have the vignette in common, a collation of the readings indicates that they are separated by an intermediate text A without vignette. The precise relationship of the three editions, wherever they occur in the periodical, therefore corresponds to one of these three stemma:

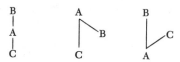

Further than this we cannot proceed by the critical method, for the potentialities of that method have now been exhausted. But if we choose to apply collateral evidence, a second series of texts is made available, and the analysis can then continue to a conclusion.

These texts, present in *The London Magazine*, *The Monthly Review*, *The Scots Magazine*, and *The Universal Magazine*,[25] abstract readings from the first two numbers of the periodical. Among the readings in the several editions of the first number the variants are accidental, amounting to a few changes in capitalization. Among those of the second, however, the variation is substantial:

	Reading	Editions			Reviews		
7,8	shine, but	A	C	MR	SM		
	shine but	B					
8,29	nothing to say	A	C	MR	SM		
	not a word to say	B					
10,32	absence;	A	B	MR	SM	LM	UM
	absence:	C					

[25] *London Magazine*, XXII (1753), 27; *Monthly Review*, VIII (1753), 40, 42–45; *Scots Magazine*, XV (1753), 30–31, 37–39; *Universal Magazine*, XII (1753), 19. The *Gentleman's Magazine* reprints only from the first number.

A collation of the seven texts now at our disposal demonstrates the literal sequence of the three editions to be of the order A-B for the one, A-C for the other. The chronological sequence, where C with the broken vignette follows the unbroken B, is therefore:

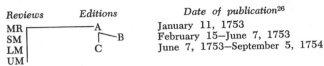

Reviews	Editions	Date of publication[26]
MR	A	January 11, 1753
SM	B	February 15–June 7, 1753
LM	C	June 7, 1753–September 5, 1754
UM		

This determination of the priority and relationship among the three editions of one number of *The World* establishes a reasonable presumption for a similar arrangement of the editions in others. Without reference to the reviews any determination, even for one number, is impossible.

From the evidence adduced in this and the preceding examples I would suggest that by one method or another, and sometimes by these methods alone, we are now in a position to discover and decide problems presently unknown or unresolved. To such a declaration it is hardly necessary to add that these several techniques do not constitute a panacea for all of the duplications and disorders to be encountered in eighteenth-century literature. Some books requiring differentiation are unfigured in uninformative patterns, or in rare instances, exactly reiterated in their figures. Some requiring arrangement are unreviewed, reviewed by a synopsis not subject to collation, or cited in portions where there are only a few or no discrepancies. For these exceptional cases other procedures must be found, or the project abandoned as insolvable. For all except these, however, the methodology now available will facilitate a solution to any problem concerning the discrimination, description, and classification of variants. Even in these elementary, though fundamental preliminaries to editorial endeavor there is much to do in the eighteenth century, and much of what has been attempted must be done again.

26 Whenever the edition with ornamental headpiece (A) is found in the volumes I have examined, it appears only for the first six numbers, and is then followed by numbers with the vignette. From this circumstance I conclude that the vignette (in edition B), especially cut for the periodical, was not ready for use until the 7th number, and that reprints of earlier numbers exhibiting this vignette, in its unbroken state, therefore must have been prepared sometime after February 15, 1753, the date of the 7th number.

VII

WILLIAM B. TODD

On the Use of Advertisements in Bibliographical Studies

In venturing a few words on newspaper advertisements I am aware of two considerations which bear upon the nature and direction of my remarks. One I owe to the honary Secretary, whose comment on the novelty of the subject has tempted me beyond the strictly limited "use of advertisements as bibliographical evidence," the original title for this paper, to the wider area of their value in studies of any kind and purpose. The other comes from the realization that even in this more extended area little has been done and less been said on the matter. When it is recalled that publishers have regularly advertised their wares for well over 300 years and have, more often than not, provided a commentary in their notices, the fact that these should be generally neglected deserves some comment. Why should we regard as new and strange material so old, so common, so relevant to the books with which we are concerned?

No response comes from bibliographers labouring in the *S.T.C.* period, for all of these are condemned to drudgery quite unenlightened by daily advertisements. Nor is much to be learned from those who, though concerned with later periods, confine their attention exclusively to the printed book. Among the latter group, especially, the tendency to depreciate the value of extraneous evidence as something of little interest to the "pure" or "analytical" bibliographer is, I would say, unwarranted and quite contrary to the practice outside our own field of investigation. When a detective is called to the scene of a crime he does more than examine the corpse: the immediate locale comes under his scrutiny and all available witnesses are summoned for their testi-

Read before the Bibliographical Society on Tuesday, 20 January 1953. Reprinted from *The Library*, 5th ser., VIII (1953), 174–87, by permission of the author and the Bibliographical Society.

mony. Similarly, when a bibliographer is called to the scene of a publication he should do more than probe around for broken letters and catchwords: all pertinent material must be examined and all contemporaneous reports brought forward as exhibits in his prosecution. As the detective would readily admit, and as the bibliographer should also acknowledge, the hardest case to prove and the easiest to reverse is one based solely on circumstantial evidence. Seemingly irrefutable facts can easily be discountenanced by the testimony of those who were there. In due course I should like to offer just such testimony and, in the presence of this court, demand another hearing for the books concerned.

For the moment, though, on the chance that there is something more of interest in it, let us continue our digression on the detective and the bibliographer. Like any analogy, this one is incomplete, for the bibliographer usually cannot avail himself of oral statements, all of which may be cross-examined, but only of recorded accounts or "depositions." Consequently, if he is to use these accounts, he must distinguish between those which appeared at the time of publication and those which were prepared at some later date. The one kind, as documentation, will always be admitted in court; the other, as mere hearsay, must always be rejected.

Now unfortunately, among those conscientious bibliographers who habitually supplement their evidence from sources outside the book, not all are careful to make this distinction. Many otherwise commendable studies thus fall short of the original papers and come to rest upon more accessible material—such as that available in biographies, memoirs, correspondence, or an occasional publisher's ledger—where the information is so variable that it affords, at best, a very irregular record of the author's work. On the facts of publication these derivative bibliographies will therefore vary according to the accuracy and extent of their references: If Prior errs in his biography of Goldsmith, if the *D.N.B.* errs in its account of Churchill, if Lockhart is a little vague about eighteen of the twenty-three Waverley Novels,[1] or if no precise information is immediately available on the early work of Galsworthy, most of Trollope, or the later collections

---

[1] This perhaps renders a disservice to Lockhart, since he usually offers more than Worthington has accepted. For items 1, 2, 3, 4, and 8 the bibliographer cites all the particulars given in the biography, for 5 only a portion, and for the remaining books nothing.

of Yeats,[2] these several errors and deficiencies reappear in the account of the author's achievements. What should have been a basic record of the books and of the circumstances of their publication (so far as these can be determined) has therefore become something less than this.

Equally commendable, but again, from the peculiar view I am now maintaining, somewhat dissatisfying, is another species of bibliography best exemplified by Sadleir's *XIX Century Fiction*. Where the compilers of other catalogues, either of a certain kind of literature or of a particular library, have usually regarded the books as separate gems apart from their historical setting, Mr. Sadleir recognizes the need for some documentation other than that supplied by the work, and offers all that his numerous authorities may provide.[3] Yet even in this magnificent bibliography, so exceptional in so many other respects, Mr. Sadleir is usually content to deal only with secondary references; and as these become less and less explicit his account necessarily grows more and more obscure. Thus, like other derivative bibliographies, the one on nineteenth-century fiction tends to give us much information on books much discussed but very little or none on those most in need of original investigation. As soon as we move into unexplored territory, should we admit defeat, concede with Mr. Sadleir, at one juncture, that the publication dates for the two forms of Kingsley's *Valentin* (1872) "cannot be established," and then follow his retreat by the purchase of both variants? Or should we carry on, find the date in the papers, discover there—as it happens—the author's own comment on the relation of one text to the other, and then choose the one variant unmistakably revealed as the first?[4] For *Valentin* and for other works, here

[2] In Marrot compare, for instance, the last 23 entries with the first several; in Sadleir such entries 2, 4, 6, 9, 10 with 14–16 or 64–69; in Wade entries 189–92 with 20–23, 202, and 211a.

[3] Though Mr. Sadleir acknowledges the necessity for accurate dating in his note preceding item 99, his references frequently have not permitted him more than an approximation. See for example, items 79, 86, 96, 286, 1144, 1152a.

[4] Sadleir 1365. On 31 August 1872 the *Athenaeum* announced that the Tinsley edition was "just ready," on 7 September advised that it was "now ready," on 21 September gave it a caustic review, and on 28 September carried this plaintive message from the author: "Will you do me the favour to state that 'Valentin: a French Boy's Story of Sedan,' which you reviewed last week, is merely a slight story for boys, written for the *Young Gentleman's Magazine*, and reprinted by Mr. Tinsley." To this the

and elsewhere, no concession should be allowed until the newspapers have presented their evidence.

So far, I must confess, my commendation of those who offer more than mere description is slightly less than enthusiastic. But while some bibliographers may rely too much on hearsay, on comment far removed from the event, others may properly distrust even the best of authorities and turn to the contemporary journals. Miss Blakey, for example, has recourse to the quarterly reviews, Courtney and Nichol Smith usually to the *Gentleman's Magazine*. Even so, though this approach provides, more consistently than the other, a regular supply of information, and thus brings us a little closer to the facts as reported at the time, the reviews are often delayed as much as a year following publication and the *Magazine* cites only the month and the price.

More immediate in reference and therefore, I believe, more accurate and comprehensive in account is such work as that of Cross on Fielding, Griffith on Pope, Pottle on Boswell, Sale on Richardson, Macdonald on Dryden, Miss Norton on Gibbon, Hazen on Walpole, and Gallup on T. S. Eliot. Here, as Griffith remarked of his own work, are bibliographies of an "amplitude and precision" far beyond the range of surveys confined to the books. Here, too, as Pottle expressly declared, is the proper base for a more extensive inquiry, a base resting not on late reports and conjectures, but on the primary material in the newspapers. From this source, as Pottle realized, one may supply for Boswell relatively more data on printing and publication than Boswell ever supplied for Johnson. All of these studies, then, enforce my own conviction that for many books, and particularly those of the

---

editor abruptly responded: "We cannot see that this accounts for the extraordinary blunders that are to be found in 'Valentin'."

The *Magazine* to which Kingsley alludes (Sadleir's reference, "Every Boy's Magazine," is to a title not adopted until 1874) was published by Routledge in penny weekly numbers, each consisting of 8 leaves and consecutively paged through the 44 numbers later bound up in one volume titled *Every Boy's Annual for 1873*. The bound copy received at the British Museum on 7 October 1872 bears on the final leaf of the 44th gathering a post-dated advertisement that "No. 1 of the New Volume [i.e. no. 45] appeared on Wednesday October 9th, 1872," a statement confirmed by a preliminary announcement in *The Times* for the 8th. It would therefore seem that, as *Valentin* was serialized in all numbers through the 43rd, the final instalment was not published until 25 September, two weeks before the 45th number of Routledge's *Magazine* and at least three weeks after the appearance of Tinsley's edition.

eighteenth century, the newspapers are more reliable than biographies written a century later, more precise than the author's own recollections, and certainly more comprehensive than any of the scattered printers' or publishers' records now extant.

So much for a cursory view of what has not been done; now for the papers and the wide variety of information they contain.

First of all, with the example of *Valentin* in mind, let us consider the simple problem of chronology. If the biographer is expected to record every significant date in the life of a person, his wife, and his children, the bibliographer has the inescapable duty of recording what are, for an author, the most important dates of all—those which mark the appearance of his books. These, as Mr. Carter aptly observes, are the all-important D-Days, the crucial times upon which may hang, not only the contemporary reputation of the author, but the later decisions of his bibliographer. Either in the date for the paper or in a notice within the advertisement, this time is easily checked, always to the month or week, usually to the day, occasionally to the very hour. Should we be content to speak in vague generalities when we can report, specifically, that a political essay was published at 8 A.M. on Saturday, 11 February; a critical letter at 10 A.M. on Monday, 28 November; Goldsmith's most famous poem at 12 noon on Saturday, 26 May; and James Thomson's first play at 4 P.M on Thursday, 12 March?[5] The mere recital of these particulars enlarges the imagination and gives it scope for various speculations. How many of us, in these days, would rise at daybreak on a wintry Saturday morning to buy a political tract? And how many of us would not have enjoyed high tea with Thomson and his friends on that spring afternoon when his play was launched in the bookstalls?

Those who would deny us this exact information and refer only to the year need to be reminded that much can happen in a very short time: that Swift's *Conduct of the Allies* and Horace Walpole's *Letter from XoHo* both went through three editions in less than a week,[6] that the authorized edition of Gray's *Elegy*

---

[5] For Erskine's *View of the Present War with France* see the *Telegraph*, 10 February 1797; for *An Expostulatory Letter to Mr. Kidgell*, the *Public Advertiser*, 28 November 1763 (cited in Norton, p. xii); for the *Deserted Village*, the *Daily Advertiser*, 26 May 1770; for *Sophonisba*, the *Monthly Chronicle*, March 1730, and the *London Evening-Post*, 10–12 March 1730.

[6] Davis, *Prose Works*, VI. 205; Hazen, item 9. As Professor Hazen has observed, the Walpole "editions" are actually impressions.

preceded a surreptitious printing by a single day, that two issues of the *Letters of Mr. Pope* appeared on the same day,[7] and that two editions of a statement from the House of Rivington were issued, I suspect, within a few hours.[8] Ignorance of the facts in any given instance may lead to serious blunders. Had he been seriously concerned about the chronology of events, or had he been properly advised by some bibliographer, the editor of the Oxford *Works* of James Thomson would have realized that the second edition of the *Castle of Indolence* was not attended by the author, for the author was in his grave a month before its issue.[9]

Lest these hardy annuals wriggle out of their predicament, I press ahead to meet them on their own ground. Assuming that the yearly date on the title-page is enough for the preparation of a bibliography, how far may we proceed? Five difficulties immediately block the way. In the first place, without advertisements or some other notation, such as that provided by a Thomason, Luttrell, or Walpole, undated items cannot be definitely assigned to any particular year.[10] Secondly, even if all the books were assigned, no method exists for sorting them out within the year. Thirdly, even if they could be segregated, the question remains for earlier works as to which calendar was in effect, Julian or Gregorian. For Prior's *Poems* the imprint date 1718 is quite acceptable, by old-style reckoning; but the advertisement is dated 17 March or, as interpreted new style, 28 March 1719.

Even more distressing to the annualists would be the many border-line cases with vacillating dates, all apparently the result of some confusion as to when one year ended and another began. Typical instances are: (1) Swift's *Conduct of the Allies*, with the first, sixth, and seventh editions reading 1712, and the second to the fifth, 1711; (2) the first octavo edition of the *Spectator*, with a third volume dated 1713 intervening between others dated

---

[7] Griffith, 374–75.

[8] These editions, both dated 13 February 1797, each represent a different version of a warning against the sale or purchase of Burke's *Letter to the Duke of Portland*, the one issued just before an injunction was obtained on the date cited, the other issued, apparently, just after. What may be unique copies of each edition are bound in the Bodleian specimen of the *Letter*, press mark Y.317 Jur.

[9] The problem is reviewed in my forthcoming study on "The Text of the *Castle of Indolence*," *English Studies*, XXXIV (1953).

[10] For books dated by advertisements see, *inter alia*, Griffith, 67 and Pottle, 11.

1712; and (3), a curious example, occurring in the year Parliament officially sanctioned the new calendar: the folio edition of the *Rambler* papers, the last dated 17 (improperly for 14) March 1752, but with general titles reading either 1751 or 1753. Though we can appreciate the printers' bewilderment in these several cases, we cannot excuse the bibliographer's failure to remove the ambiguity. For a Chesterfield tract, variously dated 1742 and 1743, the arbitrary assignment of the later year is refuted by advertisements indicating that at least three and possibly six editions appeared before the end of the year preceding.[11]

Another difficulty, the fourth, concerns books which, for one reason or another, are delayed in publication. Thus, as Miss Norton has demonstrated, the second "1814" edition of Gibbon's *Miscellaneous Works* obviously was not issued until early in 1815. On the other hand, those who read the papers would know that Goldsmith's *Millenium Hall* (1762) could not have been issued in March of the year following the date of its imprint, as alleged in the biography and thence in the bibliography, nor even in the preceding December, as might be presumed from an inscription recently reported for one copy, but as early as 28 October 1762.[12] Nor could Charles Churchill's *Night: An Epistle* (1761) have been delayed until the year after its imprint, though this would be our presumption if we relied upon the *D.N.B.* and thence, again, the bibliography, for a second edition was announced in December of the imprinted year.[13] While demonstrable cases of predating (as distinguished from the two fictitious ones just cited) are quite exceptional and quite unintended, the converse situation, or issue of books prior to the date assigned, is customary and deliberate. "The Rule in general observed among Printers," Nichols reports, "is, that when a Book happens

[11] See my notes on the *Case of the Hanover Forces* in *Papers of the Bibliographical Society of America*, XLIV (1950), 224–38.

[12] Cf. notes by Muir and Todd, *Book Collector*, I (1952), 265–66, and II (1953), 72.

[13] As the first edition seems not to have been advertised in any of the papers it may possibly have been privately distributed. The second edition "Revised and Corrected" is announced in the *Public Advertiser* for 29 December 1761 as to be published on "Monday next" but not listed thereafter until 6 January, two days after the projected date. In anticipation of later comment on imprints it might be noticed that the original announcement has "Printed for William Flexney," Churchill's usual publisher; the second announcement, "Printed for the Author."

not to be ready for publication before November, the date of the ensuing year is used."[14] Throughout the earlier periods, then through the nineteenth century—as witnessed in certain novels by Jane Austen, Trollope, and Meredith[15]—and on into the twentieth in various magazines, the custom invalidates one out of every six imprints.

Again, and finally, there is still another difficulty when the printer intentionally falsifies the date and issues on 26 July 1726 a book imprinted 1727, or some time after 1 July 1773 one imprinted 1771, or some time after November 1797 one imprinted 1796.[16] Fortunately, in two of these instances, the bibliographers referred to the advestisements and spotted the deception. Most unfortunately, in the third, relating to Lewis's *The Monk,* ignorance of the advertisements and other simple facts has led several persons to regard the first edition as the second, the third as the first, a surreptitious issue as legitimate, Lewis's revisions as his original readings, his original text as the revision, and so on. For all these reasons we are forced to conclude that any bibliography which pretends to offer a consecutive account of the author's work, but neglects the most essential evidence of this order, simply remains a pretence.

Once the advertisements are found, and the date noted, much more of interest may be divulged to the attentive reader. Now and then they may allude to the original binding, to large paper or "superfine" issues, to work intended but never brought to fruition,[17] to piracies or spurious continuations then in prospect or already produced,[18] to several errata or entire passages belatedly recognized as requiring correction,[19] to various attributions which otherwise may have gone unnoticed[20] and to work

[14] *Anecdotes,* iii. 249.

[15] Keynes, 9; Sadleir, 4, 6, 13; Forman, 2.

[16] Griffith, 177; Pottle, 47; Todd, *Studies in Bibliography,* II (1949), 3–24.

[17] Cross, iii. 324.

[18] Macdonald, *Dryden,* 214; Pottle, 20; Sale, 15.

[19] See, for example, the errata provided in the *London Evening-Post,* 1–3 March 1739; the *General Advertiser,* 30 April 1748; and the *Public Advertiser,* 29 December 1761. For more extensive correction, apparently not as yet traced to the paper to which it was sent, see the note to item 389 in Chapman's *Letters of Samuel Johnson.*

[20] Cross (iii. 339), Macdonald (205a), and Sale (1, 21) exemplify the use of advertisements for this purpose. For some authors, notably Defoe,

issued but unknown to the bibliographer until he is alerted by this information and goes looking for it.[21] They may also refer, for Collins's *Epistle to the Editor of Fairfax*, to a poem on the verge of publication, but then suppressed; for the third edition of Boswell's *Account of Corsica*, to the number of copies in preceding editions and to several translations then in print; and for Fielding's *Amelia*, to the number of presses employed in the work.[22] Furthermore, almost invariably, they will cite the price; and with this we come upon some other problems misrepresented in earlier studies.

On the priority of two issues of Crabbe's *Works*, one with labels reading £2. 12s. 6d., the other with engravings at £5. 12s. 6d., it is easy to accept Mr. Sparrow's judgement that these particulars allow no conclusion. But it is just as easy to look beyond the book to the advertisements, where we discover that upon issue the volumes are cited only at the lower price. Not until a week later are illustrations mentioned, when they were offered at £2. 2s. for insertion in the books then on sale. So informed, our inference should be that the issue containing the plates appeared somewhat later, and that those who bought this issue therefore paid 18 shillings more than the total cost of the volumes and engravings, if purchased separately. While the book permits no deduction, the advertisements, it would seem, have allowed several valid conclusions.[23]

If Mr. Sparrow is properly noncommittal on the facts known to him, others may not be so restrained and confidently propose, for a second problem, a theory wholly unsubstantiated by the advertisements. On the priorty of two editions of Charles Hanbury Williams's *Country Girl*, one with the title-page reading "Threepence," and the other "Sixpence" altered in manuscript

---

Swift, and Franklin, a thorough search of the newspapers may reveal attributions as yet unnoticed. One recently disclosed by this means is reported in my note on Swift, *Papers of the Bibliographical Society of America*, XLV (1951), 82–83.

[21] Works lost but subsequently recovered: Courtney, p. 78, Pottle, 46, Sale, 82; apparently still lost: Cross, iii. 313, 316, Griffiths, 53, 65, 68, 69, 197a, Pottle, 31, Sale, 22, 76, 87.

[22] McKillop, *TLS*, 6 December 1928, p. 965; Pottle, p. 62; Cross, ii. 307. For *Amelia* see also my note in *The Library*, 5th ser., VII (1952), 283.

[23] Todd, *Papers of the Bibliographical Society of America*, XLV (1951), 250–51.

to the lower price, the assumption has been that the revision corrects a misprint in the second edition. For this there is a suitable argument, which I shall not repeat here since it derives from insufficient data within the book. From the advertisements we see that the confusion existed at the time of original issue, not later. After some of the notices had been distributed, but before any of the copies went on sale, it was decided, apparently, that as another of Williams's poems had just been issued at sixpence, it might be expedient to sell this at half-price. Without the advertisements none of this is apparent. With them the facts immediately appear, the assumption logically follows, and the order, as given, is necessarily reversed.[24]

Apart from the date, the price, and other miscellaneous information they may contain, the advertisements will also reveal, more accurately than any imprint, the shifting arrangements for publication. What the title-page represents are the conditions momentarily in effect as of the time it was printed—a day, a week, or a month prior to issue, not the preliminary negotiations which have gone before, or the later negotiations which may come after. Possibly these conditions prevail from the very beginning and continue throughout the course of issue, possibly not. The only way the bibliographer can be sure is to emulate the practice of those who wished to buy the book, and read the public notices. These, he will find, exhibit all kinds of discrepancies, all relevant to a description of the work. The following list of variant imprints, while by no means exhaustive, illustrates some of the differences which appear and some of the inferences that may be drawn from them.

I. Advertisements of a "state" earlier than that of the imprint.
[Asterisk denotes date of issue]

Gibbon, *Memoire Justificatif* [2d ed.], 1780.   Norton,
pp. 28 f.

Adv. Printed by T. Harrison and S. Brooke   18 Dec. 1779
Imp. ... and sold by L. Davies, T. Longman,   *24 Feb.
and J. Dodsley.   1780

Agreement for distribution concluded after original announcement.[25]

[24] Todd, ibid. XLVII (1953), 159–60.

[25] In a recent note on this book (*Studies in Bibliography*, V [1952], 194–97) Mr. Robert R. Rea has suggested that the true second edition is a

Parry, *The True Anti-Pamela*, 1741. Sale 66
　Adv. Printed for J. Torbuck, H. Slater, F. Noble,
　　J. Rowlands, T. Wright, and J. Duncan. 12 June
　Imp. "Sold by the booksellers in Town and Country." *27 June

Here, as Sale observes, the scandalous nature of the work prompted the booksellers to conceal their identity.

II. Advertisements of a "state" later than that of the imprint.

Letters of Mr. Pope, 1735. Griffith
　Imp. "Printed and Sold by the Booksellers of London 378
　　and Westminster."
　Adv. "to be had of T. Cooper." *28 May

Cooper was undoubtedly the principal agent, and the only one recognized in succeeding editions. On the basis of the advertisements Griffith was able to reclassify this edition as the fourth, and not the first, as previously supposed.

Pope, *Essay on Criticism* [1st issue], 1711. Griffith 2
　Imp. Printed for W. Lewis, sold by W. Taylor,
　　T. Osborne, J. Graves.
　Adv. ... and J. Morphew. *15 May

Pope, *Essay on Criticism* [2d issue], 1711. Griffith 3
　Imp. Printed for W. Lewis
　Adv. ... and sold by J. Morphew. *1 Jan.
　　　　　　　　　　　　　　　　　　　　　　　　　1712

Again, from the evidence of the advertisements, Griffith arranges these issues for the first time in their proper order, an order subsequently confirmed by the discovery that the title-page for the second issue is a cancel.

Goldsmith (trans.?), *The Comic Romance of Monsieur Scarron*, 1775.
　Imp. Printed for W. Griffin.
　Adv. Printed by W. Griffin, and sold by J. Johnson, *7 Dec.
　　R. Baldwin, and J. Bew. *London*
　　　　　　　　　　　　　　　　　　　　　　　　　Chronicle

"1779 publication issued by one William Hallhead of Dublin." Before it displaces Miss Norton's candidate for the position, however, both the date and the authority of this printing need to be verified. In the meantime, from the evidence now before us, the more plausible assumption is that, like many other Dublin editions, this is a falsely dated piracy.

Once the actual date of publication is known, and attested by the register in the December number of the *Gentleman's Magazine*, this questionable performance becomes even more suspicious. Let it be noted that it appears twenty months after the death of the translator identified on the title-page and six months after the death of the publisher named in the imprint.[26]

Walpole, *Letter from XoHo*, 1757.	Hazen 9
Imp. Printed for N. Middleton.	18 May
Adv. Printed for J. Graham.	*19 May?

Though the date of issue cannot be exactly determined—Walpole gives it as the 17th, the *Public Advertiser* as the 18th, and all other newspapers as the 19th—it would seem that this shift occurred at about the time the copies went on sale. Only the notice of the 18th lists Middleton; the same paper for the 19th, all others, the journals, and the reviews cite Graham, the publisher named in subsequent impressions.[27]

III. Advertisements disclosing arrangements after publication.

Pope, *Works*, 1735, vol. II.	Griffith
Early imp. Printed by J. Wright for L. Gilliver	370
Adv. upon issue. . . . J. Brindley and sold by R.	
Dodsley	*24 Apr.
Later adv. . . . J. J. and P. Knapton, J. and J. Brotherton, and W. Meadows.	13 May

[26] To illustrate how far one can be misled by secondary references I cite, to my shame, the original comment on this imprint. "At this time, as we know from other sources, Griffin was closing out his retail business to devote his energies to the printing of several newspapers." What "we" were supposed to know was what I had presumed from accounts in Morison's *English Newspaper* (p. 157) and Plomer's *Dictionary* (p. 111). But what we should now understand is that, while no obituary for Griffin appears, even in his own newspapers, various other indications fix the date of his death at about 14 June 1775. For a summary of the evidence see note 13 to my article on Goldsmith, forthcoming in *Studies in Bibliography*, VI (1953).

[27] As the review copies were normally among the first to be delivered, I rather believe that they might have been, in this instance, of the first issue with Middleton altered in ink to Graham, and not, as Professor Hazen has suggested, of the second impression. With these "publicity" copies, as with the advertisements, an immediate correction would be required, in ink, if necessary, so as to avert any misunderstanding among prospective customers.

Pope, *Miscellanea*, "1727" [1726].   Griffith
177

   Imp. "Printed in the Year, 1727."   *26 July
1726

   Adv. Printed for H. Curll   6 Aug.
1726

Another instance of Curll's surreptitious activities.

Lewis, *The Monk*, 1796.
   Imp. Printed for J. Bell.   *12 Mar.
*Morning
Herald*

   Adv. . . . E. Booker, and C. Law.   4 Apr.
The Times

Chambers, *Cyclopaedia*, 2nd ed., 1738.
   Imp. Printed for D. Midwinter, A. Bettesworth and
     C. Hitch, J. Senex, R. Gosling, W. Innys and R.
     Manby, J. and J. Pemberton, R. Robinson, C.
     Rivington, A. Ward, J. and P. Knapton, E. Symon,
     D. Brown, T. Longman, H. Lintott, and the
     Executors of J. Darby and F. Clay.
Prelim. advs. (Exclude Clay, add S. Birt, J. Shuck-   3 Oct.
   burgh, and A. Millar.)   *Daily Post*
Advs. upon issue (As for prelims.)   *6 Nov.
Daily Post
Later advs. (Also exclude Bettesworth, J. Pemberton 23 Aug.—
   the elder, and Lintot.)   11 Dec.
1739
*Evening-
Post*

In view of Mr. Blagden's paper[28] it is not without interest to note that of the twenty publishers originally concerned with this enterprise, thirteen were members of the Castle Conger. But the listing in the imprint, while it may reflect conditions at the time the book was put to press, was quickly superseded by developments beginning at least a month before issue and continuing some months afterwards. By 3 October, as we may infer from the advertisements, the estate of F. Clay had been settled and his share in the *Cyclopaedia* apparently bought out by three newcomers. Then by 23 August of the following year, as the adver-

[28] "Some XVIIIth Century Booksellers" Associations called "Congers" (read before the Society, 16 December 1952).

tisements further suggest, Bettesworth's share had passed to his
son-in-law, John Pemberton's to his son, and H. Lintot's to one
or more of the proprietors remaining. Not until the publication
of the succeeding edition are any of these substitutions recorded
in the imprint.

A review of these imprints, as they appear in one form or another, suggests that, in effect, the title-pages in Group I cancel .
the preliminary announcements, while the pages in Groups II
and III are in turn cancelled by the later advertisements at the
time of issue or reissue. Whether early or late, the notices in the
papers give the publisher the opportunity of indicating his intentions from day to day and, if necessary, of altering the fixed
statement on the title-page, all without extra cost to himself and
without bother to his own printer. In any bibliographical description they should be regarded, therefore, not only as alternative
imprints but, in view of their greater accuracy, as of greater importance than those within the book.

Having just disavowed the sanctity of a page revered in all
orthodox bibliographies, I must admit the logical consequence of
these remarks and commit another heresy. If this page can mis-
represent the date and the arrangements for publication, as exhibited in the imprint, it may also falsely represent the title.
When this has been printed but the half-title remains to be done,
there is still time for Alexander Pope to prefix "Of Taste" to his
Epistle to Burlington.[29] When all the printing has been completed, however, the time and the occasion have passed and, like
the publisher, the author may then find in the public notices an
economical expedient for his revisions. Thus the title to Fielding's pamphlet, originally reading *A Proper Answer to a Late
Scurrilous Libel*, is changed to read, in all the advertisements and
journals, *A Full Answer;* the essay titled *Critical Remarks on Sir
Charles Grandison* has added to the reading in the advertisements,
With some Reflections on two late Inspectors;[30] and the Chesterfield tract on *The Case of the Hanover Forces* reads in the advertisements, journals, an abstract, and in the sequels, *The Case of
the Hanover Troops*.[31] Moving on to the next century, we ob-

[29] Somewhat later, as we know, the prefix was altered to "Of False
Taste," and then incorporated in the title of the "Third Edition."

[30] Cross, iii. 315; Sale, 85.

[31] The fact that *Troops* is adopted in the titles of the *Vindication* and
the *Farther Vindication* but not in the corrected "Second" and "Third"

serve that in its transcription the initial review of the *Memoir of the Early Life of William Cowper* substitutes "original Letters" for "religious Letters" and adds the expression "Published by Permission of the Proprietors." Apparently the editor of the *Memoir* desired, by the first change, to attract a greater number of readers and, by the second, to warn them that a rival edition had not been authorized.[32] From these several examples it would appear that such deliberate alterations so persistently reported must reflect the author's (or editor's) final decision and should, therefore, be noted in the record of his work. Hence for the titles, as well as for all the other particulars I have mentioned, the advertisements may prove to be more reliable than the books.

Beyond the present stage of our discussion, as it is now directed, only one observation remains, and that is to throw away the books and read the newspapers. Since I am not prepared to go quite so far at the moment, I withdraw to consider certain other matters. One of some interest pertains to groups of advertisements. Whenever these appear in definite series, distinguished by certain intervals of time or certain modifications in text, the recurrence may possibly indicate a reissue, a new issue, or a new edition. Entries appearing haphazardly probably indicate nothing other than the publisher's desultory attempts to clear his shelves. But those appearing in a regular pattern suggest repeated deliveries of stock and renewed efforts to move this in the market. Oftentimes a distinction in the notices will not be confirmed in the books. Though frequently thwarted by similarities when he expects some difference, the ever-watchful bibliographer should nevertheless continue to track down every clue to see where it will lead.

One that seemed rather promising to me—if I may again allude to an example cited on another occasion—concerns the undes-

---

editions of the original *Case* gives further weight to my argument (in *Papers of the Bibliographical Society of America,* XLIV [1950], 224–38) against the commonly assumed collaboration of Waller and Chesterfield in this series of pamphlets. If *Troops* is Waller's revision, it would naturally occur only with reference to the issues for which he was directly responsible, and not for those revised and published at Chesterfield's instigation.

[32] See the *British Critic* for July 1816, p. 110. There is some reason to believe, however, that the edition cited in the *Critic* is less authoritative than the other.

ignated editions of Chesterfield's *Case of the Hanover Troops.*
(Following my own recommendation, I now adopt as the title
the reading of the advertisements, *not* that of the book.) Of
these the *Daily Advertiser* carries over the first several months
some fifteen notices, equally divided into three groups, and each
group further divided as a sequence of three references, a break
of about a week, and then two more. Thus we have three pairs of
references and now, to match them, three pairs of editions.
Where the Chesterfield bibliography records only two editions
before the "second," these notices have prompted the search for
and the eventual discovery of six.

A similar problem, not mentioned before, appears in Samuel
Johnson's *False Alarm.* Concerning this, his earliest political
essay, the bibliographers identify only two editions, a biographical note refers to three, and the advertisements indicate
four. Again, as in the previous instance, the notices occur in
several series, separate in time and distinct in text. And again,
with the added assistance of the press figures in the book, the
search is completely successful, not in the discovery of four editions, nor even of the two commonly and (as we should now say)
erroneously reported, but of one edition existing in four undifferentiated impressions.[33]

I come now to the last of the several ways known to me in
which the newspapers can be used to serve our purpose. On a
question of priority, the most intriguing problem for a bibliographer, and one summoning all the resources at his command, it
occasionally happens that his all is not enough. For some books,
certainly, little can be deduced from the type, ornaments, and
paper, from a collation with other texts, or from any single
advertisement. Yet if the book contains, in the absence of the
usual evidence, notices of others then on sale, the known date of
the others will fix the time of the one in which they are advertised. By checking the papers for a reference to these others we
may therefore learn much of the one book not specifically identified and, with this knowledge, overturn many a pretty theory
based on less extensive evidence.

To illustrate what can be done by this means I present five examples, two recently offered in the proceedings of other societies,

[33] Todd, *Book Collector,* II (1953), 59–65. For directing my attention to
the advertisements, all in the *London Chronicle,* I am indebted to Professor
Hazen.

and three now disclosed for your consideration. One, as we should know from Professor Bowers's researches, is the second edition of D'Urfey's *Comical History of Don Quixote*, dated 1694, but representing a book not published until 31 March 1698.[34] Another is Lewis's *The Monk*, of which the issue long regarded as the one published early in 1796 is now shown, by its notice of books not published before 18 March 1797, to be a debased variant of the third issue, third edition.[35] Another relates to Pope's essay *Of False Taste*. As the author's many bibliographers have failed to realize, this exists in two different first editions, a second, and three different third editions, all dated 1731.[36] Ignoring the several later variants, the order of which is easily determined, we perceive in the earlier editions only a single distinction: a list of ten books in the one to be called "A," the same ten and two others in "B." That "B" is of later date is demonstrated by the fact that whereas the actual first edition is known to have been issued on 14 December, one of the extra books described in "B" was not published until the 20th, and the other not for some time after that. The next instance concerns another of Pope's essays, *Of the Use of Riches*, where two second editions have been recognized, but arranged, I believe, in the wrong order.[37] Of these, edition "A," listing ten books, was issued before 16 January 1733; and "B," listing twelve books, after the 8th of March, the date when a new book cited as Bramston's *Man of Taste* made its appearance.

Mention of Bramston's poem brings me to the final example, one of slight literary importance, perhaps, though certainly of great interest bibliographically. In asserting for the *Man of Taste* an order contrary to the one I shall propose, Iolo Williams gathers up every inference to be derived from the two editions and observes without hesitation that all "point to the same conclusion."[38] That he has advanced, in the opinion of a recent commentator, a cogent argument, I will not deny. Undoubtedly it has wide application and may be extended to many books but,

[34] Bowers, *Papers of the Bibliographical Society of America*, XLII (1949), 191–95.

[35] Todd, *Studies in Bibliography*, II (1949), 3–24.

[36] In items 259, 265, 267 Griffith notes only one of each "edition."

[37] As re-ordered, Griffith 324b, 323a. A study of these and certain other of Pope's poems is now in preparation.

[38] *Points in Eighteenth-Century Verse* (London, 1934), pp. 67–69.

unfortunately, not to this. Once again we have recourse to the newspapers, and once more the evidence there turns against the present arrangement, on this occasion overwhelmingly.

So that the application of this new evidence may be fully understood, it should be observed that all the books advertised in the papers and the two editions appeared prior to 8 March, the date of the original issue. Thus the solution to this problem must depend upon the citation, not of a single book of later date, but of several in a combination like that in one of the editions. Among the various books available for sale, all 17 are listed in edition "A" (one below the imprint and 16 on the last page), 15 in edition "B" (all on the last page), and 5 in the advertisements. If an identifying letter is assigned to each book, wherever it may appear, and the earlier portions of the lists arranged in parallel columns, this is the result:

	Advertisement[39]		Edition "A"		Edition "B"
a	Of False Taste	a	Of False Taste	a	Of False Taste
b	The Use of Riches	b	The Use of Riches	b	Dunciad
c	First Satire of Second Book of Horace	c	First Satire of Second Book of Horace	e	Collection of Pieces
m	Gardens of Lord Cobham	d	Dunciad	f	Essay on Satyre
l	Progress of Love	e	Collection of Pieces	q	Art of Politicks
Also listed:		$f-p$		$g-p$	
Below imprint:		q			

Now for those who contend that all the evidence points to "B" as the first edition, the remarkable correlation between the advertisements and "A" must be dismissed as mere coincidence. Anticipating this evasion, I have sought expert advice on the permutations involved in such an accident, and am informed that in any random selection there is one chance in 17 that the first item in the paper should correspond to that in edition "A" (or "B," for that matter); only one chance in 680, however, that the first three should be chosen; and only one in 4,080 that the three should be selected in exactly the same order.[40] Under the

---

[39] The *Man of Taste* was announced as to be published "on Thursday next" (8 March) in the *London Evening–Post* for 24–26 February; noted as published, with a list of the other works cited, in the *Post* for 8–10 March, and in the *Daily Advertiser* for 8, 12, and 15 March; and further mentioned as in "a New Edition" in the *Advertiser* for 24 March. Very probably the last notice refers to edition "B."

[40] The three formulae are: (1) $\frac{1}{17}$; (2) $\frac{3}{17} \cdot \frac{2}{16} \cdot \frac{1}{15} = \frac{6}{4080} = \frac{1}{680}$; (3) $\frac{1}{17} \cdot \frac{1}{16} \cdot \frac{1}{15} = \frac{1}{4080}$.

crushing weight of these figures all of Mr. Williams's arguments are squashed to nothing and may be swept away along with the views of others who fail to read the advertisements. For the *Man of Taste* the only plausible explanation is that in the preparation of the notices for the daily papers the copy-boy transcribed first the three entries at the top of the "A" list and then several others towards the bottom; and by this simple act he gives us the clue, the sole clue, as to the priority of the editions.

Enough has been said, I believe, to convince even the most sceptical that the data provided in the book may be insufficient for an analysis of its production and certainly inadequate for any record of the circumstances attending its issue. As Macaulay once said of history, so I would say of bibliography, that the only true account of it is to be found in the newspapers, the daily record of events as they occur.[41]

[41] In the discussion following the reading of this paper I was reminded of various journals known to exist in several settings [see comment on *The Bee* in *N. & Q.*, CLXXXVII (1944), 276, and *Philological Quarterly*, XXIV (1945), 143; also on the *Gentleman's Magazine* and *The World* in *Studies in Bibliography*, IV (1951), p. 49, n. 15a and pp. 52–55]; but since advertisements do not occur in one periodical and apparently remain unaffected in the others, all these were dismissed as irrelevant to the present study. It is now evident, however, that for at least one other journal, *The Examiner*, there may be as many as four editions of certain numbers, each representing a different group of advertisements. This discovery introduces several complications which I hope to review in a further note to *The Library*. ["The Printing of Eighteenth-Century Periodicals: With Notes on the *Examiner* and the *World*," *The Library*, 5th ser., X (1955), pp. 49–54.]

VIII

WILLIAM B. TODD

Early Editions of The Tatler

The earliest printings of *The Tatler*, in folio, octavo, and duo-decimo, all exhibit numerous undifferentiated editions and, in the course of issue, various textual alterations. Of the original 1709-1711 editions in folio, chance observation has already elicited some comment, one writer noting Steele's own reference to printing on different presses, another remarking two or more variant settings in at least 82 numbers, a third reporting variation after the 117th number.[1] Further examination, here extending to eighteen copies,[2] discloses a situation more remarkable than any yet envisaged, but still amenable to bibliographical analysis. Altogether, as we now may demonstrate, the 271 folio issues reveal three orders of presswork.

	Numbers Range	Total	Settings Each no.	Total	Printing
(1)	1-32	32	2-4	76	Successive, in one shop
(2)	33-117	85	1	85	Single, in one shop
(3)	118-271	154	2	308	Simultaneous, in two shops

The several variants of folio numbers 1–32 occur in definite patterns of a kind never encountered in simultaneous, but always appearing in successive issues.[3] Obviously with *The Tatler*, as with other literary periodicals, the demands of later subscribers

Reprinted from *Studies in Bibliography*, XV (1962), 121–33, by permission of the author and the Bibliographical Society of the University of Virginia.

[1] F. W. Bateson, *RES*, V (1929), 155–166; Graham Pollard, *The Library*, 4th ser., XXII (1941), 121; Todd, *ibid.*, 5th ser., X (1955), 49–50.

[2] To Professor Richmond P. Bond I am greatly indebted for microfilms of folio sets *j-m* and for a detailed account of the 8° and 12° editions in the British Museum, the Bodleian Library, and his personal collection. Without these and other encouragements it is doubtful whether I should ever have concluded the "further investigation" I had some years ago invited others to pursue.

[3] Todd, *loc. cit.*

required later settings, here represented, exclusively, in collections lately assembled. Certain of these subsequent editions may be identified by an advertisement entered intermittently from 14 to 114 and announcing "A New Set of CUTS for the Common Prayer." Though essentially of an identical setting throughout, this notice in issues of a single edition displays in the first line, from 33 to 54 a pointing hand and the reading "CUTS," from 59 to 114 triple stars and the reading "Cuts." Among earlier numbers 1–32 in variant settings the hand is exhibited in 14, 16, 20 of all printings, in 22, 27, 29, 32 only of one. Thus, we may conclude, numbers 22–32 with the starred variant must be of a second (or third) setting printed after 54, the last number of an invariant setting to display the hand. Collections of this later order are the ones identified in Table I as d, m, r, e, i, all with stars, the first two in 29 only, the third in 22 only, the last two in all four numbers. The three series r, e, i, also share in numbers 6, 11, and 18 a common third setting with f, an uncut presentation copy collated and bound only after completion of issue, and in numbers 1–2 a common fourth setting not only with this same f but with various other copies. Hence all of these, in more or less degree, appear to have been collected at some time after original issue, and to contain, at least in five of these collections, the latest of several printings.

Once the latest settings are identified all others fall into an inalterable sequence, the earliest A with certain typographical features successively modified to the state represented by later editions B, C, D. Table II illustrates several peculiarities evident in the first four numbers, where in 1–3 a preliminary italic notice on recto occurs in three successive settings, all interrelated with 1–4 imprints on verso in seven different impositions or arrangements of type. The sequence there defined is confirmed and, on the evidence of heading rules, extended in this same Table beyond 32 to invariant settings. From the rules, all of one arrangement until superseded by another, it may be deduced that 1–3 of B edition are coeval with 2–18 of A, 1–3C with 19–29A, and 1–3D with 36–38 or later numbers of the single printing. How much later can be determined, for some editions, again by reference to the hand-star variants previously described, all of which are affiliated with certain others not bearing the advertisement. These affiliations, also noted in Table II, indicate that thirteen of the B editions 15–32, the five C editions 4–18, C edition 32, and

D editions 2–3 were issued after number 54, dated 13 August 1709.

The chronology as established for 1–32 is specified in Table III along with a summary record of the points which most easily distinguish the editions. Of first priority, it will be noted, is an original number not in any sequence: an odd circumstance, but one not without precedent, and not unexpected here since the earlier papers were distributed gratis and—among these eighteen subscribers, at any rate—before anyone had decided to collect the issues.[4] Also to be noted, though not readily apparent in the Table, are unmistakable signs of revision, all again substantiating the order adduced from typographical evidence and waiting to bedevil any future editor of *The Tatler*. A few specimens from number 2 will suffice, at this time, to exemplify the complexities in these 76 settings—and in the book editions yet to be considered.

Col. line	2.12		4.19			
F° (A)	ungraceful		in	the		
(B)	ungrateful		,,	,,		
(C)		,,	on	the		
(D)		,,	,,	,,		
12° (A)		,,	in	Behalf	of	the
8° (B)		,,	,,	,,	,,	,,
12° (C)		,,	,,	,,	,,	,,

Col. line	4.45					4.75		
F° (A)	as	to make	him	hope		People	of *France*	
(B)	,,	,, ,,	,,	,,		,,	,,	,,
(C)	,,	,, ,,	,,	,,		,,	,,	,,
(D)	as	to hope				People	.	
12° (A)	or	make	any	Hope		People	of *France*	
8° (B)	or	conceive	any	Hope		,,	,,	,,
12° (C)	,,	,,	,,	,,		,,	,,	,,

From 33 to 117 the publisher, John Morphew, was able to provide in a single edition sufficient copies for all needs present and prospective. With an ever-increasing circulation, however, he finally realized that, even with a two-day interval between

[4] Among the *Tatlers* the original edition of numbers 2 and 3, though long anticipated from certain peculiarities in 4, did not appear before the 10th copy examined (*j*), the original setting of 1 not before the 16th (*p*) and then only in an odd lot assembled from various sources. Among early numbers of the *Gentleman's Magazine*, also at first "Printed for the Author," the original issue of March 1731 occurs only in five of the 36 sets I have inspected, the issue for February only in one, the issue for January not at all.

numbers, the press could no longer meet the demand. Thus from 118 to 271 two settings appear, both of simultaneous issue and therefore mixed indiscriminately in all collected series. Since there is no priority of issue (and, as we may determine, no certain order of impression) it will be convenient in Table IV to label as edition A the one typographically equivalent to those earlier printed for Morphew,[5] and as B the alternate setting composed at his direction in another office. Whatever the order of printing, there can be little doubt that the editions come from separate establishments, since all type-matter, even including advertisements at end of text, is invariably of two different settings and never interchanged between A and B. It is also evident that, despite the highly variable distribution, the editions were of equal size, for the 924 specimens cited in the Table are almost evenly divided, 466 being of the A type and 458 of the B. It further appears that one setting was composed from an early run (or proof-sheet) of the other, since the lineation in both is, normally, identical. In certain numbers, however, the shift of a word may displace subsequent lines; and by means of this variation we may ascertain that Steele examined setting A of numbers 120, 153, 157, 164, and 226, because the line references in the errata later supplied for these are occasionally inapplicable to setting B. Conversely, and to the despair of anyone speculating upon this circumstance, similar variation in other numbers indicates that Steele was reading edition B of 139, 148, 151, 227, 242, and 259, all with referents at times inapplicable to A. From this conflicting evidence the only deduction is that the author, like his readers, received some numbers of one setting, some of the other.

Of greater interest, and possibly of greater significance, are those numbers where Steele was allowed copy in time to amend in the later certain misprints occurring in the earlier setting. Twice in errata accounts the author notes that the errors then cited will be found only in the "faulty impression" (or first edition), a setting easily identified as B of 154 and A of 254. At another time, however, he fails to indicate that the correction pertains only to one setting, in this case to B of 166. And on

---

[5] On 2 May 1710 John Nutt, the first printer, entered in the Stationers' Register his copyright to all issues, folio, octavo, and duodecimo. This notice, supplied over a year after original issue of number 1, doubtless was prompted either by the folio reprinting begun in Edinburgh 13 February, or by the pending book edition which Hills issued before 4 July.

numerous other occasions he neglects to supply errata notices of any kind, though alterations have again been entered only in one of the two settings. Instances of this silent correction appeared immediately in a random collation of two consecutive numbers, both of which, as it happens, also illustrate the variable order of editions.

No. 190 Col. line	Editions A	B (corrected)	No. 191 Col. line	Editions B	A (corrected)
1.16	on	upon	2.51	Artifice	Artifices
2.43	me I	me that I	3.11	Ornament	Ornaments
3.58	Circumference	Circumstance	3.21	draw out of	draw of
			3.33	off the	of the

However variable the order of impression—a matter determined, it seems, entirely by the convenience of the printers—and however erratic Steele's own editorial procedure, the author appears to have exercised the greatest care in selecting the better text as copy for the collected book editions then going through the press. Whether that copy is of the original impression A or B with the author's own MS corrections, or the second setting B or A in amended form, is a question which a future editor must decide on the evidence of all the 154 numbers so affected. Any evasion of the problem will leave him with two alternatives, either to designate folio A as standard copy (since this preserves, at least in accidentals, the "house style" of the earlier single edition) or to adopt octavo or duodecimo as basic text.

The latter expedient, though always followed in times past, is particularly unwise because, as we now discover, both of these formats also exist in variable settings, all with different readings, and none with text in definitive state. The original book edition A doubtless is the 12° with errata lists in all four volumes and bearing a text, as the title declares, "Revised and Corrected by the Author." Most of the errata are corrected in later printings 8° and 12°, and the text further revised, with each edition set from copy of the same format yet incorporating, with some exceptions, amendments in a subsequent setting of another size. From the original printing A derives the octavo "subscription" edition of royal and medium paper issue $B1,2$: a text which in earliest numbers volumes I-II adopts or further improves 26 readings first introduced in 12° (Table V, order 1222, 1232, 1234), supplies 13 additional readings (1121, 1122, 1123), but fails to transmit 6 others revised in 12° (1211, 1212). These others, all rather insignificant, may represent entries in a 12° proof later than the one used as copy for subsequent editions, or readings entered in good time but deliberately rejected upon second printing and any copy dependent upon this. From the original printing also derives another 12° C, a supplementary issue presenting a text which, among the readings now under inspection, adopts or improves upon 30 entries in 12° A, including 6 not accumulated in 8° B (1222, 1121, 1123, 1212, 1232), incorporates 14 others first entered or reinserted in B (1122, 1211), and further amends a new reading first cited there (1234). Still another supplementary issue D, identical with C except for a resetting of volume I sheets B-F, occasionally in this resetting improves upon accidentals, *e.g.*, at page 2, line 36, in the alteration of "*dated from my own* Apartment" to "*dated,* From my own Apartment." Supplementary to 8° B—and of all printings the only ones seemingly unattended by the author[6]—are two later issues each also of two impressions, one with an undifferentiated resetting of volume II and volume I dated 1713 ($E1,2$), the other with volume II reissued under title also dated 1713 ($F1,2$). Points distinguishing the several issues are given, for 12° in Table VI, for 8° in Table VII.

Order of publication, as determined from advertisements in the folio *Tatlers*, confirms the textual relationship just described. Preceding any of the legitimate issues is a pirated two-volume 12° edition,[7] cited on 4 July 1710 in the same notice announcing as of "Monday next," or the 10th, the simultaneous issue of the authentic 12° and 8° (A,B). But where two 8° volumes had been proposed on 31 January, it is now admitted that only the first would appear, the second—according to an announcement of 6 July—"being necessarily defer'd for Want of Paper, which is just come by the Fleet now arriv'd from Holland." This volume B, then promised "in about a Fortnight," actually was delayed until 1 September, and thus follows the second 12° volume A, on ordinary paper, by seven weeks. Though the 12° goes unmentioned in later advertisements, it may be presumed that volumes III

[6] Through the first number the later 8° exactly reprints B except for the accidental omission at 7.12 of the "s" in "Preparations."

[7] This uncommon edition, issued by Henry Hills, reprints folios 1–100. The piracy is represented at the University of Texas, the Bodleian Library, and in Professor Bond's collection.

and IV in this format were issued, according to original intention, simultaneously with the 8° edition, III of this being announced (in final *Tatler* number 271) on 2 January 1711, and IV (in Harrison *Tatler* 316) 17 April 1711. The price of each volume of these several impressions is cited (in *Tatler* 196) as 2*s*.6*d*. for the 12° and (in *Spectator* 227) as 21*s* for 8° royal paper, 10*s*.6*d*. for 8° medium paper.

With all issues on record, it may be conceded that a definitive edition of *The Tatler* should take into account every printing except, perhaps, *E* and *F* of the collected series, and offer from a conflation of these an eclectic text. A full accounting, as calculated in this final summary, will range for any one number to as many as eight editions, for all numbers to some 1162 settings.

Volume	I			II	III		IV	Total
	1-	18-	33-	51-	115-	118-	190-	
Numbers	17[8]	32	50	114	117	189	271	
Total settings each no.								
Folio editions A-D	2-4	2-3	1	1	1	2	2	469
12° issues A,C,D	3	2	2	2	1	1	1	422
8° issue B	1	1	1	1	1	1	1	271
Totals	6-8	5-6	4	4	3	4	4	1162

[8] 12° issue *C* is reset only through the first page of number 17.

TABLE I ARRANGEMENT OF FOLIO SETTINGS, NUMBERS 1–32

Note. Identifying letters merely signify order in which the following copies were examined:

- a-f. Harvard: *57-1691F; 16441.3.9*; 16441.4*; 16441.4.6* (nos. 1-235 only); P84.840; Widener (presentation copy, 2 vols, in green vellum gilt)
- g-i. Texas:q052.T188; 2d copy; 3d copy (nos. 1-229 only)
- j-k. North Carolina: Whitaker; T824.05/T219 (nos. 1-100 only)
- l-m. Professor Richmond P. Bond: Blue and Butler copies
- n-p. New York Public Library: Berg (Jerome Kern); Berg (Owen D. Young); reserve collection (miscellaneous lot, lacking early nos. 2, 4-5, 7-39)
- q-r. Columbia: special collection; Medical School

Rules define the point where, except for an occasional purchase of missing copies, successive groups of readers appear to have collected numbers as issued. Certain collections, however, including presentation set *f*, may have been assembled later in the publisher's warehouse.

Copy No.	p Settings	n	j	b	g	q	a	h	d	k	m	l	o	c	f	r	e	i
1	1	2	2	3	3	4	4	4	4	4	4	4	3	4	4	4	4	4
2		1	1	2	2	2	3	4	3	3	4	3	3	3	4	4	4	4
3	3	1	1	2	2	2	2	3	1	1	3	3	3	3	3	3	4	4
4		1	1	1	1	1	1	2	1	2	2	2	2	2	2	2	3	3
5		1	1	1	1	1	1	1	1	2	1	2	2	2	2	2	3	3
6	1	1	1	1	1	1	1	1	2	2	1	2	2	2	3	3	3	3
7		1	1	1	1	1	1	1	1	1	2	2	2	2	2	2	2	2
8		1	1	1	1	1	1	1	1	1	2	1	2	2	2	2	2	2
9		1	1	1	1	1	1	1	1	1	2	2	2	2	2	2	2	2
10		1	1	1	1	1	1	1	1	1	1	2	2	2	2	2	2	2
11		1	1	1	1	2	1	2	1	1	2	1	3	3	3	3	3	
12		1	1	1	1	1	1	1	1	2	2	2	2	2	2	1	2	
13		1	1	1	1	1	1	1	2	2	2	2	2	2	2	2	2	
14		1	1	1	1	1	1	1	1	2	2	2	2	2	2	2	2	
15		1	1	1	1	1	1	1	2	2	2	2	2	2	2	2	2	
16		1	1	1	1	1	1	1	2	2	2	2	2	2	2	2	2	
17		1	1	1	1	1	1	1	2	1	2	2	2	2	2	2	2	
18		1	1	1	1	1	1	1	2	2	2	2	2	3	3	3	3	
19		1	1	1	1	1	1	1	1	1	2	2	2	2	2	2	2	
20		1	1	1	1	1	1	2	2	1	2	1	2	2	2	2	2	
21		1	1	1	1	1	1	1	2	1	2	1	2	2	2	2	2	
22		1	1	1	1	1	1	1	1	1	1	1	1	2	2	2	2	
23		1	1	1	1	1	1	1	1	1	1	1	1	2	2	2	2	
24		1	1	1	1	1	1	1	1	2	1	1	1	2	2	2	2	
25		1	1	1	1	1	1	1	1	1	1	1	1	2	2	2	2	
26		1	1	1	1	1	1	1	1	1	1	1	1	1	1	2	2	
27		1	1	1	1	1	1	1	1	1	1	1	1	1	1	2	2	
28		1	1	1	1	1	1	1	1	2	1	1	1	1	1	2	2	
29		1	1	1	1	1	1	2	1	2	1	1	1	1	1	2	2	
30		1	1	1	1	1	1	1	1	1	1	1	1	1	2	2	2	
31		1	1	1	1	1	1	1	1	1	1	1	1	1	1	2	2	
32		1	1	1	1	1	1	1	1	1	1	1	1	1	1	2	3	

Recto, 1st ¶ lines 3 7	Verso, imprint rule, 7mm segment	length of imprint	place	interval between comma and date	Edition and Number (*=verso point only)			
					A	B	C	D
Main think:	right	86mm	*LONDON:*	2mm	1,2	1		
„ „	„	88mm	„	„	3	2,3	1	1
„ „	left	„	„	„			2,3	2
main think:	solid	„	„	5mm	*4	*4	*4	3
main think:	„	92mm	*LONDON:*	3mm				

Numbers 1-32

Recto, rules of single or broken lines

Order	rule 1	rule 2	rule 3	Edition and Number			
				A	B	C	D
1	158mm	158mm	20.138mm	1	1-3	1-3	1
2	„	138.18	„	2-18	4-6, 11, 18		
3	148.7	„	„	19-29	8, 12-13, 19		
4	7.148	„	„	30-35	7, 9		
5	148	„	„	36-38	10, 14	18	
6	153	153	„		15-17, 20-31	4-6, 11	2-3
7	158	157	158		32	32	
8		133.20	133.20				

Notes: All measure approximate, paper shrinkage accounting for 1-2mm variation. For some reason the rules for single setting, no. 39 onward, follow no definite pattern.

Correlation among orders 6-8

Recto, title (broken letters indicated by italics)

	Verso, imprint	Edition and Number		
		B	C	D
(numbers with 'hand' advt (†) printed before issue 59)				
TATLER	*Advertisements*	10, †14	6,18	2
The	Advertisements	†16, †20,21		
(numbers with 'star' advt (*) printed after issue 54)				
The	*Advertisements*	15,17, *22, 23-26 / *27,28,30-31		
TATLER	Advertisements	*29, *32	4-5,11, *32	3

Note. Aberrant title setting with broken 'e' in 'The' is also found in single edition of nos. 41-42, occasionally in later editions of 2-32, but in conjunction with roman type 'Advertisements' only, as specified in Table, in B setting of nos. 16, 20, 21. All of these occurrences perhaps indicate an alternate setting of heading and/or imprint used when regular type was already at press for another number.

TABLE III FOLIO EDITIONS 1–32, CHRONOLOGY AND POINTS

No.	Ed.	Issued‡	Variations in text line 3 / line 7		No.	Ed.	Issued‡	Variations in text
								2.8|9
1	A	12	Apr	*Main* think: come	15	A	14 May	a Bed-|Side
	B	16	Apr	*Main* think: ding		B	13 Aug	a | Bed-Side
	C	24	May	*main* think: ding				2.2|3
	D	2	July	*main* think: ding	16	A	17 May	to come,|As
			2.11	3.73		B	2 July	to | come, *As*
								1.8
2	A	14	Apr	Home--- *Molly,*----	17	A	19 May	from
	B	19	Apr	Home--- *Molly,*----		B	13 Aug	(from
	C	24	May	Home--- *Molly,*---				2.20|21 3.1st wor⸱
	D	13	Aug	Home--- *Molly,*	18*	A	21 May	Place,|'tis he
			line 3	1.1|2		B	24 May	Place,|'tis the
						C	13 Aug	the | Place, the
3	A	16	Apr	*Main* Country|				1.10
	B	19	Apr	*Main* Country-|	19	A	24 May	Derision;
	C	24	May	*main* Country|		B	18 June	Derision:
	D	13	Aug	*main* Coun-|try				1.9
			3.last		20	A	26 May	Brown
4	A	19	Apr	notice		B	2 July	brown
	B	13	Aug	Notice				2.1
	C	13	Aug	Notice [*4 from last*]	21	A	28 May	Comedy
			1.1	4. penult		B	2 July	Comedy,
5	A	21	Apr	(*out* this				4.10|11
	B	24	May	*out* this,	22	A	31 May	many | Virgins
	C	13	Aug	(*out* this,		B	13 Aug	ma-|ny Virgins
			3.15	4.1				2.6|7
6	A	23	Apr	*Trojans;* Tranquility	23	A	2 June	a-|gainst
	B	24	May	*Trojans:* Tranquillity		B	13 Aug	|against
	C	13	Aug	*Trojans:* Tranquility				1.6
			4.2|3		24	A	4 June	Letter
7	A	26	Apr	Tran-|quility		B	13 Aug	Letter,
	B	2	July	Tran-|quillity				2.8
			3.17		25	A	7 June	The Tale
8	A	28	Apr	care		B	13 Aug	*The Tale*
	B	18	June	Care				4.10
			4.21		26	A	9 June	Death:
9	A	30	Apr	supposed		B	13 Aug	Death?
	B	2	July	suppos'd				2.1st word
			2.19		27	A	11 June	see
10	A	3	May	pairing		B	13 Aug	we
	B	2	July	paring				2.cw
			2.2|3	4.4	28	A	14 June	a
11	A	5	May	Greatness| *Wollen*		B	13 Aug	a Man's
	B	24	May	Great-|ness *Woollen*				2.1st word
	C	13	Aug	Greatness| *Woollen*	29	A	16 June	*sters*
			1.cw			B	13 Aug	*and*
12	A	7	May	[*none*]				3.13
	B	18	June	Place	30	A	18 June	Tender
			1.penult			B	13 Aug	tender
13	A	10	May	Glasses				2.11
	B	18	June	glasses	31	A	21 June	perform'd
			1.1|2			B	13 Aug	performed
14	A	12	May	had | appear'd				1.11 1.15
	B	30	June	had ap-|pear'd	32	A	23 June	*Norris,* Idea's
						B	13 Aug	*Norris,* Idea's
						C	13 Aug	*Norris,* Ideas

‡ Edition 'A' issued as dated; editions B-D, though bearing same date, from evidence of Table II issued on or after date now assigned.

* Edition B columns 1,2,4 of same setting as A and therefore issued immediately after A.

TABLE IV Simultaneous Folio Issues, Numbers 118–271

The following account lists in order the settings represented in the four Harvard and two Texas copies designated in Table I as *abcegh*. Points differentiating the two editions:

	imprint reading, nos. 118-174*	TATLER heading, nos. 132-271†
A	*Advertisements*	'R' perfect
B	Advertisements	'R' gouged

118	BBBBAA	149	BBAAAB	180	ABBBAB	211	AAABAA	242	BABBAB
119	BBAABB	150	BAABAA	181	BBABBA	212	ABAAAA	243	AABABB
120	BAABBB	151	BAABAB	182	BBBABA	213	BABBBB	244	BAABBA
121	BABBAA	152	BAABBB	183	BAABBA	214	BAABAA	245	ABBABA
122	BBBBAB	153	BAABAA	184	BABBBA	215	AAAAAA‡	246	BABABB
123	ABBBBA	154	BBAABB	185	ABAAAB	216	AABAAB	247	BABBBA
124	BAABBB	155	ABABBB	186	AAAABA	217	AABBBA	248	ABBAAA
125	BBBABB	156	AABABA	187	AAAAAA‡	218	ABBBAA	249	BBAABB
126	ABABAA	157	AAABBB	188	AABBBA	219	BABABA	250	BAAAAB
127	BABABB	158	ABABAB	189	ABBBAA	220	BBBBBA	251	BBAAAA
128	BABAAB	159	BAAAAA	190	BBAABA	221	AAABBA	252	ABABAA
129	BAAABA	160	AAABAB	191	BBBABA	222	BABAAA	253	ABAAAA
130	AABBBA	161	BBAAAA	192	ABAABA	223	BBAABB	254	AABBBA
131	BAABAB	162	ABBBBA	193	BBAAAB	224	ABAAAB	255	ABABAA
132	BABABB	163	AABBBA	194	AAAABB	225	BBAABB	256	BBAAAA
133	BABAAB	164	ABABBB	195	AABBAB	226	AAAAAB	257	BAAABA
134	BAAAAB	165	AAABAA	196	BBAABB	227	ABAABB	258	ABBBAB
135	BBBBBA	166	BABBBA	197	BAABAB	228	AABABA	259	BABBBB
136	ABABBA	167	BABAAB	198	BAABAA	229	AAAABB	260	ABBBBA
137	BBAABB	168	BABABB	199	BABBAB	230	BAAAAA	261	AABAAB
138	BBBBAB	169	AABABA	200	AABBAA	231	BBAAAA	262	BBBBAB
139	AAAABA	170	BABABB	201	BABBBA	232	ABBAAA	263	ABAABA
140	ABAAAA	171	BBBBBB‡	202	AABBAA	233	BAAAAB	264	AAABBB
141	BBAABA	172	AABBBB	203	BABABB	234	ABBBAA	265	ABAABB
142	AABBAB	173	ABABAB	204	BABBBA	235	ABABBA	266	BAABAB
143	ABBBBA	174	AABAAA	205	BABBAA	236	BABBBA	267	BBBBBA
144	ABBBAA	175	BAAABA	206	BABABB	237	BBAAAB	268	AAABBA
145	AABBAB	176	AABBAB	207	AAAABA	238	BABABA	269	BAAABA
146	ABABAA	177	BABAAA	208	BABBBA	239	BABAAB	270	ABBABB
147	BBBABB	178	ABAAAA	209	BABABA	240	AABAAA	271	AAABBB
148	BBAABB	179	AABABB	210	BABBAA	241	BABBBA		

* Thereafter both settings have "Advertisements" in roman letter.

† In the continuation bearing Morphew imprint the combined number 272-273 also was issued in two settings *A* and *B*, numbers 274-330 only in *A*.

‡ The alternate setting not represented in these numbers will be found, A171 in Texas copy *i*, B187 and 215 in Harvard copy *f*.

TABLE V REVISION IN 12° AND 8° EDITIONS, VOLUMES I–II

The "order" identifies readings successively appearing in f°, 12° (A), 8° (B), and 12° (C), numbers 1 and 51. All page and line references are to 12°

Order	Ref.	Readings
Volume I		
1211	1.5	Kinds, they] Kinds, yet they
1212	1.11	being Persons] being Men
1234	2.7	It is also resolv'd by me] I have also resolved] I resolve also] I resolved also
1121	2.9	taken] invented
1211	2.14	all Persons] my Readers
1122	2.35	I shall on any other Subject offer] I have to offer on any other Subject
1211	2.37	Reader] Readers
1122	3.13	Helps] Force
1122	3.17	not speak of any Think 'till it is pass'd] speak but of few Things 'till they are pass'd
1211	3.20	April 7] April 11
1122	3.33	he sits] sits
1122	4.4	Play-house all the Week] Play-house every Night in the Week
1222	4.21	he's] he is
1222	4.22	he's] he is
1222	4.23	The Reader is desir'd . . . in Love.] *omit*
1211	4.23	acted] presented
1222	4.30	Distinction, the] as at that Time; the
1222	4.32	there appear'd also] it discovered even there
1222	5.2	Perfection, and there seem'd a peculiar Regard had to their Behaviour on this occasion: No one] Perfection; the Actors were careful of their Carriage, and no one
1222	5.5	Respect had] Respect was had
1222	5.33	late Favour] Favour
1222	5.36	may not] should be
1222	6.6	and is] wherein he is
1222	6.9	said] say
1222	6.24	Hand; which] Hand. This
1222	6.30	who come] that come
1222	6.37	Prince Eugene was then . . . Seven Vessels.] *omit*
1122	7.26	and that not] and not
1222	8.5	Penetration] Skill
1222	8.15	Advertisement. A Vindication . . . Year 1709.] *omit*
Volume II		
1222	1.1	suitable] equal
1222	2.20	when a] by a
1122	3.1	and find] and to find
1121	3.5	the College] his College
1222	3.14	near] nearly
1122	3.16	A great deal of good Company] A good Company
1222	3.19	he presented us with] wherewith he presented us
1122	4.18	or how] and how
1222	5.18	Street] Secret
1222	6.18	a Bar] the Bar
1222	6.30	which will] that will
1222	6.34	is said] I said
1121	7.7	Last Night arrived . . . Common Cause.] *omit*
1232	7.12	is arriv'd] was arriv'd] *omit*
1123	7.14	taking] *omit*] making]

TABLE VI Variant Issues A,C,D, First 12° Edition

All issues original and supplementary of invariant impressions I-II of original on full sheets of ordinary paper with horizontal chainlines, III-IV and all reprints on half sheets of double-size paper with vertical lines. Originally published I-II on 10 July 1710, III 2 January 1711, IV 20 November 1711.

A. Volumes I-II of setting *a*, III of variant *a*, IV (all issues) with superfluous press figure page 286. *Copy:* Texas (the set used by George A. Aitken for his 1898-99 edition).

Mr. D. G. Neill, who is now preparing a more detailed analysis of this issue, kindly advises me that volume II of his copy has in addition to the figures cited below a number 1 on page 22.

C. Apparently subsequent to octavo issue, volumes I-II of setting *b*, III of variant *b* with formes B and C (o) reimpressed, C (i) reset, figure on page 3 occasionally lacking. *Copies:* Bodleian, Columbia, Harvard, Todd.

D. As for preceding issue except volume I of variant *c* with sheets B-F reset. *Copy:* Professor Richmond P. Bond.

The following list cites by page-number the press figures in sheets so marked, by the letter(s) immediately above first signature a convenient point for unfigured sheets.

	I*a* 1710	I*b* 1710	I*c* 1710	II*a* 1710	II*b* 1710	III*a* 1711	III*b* 1711	IV 1711
A	d	d	d					
B	he	22-2	11-3		23-5	24-1	3-5	4-5
		24-1	16-3	24-2	24-1		24-1	22-1
C	B	36-3	46-2	25-1	45-4	28-2	45-2	45-5
		46-1		46-4	46-4		46-1	46-4
D	fr	52-2	70-4	70-1	69-5	52-2		70-1
		71-5	72-4	72-1	71-5	70-5		72-1
E	ng	95-2	93-1	94-4	93-1	94-4		82-3
		96-4	98-5	96-1	95-2	96-3		96-4
F	e	118-3	100-5	118-3	118-4	98-2		118-5
		120-3			120-4	120-3		120-1
G			122-5	142-4	124-5	141-5		134-3
			144-4	144-3	142-5	142-2		141-2
H	ed		165-5	166-4	166-4	165-5		158-5
			166-2	168-3	168-1	166-2		168-4
I	•		190-3	190-3	190-3	191-5		190-3
			192-5	192-4	192-3	192-4		192-2
K	e i		213-5	215-3	214-4	214-2		203-5
				216-4	216-1	216-4		205-4
L	n		238-4	238-4	220-3	218-3		238-2
			240-5	240-3	238-4	240-5		240-1
M	ou		262-2	261-3	262-3	256-3		253-3
			264-3	262-4	264-5	262-2		262-4
N	ou		286-3	287-3	280-5	278-3		275-5
			288-4	288-4	286-1	285-4		288-1
O	a		310-5	302-3	292-2	310-2		304-2
			312-5	312-4	302-3	312-5		310-3
P	e		327-3	334-3	335-4	325-3		316-4
			333-3	336-4	336-2	334-4		334-5
Q	358-1		358-3	352-3	357-5	340-2		357-1
	360-2		360-4	358-4	358-1	358-4		359-2
R	364-3		374-5	364-3	382-4	381-2		374-5
	382-1		376-3	382-2	384-4	382-3		
S				388-3	397-5	388-3		
				398-4	398-4			

TABLE VII VARIANT ISSUES B,E,F, FIRST 8° EDITION

All issues original and supplementary of royal (22.3 x 14cm.) and medium paper (20 x 12.5cm.) impressions.° Original series published simultaneously with 12° edition A except for delayed issue of 2d volume, 1 September 1710.

B. Volume I dated 1710, II of setting a. 1. *Royal-paper:* BM (4 copies, one of vols. I-II only), Harvard, New York Public (Berg copy vols. I-II only), Bond. 2. *Medium-paper:* Bodleian (2 copies), Harvard, Texas (2 copies, one of vol. I only), Bond.

E. Volume I reset and dated 1713, II of setting b except for sheet S which, in the one copy examined, is of a setting. 1. *Royal-paper:* none observed. 2. *Medium-paper:* Todd.

F. Volume I as in preceding issue, II reissued with reset prelims and title also dated 1713. 1. *Royal-paper:* BM, Bodleian. 2. *Medium-paper:* Columbia.

The following list cites by page-number the press figures in sheets so marked, by the letter(s) immediately above first signature a convenient point for unfigured sheets.

	I 1710	IIa 1710	IIb 1710	III 1711	IV 1711
A	y,	s	s	m	e
B	id	14-2 16-1	he	e o	s
C	,	30-2 32-1	rk	Ho	o w
D	of	46-2 48-1	s D	V	st
E	i	62-1 64-2	r	i	o h
F	e	78-1 80-2	at	r	nc
G	94-1 96-2	94-1 96-1	u	n	s,
H	110-2 112-1	110-1 112-1	th	R	E
I	126-1 128-2	126-2 128-1	r	e	ed
K	142-1 144-1	142-2 144-1	s	r	142-1 144-1
L	158-2 160-1	158-2 160-1	e C	ig	158-2 160-1
M	174-1 176-2	174-2 176-1	ms	s s	174-1 176-1
N	190-1 192-1	190-1 192-1	i	n f	190-1 192-1
O	206-2 208-1	206-2 208-1	, a	d s	207-2
P	222-1 224-2	222-1 224-2	t	v	219-2 224-1
Q	238-2 240-1	238-2 240-1	y	l o	238-2 240-1

TABLE VII—*Continued*

	I 1710	IIa 1710	IIb 1710	III 1711	IV 1711
R	254-1 256-2	254-1 256-2	m	ho	254-1 256-2
S	270-1 272-2	270-1 272-2	s	n	270-1 272-2
T	286-2 288-1	286-1 288-1	o	st	284-2 286-1
U	302-1 304-1	302-1 304-1	m	g I	302-2 304-1
X	318-1 320-2	318-1 320-1	n	s w	318-2 320-1
Y	334-2 336-1	wn	e	wh	334-1 336-2
Z	350-1 352-1	, C	, C	e d	350-2 352-1
2A	366-2 368-1	I	. I	o	367-2
2B	382-2 384-1	h	he	d w	382-1 384-2
2C	398-2 400-1	w	n	e E	396-2 398-1
2D		g	ei	d	413-2 415-1
2E		t	p	ec	431-2 432-1
2F		m	me	he	445-2 446-1
2G		•	Mi	s o	460-1 463-2
2H				g t	t b
2I					e

* Vol. I page 368, originally misnumbered 863, is corrected in some copies of royal and all copies of medium paper impression; one or more of figures 96–2, 112–1, 128–2, 190–1 dropped in later copies of medium; vol. II page 96 figure 1 altered to 2 in some copies of royal and all copies of medium; vol. IV 284–2 added after early copies of royal.

IX

ARTHUR FRIEDMAN

The Problem of Indifferent Readings in the Eighteenth Century, with a Solution from The Deserted Village

The arguments in recent years in favor of using the first edition as copy-text have been concerned to a considerable extent with showing that the accidentals of the author's manuscript will thus be most closely approximated. For the substantive readings it would seem in theory to make very little difference what copy-text is chosen. The editor who selects the first edition will normally introduce into his edited text all changes in later editions for which he thinks the author is responsible, and the editor who chooses the last edition revised by the author will revert to earlier readings when he is sure the changes were made by the compositor or printing-house editor; so the difference would seem to be largely one of emphasis. In practice, however, the choice of copy-text may be of great importance for the substantive readings, for when he comes to the actual business of making his text the editor finds himself strongly influenced by two sometimes conflicting considerations: he wants to depart from his copy-text only when there is a compelling reason to do so, and he wants (except in unusual circumstances) to include in the edited text all revisions made by the author. Now when the last revised edition is chosen, these two considerations merely reinforce each other, since—except for obvious misprints—all the readings of the copy-text may possibly be authorial. The editor, consequently, is likely to avoid decisions by reproducing his copy-text with a minimum of change, and he can then pretend that by placing the

Reprinted with slight changes from *Studies in Bibliography*, XIII (1960), 143–47, by permission of the author and the Bibliographical Society of the University of Virginia. Part of the paper appears in a somewhat different form in the Introduction to *Collected Works of Oliver Goldsmith* (Oxford, 1966).

earlier readings in the textual notes the reader—who can have no detailed knowledge of the textual problems involved—will in some obscure way be able to make up his own mind about difficult variants. When, however, the first edition is chosen, the two considerations oppose each other, for to depart from the copy-text may be to introduce compositorial error and to follow it may be to neglect authorial revision. Thus each variant reading offers a new problem to be solved, and the excellence of the edited text will largely depend on the skill with which these solutions are made.

This argument for the use of the first edition as copy-text rests on the assumption that it is possible in most cases to distinguish with a high degree of probability between substantive revisions made by the author and changes made in the printing-house. Unless this assumption is correct—unless, in other words, the distinction can be made on the basis of something more certain than personal taste or vague questions of style—then it would be better to print with a minimum of change the substantive readings of the last revised edition.

In attempting to distinguish between author and compositor, one kind of variant that proves most troublesome, in part because of the frequency with which it occurs, is what may be called the indifferent reading, where one reading is not obviously superior to the other.[1] These changes are usually small and most fre-

---

[1] I do not wish to suggest that a change can be assigned to author or compositor merely according to whether or not it is an improvement, for the kind of change I find no satisfactory way of assigning is the one where improvement is most obvious. This is the correction of a mistake or infelicity—usually of a slip in grammar or a violation of idiom. Should we, to choose examples from Goldsmith's *Essays*, assign the correction of "one of his legs were cut off" or "I would desire . . . to imitate that fat man who I have somewhere heard of" to the author or the compositor? All we could say, if the corrections first appeared in a revised edition, would be that Goldsmith probably changed the readings if he noticed them and that the compositor changed them without hesitation if Goldsmith left them uncorrected. Actually Goldsmith let the first reading stand through two revisions and passed over the second while revising the sentence in which it appears; the compositors of two authorized editions left the readings unchanged; and they were corrected only in a pirated edition. An editor will almost inevitably admit into the edited text the corrections of mistakes and infelicities if these corrections first appear in revised editions, but in so doing he may be following the compositor as frequently as the author. Indeed we may set it down as a rule that the more obvious the change, the more impossible to assign it either to author or to compositor.

quently consist in the alteration of a single word or a change in word order ("soldiers and sailors" or "sailors and soldiers") or the addition or omission of a word ("in town and in country" or "in town and country"). This kind of change is one that authors often make deliberately, but it is also one that compositors frequently make through carelessness. By their very number these variants take on an importance that they do not have singly; at least if we believe that the excellence of an author depends in some degree on small points of style, we cannot consider these readings truly indifferent. We do not wish to reject a large number of authorial revisions, but equally we do not want to load the text with compositorial errors, and for any particular reading there is usually no good basis for choice.

Fortunately, in the case of Oliver Goldsmith—and, I imagine, of some other authors of his period—what cannot be done with any degree of confidence by considering single instances can be done with a high degree of probability by treating this kind of reading as a class. In the third quarter of the eighteenth century compositors of authorized editions followed their copy with great care, and in unrevised reprints of Goldsmith's writings they introduced on an average one substantive change only every five or ten or even twenty pages. In most revised editions of his works, on the other hand, new substantive readings occur on an average of two to five or more a page. If we assume that compositors were as careful in revised as in unrevised reprints, then the compositor would introduce on an average only one new substantive reading while Goldsmith was introducing anywhere from ten to a hundred; and if we were to limit ourselves to indifferent readings I think the proportion of authorial changes would be at least as high. To be particular, in the revised 1762 edition of *The Citizen of the World* there are literally hundreds of new indifferent readings; but in the unrevised edition of 1774, though the compositor introduced substantive changes of all sorts on an average of one in five pages, there are hardly more than a dozen new indifferent readings in the two volumes (I exclude from the count of indifferent readings here the very frequent expansion of contractions of the kind discussed below). In editing the text of Goldsmith I have consequently—except in special cases where I was reasonably sure of compositorial intervention—admitted into the edited text all indifferent readings that first made their appearance in revised reprints. By so doing I have no doubt followed a few errors, but I was willing to spare an occasional compositorial enemy for the sake of preserving a host of authorial friends.

This is my general practice, but I have been able to refine it by taking certain other habits of Goldsmith and his printers into account.

1. Although it may be an author's practice to make very numerous changes when he revises, he may not give equal attention to all parts of a text. In revising for the second edition of his *Essays*, for example, Goldsmith made extensive alterations in some of the pieces, but the only changes that appear in some of the others are infrequent new indifferent readings. These latter changes I have tended to ascribe to the compositor, as I have all occasional indifferent readings in an extended section of a revised text which shows no other signs of having received the author's attention.

2. In a particular period compositors may show a curious uniformity in making certain kinds of changes. In Goldsmith's writings the expansion of contractions such as "I'm" and "he's" and "can't" and the change of "an" in such a phrase as "an horse" to "a" appear with approximately equal regularity in unrevised and revised reprints made for various booksellers. I have consequently assigned all such changes to the compositor and retained the original readings from the edition set from manuscript.

3. In *The Deserted Village* analytical bibliography has come to my aid in the case of two difficult indifferent readings, and I imagine the method of my solution is applicable to many works of the period.

In recent years Professor Todd has made us increasingly aware of the fact that in the later eighteenth century type was frequently left standing, particularly for shorter works such as poems, plays, and pamphlets, to be reimpressed when a reprint was needed. Of course changes that originated either with the author or in the printing-house could be made in the standing type before it was reimpressed. The author could request any changes he liked, though he might be asked not to call for additions or deletion that would seriously disturb the make-up, just as a modern author is warned not to make extensive revisions in page proof. An editor employed in the printing-house might order various kinds of changes to be made—corrections of misprints, regularization of punctuation and spelling, alteration of what appeared to him to be errors or infelicities; it is extremely unlikely, however, that he would introduce new indifferent readings, where the new readings did not appear to be obviously superior to the old. The compositor, finally, would not, except in most unusual circumstances, introduce new readings through carelessness, since any changes he made in standing type would be deliberate. When, therefore, new indifferent readings are introduced in standing type, we can with a very high degree of probability assign them to the author.

Of the five editions of *The Deserted Village* that followed the first edition in 1770, each was printed in part or in whole from type left standing from the edition that preceded it.[2] Of these editions Goldsmith revised only for the second and the fourth. In the second edition there are two new indifferent readings (p. 7, l. 4: "the" for "his"; p. 11, l. 2: "steady" for "ready"), but both appear in sections where the type was newly set. In the fourth edition there are four new indifferent readings. One of these (p. 19, l. 5: "Through" for "To") occurs where the type was reset. A second—"sweet" for "soft" (p. 8, l. 1)—does not seem to be the kind of change that a compositor would make carelessly, and consequently the fact that the alteration was made in standing type merely confirms our belief that the author was responsible. The other readings would, without the aid of analytical bibliography, offer difficult choices. In the first three editions the last line on page 20 reads: "And left a lover's for her father's arms"; in the fourth edition the reading is "a father's." The change from "her" to "a" is just the kind of repetition (from "a lover's") that compositors frequently introduce through faulty memory; but since it was made in standing type, we can be confident that it was ordered by the author. Finally, there is

---

[2] All the early editions of *The Deserted Village* have the same collation: 4°, A^2 a^2 B–G^2. In the second edition all of a, B, and G and probably E_2^r are from the same setting as the first. In the third edition a–G are from the same setting as the second with no alterations in the text, but the evidence, as far as it goes, suggests that the sheets for the two were not continuously impressed: both have the same press figure on E_2^r, but in the second edition either E_1 or E_2 is a cancel; and G_1^v has a figure in the third but not in the second edition. In the fourth edition all of C and D, F_2^v, and probably F_1^r are from the same setting as the third. In the fifth edition all of a and B and E_1^r and E_2^v are from the same setting as the fourth. In the sixth edition all of D and F are from the same setting as the fifth.

a more important change. In the first three editions a passage on page 5 appears as follows:

> Here as I take my solitary rounds,
> Amidst thy tangling walks, and ruined grounds,
> And, many a year elapsed, return to view
> Where once the cottage stood, the hawthorn grew,
> Here, as with doubtful, pensive steps I range,
> Trace every scene, and wonder at the change,
> Remembrance wakes with all her busy train,
> Swells at my breast, and turns the past to pain.

In the fourth edition the penultimate couplet is omitted. The passage is certainly satisfactory without the couplet; on the other hand, it would be hard to show that the couplet is more redundant than many left standing in the poem. Certainly it is not so obviously bad that an editor in the printing-house would have had it struck out. Again, it does not seem probable that the type fell out by accident, for in the third edition the couplet does not appear at the very top or bottom of the page, and the lines that preceded and followed it do not appear in the fourth edition to have been disarranged. If the passage had been newly set, it would seem not improbable that the compositor omitted the couplet through negligence; but since it was printed from standing type, the most probable solution is that Goldsmith marked the couplet for deletion when he revised for the fourth edition.

X

FREDSON BOWERS

Some Principles for Scholarly Editions of Nineteenth-Century American Authors

The first problem that faces any editor of a text from the nineteenth century, or earlier, is whether to modernize. For nineteenth-century American books there is only one answer: no gain results from modernizing, and much is lost that is characteristic of the author. One may safely say that nothing in the spelling, punctuation, capitalization, word-division, or paragraphing of nineteenth-century books is likely to cause a presentday reader any difficulty, whereas an attempt at modernization is certain to destroy a number of the values of the original. Every reason exists to preserve these classic texts in as close a form as possible to the authors' intentions, to the extent that the surviving documents for each individual work permit of such reconstruction. Indeed, one may flatly assert that any text that is modernized can never pretend to be scholarly, no matter at what audience it is aimed.

The second problem is whether to edit the text critically or to content oneself with a reprint of some single document. Again, an argument cannot really exist in favor of a mere reprint, no matter how neatly such a procedure enables an editor to dodge his basic responsibility. It is probably safe to say that no nineteenth-century text of any length exists that is not in need of some correction, and possibly even of revisory emendation. Once an editor tinkers in any way with his original, he has entered upon the province of critical editing; and he had better go the whole way and be consistent than dip his big toe in the water

Read on 22 November 1962 before the American Literature section of the South Atlantic Modern Language Association, meeting in Miami Beach, Florida. Reprinted from *Studies in Bibliography*, XVII (1964), 223–28, by permission of the author and the Bibliographical Society of the University of Virginia.

and then draw back in alarm lest he suddenly find himself out of his depth.

The first step in critical editing is the so-called establishment of the text. The first step in *this* process is the determination of the exact forms of the early documents in which the text is preserved and of the facts about their relationship to one another. That is, the early editions within an author's lifetime, and within a sufficient time after his death to give the opportunity for testamentary documents to be produced, must be collated and the authoritative editions isolated. An authoritative edition is one set directly from manuscript, or a later edition that contains corrections or revisions that proceeded from the author. Authority divides itself between the words as meaningful units (i.e., the substantives) and the accidentals, that is, the forms that the words take in respect to spelling, punctuation, capitalization, and division. In this question the theory of copy-text proposed by Sir Walter Greg rules supreme. Greg distinguished between the authority of the substantives and of the forms, or accidentals, assumed by these substantives. If only the first edition, set from manuscript, has authority, as being the closest in each of these two respects to the author's lost manuscript, then both authorities are combined in one edition. On the other hand, a revised edition may alter the authority of some of the substantives; but the transmission of the author's accidentals through the hands, and mind, of still another compositor destroys the authority of these features of the first edition, set from manuscript. An eclectic text must be constructed which combines the superior authority of most of the words in the revised edition with the superior authority of the forms of words in the first edition.

The determination of authority is not always easy in a later edition. For example, in Hawthorne's *Scarlet Letter* three editions (i.e., three different typesettings) were made during his lifetime. In the second edition, set and printed in 1850 within two months of the first, 226 pages were completely reset, but 96 pages were printed from the standing type of the first edition. In the 226 pages of the resetting occur 62 variants from the first edition, of which three are corrections of first-edition typographical errors and four are typographical errors in the second edition. Twelve different words (i.e., variant substantive readings) appear in these pages, and there are 43 changes in spelling, capitalization, and word-division.

Of more import, in the 96 pages of standing type, someone ordered eight variants, of which three are spelling, four are punctuation, and one is division. Here if anywhere the author's intentions would be visible if he had ordered these changes in standing type; but an editor will find no clearcut authority in the changes, and indeed some evidence that at least two of them go contrary to Hawthorne's observed characteristics. Once these variants are rejected as non-authorial, therefore, the conclusion must be drawn that Hawthorne did not supervise the production of the second edition and hence no revisions can be accepted from the reset type-pages, although a few corrections will prove useful.

Nor does the third edition, the last in Hawthorne's lifetime, yield any readings other than a continuation of corruption, and some necessary but obvious correction. None of the 37 additional alterations in the words seems to have any chance of being an authorial revision, and most are clearly errors.

In these circumstances, the editor is forced back to the first edition as the sole authority. But the question then arises, what is the specific authority of each page of this first edition, for it is possible for copies to vary because of changes made during the course of printing. Mechanical collation on the Hinman Machine of eight copies of *The Scarlet Letter* discloses four differences in readings, but all of these seem to have resulted from type being loosensed during the course of printing so that the progression is from correctness to error. However, unless an editor had established the correct readings where these errors exist, he would wrongly have imputed the errors to the first edition; and it is possible that he might have emended differently from the original reading. For example, because an exclamation point dropped out very early in the printing of page 228, no edition before the Centenary recovered this original authoritative punctuation, for all editors were content to follow the second-edition comma that the later compositor inserted when he came to the blank space in his copy.

The collation of multiple copies reveals other possibilities for variation. In *The Scarlet Letter*, interestingly enough, economy of printing led the printer of the first edition to typeset the last two text pages in duplicate. Fortunately no differences appear in these two settings, but the possibility of variation is always present. For example, the new Preface to the second edition was also set in duplicate, and here one typesetting has a comma that appears to be authoritative, whereas the other omits it. An editor who neglected to collate a number of copies might have reprinted arbitrarily from the wrong typesetting and thus, even though in a small matter, have departed from Hawthorne's intention.

Even if the first edition were printed from plates, machine collation is necessary to discover concealed printings within the so-called first edition, for the possibility exists that plates may be altered between impressions. For example, the Ticknor and Field cost books list four printings from plates in 1851 of *The House of the Seven Gables*, and one printing in 1852. Since no copy of an 1852 printing has turned up, it seems clear that one of the unidentified 1851 printings represents the fifth impression with a title-page date unchanged. No book collector or librarian has the least idea which printing his precious first-edition copy represents, but the Hinman Machine discloses the order by combining the evidence of type batter with the evidence for resetting of damaged plates as well as various mendings. It is pure luck that these extensive plate repairs were carried out without producing any changes in the text to baffle the non-bibliographical editor, and it is clear that Hawthorne (if he saw any errors) ordered no revisions between these printings.

But not all changes made in plates from printing to printing are so respectful of the text. For instance, the third edition of *The Scarlet Letter* was printed from plates in 1850 and these plates remained in use at least as late as 1886. In the course of the various repairs made in this interval, five different words got altered so that the text of the final printings from these plates differs from that of the initial printings in this respect as well as in dozens and dozens of punctuation marks worn off or quite altered by batter. These changes have no authority, but it is clear that Hawthorne himself made some alterations in the plates for one of the later printings of *The Marble Faun*, revisions of which an editor must take account of if he knows about them.

When an author's manuscript is preserved, this has paramount authority, of course. Yet the fallacy is still maintained that since the first edition was proofread by the author, it must represent his final intentions and hence should be chosen as copy-text. Practical experience shows the contrary. When one collates the manuscript of *The House of the Seven Gables* against the first printed edition, one finds an average of ten to fifteen differences per page between the manuscript and the print, many of them consistent alterations from the manuscript system of punctuation, capitalization, spelling, and word-division. It would be ridiculous to argue that Hawthorne made approximately three to four thousand small changes in proof, and then wrote the manuscript of *The Blithedale Romance* according to the same system as the manuscript of the *Seven Gables*, a system that he had rejected in proof.

A close study'of the several thousand variants in *Seven Gables* demonstrates that almost every one can be attributed to the printer. That Hawthorne passed them in proof is indisputable, but that they differ from what he wrote in the manuscript and manifestly preferred is also indisputable. Thus the editor must choose the manuscript as his major authority, correcting from the first edition only what are positive errors in the accidentals of the manuscript.

However, when words differ in the print from the manuscript, as they do a certain number of times, the question of authority arises. Any difference in words can arise only by reason of printer's error that Hawthorne did not catch in proof, or by reason of changes that Hawthorne himself made in the lost proof-sheets. Each variant, thus, becomes an editorial responsibility, to be adjudicated on the evidence available. In *The Blithedale Romance* Hawthorne can be assigned twenty-four of the verbal proof-changes between manuscript and first edition. The printer is responsible, fairly clearly, for the remaining seven of the thirty-one differences in wording.

Here we encounter the theory of a critical edition. Obviously, an editor cannot simply reprint the manuscript, and he must substitute for its readings any words that he believes Hawthorne changed in proof. Once more, if one argues why not reprint the first edition and be done with it—then two questions of evidence are pertinent. First, in reprinting the first edition of *The Blithe-dale Romance*, one would be attributing to Hawthorne seven words that are actually printer's errors. Secondly, if an author's habits of expression go beyond words and into the forms that these take, together with the punctuation that helps to shape the relationships of these words, then one is foolish to prefer a print-ing-house style to the author's style. This distinction is not the-ory, but fact. Hawthorne's punctuation, for example, is much more meaningful in respect to emphasis and to delicate matters of parenthesis and subordination than is the printing-house style in which *Seven Gables* and *The Blithedale Romance* appeared. In each book, the real flavor of Hawthorne, cumulatively developing in several thousand small distinctions, can be found only in the manuscript.

Sometimes the Greg formula that authors' substantive revisions in later editions must always be followed, when identified, but that the best authority for the accidentals remains the edition set directly from manuscript, produces some complexity, and the result will agree in a number of details with no preserved document, even though it will represent the nearest approximation in every respect of the author's final intentions. An eclectic editor must be prepared for any eventuality. In *The Marble Faun*, for example, Hawthorne seems to have proofread the original English edition rather carelessly, because he made a number of corrections, and a few revisions, in the first American edition, which was set up from the English sheets. Fortunately, we have the manuscript preserved (though lost sight of for many years). Hence an editor will base his edition on the manuscript copy-text but will substitute, first, any words from the English first edition that he thinks are authorial proof changes, and then, in addition, any variant readings from the first American edition that appear to him, also, to represent the author's alterations, and then, in addition, the authoritative Hawthorne revisions and corrections made later in the first-edition plates. This is indeed an eclectic text, but the unique results will be closer to Hawthorne's characteristics than any single preserved document, not only in respect to the insertion of Hawthorne's final intentions within the framework of his original accidentals but also in respect to the scholarly refusal to reprint errors from either the first English or the first American edition any more than the rejected readings of the manuscript.

Granted that an editor has established a critical text that will stand up under the most searching investigation of scholarship, then what will scholars want from his apparatus? First, a list of the internal variants in the first and in any other authoritative edition as revealed by the collation of a number of copies of each, preferably on the Hinman Machine. Secondly, a complete list of all editorial changes in the selected copy-text. These changes comprise corrections and revisions admitted from later editions as well as the editor's own alterations. For the sake of the record, the editor should list the earliest edition from which he draws any alteration. Textual notes should discuss briefly any arguable emendations, or failure to emend.

The next item is the Historical Collation. This should contain all the substantive alterations from the established edited text found in a group of significant later editions. An edition is to be defined as any new typesetting. Obviously, any edition within the author's lifetime may be significant and must be collated. Thereafter the editor's discretion may enter. Usually it is important to select editions that have been influential in the formation of the text, or that have been commonly used by critics. For instance, the decision was made by the Centenary editors of Hawthorne to confine the Historical Collation largely to the Boston collected editions published in the Ticknor and Field line to Houghton Mifflin, as well as any separate editions published within the author's lifetime. For *The Scarlet Letter*, therefore, the Centenary Edition records the readings from the second edition of 1850, the third edition of 1850, the Little Classics edition of 1875, the Riverside of 1883, and ends with the Autograph of 1900. Included always are the first English editions in case any authoritative changes were made in the copy sent abroad, and usually any modern edition that has been freshly edited in fact instead of in theory.

To insure accuracy, the sets of plates are taken as representing the various editions, and the earliest and latest printings from each edition-set of plates have been collated on the Hinman Machine and their variants recorded in the Centenary apparatus. All printings from plates within the author's lifetime have also been collated whenever variants appeared between the first and last impressions of any set of plates instituted before his death.

Although this Historical Collation is chiefly a record of the corruption of the text, it serves as a useful object lesson in the untrustworthy nature of various commonly esteemed editions. More important, however, this list insures that all cards are on the table. If any collated edition has authority not recognized by the editor, the critic will find the record of its variants and all the evidence on which, throughout, the editor made up his mind about the details of the text.

When a manuscript is preserved, an important separate list will contain a record of all the rejected readings and revisions during the process of inscription. Moreover, the variants in any preserved proof-sheets should be recorded with the same scrupulousness and for the same critical purpose.

So far as I know, a problem that no editor has faced concerns the word-division whenever a compound in the copy-text is divided at the end of one line and the start of the next. The exact form of all such compounds must be settled so that the edited text will contain that one that is characteristic of the author. Since editorial judgment is sometimes involved in this process, a list of such divided possible compounds should be provided. Correspondingly, the modern printer will divide a number of compounds so that a reader will not always know the exact form in the original. A second section of the compound list should note the copy-text reading in all such cases.

The amount of collating and checking in such an edition as has been outlined is very heavy indeed; but only this editorial process scrupulously carried out will produce editions of American classics that will stand the test of time and, heaven willing, need never be edited again from the ground up. When scholars editing American literature will bring to their task the careful effort that has been established as necessary for English Renaissance texts, say, then the editing of American texts will become a respectable occupation at long last, and not a piece of hack work for the paperbacks.

XI

WILLIAM B. TODD

Problems in Editing Mark Twain

On July ninth of last year various Innocents at Home progressed
to Iowa City, headquarters of the forthcoming Mark Twain edition, there to consider the rapidly developing complications of
the project entrusted to their care. On the way some editors, I
believe, found solace in the thought that there was really nothing
to do. *Life* magazine had just declared that all of Twain was
written by Longfellow.[1] The present writer worried over quite
a different report, Henry M. and D. C. Partridge's *The Most
Remarkable Echo in the World,* which not only authenticated
all of Twain's writings but assigned to him the work of Edgar
Allan Poe, Nathaniel Hawthorne, and Lewis Carroll.[2] The year
after this great disclosure, in 1934, one of these authors also
attributed to Twain the entire corpus of Rudyard Kipling and
the forgeries of Thomas J. Wise.[3] Somewhere within these luna-
tic fringes, we may be assured, lies the real Twain: a vast international territory demanding, for its proper government, a
ministry of all the talents, a search through countless newspapers
and journals, an inspection of hundreds of reference works, the
collation by machine and by eye of perhaps 400 texts—this an
estimate for major works only—the compilation of thousands of
variant readings and, at last, the production of some thirty-six
volumes, the twelve from the University of California at Berkeley representing work not previously in print, twenty-three

This paper was read at the annual meeting of the Modern Language
Association in New York 27 December 1964. Reprinted from *Books at
Iowa, no. 2* (April, 1965), 3–8, by permission of the author and The Friends
of The University of Iowa Libraries.

[1] D. J. Hamblin, "Mark (ye) (the) Twain," *Life,* 10 July 1964, p. 13.

[2] Henry M. and D. C. Partridge, *The Most Remarkable Echo in the
World* (New York, 1933). Privately printed in 100 copies.

[3] Henry M. Partridge, "Did Mark Twain Perpetrate Literary Hoaxes?"
American Book Collector, V (December 1934), 351–57; VI (January 1935),
20–23; (February 1935), pp. 50–53.

others from Iowa exhibiting in definitive form work already published, and a final volume providing for the whole a bibliography and index. Except in one important particular, to be considered last of all, the editorial board has accepted and intends to apply the principles recently expounded by Professor Bowers at Miami Beach and more recently demonstrated in the Hawthorne (if it is really Hawthorne) edition now issuing from the press.[4]

Of first importance is a means of bringing under control and then refining in a certain procedure the diverse materials to be examined. The entire output of Twain, as measured only by cards filed at the Union Catalogue, Library of Congress, consists of some 2,650 variant issues. Even if this total is reduced first to issues in Twain's lifetime, then to the variants of a single work— *The Innocents Abroad*, let us say—the count still runs to forty issues, twenty-six beyond the count in the *Bibliography of American Literature*. Viewed as arithmetic totals these figures are rather unmanageable, however talented the ministry, but regarded as multitudinous printings from relatively few electrotype plates, the usual condition, the situation is brought within easy compass and can be expressed in formulae applicable at least to Twain's major works. An analogical scheme is now also being devised for the minor writings. Thus for any book the sigla may consist of from one to three elements:

1. A *capital letter* designating the national origin of the setting and comprising all plates of that setting, including those used earlier or later at some distant time or place. For separate authorized settings four letters will be used, ACEG, representing plates originating in America, Canada, England, and Germany. In this arrangement such variants as the earlier Canadian issue of *Adventures of Huckleberry Finn*, or the later English issue of *Christian Science*, can be subsumed under *A*, the original American setting, and then machine-collated as a part of the *A* sequence. As for *G*, the editions issued by Tauchnitz in Leipzig, the fact that Twain once here provided a new introduction, and then expressed some inclination to revise the text, obliges us to read all thirty-three volumes in this series.

2. If there is more than one setting of the same nationality, the letter will be followed by a numeral. This numeral, however,

[4] Fredson Bowers, "Some Principles for Scholarly Editions of Nineteenth-Century American Authors," *Studies in Bibliography*, XVII (1964), 223–28.

does not signify any textual relationship between the two editions. Text E2 of *Innocents Abroad* (Chatto and Windus, 1881) for some odd reason does not derive from the earlier and revised E1 (Routledge, 1872), but from the original unrevised *A* (Hartford, 1869). Again in *The Adventures of Tom Sawyer*, E2 derives directly from *A*, and now with good reason, for *A* here represents some textual improvement over E1.

3. Within a given setting A, E1, or whatever, any variant state will be signified by a lower-case letter. This reference applies only to textual variation in any group of impressions, all comment on typographical peculiarities, including reset but invariant words, lines, paragraphs, being reserved for the Bibliography. Thus for *The Gilded Age*, a highly complicated *A* setting, the textual state may be simply represented as a, b, c, with *a* for the 1873 "Eschol" state, *b* for the "Beriah" state, and *c* for the state further revised in 1895. A later printing of 1901 comes also from the earliest plates and thus is classified as of the *a* group.

Now with these three-element sigla we can defer, until after collation, the assignment of the final a, b, c orders, and classify beforehand all the books to be considered. Of printed texts the total authorized settings are, at the one extreme, *Christian Science*, only two, and at the other extreme, *The Prince and the Pauper*, no less than eight.

Beyond the early printed texts there also lie a seemingly unending series of collected editions, at last count extending to twenty-seven issues under sixteen names and published by at least five different firms. Again, however, a plate analysis reduces all this confusion to three settings, now to be assigned the terminal letters X, Y, Z. The relevance of these texts to a definitive edition requires separate comment.

X. An abortive series of five volumes produced in the so-called Harper "Uniform" edition and reviewed by W. D. Howells in the 13 February 1897 issue of *Harper's Weekly*. All of these are undated and bear no helpful code-reference. At the time of the Iowa meeting only one exemplar had been identified—a solitary copy among some 5,000 specimens at Texas—but that one, of *The Prince and the Pauper*, exhibited a distinctive house-style which has since enabled us to locate all the others. Doubtless setting X will contribute little toward a definition of the text; yet as an authorized edition it must be collated in the automatic, unvarying process devised for all works.

Y. A sequence extending from twenty-two to thirty-seven volumes, issued initially by the American Publishing Company in 1899, then by several other firms, and finally by Harper in a series of coded issues the last reading D-R, or April 1917. Thus the impressions range over nineteen years, twelve before and seven years after the death of the author. Of all the complications in *Y* the pitiful sum of our knowledge, at the time of the Iowa conference, was that different issues of the first volume immediately exhibited a score of variants, the first appearing in the very first sentence. Since then the Hinman Collator has been scanning first and last issues and, though only one-third the way through the job, promises to extract a phenomenal number of readings far exceeding the total exposed in any other editorial enterprise. Thus far the count is 92 for *A Connecticut Yankee in King Arthur's Court*, 152 for *The Prince and the Pauper*, 212 for *Joan of Arc*, 315 for *A Tramp Abroad*, 338 for *Roughing It*, and 367 for *The Gilded Age*. At this rate the corrected plates in the twenty-two volumes should produce some 4,500 variants, all these *within* the last setting in Twain's lifetime and—since the edition is plated—all therefore representing deliberate alterations unsullied (or unsallied if you prefer) by the corrupting effects of new composition. This situation, unparalleled, I believe, in editorial history, for awhile sent the editors, already exhausted by earlier labors, reeling into a state of shock. Most of them recovered somewhat when it was determined that 80 per cent of the variants restored the first edition text, one grossly abused by those who prepared the 1899 plates. But what authority, if any, resided in the other 20 per cent now first appearing?

No sooner was the question raised than Professor Salomon found an answer in a marked set at Yale. This issue of 1899, called the "Royal Edition," obviously served if not directly as copy for the corrected impressions, then certainly as the text where all problems were decided. To simplify considerably, green crayon marks in this signify restorations, all billed against the firm of Case, Lockwood, and Brainard, printer of the original "Autograph" impression, and red crayon marks designate new readings, all charged to the publisher. The copy also reports, for many readings, a lively debate between one "FM," a learned and opinionated corrector, and "FEB," or Frank E. Bliss, the proprietor of the American Publishing Company, here often forced to consult with the final authority, Twain. Thus in a short story, where reference is made to "the creator of Frankenstein," FM retorts "This is terrible, for it shows Twain has never read Frankenstein. Frankenstein was the name of the creator, not the man monster, who is nameless." FEB then remarks, "Twain indicates that the phrase 'the creator of' is to be struck out." At other times FM expresses his dismay in such terms as "absurd," "ludicrous," "This is awful," or "This is an awfully stupid blunder." All this leads FEB to telephone Twain, to consult Webster's Dictionary, to peruse the *Book of Mormon*, to admit some doubt "I reckon so," or simply to concede defeat "Dunno." As the dialogue proceeds we stand as delighted witnesses, here observing much of what we would otherwise have to do in 1965, now being done, indirectly with Twain's approval, in 1899. Coincidentally Y (or rather Yb, second state) is an appropriate symbol for this edition, for it constantly reminds us of the Yale text, the final arbiter on many doubtful matters.

Z. A setting first plated as the code would indicate in July 1917 (three months after the last impression of Y) and still available, from other plates, in this year 1965. The collation of this setting proceeds in observance of the principle that inspection should extend to one edition beyond the last in the author's lifetime. Moreover, even if there were no such principle, the editors of Twain would be forced to consider, in this setting, two impressions, the "Definitive Edition" of 1922–1925 and the "Stormfield Edition" of 1929, this last an issue fondly regarded by some Twainians as even more definitive than the "Definitive." Actually, of course, both are the same, and both textually inferior to anything that has gone before.

Apart from all other sigla, ACEG for separate editions, XYZ for collected, there appears among collational symbols one other letter, I. This could be understood as I the editor, I the intermediary, or I Claudius, the final judge of Twain's destiny. Formally it denotes no personal act, but the necessary intrusion of the editor, with the concurrence of the Iowa board, to correct *manifest* error or ambiguity. Despite the tendency of FEB, in the Y setting, to normalize the abnormal, and particularly to alter on his own authority a number of accidentals—some fifty-three, for example, in *The Gilded Age*—the editor will reject all such attempts and, so long as the earlier reading is defensible, even on the most tenuous grounds, preserve the reading against every assault. All optional spellings, idiosyncratic pointing, and misquotation, purposeful or not, must remain and then, if necessary, be explained in the notes. Even a misspelling, "straightened" for "straitened" in *The Gilded Age*, should be tolerated, I believe, if it represents a common fault or possibly, as here, a pun. But the misspelling of a proper name if unintentional, Russell for Russel, Septimius for Septimus, should be amended, for in these instances, surely, Twain would wish to be right or, at least, would have nothing to gain by being wrong. Pointing which is inconsistently employed, *e.g.* end quotes before period, or which distorts the meaning, must also be set aright, as Twain again would approve. Beyond these trivialities, however, these evident mistakes, these mechanical errors, the editor will not go.

With Twain the editor also dares not proceed very far in the other direction, that is, in substituting for first readings those of anterior texts in manuscript, typescript, proof, or other printer's copy. Unlike Hawthorne's carefully fashioned manuscripts, Twain's essentially are drafts, more often than not hurriedly written with ampersands, dashes, abbreviations, and other kinds of shorthand, then in this form amended, cancelled, extended, and then again as all evidence indicates gradually refined to the form perfected in print. For Twain the printed form was the ultimate state, a condition in which, given his own expertise as printer and publisher, he was fully competent to perform—when he chose to do so. Thus, contrary to practice in the Hawthorne edition, the editors of Twain have good reason to rely primarily on the earliest printing.

Even so, the editors will scrutinize every word before that printing, convey in notes every reading thereafter amended, and again, if necessity requires, intrude upon the text certain trivialities overlooked in the larger effort. When Jean Clemens, in typing her father's manuscript of *Christian Science*, silently elides a word or two, the loss, though not affecting the sense, must still be made good. And when C. D. Warner, while attending the American edition of *The Gilded Age*, alters a Twainian reading Twain himself retains in the English issue, again the intent here thwarted must prevail. But when Twain declares that his wife was "perfectly right" in suppressing a chapter of *Following the Equator*, or allows W. D. Howells to revise the proofs of *The Prince and the Pauper*, then we may not claim an authority which Twain has expressly delegated to others. The confidence in others may be misplaced, the passage deleted of greater interest than anything retained; but whatever the significance of the reading we may not restore it even in brown ink, according to the latest fashion—and thus violate Twain's will in the matter. Throughout the edition, then, through the entire mass of variants before and after original printing, our constant endeavor will be to represent Twain, not as our present inclination might suggest, but as he in his own time would have us do it, with warts and all.

XII

JOHN M. ROBSON

Textual Introduction to John Stuart Mill's
Principles of Political Economy

I. The Text of the *Principles*

John Stuart Mill's *Principles of Political Economy, with Some of Their Applications to Social Philosophy*, went through seven Library editions (in two volumes) in his lifetime, plus a People's edition (in one volume of difficult double-column type) which was frequently reissued. The first five editions were published by Parker; the last two Library editions and the People's editions by Longmans.[1]

Mill, evidently encouraged by Parker's willingness to publish his *Essays on Some Unsettled Questions of Political Economy* in 1844 (consequent upon the success of his *System of Logic* in the preceding year), decided to write "a systematic treatise on Political Economy" as early as April, 1844,[2] and as his letters to Comte in the spring of that year show, he already had his line of approach in mind. Not until the autumn of 1845, however, did he begin to write the first draft, which was completed early in March, 1847. Mill expected to finish the book in a few months,[3]

From the *Collected Works of John Stuart Mill*, Vol. II: *Principles of Political Economy*, Bks. I-II (Toronto, 1965). Reprinted by permission of the author, University of Toronto Press, and Routledge & Kegan Paul.

[1] The printers for all editions except the 1st were Savill and Edwards, Chandos Street, Covent Garden; the 1st was printed by Harrison and Co., St. Martin's Lane. Such trivia have some point: see Appendix G [*Collected Works of John Stuart Mill*] II. 1029–30.

[2] The quotation is from a letter to Sterling (29/5/44), but the intention is shown in the letter to Comte mentioned in the next note. See Francis E. Mineka (ed.), *The Earlier Letters of John Stuart Mill*, in *Collected Works* (University of Toronto Press, 1963), XIII, 630.

[3] Letters to Comte (3/4/44) and Chapman (12/11/45), in Mineka, XIII, 626 and 687.

and probably he spent little more than a few months on it, for in this period of less than a year and a half he took a two-month holiday, revised and published the 2nd edition of his *Logic*, wrote two long articles for the *Edinburgh Review* and a notice in the *Spectator*, and supplied fifty-eight leaders for the *Morning Chronicle*, forty-three of them (5 Oct., 1846-Jan. 1847) on Irish affairs.[4] He also, of course, continued his duties at the East India House. From the account in Alexander Bain's *John Stuart Mill* (London: Longmans, Green, 1882), 84-7, we learn that "the third part" is written by February, 1846; in September of the same year (after the appearance of the 2nd edition of the *Logic*, and his holiday) he writes to Bain that he is "on the point of finishing the third book ('Exchange')." And in December he says: "I continue to carry on the *Pol. Econ.* as well as I can with the articles in the *Chronicle*."

The rewriting, from March to December, 1847 (when the work went to press), was less interrupted, Mill publishing only five leaders, a notice, and a letter during this period. The *Principles* was published in April, 1848, in an edition of one thousand copies. This was sold out within a year, and a second edition, also of a thousand copies, appeared a year later (having been revised during February and March).[5] The third edition, of 1200 copies, the Preface dated July, 1852,[6] was the most extensively revised of all the editions. Further Library editions appeared in 1857 (4th),[7] 1862 (5th), 1865 (6th), and 1871 (7th). Also, in 1865, "in compliance with a wish frequently expressed to [him] by working men" (*Autobiography*, 195), Mill pub-

---

[4] In the *Autobiography* ([Columbia University Press, 1924], 164-65), Mill says he took six months (rather than the actual three) from the writing of the *Principles* to concentrate on these leaders. Three of his long leaders on French agriculture (11, 13, and 16 Jan., 1847) appeared in modified form as the Appendix to Volume I of the *Principles*, and so, all unknowing, he was for a short time carrying on both tasks simultaneously. Cf. Michael St. J. Packe, *Life of John Stuart Mill* (London: Secker and Warburg, 1954), 296.

[5] See F. A. Hayek, *John Stuart Mill and Harriet Taylor* (London: Routledge and Kegan Paul, 1951), 134-48, and Appendix G [*Collected Works*].

[6] Packe (359) gives March as the month of publication.

[7] It was being revised during Feb., 1857 (see [*Collected Works*] II. 1037), although Mill, beginning a revision of II, x, §2, says in 1862: "Thus far I had written in 1856."

lished a cheap People's edition of the *Principles* which went through several reprintings.[8]

The early draft seems to have disappeared, along with all proof sheets, and the manuscript of the press copy contains only Volume I of the published work (Books I and II, and Chapters i-vi of Book III, with the Appendix to Volume I).

The editions vary little in length (there is a slight increase in bulk over the years, the 7th edition being eighty-three pages longer than the 1st), but a word by word collation of the Library editions reveals a huge number of variants: there are over 500 substantive variants between the MS and Volume I of the 1st edition; between the 1st and 7th editions there are nearly 3000: making about 3500 in all.[9]

Mill's successive prefaces call attention to the fact of revision, but except in the major instances, do not indicate where changes will be found, and rather disguise their extent. In each preface after the first, following six paragraphs of explanation found in all editions, a brief account of the current edition is given. As these accounts supplant one another, only one is found in each edition.

The Preface to the 2nd edition says, "The additions and alterations in the present edition are generally of little moment," except for those in the chapter on the "Socialist controversy" (II, i, "On Property"), but Mill lessens the apparent importance of the chapter and the changes by concluding: "A full appreciation of Socialism, and of the questions which it raises, can only be advantageously attempted in a separate work"—which he, of course, did not live to complete, the posthumous *Chapters on Socialism* being fragmentary.

[8] The People's edition sold at 7s., falling to 5s. after the first 4000. Mill resigned his usual one-half share of the net profit to lower the price, but Longmans insisted that he accept one-half profits after 10,000 copies were sold, as they were before he wrote his account in the *Autobiography* (195–96) in 1869–70.

[9] This count (like all subsequent ones, unless otherwise indicated) excludes typographical errors, variations in punctuation and spelling (including capitalization and hyphenation), alterations in the form of footnotes, and variants within quotations (which are considered separately). Perhaps no two people would agree as to the number of variants: I have counted (as many would not) changes which are entailed by other changes (e.g., changes in tense are counted each time they occur, rather than just once for a passage).

The 3rd edition's Preface, the longest, most detailed, and most important, is dignified by a separate heading. Here Mill calls attention to chapters "either materially added to or entirely recast," mentioning II, i ("On Property"), II, x ("Means of Abolishing Cottier Tenantry"),[10] III, xviii ("Of International Values"), and IV, vii ("On the Probable Futurity of the Labouring Classes"). An important paragraph in this Preface is devoted to each of II, i, and IV, vii.

In the 4th edition, the Preface says, as do all those from the 3rd through the 6th, that the text has been revised throughout; without detail, it mentions specially III, xii ("Influence of Credit on Prices") and III, xxiv ("On the Regulation of a Convertible Paper Currency"). The Preface to the 5th edition mentions no specific chapters. That to the 6th calls attention to III, xxiii ("Of the Rate of Interest"), and to the help given to the author by Professor J. E. Cairnes.[11] The People's edition, published in the same year as the 6th, announces in its Preface that, except for the translation of "all extracts and most phrases in foreign languages" into English, the removal of a small number of superfluous quotations or parts of quotations, and the cancelling of the Appendix to Volume I, it "is an exact transcript from the sixth." And finally, the 7th edition, Mill says in its Preface, "with the exception of a few verbal corrections, corresponds exactly" with the 6th and People's editions. (He also remarks that alterations in the accounts of the Wages Fund and the land laws of Ireland are deferred by him until more trustworthy facts are available.)

Only when Mill's text had been superseded by others, that is, when it became really a text in the *history* of political economy, was attention called to the presence and importance of revisions by Miriam A. Ellis, in "Variations in the Editions of J. S. Mill's Principles of Political Economy" (*Economic Journal*, XVI [June, 1906], 291-302). Miss Ellis was partly interested in assessing the validity of the posthumous 8th (1878) and 9th (1886)

[10] Except here, this chapter is called throughout all editions, "Means of Abolishing Cottier Tenancy." Here he also calls IV, vii simply "Futurity of the Labouring Classes," in an uncharacteristic burst of confidence.

[11] For Cairnes' part in the revisions for the 6th edition, see Appendix H [*Collected Works*, Vol. II].

editions,[12] but her main concerns were to discuss the importance of some of the differences between the 2nd and 3rd editions, to mention those changes in the 4th, 5th, 6th, and 7th to which Mill's prefaces refer, and to point out the confusion caused by the unindicated gap of years between different parts of the text. As she gives no clue to her method, it may be assumed that she worked, originally at least, from Mill's prefatory accounts. In any case, she calls attention to the chapters in which the most important changes occur, that is, those listed above in the account of Mill's prefaces.[13] In looking at these chapters, she mentions some sixty passages which were altered, of which forty-five were rewritten in the 3rd edition. Her "notes" are obviously not intended as a comprehensive account of the variants, or even as a detailed discussion of those she mentions; but actually her article had more effect than most do, for it led to W. J. Ashley's important one-volume edition (London: Longmans, Green, 1909).

Ashley's edition has been of great value, and has justifiably become *the* text for students of Mill. His introduction is illuminating and forceful, and his appendices, containing some of Mill's opinions, expressed elsewhere, on the Wages Fund and Socialism, and opinions of later economists on a variety of topics, are very useful to students. But Professor Ashley's greatest service was to indicate in footnotes Mill's revisions of the text.

He made no attempt to provide a fully collated text, but tried, he says in his Introduction (xxv), to give "indications" of "all the significant changes or additions," erring "rather in the direction of including than of excluding every apparent indication of change of opinion or even of mood." His editorial discretion was good, and considering the short time he took to prepare the edition, with the help only of Miss Ellis' notes, his comprehensiveness is surprising. The edition has, however, limitations, some of which will be suggested by the words *indication, significant,* and *apparent.*

As the present edition is intended to correct these limitations (without, it is hoped, revealing new ones), a few words in criti-

[12] She also points out that the edition (1891) edited by Sir John Lubbock is a bad reprint of the 2nd edition.

[13] She wrongly identifies III, xxiv ("On the Regulation of a Convertible Paper Currency") as III, xiii ("Of an Inconvertible Paper Currency").

cism are offered, without any intention of denigrating Ashley's work.

From the standpoint of the textual scholar, the text is faulty in that, while purporting to be that of the 7th edition, there is in fact a slight admixture of texts, especially of that of the People's edition, and there are a few unsupported readings. His treatment of punctuation will seem cavalier to the purist, and some erroneous readings in the 7th edition are preserved.

More serious is his indication of only some 16 per cent of the variant readings. While it is true that he calls attention to almost all of those which would be admitted to be of major importance by everyone, he does not pay heed to a large number which to many people are highly significant. There are also (inevitably?) some mistakes in wording and placing of variants and dates.

But the main fault, from the standpoint of the student of Mill, is that the text of the earlier editions, even in the most important places, cannot be reconstructed with acceptable accuracy. Constant reference to the earlier editions, which are seldom available, is necessary. The final judgment must be that Ashley's notes are most useful as guides *to* the places where most of the important variants will be found, but they are not adequate as guides *through* the variants. In this respect, as in others, the present edition is intended to be definitive. For this reason, all substantive variants (described below) are given in a form permitting of easy reconstruction.

The full extent of the revisions is revealed only by a full collation,[14] which yields the following results:

CHANGES INTRODUCED IN EACH EDITION

	Preliminary remarks	Book I	Book II	Book III	Book IV	Book V	Total
1848[15]	9	188	266	64			527
1849	4	46	104	42	38	53	287
1852	29	230	431	197	115	319	1321
1857	1	35	86	77	54	98	351
1862	11	76	151	82	38	116	474
1865	8	84	79	67	48	48	334
1871	0	18	47	47	25	41	178
Total	62	677	1164	576	318	675	3472

[14] For a brief account of the initial collating procedures, see my "Editing J. S. Mill's *Principles of Political Economy*," *University of Toronto Press Notes*, III (Sept., 1961).

[15] Changes between the MS and the 1st edition; that is, proof changes.

The table speaks for itself, but it should be noted that, as expected, by far the largest number of changes comes in the 3rd
edition;[16] it is surprising that (after the MS revisions for the 1st)
the 5th is third in total number, for Mill's preface would indicate
that it, like the 7th, was little altered. Again it was to be expected that Book II should contain most altered passages, but it
is surprising that Book V has such a large number of revisions,
for the prefaces do not mention it at all.[17] Such figures are of
little help, however, until the content of the changes is considered, but it can be seen that the book containing most economic analysis, Book III, is least altered, and that the heavy revision of Book II can be related to Mill's strong belief that the laws
of distribution are more amendable to human control than those
of production, and hence their description is more liable to
change.

A complete account of the changes is not here possible, and
opinions about them are certain to be varied, if not idiosyncratic.
Such opinions properly derive only from a careful study of the
collated text in the present volumes, but a few general remarks
may be useful preliminaries.

First, the changes in the manuscript: almost every folio contains cancellations and interlineations, with occasional inter-
polations of passages on the verso of the previous folio, all of
which indicate again the careful attention Mill paid to rewriting.
(It should be remembered, in view of the heavy revisions, that
this is undoubtedly not the first draft of the work.) Apart from
the cancellations (which are discussed in Appendix F), there are
many places where the manuscript version and the 1st edition
differ. In analyzing such variants, I separate them, in decreasing
order of importance, into the following categories (which are
also used in the subsequent discussion of alterations amongst
editions): (1) alterations in opinion or fact, including major
amplifications and corrections of information; (2) alterations
resulting from the time between writings, including changes

[16] Miss Ellis says (302), "the third edition forms the chief bulk of the
seventh," a misleading comment, because even with all the changes, by far
the "chief bulk" of the 7th is formed by the 1st.

[17] A more accurate indication, if still not the most meaningful one, is
seen when the length of the books is taken into account. The overall figure
of 2.5 variants per page is made up of Book I, 2.3; Book II, 3.2; Book III,
1.6; Book IV, 2.8; Book V, 3.0.

in statement of fact resulting from the passage of time and new publications; (3) alterations which qualify, emphasize, or give technical clarity; and (4) alterations which are purely verbal, or give semantic clarity, or result from changes in word usage.

In summary statement, it appears that more than one-half of the changes between the manuscript and the 1st edition[18] are of the fourth kind, and almost all the rest are of the third (some of them quite interesting), only a very few being of the first.[19] Two of these last may be mentioned: after the quotation from Babbage at I.111n, the MS has a passage praising in strong terms Dunoyer's *De la liberté du travail*; the greatest alteration is the deletion of a long paragraph from Thornton's *Over-Population and its Remedy* at II.997[a] (the whole passage was deleted in 1852).

A few of the lesser changes merit comment. In all his writings Mill limits reference to himself, but one kind of variant here shows his extreme sensitivity: at I.26[c−c], where the printed text reads "upper stone", the manuscript reads "upper millstone"; at I.28[m−m], "machine" is substituted for "windmill or watermill"; and in four other cases within five pages the possible pun is deleted. (It does, of course, appear in other places in the *Principles*.)[20] The peculiar reading of the first two editions, "approximatively" for "approximately" (II.483.11-2) is found in the manuscript. In only three cases did Mill revert to a manuscript reading which differs from that of the 1st edition where no error is involved, and in two of these he restores the manuscript reading only in 1862 (5th edition). It seems certain that he corrected the editions without reference to the earlier texts or the manu-

[18] The discussion of the changes in all editions is based on Book I, which contains typical examples of all kinds; examples from other books are used exceptionally and noted.

[19] No obvious examples of the second kind occur, because of the short time between the completions of this MS and the appearance of the volume. A general discussion of the third and fourth kinds is reserved for the moment, as those in the MS are not unusual, and the most interesting ones occur later.

[20] This peculiarity was first noted by Mr. John Willoughby, to whom I am much indebted.

script (the changes in punctuation discussed below support this conclusion). Of the four cases in which the 2nd edition, correcting errors in the 1st, returns to the MS reading, only one is of importance: at I.121^{e-e}, the correct "superior" replaces "inferior."

It would be reckless to attempt extensive inference from the changes in punctuation between the MS and the 1st edition, but some guesses may be made about them. Of 672 changes in Book I, 329 involve the addition of a comma (or two enclosing commas), and 212 the deletion of a comma (or two enclosing commas). The vast majority of these are possibly the result of printers' decisions and of the normal transition from MS to printed page in the nineteenth century, but more than a few must reflect Mill's dedication to precision. His attention to this sort of detail is surely seen in the return in the 2nd edition to the MS reading in thirty-seven places. Similarly, a large number of the 102 changes which suggest choice rather than printers' practice or misreading are likely Mill's, especially those which involve a full stop.[21]

Many other changes are probably caused by difficulties in reading Mill's hand, and by printing-house practice.[22] A final trivial example will indicate the amount of work that went into revision: in just over one hundred places in Books I-III, a hyphen was added in the 1st edition, almost always, I would think, by the printer (in only two cases is a hyphen removed). One conclusion is unquestionable: if most of these changes in punctuation and spelling were made by Mill, the printers had just cause for complaint—and vice versa.

Leaving the MS changes for those in the printed editions, I again choose Book I to illustrate the pattern:

[21] I recognize the germ of circularity: Mill's finickiness elsewhere suggests it here; his finickiness here supports the evidence for it elsewhere. Nonetheless, finick he did.

[22] Of the former, the most frequent, in this MS and elsewhere, are almost impossible decisions between "show" and "shew," "where" and "when," "everything" and "every thing." Of the latter, four likely cases may be mentioned: MS "premisses," 1st edition, "premises"; MS, "plowman," 1st edition, "ploughman"; MS, "MacCulloch," 1st edition, "M'Culloch"; MS, "potato," 1st edition, "potatoe" (this last not uniform, and the MS version restored later).

CHANGES IN BOOK I

	Opinion, fact, etc.	Time, etc.	Qualification, etc.	Verbal, etc.	Total
1849	3	5	10	28	46
1852	11	23	88	108	230
1857	2	5	11	17	35
1862	4	9	28	35	76
1865	7	11	42	24	84
1871	1	4	5	8	18
Total	28	57	184	220	489[23]

When this table is compared with the former one, it is seen that Book I is fairly typical of the work as a whole, although there are relatively fewer changes in the 1857 and 1871 editions, and relatively more (nearly twice as many) in the 1865 edition. But the main point the table makes is that almost half the changes could be called stylistic. These do not here claim attention, but I append a few samples in a note.[24]

The alterations caused by time are easily accounted for: most of them are simple changes of tense, or of adjectives of time (1.159 $^{p-p}$ reads "forty years"; in 1852 and 1857 it reads "thirty

[23] Of these, 52 are noted in Ashley's edition (14 in the first category, 16 in the second, 18 in the third, and 4 in the fourth); given his intention, it is my opinion that he should have noted all in the first two categories, and a much higher proportion of the third.

[24] The most trival examples are the substitution, almost always in the 2nd edition, of "though" for "although" (64 times). At I.25^{a-a} "culinary process" is substituted for "process of cookery" in 1862. At I.54^{a-a} "can only be a subject" is substituted for "is a subject only" in 1852. In 1862 "later" replaces "latter" at I.189^{t-t}; "later" is the right word, and one wonders why the other appeared, until one sees that a revision of this sentence between the MS and the 1st edition removed "(compared with the former)"; Mill evidently missed the word in his intervening revisions. Included in this same category are the few cases where punctuation makes a slight differences: e.g., I.181^{c-c}, where in 1865 "have, apparently at least," replaced "have apparently, at least," which replaced "have (apparently at least)" in 1862.

A few of these changes have some philological interest: at I.74^{b-b}, "manufactories" replaces "factories" in 1862—one would expect the reverse, as one would at I.282^{h-h}, where "leathern" replaces "leather" in 1849. The useful word "cotemporaries" replaces the more common "contemporaries" at I.189^{v-v} in 1849. At I.171^{h-h}, "middle-class" replaces "bourgeois" in 1865. Some of the changes point out the weakness of my classification; how should the substitution (I.183^{q-q}) in 1865 of "industrial classes" for "industrious classes" be described?

years"; in MS, 1848, and 1849, "sixteen years"). Slightly different are those like that at I.148^{k-k}, where "as until lately in Ireland" read "as hitherto in Ireland" in 1857, and "as in Ireland" in MS, 1848, 1849, and 1852. Such changes as the inclusion of the note to I.37 in 1849, quoting a review of the 1st edition, are not infrequent, and there are a few like that at I.65^{b-b}, where in 1862 the words "(now called Western Australia)" were added after "the Swan River settlement."

The changes which are most characteristic of Mill are those which I have described as alterations which qualify, emphasize, or give technical clarity. Professional interest and personal taste will determine one's attitude towards these, and they spread (whatever one's interests and tastes) from the territory of stylistics to that of factual interpretation. An extreme example of Mill's worry over apparently small matters is found in his revisions of the following sentence (I.42^{c-c}): "The stupidest hodman, who repeats from day to day the mechanical act of climbing a ladder, performs a function partly intellectual; so much so, indeed, that the most intelligent dog or elephant could not, probably, be taught to do it." In the MS, the sentence ends, "could not be taught to do it"; in 1848 and 1849, "probably could not be taught to do it"; in 1852 and 1857, "could not, perhaps, be taught to do it"; the final reading appeared in 1862. More typical is the introduction in 1852 of the qualifying "in some degree" at I.52^{o-o}, or the alteration on the next page, $^{g-g}$ and $^{h-h}$, of "no labour really tends to the enrichment of society, which . . ." to "no labour tends to the permanent enrichment of society, which . . ." in 1865. Small changes presumably in the interest of technical clarity may be illustrated by the substitution in 1857 of "productive reinvestment" for "productive employment" at I.57^{g-g}. An alteration in 1865 which would interest few (and which may even be accidental), but which I would argue reveals Mill's adherence to part of his father's training, is the reversing, in a persuasive context, of "stronger and clearer" to read "clearer and stronger" (I.59^{a-a}). Another change, and a typical one, appears to me indicative of his movement away from his father's modes of thought: at I.79^{e-e}, the final reading, "This theorem, that to purchase produce is not to employ labour . . . , replaced in 1852 the original, "This truth, that purchasing produce is not employing labour . . . ." The following case is, I suppose, a factual correction, but of a very minor kind: at

I.101^{b-b}, when Mill is listing agricultural products found as one moves to the south and east in Europe, the final reading of part of the list, "silk, figs, olives," appeared only in 1871, as a correction of "figs, olives, silk." Another kind of change could be the result of altered opinion or simply of a desire for precision: these are typified at I.109^{g-g} where in the sentence, "As soon as any idea of equality enters the mind of an uneducated English working man, his head is turned by it," the reading until 1865 was "ordinary English working man."[25]

The most important changes, those which I have described as alterations in opinion or fact, including major amplifications and corrections of information, occur mainly in the chapters mentioned by Mill in his prefaces, and should be studied in close detail. But the grossest changes can be briefly described. In II, i, the first major change occurs in §2 ("Statement of the Question") in the 2nd edition. The 1st edition here contained a short account of St. Simonism, which was deleted in the 2nd, and replaced by a longer and more favourable account of all kinds of socialism; this account remained throughout all editions (with minor changes). The long preceding sentence which argued that attacks on property will necessarily increase until laws of property are made just, was cut down in the 3rd edition to a clause of no special weight. In §3 ("Examination of Communism") only a few sentences from the 1st and 2nd editions correspond to those in later versions; parts of the section are roughly equivalent but in different order, and some parts of §6 in the edition of 1849 are here incorporated in later editions. The general tone in 1852 is more favourable to socialism, but the change is less dramatic than might be thought. In both early and late versions the emphasis is on liberty. An interesting change in 1849 is the deletion of one long and one short passage emphasizing the comparative advantages of a competitive economy. In 1852 the account of Fourierism which was added in 1849 as §5 was combined with the account of St. Simonism in §4, and a long introductory paragraph was added to point out more clearly the differences between St. Simonism and Fourierism on the one hand, and strict and theoretical Communism on the other. Also in 1852 Mill

[25] That this was less than a change of opinion is probable, for in 1852 the passage containing this sentence replaced the concluding part of a quotation from Escher, in which a contrary opinion is affirmed of the "educated English workmen."

deleted his recommendation of St. Simonism as a probable stimulant to social diversity. Finally, the concluding paragraph of §4 (the last section) in 1852 replaced the end of §5 in the version of 1849, and all of §6 in the versions of 1848 and 1849.

In II, x, the eight sections of 1848 and 1849 were reduced in 1852 to three, and in 1862 to two. In 1852, §1 is a rewriting of §§1–3 in the earlier versions; in 1862, §1 is a further rewriting of §§1–7 in the 1848 and 1849 versions (§§1–2 of 1852 and 1857); the final §2 (which was further rewritten in 1865) replaces §8 of 1848 and 1849 (§3 of 1852 and 1857). This final section contained in its early versions a long footnote which was incorporated in II, vii from 1862 on.

Book III contains many alterations in sections, mostly additions to the early text. In III, xii, for example, §7 ("Are bank notes money?") was added in 1857. In III, xviii, §6 ("The preceding theory not complete"), §7 ("International values depend not solely on the quantities demanded, but also on the means of production available in each country for the supply of foreign markets"), and §8 ("The practical result little affected by this additional element") were added in 1852. In III, xxiii, most of §4 ("The rate of interest, how far, and in what sense connected with the value of money") was rewritten in 1865; it was formerly entitled: "The rate of interest not really connected with the value of money, but often confounded with it." The other chapter in Book III to which Mill calls attention, xxiv, was not altered in its sections, the rewriting being mostly of paragraphs in §§3, 4, and 6 (most of which took place in 1857, as Mill indicates, but §3 was as much altered again in 1865).

Finally, in Book IV, Chapter vii, the main changes are in the final sections: §5 ("Examples of the association of labourers with capitalists"), §6 ("Examples of the association of labourers among themselves"), and §7 ("Competition not pernicious, but useful and indispensable"); these replaced in 1852 §5 ("Examples of the association of the labourers in the profits of industrial undertakings") and §6 ("Probable future developement of this principle").

Other gross changes, involving new or greatly altered sections, but not mentioned by Mill in his prefaces, are in II, vi (§6 added in 1849), II, xv (§5 added in 1857), and III, xiii (§4 added in 1849 and deleted in 1862).

A few remarks should be made about changes in spelling and

punctuation. The changes in spelling seem to indicate indecision rather than careless proofreading. Such changes as "recognise" (7th edition) for "recognize" occur in the 3rd, 5th, and 6th editions, the earlier form remaining in isolated places until these editions. The earlier "shews," "shewed," etc., are altered in the 2nd, 3rd, 4th, and 5th editions. And "artisan(s)" is replaced by "artizan(s)" sixteen times, with the reverse change occurring once in the 2nd edition. The only other frequent change is the substitution of initial "e" for initial "i" in such words as "enclosure" and "encumbrance," and the reverse change in such words as "inquiry" and "insure" (fifty-five words in all are altered). There is also (especially in the later editions) an increase in initial capitalization and in hyphenation. A common change, especially in the 6th edition, is from the simple adjectival or singular possessive forms to the plural possessive in such words as "days'."

Concerning punctuation little need be said, and again little can be inferred, because the printers may be responsible for most of the changes. There is an increase in the number of commas (especially in the 2nd edition) until the 5th, and a decrease in the last two editions (which were published, it will be recalled, by Longmans rather than Parker). There is a tendency throughout to substitute semi-colons for colons and (less frequently) for commas. After the first two editions, the one showing most revision is the 5th; and the 7th, apart from a few comma changes, is almost free from alteration.

About one hundred sources are quoted by Mill, some of them at considerable length. The notes to these quotations are typical of nineteenth-century practice, in being often too slender for accurate identification, and not infrequently wrong in page reference. The quotations themselves are fairly accurate by nineteenth-century standards; that is, there is considerable variation in punctuation and paragraphing, occasional words are wrongly transcribed, passages are sometimes summarized or rearranged within quotation marks, and words and sentences and even paragraphs are omitted without indication. (See Appendix I) A few of the word errors show once more the printers' difficulty in reading Mill's hand; in other cases the printer has simply made an error not justified by such difficulty; in others the error is Mill's.[26] Summary and rearrangement within quotation marks,

[26] Examples of the first kind: I.263.19, "heavy" should read "hung"; I.264*f−1*, "when" should read "where"—in both cases, in my opinion, the

without indication, which are not common, are both found in one passage, I.168.13–4, where the interpolation "(who seems . . . all classes,)" is a summary of the note which occurs a page further on in the original (John Rae, *Statement of Some New Principles . . . of Political Economy*).

Omission of words, sentences, and notes is quite common, and longer omissions are not rare. For example, at I.382.19–20, after "employment," he omits two of Adam Smith's paragraphs, and at II.780.n2–3, he omits one of Cherbuliez's. These omissions suggest again carelessness and also a desire for brevity, rather than suppression or distortion.[27] Some but by no means all of the longer omissions actually are indicated in the MS by two or more dots which the printer ignored (e.g., I.129[i], where six sentences are omitted). But occasionally an omission, or the point at which a quotation ends, suggests that bias is involved. For example, his attitude towards religion is surely evident when, in quoting (II.770) from Samuel Laing, Mill ends the praise of the Cornish miners with the word "miners," whereas the original, after a semi-colon and quotation marks, continues:

and finally, they are, as a class, "religious people, leading habitually excellent and religious lives, and giving conclusive evidence of the real influence of the great doctrines of revelation on their hearts, by their equanimity under suffering and privation, and in calmness and resignation when death is known to be inevitable." This is, by many degrees, the brightest picture we have ever met with of the condition of any considerable portion of the labouring class in England at the present day.

To this, Laing appends a note (which, of course, is also omitted by Mill), beginning: "The reasons assigned for the high moral standard among a large proportion of the Cornish Miners are 'the ministration of the Church of England, exercised by an able

---

MS gives the correct reading, but certainly in the second case the other is possible. An example of the second kind: I.263[b–b], "among" should read "amongst". An example of the third kind: I.257.6, "two, or three" is an incorrect transcription of "two and four".

[27] In quoting from his own *Essays on Some Unsettled Questions of Political Economy*, he—or the printer, as the MS is not known—three times, at II.633.n14, II.634.n6, and II.851.15, omits a sentence; in each case the omited sentence ends with the same word as the previous sentence, an easily explained confusion.

and excellent body of clergy, and the persevering zeal of the Wesleyan methodists. . . .'"[28]

The omission of one long note by Mill is as indicative of his tastes (and his sense of relevance) as the note is of its author's: in quoting the passage from de Quincey's *Logic of Political Economy* about musical snuffboxes (II.463), Mill omits a long note concerning de Quincey's personal acquaintance with snuffboxes and their owners.[29]

One final matter merits mention: the text of the People's edition, which has some peculiarities.[30] Its Preface, after the paragraphs common to all the prefaces, reads:

> The present edition is an exact transcript from the sixth, except that all extracts and most phrases in foreign languages have been translated into English, and a very small number of quotations, or parts of quotations, which appeared superfluous, have been struck out. A reprint of an old controversy with the "Quarterly Review" on the condition of landed property in France, which had been subjoined as an Appendix, has been dispensed with.

As indicated in the discussion of Ashley's edition, this description is partly accurate: the People's edition does translate passages from foreign languages (usually including book titles), and omits the Appendix to Volume I. A few, but only a few, quotations or parts of quotations are deleted (e.g., I.123n—People's, 76n—where only the identification of the source remains). Many titles are italicized, as they are not in the Library editions, and the English equivalents of French measures are usually given in square brackets following the French (Ashley adopts this practice). The foreign phrases and tags in the text are occasionally translated, but Mill is erratic.[31] The main point of interest, how-

[28] In these quotations I omit two referential footnotes. Laing is quoting from the *Appendix to the Report of the Children's Employment Commission in Mines and Collieries*.

[29] It might also be noted that occasionally in the Library editions Mill translates from the French without indication (in one of these cases, I.285n, the MS note says "Translated from the").

[30] The following remarks are based on partial comparison, not on complete collation.

[31] For example, "*cœteris paribus*" is rendered at I.148.31 as "other things being the same" (People's, 93), and at II. 807.6 as "on the average" (People's, 484), but elsewhere is not translated. Similarly, *inter vivos*" (II.811.26) rendered as "during life" (People's, 487), is not translated at II.895.15 (People's, 541).

ever, is that—admitting the exceptions—the description of the text as "an exact transcript from the sixth" edition is not accurate. A paragraph added (1.9^{w-w}) in 1865 is, as Miss Ellis notes, interchanged with the following one (People's, 5–6), and in three of the four other places where the paragraphing differs from that in the 6th edition, the relevant passage was added in or rewritten for the 6th edition. In two other cases, the paragraphing of Mill's translations in the People's edition differs from that of his rendering of the original in the Library editions. These differences suggest that others exist, and a check of those places in Book I where the 5th and 6th editions differ shows that the People's edition follows the 5th rather than the 6th in fourteen of eighty-four cases.[32] The destruction of Longmans' records during the London Blitz makes explanation uncertain, but it is clear at least that the People's edition is properly seen as intermediate between the 5th and 6th rather than as an altered version of the 6th. Certainly the People's and the 6th editions cannot have used the same proof.

It can safely be concluded, from all the evidence above, that second versions were second nature to Mill. He could not, of course, remember the vast number of minor changes which he made as successive editions passed through his hands. New knowledge and new opponents led to important changes (though not so many as in his *Logic*), as did a few second and third thoughts; and these will provide the main interest in the collated text. But the rewriting as a whole should be seen as rhetorical—and that, of course, not in a pejorative sense. Isolation of analytical, descriptive, and normative approaches in social science is possible, and the twentieth century has seen a plethora of works in which persuasion towards a "better" point of view is expressly excluded, although often the exclusion is specious or founded on a naive attitude towards structural analysis and statistics. But Mill in his Preface states his determination to go beyond the "theory of the subject" and "abstract speculation"

[32] Two cases might be mentioned: at 1.49^{c-c}, the reading is, "as most conducive to the ends of classification; and I am still of that opinion." In 1862 the reading was, "as the most conducive to the ends of classification, though not strictly conformable to the customs of language." The People's edition follows the 5th in retaining "the" after "as", but follows the 6th in the clause following "classification". And at I.195.4, the People's edition follows the 6th in rejecting one sentence and its footnote (a reference to another part of the *Principles*,) but incorporates the footnote of the 6th in its text.

in order to challenge and indeed surpass Adam Smith on his own grounds, by associating the applications of the theory with the principles. And his reference to the "improved ideas of the present age" and "the best social ideas of the present time" surely suggests that he hopes his book will be "better" than Adam Smith's not simply in an economic way. In fact, his determination to subordinate such special sciences as economics to sociology, and further to subordinate sociology to ethics, makes it impossible for him to keep theoretical, actual, and ideal models separate, and while he aims at honesty (a more valid goal than objectivity) in his account of economic phenomena, he is deeply concerned with the furthering of social justice. His attempt to be honest prevents him, for the most part, from ignoring facts and tendencies which he dislikes, but not from presenting those which he likes in the most persuasive form.

His dedication of the *Principles* to Harriet Taylor (quoted in full in Appendix G) again indicates, both in tone and implication, his purpose. He praises her for her ability "to originate" and "to appreciate speculations on social improvement," and says the *Principles* is an "attempt to explain and diffuse ideas many of which were first learned from herself. . . ." The implications here[33] are made explicit in the Preface, where Mill states that his intention has been to write a "practical" and "popular" work, without sacrificing "strict scientific reasoning." The *Principles of Political Economy* is not simply a textbook; it is also a measured polemic. As such, it was open to endless revision, always in the direction of clarity and effective persuasion, and also in response to the changing climate of opinion. The successive revisions show this, as they show in their relative density in certain parts of the work just what Mill felt most deeply about. The cumulative effects of nearly 3500 changes over a period of twenty-four years cannot be precisely assessed, but the *Principles* was, in its final form, undeniably a more satisfactory work. He would not, and I cannot, consider that the revisions were wasted effort.

II. THE PRESENT TEXT

There will always be arguments about the "best" text of any work, centering on two main issues: which text represents the

---

[33] Cf. Dean Bladen's argument in the first two sections of his Introduction [*Collected Works*, Vol. II].

author at his best; and which most accurately reproduces what the author wrote. When a book has gone through as many authorial revisions as the *Principles* has, a consensus of opinion on the first of these issues is hard to achieve. For the reasons stated above and below, and because Mill was not senile when the 7th edition was prepared, I believe it shows him at his best.

With the intention of producing texts which most closely approximate accuracy, literary scholars now, following the lead of Sir Walter Greg and Professor Fredson Bowers, commonly use as a basic text the manuscript or (if it is not known, or in conjunction with it) the earliest edition known to have been supervised by the author. The virtues of this approach need not be presented here, but it should be made clear why it has not been adopted. The method was devised to deal with Elizabethan and other early texts in which, because of printing-house and publishing practices, there is demonstrable evidence of corruption. Seldom did an author see his work through the press for edition after edition, and reprinting almost always took the text further away from the author's intention.

A different approach is valid for nineteenth-century works such as the *Principles*. Each edition was revised by Mill himself, who read and altered the proofs carefully; there is no question of substantial corruption in the editions published during his lifetime. The manuscript and 1st edition have validity primarily as a starting point, as an indication of the state of economic thought in 1848, and of Mill's knowledge of, and attitude towards, economic phenomena and theory at that time. There can surely be few who believe in plenary economic inspiration. Each successive edition reveals more information, as well as changed attitudes, and therefore, considered primarily as a textbook of economics, the 7th edition best represents Mill's considered judgment, and is, because of the constant re-readings, more reliable than any previous edition. For him, and for the student of political economy from 1871 to the present, this is the best text, and it has been adopted in this edition.

The *Principles*, however, must now appear in a light different from that of the years immediately following its publication. Both in evidence and analysis, the science of economics has advanced beyond Mill, and its primacy as a textbook cannot be asserted, although, as Dean Bladen argues in his Introduction, its value purely as an economic text has been under-exploited.

Its importance in other areas, however, has steadily increased. It served as an economic text to several generations of policy framers and law makers, even into the twentieth century, and its influence on them must be recognized. If one is to study the effect of political and economic thought on events, the changes in such thought are of obvious importance. Each edition of the *Principles* takes on separate value then, as do the changes from edition to edition. Similarly, the way in which events alter theory is shown by a comparison of the various editions. One might examine, for example, the changes in Mill's expressed opinions about socialism after the French Revolution of 1848, or the effect of Irish experience on his views concerning land tenure. Again, any study in the history of economic and social ideas can benefit from a close study of the changing attitudes revealed by a comparison of the various editions. Here one might look at Mill's remarks on slavery in the years before and during the American Civil War. And most obviously, the development of Mill's own thought is demonstrated by such a comparison. For example, his increased attention to co-operative experiments is evident in the revisions of IV, vii.

We have, therefore, while accepting the 7th edition as the best in both senses, incorporated the textual changes found in a complete collation of the seven Library editions of the *Principles*. Of all editorial practices, the recording of variants is most obviously a matter of diminishing returns. Furthermore, the returns, defying all quantification, do not accrue to one person or group, and are certainly not monetary. There is no clear distinction between the significant and the insignificant, between stylistic orchestration and mere fiddling. Given the exigencies of printing and the frailty of editors, which make it impossible to record all changes, and the justifiable impatience of readers who cannot follow the text through jungles of textual apparatus, some compromise is necessary. The one adopted for this edition is intended to meet the needs of all potential readers and does not represent a licentious acceptance of particular views (including those of the editors).

In simple statement, the following pages contain all substantive variants amongst the various editions. "Substantive" here means all changes of text except spelling, capitalization, hyphenation, punctuation, demonstrable typographical errors, such necessary alterations as changed footnote references to the *Principles* itself, and such printing-house concerns as type size, etc. (There are two exceptions—to prove the rule—Mill's frequent changes between "though" and "although" and between "on" and "upon" are not recorded.)

A glance at any of the heavily revised pages in this edition will reveal the difficulties involved in providing variant readings without at the same time making the text difficult if not impossible to follow. The method adopted, after considerable trial, has these objectives: a text as little interrupted by editorial apparatus as possible; variant readings which allow reconstruction of the earlier texts without separate instructions for each variant; the minimum number of levels of text on each page consistent with accuracy and with the above objectives. The method is, I believe, harder to describe than to apply, and I beg the reader's indulgence in the following account.

On a typical page, there will be three levels of text: the text of the 7th edition; in slightly smaller type, Mill's own notes; in smaller type again, notes containing the variant readings. In the text itself, the usual indicators (*, †, etc.) call attention to Mill's notes, while small italic superscript letters, in alphabetical sequence (beginning anew in each section) call attention to variant readings. These variants are of three kinds: addition of a word or words, substitution of a word or words, deletion of a word or words. Examples to illustrate these three kinds will be drawn from the "Preliminary Remarks."

Addition of a word or words: see I.7^{p-p}. In the text, the word "power" appears as "^{p}power^{p}"; the variant note reads "$^{p-p}+65$, 71". Here the plus sign indicates that the word "power" was added; the following numbers (65, 71) indicate the editions in which it appears. The editions are always indicated by the last two numbers of the year of publication, as follows: 48 = 1848 (1st edition), 49 = 1849 (2nd edition), 52 = 1852 (3rd edition), 57 = 1857 (4th edition), 62 = 1862 (5th edition), 65 = 1865 (6th edition), 71 = 1871 (7th edition). The manuscript is indicated by MS. (This indicator does not appear in variants after Book III, Chapter vi, where the manuscript ends.) If the variant occurs within a quotation, and the earlier version (i.e., that in the variant note) is the reading of the source from which Mill is quoting, the word "Source" precedes the manuscript and edition indicators in the variant note. If the reading in the text, as opposed to that in the variant note, is the same as that of the source, no indicator is needed. If the text varies from the source, but not amongst editions, there is no variant note; the variant will, however, appear in Appendix I.

Placing the example above ($I.7^{p-p}$) in context, then, the interpretation is that from the manuscript through the 5th edition, the reading is "grinding by water instead of by hand"; in the 6th edition (65) this is altered to "grinding by water power instead of by hand," and the reading of the 6th edition is retained (as is clear in the text) in the 7th edition (71).

Before going on to the second kind of variant, it should be noted that in all cases, any added editorial information, except "Source," "MS," the edition indicators, and page references, is in italics. Also, in the case of long added or substituted passages, the second enclosing superscript may be found on the next page, or even several pages, after the first; when necessary, the superscript notation in the footnote will give the page number on which the variant passage concludes (see, e.g., $I.8^{l-184}$).

Substitution of a word or words: see $I.5^{e-e}$. In the text the word "promoting" appears as "^{e}promoting^{e}"; the variant note reads "$^{e-e}$MS, 48, 49, 52, 57, 62 favouring". Here the word following the edition indicators is that for which "promoting" was substituted; again applying the same rules and putting the variant in context, the interpretation is that from the manuscript through the 5th edition the reading is "concurred in favouring it"; in the 6th edition this was altered to "concurred in promoting it," and the reading of the 6th edition was retained (as is clear in the text) in the 7th edition.

Deletion of a word or words: see $I.5^{f}$. In the text, a *single* superscript ^{f} appears *centered* between "absurdity" and "seemed"; the variant note reads "^{f}MS, 48, 49 must have." Here the words following the edition indicators are those deleted; applying the same rules and putting the variant in context, the interpretation is that the manuscript (MS), 1st edition (48), and 2nd edition (49) read "absurdity must have seemed"; the words "must have" were deleted in the 3rd edition and the reading of the 3rd edition was retained through all subsequent editions.

Variants within variants: see $I.10^{a-a}$. Often, of course, Mill altered a passage more than once. In this case the text reads "^{a}among most savages^{a}"; the variant note reads "$^{a-a}$MS even in the most savage state] 48, 49 in most savage states". The different readings are given in chronological order, with a square bracket separating them, and the interpretation is that in the manuscript the reading is "exists even in the most savage state"; in the 1st and 2nd editions the reading is "exists in most savage states"; and the final reading is found in all editions from the 3rd through the 7th. In longer variants of this sort, it seems unnecessary to repeat the whole passage, and so such variant notes as those at I.7^{n-n} and I.21^{m-m} appear. In the first of these the note reads "$^{n-n}$MS want, answers no purpose whatsoever:] 48, 49 *as* MS . . . purpose:"—the interpretation is that the 1st and 2nd editions have the same reading as the manuscript up to and including the word "purpose" and end in the same way (i.e., with a colon); in other words, "whatsoever" is found in the manuscript but not in the 1st and 2nd editions. At I.21^{m-m} the variant note reads "$^{m-m}$MS determined by laws as rigid, & as independent of human control, as those of Production itself] 48, 49 *as* MS . . . rigid as those . . . *as* MS"—the interpretation is, similarly, that the passage ", & as independent of human control," which appears in the manuscript, is not in the 1st and 2nd editions.

Variants in Mill's footnotes. To avoid four levels of text on the page, a different method has been used to indicate changes in the notes supplied by Mill. An example will be seen at I.37^n, where the footnote reads in part ". . . According to these definitions [49 this distinction], the . . . ." Here a simple substitution of "these definitions" for "this distinction" took place in the 3rd edition. Often, to allow for accurate placing of the variant, the words before and/or after the altered passage are given (see the other variants in the same note).

Dates of footnotes. Here the practice (borrowed from Ashley's edition, but applied more rigorously) is to place immediately after the footnote indicator, in square brackets, the figure indicating the edition in which the note first appeared. In the last cited example, for instance, the beginning of the note reads "*[49] The . . .", indicating that the note was added in the 2nd edition. If no such figure appears, the note is in the first version (manuscript or 1st edition) and in all subsequent editions. If a note was deleted, it will appear in the variant notes at the bottom of the page, with suitable indication (see, for example, I.27^b). If a note was lengthened in a subsequent edition, the appropriate date is given, again in square brackets, before the added passage (see, for example, I.174n, where the original MS note was added to in the 1st edition).

Punctuation and spelling. In general, changes in punctuation and spelling (including capitalization and hyphenation) are ignored. Those changes which occur as part of a substantive variant are included in that variant, and the superscript letters in the text are placed exactly with reference to punctuation. Changes *within* variants are ignored, however, so that if a reference is, say, to MS, 48, 49 the punctuation and spelling derive from the 2nd edition, the last cited. In a few cases changes in capitalization and punctuation (especially terminal punctuation) reveal at least a change in emphasis, and these are noted as normal variants. Changes from or to italic type are noted.

Prefaces. After the Preface to the 1st edition, the additional prefatory passages have been added in chronological order (as in Ashley's edition).

Other textual liberties. The typographical errors in the 7th edition have been silently corrected.[34] Mill's section titles in the Table of Contents have been introduced, in square brackets and italics, after each section number. (The wording has been slightly altered in a few cases for the sake of brevity and clarity.) The volumes are divided between Books II and III, instead of between Chapters vi and vii of Book III, and the Appendix to Volume I has been moved to the end of Book II, to which it has

---

[34]Typographical errors in earlier editions are ignored. It should be noted that no correction has been made in such matters as French accents unless there is authority in the earlier editions or the MS. The errors which have been corrected are (with the reading of the 7th edition first, followed by the corrected reading in square brackets):

VOLUME I

43.13 individnal [individual]	307.n14 epoux [époux]
146.n5 côte [côté]	308.21 pour [par]
147.n1 recemment [récemment]	308.25 diner [dîner]
157.35 concientious [conscientious]	378.5 he [be]
165.31 St [St.]	445.19 opuleut [opulent]
284.11 , [.]	446.n10 , fr.; et [fr.; et]
387.2 farmers' [farmer's]	447.n2 corréspond [correspond]
300.n14 opére [opère]	449.35 farms [farms.]
301.34 : [:"]	

VOLUME II

461.4 often [oftener]	777.6 resterènt [restèrent]
475.2 people [people;]	777.22 plias [plais]
540.32 obstruction [obstructions]	781.n28 *total omitted* [66,752]
543.4 latter [later]	794.n10 order. [order."]
640.17 due, [due;]	866.25 dlrect [direct]
660.7 alterations [alternations]	944.24 Unhapily [Unhappily]

reference. Mill occasionally uses square brackets in his footnotes; these have been altered to round brackets to avoid confusion with editorial information. Mill's footnotes referring to sources have been completed and corrected, with all added information being placed in square brackets. Also in Mill's footnotes, the page references to other parts of the *Principles* have been altered to apply to the present edition. A few alterations in printing style have been made: for example, small capitals for proper names have been replaced by lower case in a few places; the form of tables has been altered; and periods have been removed after section titles. The running heads and the style of chapter headings, etc., have been altered when necessary or desirable.

III. APPENDICES

Appendices A to D. Further to avoid difficulty in reading and reconstruction, those sections most heavily revised by Mill have been printed separately as appendices. *Appendix A* contains Book II, Chapter i, §§3–6 in the 2nd edition, with variant notes giving the readings of the manuscript and 1st edition. *Appendix B* contains Book II, Chapter x, §§1–7 in the 2nd edition, again with variants from the manuscript and 1st edition. *Appendix C* contains (from the same heavily revised chapter) Book II, Chapter x, §3 in the 4th edition, with variants from the manuscript, 1st, 2nd, and 3rd editions. *Appendix D* contains Book IV, Chapter vii, §§5–6 in the 2nd edition, with variants from the 1st edition. For all these passages, then, the text itself (as is indicated at the appropriate places) does not indicate variants from editions earlier than that reproduced in the appendices; that is, variants in Book II, Chapter i, §3, for example, will be found in the text proper only for the 3rd and later editions—the earlier variants will be found only in Appendix A. To facilitate comparison of the appendices with the text, square brackets have been placed around those passages which are retained into the 7th edition, with referential notes. Again, the rule is more complicated than its application, and it will easily be seen that to include these long and complicated variants in the notes would make normal reading impossible.

Appendix E. In an appendix to Volume II of the 4th edition, Mill included information he had lately gathered from Villiaumé, which he incorporated into Book IV, Chapter vii in the 5th and subsequent editions. This appendix is reproduced in its original form, with square brackets in the text indicating those passages which were later used in IV, vii.

Appendix F. In this appendix the press-copy manuscript of the *Principles* is described and discussed, and examples of cancelled readings are given.

Appendix G. Little is known about the specific role played by Harriet Taylor in the writing and revision of the *Principles*, but the epistolary evidence (mostly quoted by Professor Hayek in his *John Stuart Mill and Harriet Taylor*) is best understood in close conjunction with the text, and so has been here included.

Appendix H. In the Preface to the 6th edition, as mentioned above, Mill pays warm tribute to John E. Cairnes for his helpful suggestions concerning revision. The extent of his debt is revealed only when one sees the lengthy and detailed letters and notes which Cairnes sent to Mill late in 1864 and early in 1865, when the revision for the 6th edition was taking place. The relevant parts of their correspondence and of Cairnes' notes are reproduced, with added references indicating which passages were being criticized, and which were altered as a result of the criticism.

Appendix I. One's admiration for the speed with which Mill wrote the *Principles* is perhaps slightly lessened when one becomes aware of the extent of his quotations. A list of the sources from which he drew material or opinions is in itself a guide to nineteenth-century economic literature, and this appendix was devised to provide such a list. At the same time, the slight disservice which the inaccuracy of the quotations does to their sources and to readers is compensated by the inclusion of substantive variants between the sources and the *Principles*. Because this appendix includes all references to authors and books, it is in effect also an index of names and titles, which are therefore omitted in the Index proper.

Index. As will be seen by reference to II.1090–1 below, Cairnes' need rather than Mill's scepticism has been recognized in the provision of an index of topics, which has been prepared by Julian Patrick.

XIII

MATTHEW J. BRUCCOLI

Concealed Printings in Hawthorne

The following work-in-progress report from the Centenary Edition of the Works of Nathaniel Hawthorne is published in the hope that it will uncover still more concealed printings in Hawthorne. The editors of the Centenary Hawthorne will be grateful for communications on this subject.[1]

The differentiating of concealed printings which have resulted from the reimpression of stereotype or electrotype plates is a wide-open subject. Much of the work that has already been done has been performed by point-hunters, and these investigators have frequently been satisfied with flimsy evidence, such as binding variants or nonintegral bound-in advertisements. But the binding or inserted advertisements of a book have no relation to the printing of the sheets, and cannot be used to establish textual priority.[2] Many old-line bookmen have shown an abhorrence for the Hinman Collating Machine, but with it the job of comparing a suspected late printing with a suspected early printing can be done with great accuracy and comparative speed.

Although the researcher engaged in work on concealed printings runs the risk of becoming involved in a kind of bibliographical solitaire—that is, he may find himself playing a game in which there are no textual stakes—unsuspected (or, at least, undifferentiated) printings abound in nineteenth-century American literature; and there is always the possibility that significant emenda-

Reprinted with revisions from the *Papers of the Bibliographical Society of America*, vol. LVII (1963) by permission of the author and the Council for the Bibliographical Society of America.

[1] A slightly different version of this paper was read before General Topics 8: Bibliographical Evidence, at the December 1962 meeting of the Modern Language Association of America.

[2] For the record: on the spine of *The House of the Seven Gables* some copies have a straight ampersand and a large *O* in *Ticknor & Co.*; others have a crooked ampersand and a small *o*. On the spine of *The Blithedale Romance* some copies have a large *O* in *CO.*; others have a small *o*.

tions are hidden in the plates of a work. In bibliography you never know what you are going to find until you find it.

As has been mentioned, the best way to attack concealed printings is by collating multiple copies on the Hinman Machine for textual variants or resettings. Since plate alteration normally occurs between printings, it is a good working rule that evidence of plate alteration is evidence of reimpression. The Hinman Machine will also reveal type batter, but batter—if it really is batter and not bad impression or bad inking—may occur in press as well as in storage and can only be used to distinguish late copies from earlier copies. Another method for identifying printings is gutter measurement. Since the two facing pages where a book is sewn had to be adjacent in the imposition of the plates on the press, any significant variation in the width of a given gutter in two copies may be taken as evidence of reimposition. Allowing for paper shrinkage, a significant difference would be three or more centimeters.

Since Nathaniel Hawthorne is a major figure in our literature, *The House of the Seven Gables* (1851), *The Blithedale Romance* (1852), and *The Marble Faun* (1860)—all printed in first editions from stereotype plates—will serve as examples of jobs worth doing. *The Scarlet Letter* (1850) was not plated until its third edition, but there are unrecorded states of the first two editions from type, which are discussed by Fredson Bowers in the Centenary Hawthorne edition of *The Scarlet Letter*. Loosely speaking, up to now a "first edition" or even a "first printing" of *Seven Gables*, *Blithedale*, or the *Faun* has been an edition bearing the year of first publication on its title-page—although some firsts have been considered "firster" than others on the basis of dated advertisements or gilt stamping. However, *The Cost Books of Ticknor and Fields* reveal that there were four printings of *Seven Gables* in 1851, two printings of *Blithedale* in 1852, and seven printings of the *Faun* in 1860.[3]

Machine collation reveals no textual variants in the 1851 *Seven Gables*, but there are three resettings which mark four printings:

	A	B	C	D
57.32-34				reset
58			reset	
149.1-3		reset		

[3] *The Cost Books of Ticknor and Fields,* ed. Warren S. Tryon and William Charvat (New York, 1949).

In the earliest form of the plates the first three lines of page 149 are battered on the right-hand margin, and the batter almost certainly occurred before printing. This area is reset in the second printing; in this printing the final letters on 149.1–3 are slightly out of line.[4] In the third printing page 58 is completely reset: the clearest difference is that in the earlier printings the question mark in line 17 is to the left of the *y* in *lady*, but in the reset page the question mark is directly beneath the *y*. The resetting of the last three lines on page 57 in the fourth printing can be readily detected on the machine; the eye may be able to tell that in line 33 of the original setting the *c* in *child* is slightly to the right of the *f* in *for*, but in the resetting the *c* is directly beneath the *f*. This division into four printings is supported by gutter measurements. The *Cost Books* also list an 1852 reprint of *Seven Gables*. Since no copy with this date has been found, it is almost certain that the 1852 reprint is hidden among the 1851 copies; and this fifth printing can be isolated by gutter measurement:

	D (1851)	E (1852)
120/121	3.3 cm.	3.8 cm.
216/217	3.3 cm.	3.7 cm.

There are two textual changes resulting from type damage in *Seven Gables*. During the second printing *apparent* becomes *apparen* (50.25) and *or* becomes *o* (278.25). There are states of the type for the second printing with *apparent/or*, *apparen/or*, and *apparen/o*. In 1865 the *o* was incorrectly emended to *of*.

An intriguing possibility for further work on *Seven Gables* is suggested by the *Cost Books* entries showing that the first printing was imposed in 22 formes and that the next four printings were imposed in eleven formes. Applying a technique developed by Oliver Steele,[5] it should be possible to reconstruct the impo-

---

[4] No copy of the first printing of *Seven Gables* with perfect type at 149.1–3 is known to me. Copies with the reset lines are from the second printing or later. Since this batter occurred before machining of the plates, copies with the broken type at 149.1–3 precede copies with the reset lines.

The private collection of C. E. Frazer Clark, Jr., includes a copy of the 1853 sixth printing with an 1851 title page—see my note, "A Sophisticated Copy of *The House of the Seven Gables*," PBSA, LIX (1965), 438–39.

[5] See *The Library*, 5th Series, XVII (Sept., 1962). I am grateful to Prof. Steele for further information which he has communicated to me.

sition of a copy of *Seven Gables* from the pattern of its rough and smooth edges—but all fifteen copies I have examined are trimmed. Imposition of inner and outer formes of 32 pages each, producing four different 16-page gatherings, would result in rough side edges on leaves 2, 3, 5–8 of each gathering, and rough bottom edges on leaves 3–6. Imposition of inner and outer formes of 16 pages each, producing two different 16-page gatherings, would result in rough side edges on leaves 5–8, and rough bottom edges on leaves 3–6. Imposition of one 16-page forme printed work-and-turn, producing two copies of the same 16-page gathering, would result in rough side edges on leaves 1–4, and rough bottom edges on leaves 1–8.

There are no resettings in the 1852 *Blithedale*—and I am morally certain of this because I have machined C. Waller Barrett's (University of Virginia) proof copy against an 1855 reprint. Neither are there significant gutter variations, so it has been impossible to differentiate the two printings listed in the *Cost Books*. But there is a neat pattern of progressive type batter that shows five states of the plates:

	A	B	C	D	E
vi.14			x	x	x
16.15					x
57.26				x	x
69.6					x
97 r.t.			x	x	x
97.1			x	x	x
108.28		x	x	x	x
229.2			x	x	x

Thus far the textual pickings have been lean; but with *The Marble Faun* we hit pay dirt, for there are 43 unrecorded textual variants in the 1860 printings of this romance.

As first issued in March 1860 the ending of the *Faun* baffled its readers, and a 5-page "Conclusion" subscribed "LEAMINGTON, March 14, 1860." was added to a later printing in that year. This conclusion has been made the distinction between the "first edition" and the "second edition" and has discouraged closer scrutiny of the book. The *Cost Books* show that the problem is considerably more complicated than has been thought: three printings were on sale during the first week of publication (all three may, in fact, have been pre-publication printings), and four more printings were required later in the year. In addition, there were two printings in 1864 and one in 1865, all three of which may have carried the 1860 date on their title-pages. Although the *Cost Books* usually manifest puritanical thrift in their attention to small charges, they unaccountably include no entry for setting and plating the conclusion; and they offer no other clue about which 1860 printing first added the conclusion. However, since the conclusion was written on 14 March in England, it could not have appeared in Boston before the fourth printing of about 7 April.[6]

Although I have not been able to differentiate all seven 1860 printings on the basis of a 50-copy sample, there is clear-cut evidence for identifying four printings of volume I and five printings of volume II—and each volume must be considered separately because there is no guarantee that any two volumes now mated are not living in sin.

The most striking thing about the 1860 printings of the *Faun* is that there were three make-ups of volume I and two of volume II before the conclusion was added—a fact that I have found noted in print only three times.[7] Both volumes are signed in twelves, but the suspected first printing of each is gathered in eights. The suspected second printing is gathered in twelves, but the misimposition of the contents before the preface produces a hiatus in the pagination of volume I. I call the order of these printings suspected because it is reversible, although some slight batter evidence supports the ordering on the chart. The third printing—that is, the third printing I have been able to identify—is gathered in twelves, and volume I has the preliminary matter correctly ordered. That this printing is later than the other two is established by the appearance of two plate changes in volume I and twelve plate changes in volume II. The fourth printing of volume II—which marks the first appearance of the conclusion—

[6] A letter from Hawthorne to Smith, Elder & Co., the publisher of the English edition of *The Marble Faun, Transformation,* reveals that he returned the proof of the conclusion to the printer on 16 March. I am deeply grateful to Professor Norman Holmes Pearson for allowing me to see his transcription of this letter, which is in the collection of Mrs. Reginald Smith.

[7] Jacob Blanck, "Nathaniel Hawthorne," *News Sheet of the Bibliographical Society of America* No. 67 (1 March 1946). Lyle H. Wright, *American Fiction 1851–1875* (San Marino, 1957). Fredson Bowers has commented on the make-ups of *The Marble Faun* in his *Principles of Bibliographical Description* (Princeton, 1949), pp. 386–87, 390, 433.

includes six errors, of which the five on page 98 almost certainly resulted from hasty repair of shop damage. Only one of these errors was corrected during the life of plates, when 98.3 was changed in 1865.

I can speak with some confidence about the first three printings of volume I and the first four of volume II; but beyond this point I am in trouble because I have not isolated all seven of the 1860 printings listed in the *Cost Books*. As the hole in my chart for the fourth printing of volume I indicates, I strongly suspect that I have not found the printing of volume I that corresponds to the fourth printing of volume II; and I further suspect that this undiscovered printing has the ten plate changes which appear in the fifth printing. It is, however, unlikely that there are any undiscovered textual variants in the missing printings of the *Faun*, for the copies bearing the legend "SEVENTEENTH THOUSAND." were printed late in 1860. Indeed, if the figure is honest—and it probably is not—it could not apply to any 1860 printing because the *Cost Books* show that only 14,500 sets were printed in 1860. However, on 2 Nov. 1860 Ticknor & Fields advertised in the *Boston Evening Transcript*, "Eighteenth Thousand. Now Ready.", so that the "SEVENTEENTH THOUSAND." legend probably marks the seventh printing of September 1860, the last printing of the year.

Of the *Faun* variants, only the one at 199.13 of volume II is of critical significance. Here Kenyon, the artist, who has been stood up by Hilda at the Vatican galleries thinks in the first printing that it was a "very cold heart to which he had devoted himself." The correction to a "very cold art" obviously changes the meaning of the passage from a lover's lament to a statement of Hawthorne's prejudice against the pictorial arts.[8]

---

[8] Although I have limited my discussion to the American edition of *The Marble Faun*, I have included the first printing of *Transformation* in the table of variants because *The Marble Faun* was set from advance sheets of *Transformation*. On 7 March 1860 Hawthorne wrote to Smith, Elder & Co., calling attention to two errors in the text of *Transformation:* II-9.7 with foot; II-30.17 literary. In the third printing of *Transformation, literary* was corrected to *literally,* but *with foot* was left unchanged. All the 1860 printings of *The Marble Faun* have *with foot* at I–198.9 and *literally* at I–212.16. Hawthorne's letter is in the collection of Mrs. Reginald Smith, and again I am indebted to Professor Pearson for allowing me to see his transcription. See the Centenary Hawthorne edition of *The Marble Faun* (Columbus, Ohio, 1968).

PLATE VARIANTS: "THE MARBLE FAUN"

VOLUME I

Centenary Page-Line	MS Reading	"Transformation" Sheet, Page-Line	"Transformation" Reading	"Marble Faun" Page-Line	A	B	C	D	E
				Prelim ....Pref-Cont	....Pref-Cont	Cont-Pref	Pref-Cont		Pref-Cont
				Gathered 8	8	12	12		12
				Signed 12	12	12	12		12
				Copyright page					SEVENTEENTH THOUSAND.
				vii	∧	1*	∧		∧
				ix	1*	∧	∧		∧
7.6	gaily	1/I,4.19	gaily	17.17	gaily	~	~		gaily
40.31	Nature	5/I,66.5	nature	56.21	nature	~	~		Nature
58.33	face;—	7/I,99.21	face∧—	78.15	face∧—	~∧—	~∧—		~,—
59.9	sensibility,	7/I,100.11	sensibility∧	78.24	sensibility,	~,	~,		~∧
68.27	bye	8/I,117.16	bye	90.4	bye	~	~		by
101.24	history∧—	12/I,177.19	history∧—	131.4	history∧—	~∧—	~∧—		~,—
101.27	ink∧—	12/I,178.1	ink∧—	131.7	ink∧—	~∧—	~∧—		~,—
152.14	slily	17/I,272.8	slily	192.12	slily	~	~		slyly
162.18	grieves	20/II,18.13	grieves	204.22	grives	~	~		grieves
180.10	for	22/II,52.1	for	225.22	for	~	on		~
204.22	them	24/II,95.14	them	252.30	there	~	them		~
218.19	nevertheless∧	26/II,122.13	nevertheless∧	269.22	nevertheless∧	~∧	~∧		~∧

Plate Variants: "The Marble Faun"

Volume II

					A	B	C	D	E
Gathered					8				
Signed					12	12	12	12	12
Copyright page									SEVENTEENTH THOUSAND.

Centenary Page-Line	MS Reading	"Transformation" Sheet, Page-Line	"Transformation" Reading	"Marble Faun" Page-Line	A	B	C	D	E
233.13	friend;	28/II,149.4	friend∧—	9.27	friend∧—	~∧—	~∧—	~∧—	~;—
233.15	woods;—	28/II,149.7	woods∧—	9.29	woods∧—	~∧—	~∧—	~∧—	~;—
239.4	era, (	28/II,160.19	era∧—	17.2	era∧—	~∧—	~∧—	~∧—	~,—
239.5	abundant,)	28/II,160.20	abundant∧—	17.3	abundant∧—	~∧—	~∧—	~∧—	~,—
294.22	intercourse,	35/II,267.12	intercourse,	84.24	intercourse,	~∧	~∧	~∧	~,
301.20	Etruscan	36/II,280.15	Etruscan	92.23	Etruscan	~	Etruscan	~	~
301.24	fall∧—	36/II,280.21	fall∧—	92.28	fall∧—	~∧—	~∧—	~∧—	~∧—
301.24	away∧—	36/II,280.21	away∧—	92.28	away∧—	~∧—	~∧—	~∧—	~∧—
302.18	country∧—	36/II,282.11	country∧—	93.27	country∧—	~∧—	~∧—	~∧—	~∧—
302.18	here∧—	36/II,282.12	here∧—	93.28	here∧—	~∧—	~∧—	~∧—	~∧—
306.3	strangely	37/II,289.9	strangely	98.3	strangely	~	~	strangelg	~
306.4	figure!	37/II,289.10	figure!	98.4	figure!	~!	~!	~;	~:
306.6	"it	37/II,289.12	"it	98.6	"it	~,	~,	'it	'it
306.7	himself.	37/II,289.13	himself.	98.7	himself.	~.	~.	~∧	~∧
306.19	Belief	37/II,290.6	belief	98.20	belief	~	~	belife	~

PLATE VARIANTS: "THE MARBLE FAUN"

VOLUME II—Continued

Centenary Page-Line	MS Reading	"Transformation" Sheet, Page-Line	"Transformation" Reading	"Marble Faun" Page-Line	A	B	C	D	E
307.3	boneless∧	37/II,291.9	boneless∧	99.10	boneless,	ʼ	ʼ,	ʼ ʼ	ʼ ʼ
307.11	dirty	37/II,291.18	dirty	99.18	dirtly	ʼ	dirty	ʼ ʼ	ʼ ʼ
322.32	ever,	39/III,27.1	ever,	118.4 / 197	ever, / 4*	ʼ, / 9*	ʼ, / <	ʼ < / < ʼ	ʼ < / < ʼ
390.16	medium.	47/III,152.4	medium.	198.16	medium,	ʼ	ʼ,	ʼ ʼ	ʼ ʼ
391.10	art	47/III,153.2	art	199.13	heart	ʼ	art	ʼ ʼ	ʼ ʼ
391.22	Errour⋯ Evil	47/III,153.17	Error⋯ Evil	199.26	error⋯ evil	ʼ⋯ ʼ	Error⋯ Evil	ʼ⋯ ʼ	ʼ⋯ ʼ
406.8	anxiety,	49/III,181.15	anxiety,	217.19	anxiety;	ʼ;	ʼ,	ʼ ʼ	ʼ ʼ
406.33	Heaven	49/III,182.22	Heaven	218.15	heaven	ʼ,	Heaven	ʼ ʼ	ʼ ʼ
410.33	before—	49/III,190.8-9	before—	223.8	before,	ʼ,	ʼ—	ʼ—	ʼ—
412.17	dead	50/III,193.10	dead	225.4	dread	ʼ	dead	ʼ ʼ	ʼ ʼ
413.18	vain;	50/III,195.10	vain;	226.11	vain;	ʼ <	ʼ <	ʼ <	ʼ <
416.23	forever?	50/III,201.14	for ever?	230.5	forever.	ʼ	ʼ,	ʼ ?	ʼ ?
416.26	aid?	50/III,201.17	aid?	230.7	aid.	ʼ	ʼ,	ʼ ʼ	ʼ ʼ
421.10	a charge	50/III,208.21	a charge	234.24	charge	ʼ	a charge	ʼ ʼ	ʼ ʼ
423.19	de'	51/III,213.8	de'	237.14	de∧	ʼ <	ʼ,	ʼ,	ʼ,
443.18	bestrewn.	53/III,250.2	bestrewn.	260.30	bestrewn∧	ʼ <	ʼ,	ʼ ʼ	ʼ ʼ
			Conclusion ⋯⋯No		No	No	No	Yes	Yes

XIV

MATTHEW J. BRUCCOLI

Some Transatlantic Texts: West to East

A practical survey of the textual problems in British editions of American novels is not possible within this space; and I am therefore limiting myself to certain twentieth-century novels. Apart from the fact that this is the area that interests me most, it seems to me that there is a good deal of complacency about the transatlantic texts of modern novels. We all know something about some of the general problems in the Anglo-American books of the nineteenth century—problems resulting from weak copyright laws, primitive printing techniques, and slow transportation. That there are textual variants in the transatlantic editions of Melville, Hawthorne, and Mark Twain is pretty much common knowledge. But most of us tend to assume that, except in special cases, we do not have to worry about the British editions of Faulkner, Fitzgerald, Hemingway, O'Hara, Salinger, or Lewis. Not so. British scholars, critics, teachers, and readers are taking chances when they scrutinize, analyze, explicate, or read only the editions of modern American novels available to them. And, indeed, in a few cases the American reader should be reading the British text of an American novel.

When an American novel is published in a British edition—and the new edition is a true edition from reset type—the text is altered. At any rate, I have not found an accurate word-for-word and punctuation-for-punctuation British resetting of any American novel. When house-styling alone occurs, the implications are serious if not necessarily overwhelming. One cannot help wondering about the point where regularization of commas, quotation marks, and spelling alters the texture of the prose and begins to have some subtle effect on the total impression the novel makes on the reader. What do 100 *our* or *re* spellings do to

This essay has been written at the editors' invitation, for inclusion in the present volume. Earlier versions of this paper were presented before the Bibliographical Society and at Pennsylvania State University.

the American-ness of an American novel? Or 300? Is there such a thing as eye-ball effect which is influenced by word forms even when word meanings are unchanged? There is, I would suggest, a special category of house-style variants which are more than accidentals in force, if less than true substantives, such as *mamma* for *mama* or *hallo* for *hello*. Whether in dialogue or narration, these substitutions do something to the reader. If the immediate effect of the house-styling or English-styling of an American novel is to make things easier for British readers, in the long run it deceives them. James Meriwether, who has done pioneering work on the subject, has made this point in discussing the Chatto & Windus edition of *The Sound and The Fury* (1931), which was inconsistently copy-edited and anglicized, though not censored:

> The English reader misses a good many of the finer shades of pronunciation and rhythm in the dialogue through changes made in spelling and punctuation. He loses the chance of the closer acquaintance with Faulkner's mind which familiarity with some of the idiosyncrasies of usage in the American text affords. And perhaps worst of all, the inconsistencies caused by careless copy editing and proofreading are apt to shake the reader's confidence in his text, and to discourage the kind of close attention the writing deserves.[1]

It is important to recognize that in addition to their cumulative effect, certain kinds of accidentals are significant in themselves—for example, the capitalization that may give symbolic force to nouns, or the use of italics for emphasis. In the case of J. D. Salinger, who uses italics very deliberately, the removal of 225 italic words between the 1951 Little, Brown and Hamish Hamilton editions of *The Catcher in the Rye* is a serious distortion of both style and meaning.

The issues are less disputable when the British text of an American novel includes authorial bowdlerizations. All of these alterations are silent, of course, so that the reader has no way—short of collating—of knowing about them. Even when an American novel has been bowdlerized with the author's permission in the first British edition, there may well be long-range consequences. The Chatto & Windus text of *Sanctuary* (1931) deleted

[1] James B. Meriwether, "Notes on the Textual History of *The Sound and the Fury*," *Papers of the Bibliographical Society of America*, LVI (1962), 285–316.

325 words with Faulkner's permission. The original text was not available in England until 1952; furthermore, the 1953 Penguin edition reverted to the censored British text.

The same problems arise in American texts of British novels, of course; and I do not suppose that my side of the Atlantic has a finer textual conscience than the other side. I am not ordering England to shape up. What I am offering is the angle of an American bibliographer whose field is American literature and who therefore knows more about the west-to-east textual flow. The only warning I can presume to issue is the old one that every serious user of printed words has to be concerned about whose words they are. Nor would I go so far as to claim that an English publisher has the duty to follow slavishly an incorrect or sloppy American copy-text. But he had better be sure that he is correcting an error—and not spoiling an American idiom. A letter from Raymond Chandler to his English publisher is instructive: "As to misprints, I think the strange lingo I write is a bit tough on English proof-readers and some of the things I say are probably changed deliberately by some type-setter or proof-reader of the printer's because they think *I* have made a mistake. For instance on Page 11, line 8 [of *The Long Good-Bye*] there appears the word 'wag,' quite meaningless in context. The real word was 'vag,' short for 'vagrant. . . .' "[2]

Although it is amusing to play the bibliographical parlor game of inventing tricky case histories of textual transmission (such as: suppose a British publisher decides to offset an American novel and obtains for photographing not two copies of the first printing or two copies of the revised second printing, but one copy of the first printing which he uses for rectos and one copy of the second printing which he uses for versos) I will confine myself to actual cases.

The most common problem by far that I have encountered involves British conservative treatment of the dirty words in American novels. These examples are sometimes silly or amusing, I admit, but in many cases the silent cleansing of American novels has quite serious results. The Hamish Hamilton first edition of *The Catcher in the Rye* substitutes dashes for the six appearances of *fuck* in the Little, Brown text. All six appearances of the word are in a passage that shows Holden Caulfield's distress

[2] *Raymond Chandler Speaking*, ed. Dorothy Gardiner and Katherine Sorley Walker (Boston: Houghton Mifflin, 1962), pp. 171–72.

at seeing *fuck* written on a wall in his young sister's school. To be squeamish about printing the word in such a context is to alter the tone of this delicately balanced section. In order to appreciate Holden's reaction we have to see the word and hear him say it. A dash, or even six dashes, may make the meaning perfectly clear; but it modifies our response to Holden's response. It is necessary that we realize that he is not afraid to use the word, although he is upset by the hopelessness of trying to rub out all of the *fuck* signs in the world, even "if you had a million years to do it in."[3] Similarly, the Collins edition of *From Here to Eternity* converts some fifty-five appearances of this same word to *f---*. Although I was tipped off by an English bibliographer that this novel had been thoroughly purged for English consumption, a fast collation reveals that only thirty-six lines were deleted from the American text—all presumably in the interest of decency. Seven of these lines deal with female physiology and twenty-nine describe a "Japanese massage."

As might be expected, the history of Ernest Hemingway's British texts is a chronicle of dashes, deletions, asterisks, and stars. As early as Cape's 1926 edition of *In Our Time* we encounter textual fumigations which were almost certainly not authorial. In "A Very Short Story," the word *enema* is purged to *enemy*, thereby ruining the point of the sentence: "When they operated on him she prepared him for the operating table; and they had a joke about friend or enema." Later in the same story *gonorrhea* is generalized to *a disease*. The original 1929 Scribners text of *A Farewell to Arms* had sixteen dashes—not the words, but dashes—standing for three different dirty words. The 1929 Cape edition retained eight of these original dashes; omitted one dash; excised the entire line in three places; and in four places substituted a word for the dash—but not the word intended. Absurd.[4]

I have not yet collated *The Green Hills of Africa*, but a check of the preliminary matter reveals interesting differences between the 1935 Scribners and 1936 Cape editions. The American edition is dedicated "To Philip, To Charles, And To Sully," and

[3] These details about *The Catcher in the Rye* are courtesy of John Manning.

[4] James B. Meriwether, "The Dashes in Hemingway's *A Farewell to Arms*," *Papers of the Bibliographical Society of America*, LVIII (1964), 449–57.

has a seventy-seven word "Foreword" which can be taken as an early entry in the "non-fiction novel" derby: "The writer has attempted to write an absolutely true book to see whether the shape of a country and the pattern of a month's action can, if truly presented, compete with a work of the imagination." The London edition omits this Foreword and replaces the triple dedication with a ninety-eight word joking note to "Mr. J. P.," the white hunter of the book. These changes had to be authorial, and one would very much like to know why they were made.

In point of fact, one would like to know more about most of the textual changes I am talking about. But the information is hard to come by. American publishers are notoriously un-cooperative about these things; English publishers are only slightly more tolerant of scholarly enquiries, and it often turns out that their records were destroyed in the Blitz.

In *To Have and Have Not* the 1937 Cape edition purifies the Scribners text through a combination of dashes and rewriting. *Shit* becomes *s---* four times; *piss p---;* an inoffensive reference to male homosexuality is deleted; and the word *lesbians* is emended to *what do you call thems.* A reference to cirrhosis of the liver is deleted—and I do not know why, unless this organ has naughty connotations in Britain. An attempt to help the British reader backfires when the phrase *Skull and Bones man* is ex-panded to *Skull and Bones fraternity man*, thereby misleading the reader. Skull and Bones is not a fraternity; it is a secret society at Yale limited to fifteen seniors. To describe it as a fraternity alters the position of the character who is being identified as a member—a meaningful point in terms of the social distinctions Hemingway is making in that section of the novel. The most important change in *To Have and Have Not* occurs in the key sentence, Harry Morgan's dying speech, which in the Scribners edition reads: "No matter how a man alone aint got no bloody fucking chance." Is this deletion of *fucking* really crucial? If the sentence is as important to the novel as most critics think, then the reader needs all the words. As late as 1961 the Penguin text of this novel followed the expurgated text.

Across the River and into the Trees raises a special problem. The Cape edition was published in London on 4 September 1950, and the Scribners edition three days later. Practically speaking, they were published simultaneously; the problem is to account for 479 variants exclusive of punctuation marks—of which fifty are substantives. The facts are not known, but the assumption is that an early corrected set of the Scribners galleys was sent to London and that Hemingway made further changes, perhaps in page proof, when it was too late to relay these changes to London. But there is an outside chance that in some way Hemingway's final revisions were sent only to Cape. The Cape edition substitutes stars not only for the author's four-letter words, but also for his own euphemisms—such as Hemingway's use of the word *fornicate*. Of the six short sentences, a total of forty-three words, present in Scribners but wanting in Cape, only one—which includes the word *urinate*—can be explained as a censorship deletion. The other five sentences are in no way offensive, and a serious reader wants to know whether Hemingway added them to the Scribners text or whether some officious hand cut them from the Cape text. On the face of it, though, there is small chance that anyone but the author would have added, or cut, Col. Cantwell's observation that Shakespeare "writes like a soldier himself" or Cantwell's statement that the Austrian army "went by the book."

After the Hemingway texts, the 1935 Faber & Faber edition of John O'Hara's *Appointment in Samarra* comes as a surprise. There are things in this novel which were no doubt upsetting or puzzling to British readers, but the London text has only twenty-five substantive departures from the 1934 Harcourt, Brace text—all minor, except, perhaps, for the effect of the eight times *ass* was emended to *arse*, for in this case spelling, pronunciation, and definition are involved. People in Gibbsville, Pennsylvania, do not say *arse*, nor do they make any verbal distinction between the word for donkey and the word for backside.

Ring Lardner is an author for whom I eagerly anticipated transmogrified English texts; but collation of the title story and "Haircut" in the 1926 Scribner's and 1928 Philip Allan editions of *The Love Nest and Other Stories* reveals no substantive changes, although the volumes include different stories. A delightful variant occurs when the dialect spelling *theayter* in the Scribner's text of "Haircut" is carefully emended to *theaytre* by Allan.

In contrast to the reliable text of *Appointment in Samarra*, the 1922 Cape edition of Sinclair Lewis's *Babbitt* distorts—indeed, butchers—American speech. Here there are 182 substantives out of 588 emendations, and the result is to make the citizens of

Zenith sound like citizens of Leeds: *lift, tram, lorry, petrol, public-house, chemist,* and even *two-penny car* for *flivver* are used. George F. Babbitt, the real-estate man, even says *let* instead of *rent.* To top off the atrocity, there is a glossary of Americanisms appended to the English edition, which explains 126 expressions of which seventeen are incorrectly or inaccurately defined. *Highball* is defined as *a tot of whiskey; hoodlum* as *crank;* and *heck* is solemnly—perhaps spoofingly—defined as "familiar for Hecuba, a New England deity."

Obviously, Lewis's unmodified vocabulary was considered difficult, if not baffling, for the British reader of 1922. Hugh Walpole's introduction to the Cape edition—which, by the way, says nothing about the textual tampering—applies the words "strange," "obscure," and "complicated" to the novel; nevertheless he urges the British reader to persevere: "For it is Mr. Lewis' triumph in this book that he has made Babbitt own brother to our Mr. Polly, Uncle Ponderovo, Denry of the Five Towns, the Forsyte family and even Mr. George Moore."

The British texts of F. Scott Fitzgerald are interesting in a special way because they show a disinclination to emend where emendation would be expected. The original Scribners editions of his books are all more or less sloppy because Fitzgerald was an inspired speller and an incompetent proofreader; and Maxwell Perkins, his editor, apparently did not worry about it. Or perhaps it is fairer to say that after Fitzgerald finished rewriting in proof there was no room for Perkins to make corrections. At any rate, the British editions of Fitzgerald perform the usual housestyling and catch a few blatant errors, but they do not systematically correct. The 1920 Scribners text of *This Side of Paradise* was messy, and thirty plate corrections were made before the seventh Scribners printing. Since the Collins 1921 edition was set from a seventh or later Scribners printing, it includes these thirty corrections; however, the Collins text makes some 650 emendations, of which two are new typos, fourteen are spelling corrections, three are incorrect corrections, and eighteen are substantive emendations. It is curious that the misspelled *Gunga Dhin* of the Scribners text is incorrectly emended to *Ghanga Dhin* by the Collins edition.

The Collins edition of *Flappers and Philosophers* has six substantive and 431 accidental variants, none of which appears to be authorial. It does, however, include the only revision Fitzgerald made in the plates of the Scribners edition, showing that it was set from the fourth or fifth Scribners printing.

By far the most interesting, and most frustrating, of Fitzgerald's British texts is the 1922 Collins edition of *The Beautiful and Damned*. Although it has the usual mixture of variants —eighty-two substantives and some 620 accidentals—this Collins text also omits four passages totalling 142 lines of type. Since all of these cuts involve the bogus philosophizing and strained wit, including the section entitled "A Flashback in Paradise" that American reviewers ridiculed, it would seem at least possible that the author ordered these deletions for the British edition. Although I have no outside evidence to indicate that Fitzgerald did in fact have anything to do with the Collins text, one other change in this text strongly suggests that he did take some interest in the British edition. The emendation of *tall steeple* to *hilarious steeple* appears only in the Collins edition and could only have been made by Fitzgerald. An editor would not make this revision, and a compositor would not make the error. Moreover, the change is pure Fitzgerald. If the four deletions were made by Fitzgerald, it is noteworthy that all American editions and both the 1950 Grey Walls (which was offset from the original Scribners edition) and the 1961 Bodley Head editions included the four passages—and all, by the way, have the reading *tall steeple*. The Scribners text included contradictory references to Gloria's age and birthday, but these were not corrected in the Collins text.

The 1935 Chatto & Windus edition of *Tender is the Night* includes five substantives and 856 accidentals. Of these five substantives, one is a correction of an error in the 1934 Scribners text; three are fresh errors; and one is possibly a correction. One of the accidentals is worth talking about, for it demonstrates how the insertion of one comma can destroy the meaning of a whole scene: *he cut through her raging* [he *cut through her, raging* This comma is not trivial. It comes in the scene near the end of the novel where Dick Diver displays his old self-control for the last time as he rescues Mary and Lady Caroline from the police. The whole point of the passage is that Dick is in command as he cuts through Lady Caroline's raging.

Tender is the Night is a novel in which liberal correcting by the Chatto & Windus copy editors would have been justified, for the Scribners edition needs emendation at 266 points; but the

Chatto & Windus edition, for all of its 861 variants, emended only twenty-nine of these 266 had readings

I can make only passing mention of novels I have not collated. The 1928 Cape edition of Cummings's *The Enormous Room* was purportedly based on the author's manuscript and is supposed to be much better than the 1922 Boni & Liveright text. According to Robert Graves's introduction to the Cape edition, it "contains a good deal of material that does not appear in the American edition, including five or six portraits in Chapter V, and corrects a very large number of misprints that do." The unexpurgated text did not appear in America until 1934.

The 1930 Heinemann edition of *Look Homeward, Angel* is said to add some forty lines that were not in the 1929 Scribners text. The British text is also said to have many omissions and some transpositions. It would seem likely that the added lines, at least, were added by Wolfe or Perkins. If so, they require attention. They do not, to my knowledge, appear in any American edition.

Although the Hamish Hamilton text of *The Thurber Carnival* is an offset reprint of the 1945 original Harper edition, it abounds in errors—probably because the photocopy was uncorrected proofs.[5]

The resetting of type for a British edition offers the American author an opportunity for revision which he may use to respond to the American reception of the book, as I think happened with *The Beautiful and Damned*. An entertaining case involves James Branch Cabell's *Jurgen*, which was published in America by McBride in 1919 and suppressed in 1920. When the first British edition, limited, was published by John Lane in 1921, Cabell interpolated into the novel more than one thousand words from his pamphlet, *The Judging of Jurgen*. This material jests about phallic symbolism, ridicules literary censorship, and cites Poe, Whitman, and Mark Twain as the victims of prudery. These words were also included in the 1923 Lane trade edition. They were added to the Foreword of the 1923 American reprint, but did not appear as an integrated part of any American text until the 1928 collected—and limited—Storisende Edition. The inclusion of the material in the Storisende text demonstrates that its appearance in the London text was not just a whim

[5] Edwin T. Bowden, "*The Thurber Carnival*: Bibliography and Printing History," *Texas Studies in Literature and Language*, IX (1968), 555–66.

and that Cabell really wanted this reply to be part of the novel.

Interesting situations arise when an American novel is pre-published in Britain. The 1934 Longmans, Green edition of James Gould Cozzens' *Castaway* has a preliminary note explaining that Mr. Lecky is alone in a department store after a catastrophe has destroyed the population of the city; and the final chapter of the novel includes a paragraph in which the author supplies the same information. Both explanations are absent from the Random House edition which appeared six weeks later.[6]

Raymond Chandler's *The Long Good-Bye* provides a splendid example of the textual permutations that can result from British prepublication of an American novel. This novel was first published by Hamish Hamilton in November 1953 and reprinted in December; the first American edition was published by Houghton Mifflin in March 1954. The text of the first Hamilton printing was careless, and Chandler made eighty-four revisions—seventy-seven of them substantive—in the plates before the second printing. Plate revision limited the author to spot substitutions, and he was able to add only one new short passage by altering the paragraphing to make room for it. But when type was set for the Houghton Mifflin edition—probably from the second Hamilton printing—914 revisions were made, of which fifty-four are substantives. A good portion of these seem to be authorial, including the restoration of the original paragraphing. As a churlish bibliographer would expect, the text of *The Long Good-Bye* in Hamilton's 1962 *Second Chandler Omnibus* was set not from the Houghton Mifflin text and not even from Hamilton's own revised second printing, but from the unrevised Hamilton first printing.

The punctuation of *The Long Good-Bye* introduces a special problem. Chandler was educated in England, and his habitual punctuation was closer to English practice than to American. Since the Hamilton edition was set from the author's corrected typescript, its punctuation, even after house-styling, is closer to the author's than is the restyled Houghton Mifflin edition set, apparently, from the Hamilton printed text.[7]

As would be expected, expatriation by an American author

[6] James B. Meriwether, "The English Editions of James Gould Cozzens," *Studies in Bibliography*, XV (1962), 207–18.

[7] My information about *The Long Good-Bye* derives from an unpublished paper by Prof. Robert Miller of the University of Louisville.

sometimes results in a British text of his novel which is markedly superior to the American text. In such a case, when simultaneous publication is intended, the British edition is the one the author sees proof for. The Heinemann edition of Harold Frederic's *Illumination* and the Stone & Kimball edition of *The Damnation of Theron Ware* were published during the same week in 1896, when Frederic was living in England. The 204 substantive differences between the two texts show that the London edition was thoroughly revised in proof. Still more significant is the Heinemann edition of Stephen Crane's *Active Service* published in 1899 one month after the Stokes edition, while Crane was living in England. Not only does the Heinemann edition present a revised text with 436 substantive emendations, nearly all of which seem to be Crane's, but it is also the only novel, except for *Maggie*, that Crane, one of the devout non-revisers in American literature, ever revised. The Heinemann *Active Service*, then, gives us a glimpse of Stephen Crane as a critic of his own prose— in this case trying to improve a poor novel.[8]

The conclusion to be drawn from these notes is not that any publisher—British or American—stands convicted of reprehensible negligence or textual chicanery. When everyone is indifferent to the ideals of textual integrity, it is useless to brand one particular culprit, or nation of culprits. Textual laxity is prevalent among publishers of fiction because they are simply not aware that they are doing anything wrong—or failing to do something right. Ignorance and complacency, not subterfuge or wickedness, are to blame.

It is not necessary for a publisher to computerize his texts, or to consult Fredson Bowers, in order to reprint trustworthy texts. What it takes is the awareness that textual reliability matters as much in a novel as in a sonnet. One reason why there is not a widespread awareness of the problems I have been noting is that the drudges who collate Anglo-American texts have, in America, been hampered by the unavailability of the English editions of American novels. Few American libraries collect them, and few dealers—in America or Britain—trouble to catalogue them unless the British edition is known to precede the American. It took seven years to acquire the six English firsts of Fitzgerald and I

---

[8] Matthew J. Bruccoli and Joseph Katz, "Scholarship and Mere Artifacts: The British and Empire Publications of Stephen Crane," *Studies in Bibliography*, XXII (1969), 277–87.

still have not seen the 1927 Collins reprints of *This Side of Paradise* and *Tales of the Jazz Age.*

It is my pious hope, that more scholarship, which will produce publisher anxiety, will triumphantly produce reliable, accurate, trustworthy British texts of American novels. And also reliable, accurate, trustworthy American texts of American novels.[9]

[9] I am obliged to James Geibel for much research assistance.

XV

DAVID HAYMAN

From Finnegans Wake: *A Sentence in Progress*

Although it has often been described as a work of destruction, James Joyce's *Finnegans Wake* was designed to be a triumphant reconstruction. It was in reference to this characteristic of his last book that Joyce is reported to have remarked during a visit to Stonehenge, "I am fourteen years trying to get here."[1] The task of reproducing with words the "nightmare of history" was an arduous one. For seventeen years Joyce labored to resolve the "proteaform" mass of modern learning in a "faustian fustian" of words. Such a process, the mixing and blending, the ordering and composing, the choosing and discarding, was necessarily a lengthy one entailing numberless revisions which bear "hermetic" testimony to the nature of the creative act while recording the artistic mind in a state of flux.

It is self-evident that Joyce's manuscripts for *Finnegans Wake* are of immense importance to the scholar.[2] They provide a basis

Reprinted with slight revisions from *PMLA*, LXIII (1958), 136–54, by permission of the author and the Modern Language Association.

[1] Statement by Mrs. Kathleen Griffin on the BBC Third Program, Pt. II, "The Artist in Maturity," 17 Feb. 1950.

[2] A remarkably complete collection of the *Finnegans Wake* MSS is now at the British Museum where it was deposited by Miss Harriet Weaver. In the course of this article, these manuscripts, BM Add MSS 47471–89, will be referred to by their catalogue numbers. For a brief account of the nature of the collection see John J. Slocum and Herbert Cahoon, *A Bibliography of James Joyce, 1882–1941* (New Haven, 1953), pp. 145–48. For more extended accounts see A. Walton Litz' *The Art of James Joyce* (New York, 1961) and *A First-Draft Version of Finnegans Wake*, ed. David Hayman (Austin, 1963). This article was among the first devoted to Joyce's manuscripts for the *Wake*. It is still the only extended exegesis in depth and despite the large amount of fine work done since, I find that the views I held in 1958 have changed very little. Nevertheless, I have made a number of changes which reflect some doubts about details in my reading, some second thoughts about my transcriptions and about my style, and

for study of Joyce's method, his progressive elaboration upon a theme. They furnish material for a close examination of the mental process behind this style and of the organization which enabled Joyce to control the chaos from which he drew his inspiration. To this end, I believe a word-by-word study which questions each aspect of a single sentence in progress would be of greater value than a more generalized discussion of a longer passage. If feasible, a series of such exegetic analyses might aid in more thoroughly illuminating the total stylistic of the book.

It is for this purpose and with the intention of casting the first stone that I have chosen to examine here a sentence of moderate length and complexity which Joyce, beginning in 1924, elaborated over a period of fourteen years. A study of the thirteen-odd stages of its development should give us a reasonable number of insights into the artistic method and into the meaning of Book III, the section of *Finnegans Wake* to which this sentence belongs.[3]

As the plan of *Finnegans Wake* was not completed until 1926[4] and as there was to be "no beginning or end,"[5] Joyce composed his chapters without regard to their final order. Consequently,

---

some random insights gathered along the way. They also reflect the advice and criticism of students at my informal *Wake* seminar at the University of Iowa.

[3] "I could sit on safe side till the bark of Saint Grouseus for hoopoe's hours, till heoll's hoerrisings, laughing lazy at the sheep's lightning and turn a widamost ear dreamily to the drummling of snipers, hearing the wireless harps of sweet old Aeriel and the mails across the nightrives (peepet! peepet!) and whippoor willy in the woody (moor park! moor park!) as peacefed as a philopotamus, and crekking jugs at the grenoulls, leaving tealeaves for the trout and belleeks till the wary till I'd followed through my upfielded neviewscope the rugaby moon cumuliously god-rolling himself westasleep amuckst the cloudscrums for to watch how carefully my nocturnal goosemother would lay her new golden sheegg for me down under in the shy orient" (New York, 1947), p. 449. For the sake of brevity I shall designate sections of *Finnegans Wake* by means of Roman capitals (Joyce's: I, II, III, IV); chapters falling within sections will be indicated by lower-case letters (Ii, Ilii, etc.); page and line numbers will be separated by a diagonal line.

[4] In a letter dated 21 May 1926, Joyce tells Miss Harriet Weaver that he finally has the book "fairly well planned out in [his] head." The final plan was fixed only after the inclusion of Ii in Dec. 1926, more than 3 years after he had begun writing (Add MS. 47489).

[5] Ibid., letter to Miss Weaver, 8 Nov. 1926.

though the first versions of some of the chapters in Book I of *Finnegans Wake* were among the earliest passages to be written, the first section to be completely planned and executed was Book III. This last is comprised of four chapters, in three of which Shaun, the dream-son of the archetypal father-hero, HCE, appears successively under the names Shaun, Jaun, and Yawn. On 24 May 1924, after he had sketched out IIIi and ii, Joyce wrote Miss Weaver that the Shaun chapters describe a postman's journey backward through the night's events, that they are "written in the form of a *via crucis* of 14 stations but in reality [they are] only [the description of] a barrel rolling down the river Liffey."[6]

The analogies mentioned in this letter only begin to indicate controls Joyce imposed upon himself and the framework within which these chapters were constructed. Aside from instituting for Shaun a set of character traits appropriate to a hero of Vico's democratic or decadent age, Joyce established at least five parody levels of which the movement is both forward and backward. Thus, while Shaun-the-post travels backward, Christ follows in their proper order the fourteen stations of the cross;[7] Buddha under the Bo tree withstands the trials of the night, passes watch by watch through the four steps of knowledge. Coincidentally, Joyce implies that the sun has disappeared and that Shaun, the shadow-son, is re-enacting the sunset in four positions: the appearance of the false sun, its static moment near the horizon, its slipping below the horizon, and its disappearance. As to the chronology of these themes, Shaun travels from deep-

[6] *Letters of James Joyce*, ed. Stuart Gilbert (New York, 1957), p. 214.

[7] In *Dublin's Joyce* (Bloomington, 1956), p. 362, Hugh Kenner convincingly develops *Finnegans Wake*'s liturgical analogies in sequential order. According to his analysis, the 14 stages of the cross are confined to Chap. IIIii. Although Kenner's arguments supporting this last contention sound very convincing, Joyce indicated clearly in his letter of 24 May 1924 (above) that he thought of the Shaun chapters as a solid unit. As it happens, the 2 other analogical levels mentioned by Joyce clearly hold for all 4 chapters. Indeed, the first 2 chapters were composed and, for 3 consecutive drafts, revised as a unit. Furthermore, Kenner's liturgical progression would be somewhat reinforced by the inclusion of IIIi and IIIiv in his calculations. For purposes of this study, therefore, I shall assume that Joyce applied the *via crucis* to both the chapter and the section simultaneously, making Jaun a priest in the smaller unit and a Christ in the other. In all events, it should be stated that no single level of analogy can provide the "key" to *Finnegans Wake*, which depends for its meaning on total effects.

est night to evening, Buddha sits from sunset till sunrise, Jesus suffers from morning to evening, and the false sun shines from the moment of the sun's disappearance till nightfall. Meanwhile, the barrel analogy links all the others: "Shaun a," or IIIi, shows us the empty barrel floating at an angle in the river; in "Shaun b" the barrel, which has begun to take water through its bunghole, is leaning on a weir or a post; "Shaun c" finds the water-logged barrel floating on its side, slowly sinking into the maternal liquid; while in "Shaun d" the barrel has been submerged and we are faced with a view of the sea of life. This barrel, slowly being infused with the dark female fluid, parallels Jesus' torment as he becomes progressively more imbued with the Holy Ghost. It also parallels the experience of the Buddha losing himself in the effort to gain nirvana. As Shaun, it journeys back through the stages of the nocturnal cycle to the Fall with which the book opens. Finally, as the sun, the barrel is slowly engulfed by night.[8]

When applied to the individual chapter, this rich superstructure becomes even more elaborate as Joyce particularizes each analogy, finds further (narrower) identities for his protagonists. Chapter IIIii's Jaun is at once a somewhat Laforguian hero—blasé and splenetic, a happy-go-lucky priest, a Don Juanish Tristan figure ("Sir Tristram, violer d'amores," p. 3/4), a boyish Tom Sawyer ("topsawyer," p. 3/7), and, to the extent that he has begun to embody his brother Shem, a Saint Patrick ("thuartpeatrick," p. 3/10) come to deliver Ireland to the day. He stands as the white hope of mankind, the product of centuries of over-civilization, the thin shadow of his forefathers' vitality. As the white hope, he naturally assumes the traits of a savior and of a sacrificial god. Also, as the white hope he is destined to carry the coals of a dying civilization, both figuratively and literally. Thus, on one level he repeats the meaningless dictums, preaches the institutionalized rules of behavior which have long since fallen into disuse and which he himself fails to honor. But on another level he revitalizes the Word, interprets God to man. As the postman, having reached the peak of his possibilities, he distributes the act-become-word which was the sin and the glory of his fallen predecessor. As the priest of cults, he re-enacts the tragedies of Osiris and the Saviour. Thus, for one hopeful moment, as the empty husk which formerly surrounded the life-

[8] This movement may also be applied to the stages of the Vichian cycle.

giving fluid Guinness, he promises to stay with us, leaning against the garnered wealth of civilization, the light of the vanished sun. This is the point at which Jaun, or the false sun which swells on the horizon, has reached the static point in his decline, the same process that will be repeated in reverse by his backward reflection and morning self, the sunrise. As the Buddha beneath the Bo tree, Jaun is being tempted by the daughters of Mara Pusana, lord of passions, who sing to him of the joys of love. He is literally tormented by devils as he loses himself in contemplation. Finally, as Christ, Jaun is carrying his cross and possibly going through steps four through nine of the *via crucis*.

Examining Chapter IIIii's most generalized plane of action, we find that Jaun, halted in his journey down the Liffey, is propped up against a weir upon which are seated twenty-nine schoolgirls.[9] As soon as he sees that the last of these girls is his sister, Issy, he sermonizes her on virtue and the Ten Commandments. He then expatiates on his mission, on his return, on the joyous prospect of seeing Issy again, and on the reforms he would like to put into effect in Dublin. At this point Joyce inserted the earliest version of the paragraph of which our sentence was to become a crucial element:[10]

> I'd ask no kinder fate than to stay where I am this moment catching trophies of sturgeon by the armful and what I'd make by poaching I'd put into the poteen & before you knew where I was I'd be rolling over in tons of cash but I'd be anxious about the terrible cold in the air that wd [would] perish the Danes.[11]

Jaun's statement is a two-part explanation of his reasons for staying where he is (i.e., his pleasant occupations during this stay and the wealth which he expects to amass) and his reasons for leaving (i.e., his fears and compulsions concerning the

[9] These too are representative symbols of many of the aspects of *Finnegans Wake*: the multiplicity of a democratic age which destroys the tendency to exert a unified effort; the nature of broken light which has lost its whiteness, being dispersed by a prism; the disappearing process of the hero, whose virtue lies in his essentially macrocosmic nature.

[10] Joyce first conceived this passage in 1924 while revising the 3rd draft of Chap. IIIii. In the course of this early revision he interpolated a multitude of additions, but as this is an attempt to isolate the fundamental elements upon which the paragraph is constructed, most secondary and tertiary revisions are omitted from the citation of what appears to be Joyce's first continuous sentence.

[11] BM Add MS. 47482b, p. 30.

future). Our hero is lazy and a wastrel; he would get rich quickly by "poaching" or capitalizing on the wealth of others, but he would drink and eat up his profits putting all of his wealth in the "poteen" or whisky. The success that he desires is also in keeping with his shadow personality. Like the crass materialist of a decadent age, the antithesis of the hero of the fairy tales or of a more active epoch Jaun would like to be "rolling over in cash" for the benefit of Issy. We find in this evocation of gold ("cash") a prediction of the glory of the sunrise and a suggestion that Shaun is, like Zeus, capable of visiting Issy-Danaë ("Danes") as a shower of gold, but we are assured that our hero remains a barrel in the river, capable perhaps of floating in water dyed by the setting sun, but nevertheless a victim of the Fates. To mask this weakness and to motivate his disappearance, Jaun expresses fear of the cold air which would destroy him. By means of a reference to "Dane," he evokes his physical aspect as a false sun, bringing out his concern over the transitory nature of the post upon which he is leaning, that is, the Viking wanderer, HCE drunk, or the light of the vanished Helios.[12] In the chapter of the lessons, IIii, which foreshadows the reappearance of HCE (absent since the beginning of the book), the speaker refers to "Mr. Dane" as "the pillar of the perished and the rock o'ralere-ality" (p. 289/3).

The pattern established by Joyce for this primary paragraph is the one which he later imposed upon each succeeding draft of our sentence. Jaun's humdrum conception of the ideal existence is pitted against the rude facts of fate and a lack of courage; his static dream is opposed to a kinetic reality:[13]

> I'd ask no kinder fate than to stay where I am at this present moment *by local option* in the birds' lodging the pheasants among till well on into the night [sic] I COULD SIT ON MY SIDE TILL THE BARK OF THE DAY. . . .[14]

12 See "King Hamlaugh's gulden dayne" (p. 79/35).

13 I have glossed over the greater part of the implications of this paragraph in an effort to simplify the presentation of the skeletal elements. In like manner I shall generally avoid indulging in too meticulous a reconstruction of the many phases of Jaun's existence as they are effected by Joyce's *retouches*. The analogical aspects which will be alluded to throughout the exegesis should suffice to establish the extent to which Joyce integrated his material.

14 Draft 4, 1924 (BM Add MS. 47482b, pp. 53b–54). Italics and small capitals indicate respectively the 1st– and 2nd–degree additions which I have felt obligated to include.

Here, our sentence—"I could sit on my side till the bark of the day"—functions as a simple reiterative statement, further limiting time, place, and condition, further developing the theme that opens the paragraph. It is inserted as a self-contained unit whose addition has little or no immediate effect on the structure of the surrounding clauses, which are elaborated by its intellectual content.[15] The whole of this new germ element hangs upon the interpretation given two vague words, "side" and "bark." Even at this early stage Joyce forces his reader to utilize the ungrammatical meanings suggested by his distortions of the language. Thus, "I could sit on my side" is at best an *ambiguous* statement of physical position. Jaun seems to be saying that he is now sitting, but he also indicates a reclining position, that of the floating barrel propped up against "a log." The force of this same nautical analogy reflects upon the rest of the clause. "Bark of the day" may refer to the solar boat of Ra to which Jaun is attached as the reflected glory of the departed sun. Again, the "bark" recalls the barking baboons (i.e., HCE or "Babau," p. 466/1) that were believed by the Egyptians to herald the sun's matinal appearance. In all of his symbolic identities, Jaun, the last surviving remnant of the disappearing male factor, would like to live through the night to greet the new day, the spring, or the new dawn of civilization.

Already, we detect some of the possibilities to be developed in the second draft. The sentence, like the paragraph, is a dual entity which opposes a desired stasis to an impending change. To elaborate the pattern, the author must now brush in the implications of the time gap, the conflict, the cataclysm, and the glory to come. He must detail the setting more carefully, describing the actions of his hero as he awaits the dawn. He must suggest not only the actual sunrise but also the emotions it arouses in the heart of the character, its significance in the book, and its relation to the book's symbolical basis.

But the process is painfully gradual. In Draft 6[16] or the heavily revised first typescript of this chapter, with corrections dating

---

[15] Most of Joyce's changes are of this order. Rather than revise an entire sentence, he customarily used his primary ideas as a base upon which to construct a more complex thought-expression unit.

[16] In Draft 5, which Joyce completed before Oct. 1924, our sentence remains unchanged.

from 1924–26, we may approximate three distinct evolutionary stages resulting from three separate revisions: [17]

> I could sit on ~~my~~ *one* side till the bark of the day *for to watch how* ~~the~~ *my* [sic] *my nocturnal goose would lay her golden egg for* [sic] *behind me in the shy orient.*[18]

Joyce's first change, "one" for "my," seems to add a note of detachment to Jaun's position—he wishes to see himself as a disinterested spectator. The "side" has become more manifestly one side of the barrel, the setting sun, the barque, or "one side" of a log or a tree. When we consider the nature of the other additions, "one" enriches the meaning of "till." Jaun would like to "sit *beside* the bark of the sun till the night prepares to give birth to the new day." The Egyptian sunboat is now associated with the goose that will lay her golden egg in the east as Jaun watches from his vantage point. The replacement of the word "the" by "my" strengthens the hero's sun aspect. Perhaps he too has been hatched out of a goose egg. His desire to watch the sunrise "behind" him (his progress as the sun's shadow is from east to west) highlights the already present, dual aspect. In spite of his reluctance to move, and like the hero of the fairy tales and myths, he will have to suffer hardships in order to bring back the goose egg upon which our happiness depends. On this level at least, he remains a reluctant hero who has no control over his own movements.

If we accept the bark-log association, Jaun is leaning against the day-post-HCE. In the beginning of IIIii his means of support is described as a "butterblond . . . exsearfaceman" (p. 429/19–20) in reference to the light and the heat of the sunfather from whom the son derives his existence. Another analogical level makes of the log a fertility symbol and of Jaun the corn or harvest god. This is clearly implied by the reception he receives from the twenty-nine pupils of St. Bride's night school. As the chapter opens, these girls have gathered about the "yellowstone landmark" (see the periodic ejaculation of Old Faithful). Jaun arrives, perfumed with "wild thyme and parsley," doffing a "hat with a reinforced crown," and wearing his hair in "golliwog

---

[17] According to his letters Joyce reworked *Shaun abc* in 1925 and again in 1926. *Letters, op. cit.* pp. 224, 241.

[18] Draft 6 (BM Add MS. 47483, p. 117). This version is only an approximation of the 2nd stage of the sentence's chronological development.

curls"; and they dance up to kiss the "post"[19] (Jaun or the log) in a simulated spring or harvest dance.[20] Again, the log is the Bodhi tree of enlightenment whose protection Buddha employed to help him withstand the terrors of the "four watches of the night." There is an evident but valid contradiction between Jaun's wish to stay, a craven desire contrary to the dictates of his mission, and the Buddha's resistance to movement, his steadfast observance of a vow.

The major addition to the draft is an account of the "goose's" laying of the dawn egg. By means of this adverbial phrase Joyce motivates his hero's action and elaborates upon the theme of the "bark of the day." We may infer from the context that the author was quite aware of the goose's wide religious significance as a soul bird. According to the Hindu institutes of Manu, Brahmā, the breath of life, "progenitor of the Universe," was hatched from a golden egg laid by the Supreme Spirit (Brahmă). For the Egyptians, whose sun was said to have been laid by "the primeval goose," Osiris was the son of Seb, an anthropomorphized goose.[21] By extension, Jaun's bird will lay the egg from which the Christian world will emerge after the culmination of Jesus' sacrifice. Gautama's Brahma will eventually provide him with the divine knowledge (Buddha means "enlightened") to which he aspires. Osiris' Seb will make possible the god's physical

[19] Page 430/6, 29, 17–18, 23, 20.

[20] Harold Bayley describes the Greek festival of the laurel bearer where the principal actor wears his hair loose under a golden wreath as he leads a band of maidens. The author cites in this connection a Guernsey harvest dance known as "A mon beau Laurier." "In this ceremony the dancers join hands, whirl round, curtsy, and kiss a central object, in later days either a man or a woman, but, in the opinion of Miss Carey, 'perhaps originally either a sacred stone or a primeval altar'" (*Archaic England*, London, 1919, p. 541). Much of the date used in this article to explicate Joyce's mythological analogies is to be found in Bayley's 2 books on symbology, *The Lost Language of Symbolism* and *Archaic England*. These rather idiosyncratic books contain such a surprising number of clues to the esoteric meanings of this sentence and, in general, to the analogies in *Finnegans Wake* that I am strongly tempted to place them among Joyce's source books. This does not, of course, rule out other possible sources such as Frazer or Harrison or even the encyclopedias.

[21] Bayley, *The Lost Language of Symbolism*, I (London, 1951; first pub. 1912), 93–94—hereafter referred to as *Lost Language*. Like Joyce, Bayley equates these with the tale of the goose that laid the golden egg. See also *Encyclopedia Britannica*, 11th edition, Vol. 4, p. 397 and Vol. 19, pp. 138–39.

renewal. While, on the material level, Jaun's goose will provide him with wealth and sustenance, his breakfast.

The second stage of the draft reads as follows:

> I could sit on one side till the bark of the day *while the rugaby moon had rolled west through her scrummages* for to watch how *carefully* my nocturnal goose*mother* would lay her *new* golden *shee*gg for [sic] ~~behind me~~ *down under* in the shy orient.[22]

Here Joyce introduces a third aspect, the dualistic interpretation of the moon's nightly journey. To describe his moon, the author evolved a rich series of play images well suited to Jaun's adolescent and childish or Tom Sawyerlike identity. But the pleasure element innate in sports was darkened for Joyce by prior associations.[23] "Rockaby" and "Rugby" are both descriptive of the moon which rolls across the sky, but "Rugby" negates the dreamy quality of the other word and evokes the turmoil of a game field. The moon is destroying the worn-out remnants of civilization, preparing for the new day, while enforcing Jaun's lazy mood, lulling him to sleep. Again, although the cloud image implicit in "scrummages," baby talk for small clouds, is primarily a restful one, the duality is confirmed by the brutally kinetic football scrimmage.

As we might expect, the lunar image yields a rich harvest of associations. For the early Christian and the ancient Hindoo the crescent moon, symbolized here by a cradle, meant the land of heaven (*Lost Language*, I, 44). Likewise, the crescent with the circle (i.e., the ambiguous shape of our moon as a Rugby-ball cradle) signified the kingdom of heaven or the ultimate perfection of the millennium (I, 56). Joyce pictures a paradise surrounded by cloudlike angels. Still faithful to Egyptian, Hindoo, and Christian symbology, he depicts the moon as preparing the

[22] Draft 6 (BM Add MS. 47483, p. 117).

[23] In *A Portrait of the Artist as a Young Man* Joyce describes Stephen's impressions of a rugby game: "He was caught in the whirl of a scrimmage and, fearful of the flashing eyes and muddy boots, bent down to look through the legs. The fellows were struggling and groaning and their legs were rubbing and kicking and stamping" (New York, 1916), p. 4. This same image reappears in *Ulysses* where a more mature Stephen watches a game from Mr. Deasy's window: "Again: a goal. I am among them, among their battling bodies in a medley, the joust of life." Joyce continues with an evocation of the "uproar of battles, the frozen deathspew of the slain . . ." (New York, 1946), p. 33.

way for the hero's return. As such, "she" is a "destroyer of foes" (I, 107–8), a powerful light image in a darkened world.

Joyce does everything he can to help the reader fill in *Finnegans Wake*'s symbolic patterns. Thus, the goose that laid the golden egg has become a nocturnal symbol for pleasant dreams and light fantasies. This marriage of images continues and amplifies the above-mentioned theme of "Rockabye Baby" while injecting a further set of conflicts. By the portentous placement of the word "mother," Joyce makes it clear that "goose mother" is more than a reference to that good old lady Mother Goose or even to the creator goose; it is also a pun on nightmare or "smother."[24] Likewise, in reference to "Rockabye Baby," we remember that the cradle will fall, and we find therein an echo of the primal fall from innocence. This is of course confirmed by the fact that Jaun is an aspect of that first man, HCE, and that he shares and relives the tragedy of the *father*'s guilt as he leans against the post of *his* memory.

Again in the Rugby-Fall context, as Joyce's friend Samuel Beckett has pointed out to me, mother goose's "she-égg" is, according to Freud, a symbol of defecation (see French argotic sense). The little boy's world of Shaun, like the subconscious world of HCE, sees defecation as a catastrophic act worthy of the closest attention and an act of creation. As the night, Shaun's goose mother lays the new sun; for the sun must, like the Phoenix, be born afresh. The goose's giving birth to the light parallels the creation of darkness by HCE defecating in Phoenix Park. Appropriately, both acts lead to the destruction or fall of their perpetrators.

In this valuable egg, laid for Jaun "down under" or in Australia (or America?), we find a new aspect of the get-rich-quick motifs present in the early versions of the paragraph. Both "down under" and "for to" remind us of the language of the adventurous emigrants whose motives the speaker shares. It would seem that he wishes to move only after his fortune has been *carefully* provided for.

The true nature of the egg's location becomes clear when we associate Joyce's sentence with Harold Bayley's discussion under the chapter heading "Down Under" of the prehistoric "*Dane*

[24] "A fiend or incubus formerly supposed to oppress people during sleep" (*Webster's New Collegiate Dictionary*).

holes"[25] which dot the English and Irish countrysides. These holes, Bayley states, had nothing to do with the Danes, whose appearance they antedate. Instead, they represent perhaps the dwelling places of some ancient troglodites, that is, "the Children of Don or Danu," the Danaan. In *Finnegans Wake*, the blood of Finn, the Dublin giant, whom Joyce patterned after the English Penrith giant, is "Danu U'Dunnell's" ale (p. 7/12).[26] Of more direct interest is the fact that the primitives "believed that the Life of the World, in the form of the Young Sun, was born yearly anew on 25th December, always in a cave: thus caves were invariably sacred to the Dawn or God of Light, and only secondarily to the engulfing powers of Darkness . . ." (*Archaic England*, p. 765). The Danaan's caves and the barrow of the Penrith giant are therefore similar in nature to the Phoenix' pyre: the home of the issuing soul or sun or race, and the testing ground of the dismembered hero. If we may presume that Joyce had these interpretations in mind, Jaun links himself not only with the sun but also with the prehistoric cradle of life, the birthplace of all ancestors. In a world where actual time and place do not exist, our protean hero visualizes himself as being in two places at once. As the false sun he is either sitting down, waiting for the daybreak or, the moon having completed her journey, he has already bridged the night and is sitting "on one side" of the sun bark, below the horizon or in a dene cave, watching his "goosemother" lay the new day. Hence, the action is, now more than ever, dualistic: the hero is at once neglecting and fulfilling his function.

With the "when" clause—"when the moon had rolled West through her scrummages"—Joyce introduced into a basic evening-morning, death-resurrection context a solid time element. He hoped thereby to complete the motivation of Jaun's behavior, suggesting the texture of the nocturnal gap: the ordeal of the sacrificial hero, his dying into evening, and the dismemberment

[25] See Joyce's "perish the Dane."

[26] In another context Bayley mentions the existence of an "Adam's Grave" or "Giant's Grave near Edenhall by Penrith . . ." (*Archaic England*, p. 746). For further information on the derivation of Joyce's Giant see Joseph Prescott, "Concerning the Genesis of *Finnegans Wake*," *PMLA*, LXIX (Dec. 1954), 1300–32, and Walton Litz, "The Genesis of *Finnegans Wake*," *N&Q* (Oct. 1953), pp. 445–47.

which must precede the recovery, that is, the nature of the hero's accomplishment. But this new element, as we have seen, only halfway fulfills its purpose. The sentence is still primarily concerned with the morning and evening worlds, the poles of its action. The new clause vacillates between these two major elements but possesses no ground of its own. Joyce was later to recognize that, in what amounts to a ritualistic or semi-incantatory situation, emotional distance must intervene between *theophany* and the ritual death.

Nevertheless, the author has established a basis for further development, a solid armature which will adhere to and generate a meaningful structure for the future. The sentence, as it first stood, was itself an elaboration on an already-existing theme. As such an elaboration should, it helped supply color and mood. Our sentence now stands in relation to its future elements, as the paragraph once stood in relation to it.

> I could sit on one side till the bark of the day *laughing at the sheep's lightning* ~~while~~ ~~when~~ *till I'd followed with my nephew-scope* the rugaby moon *cumuliously* ~~had~~ *roll*~~ed~~*ing himself* west through ~~her~~ *the* scrummages for to watch how carefully my nocturnal goosemother would lay her new golden sheegg for [sic] down under in the shy orient.[27]

The two major addenda in this revision both contribute to the sense of chronological continuity required by the dramatic context. The first, "*laughing at the sheep's lightning*," gives Jaun at least two occupations as he awaits the dawn. He will continue to enjoy the fireworks that accompany the sunset, that is, the lightning of the sunboat or ship. He will count sheep. But in spite of his flippant manner, uneasy rests our hero's head; for the sheep in question are jumping over the insomniac's proverbial fence and the sheet lightning, though in itself harmless, is frequently a presage of trouble and may well be a result of the moon's battle with the clouds. A further aspersion is cast on Jaun's courage by an earlier association. In the "Circe" chapter of *Ulysses*, Zoe, the harlot, sees courage in Stephen Dedalus' palm. This he denies while his friend Lynch quips, "Sheet lightning courage" (p. 547). We may also see in the lightning a symbol both of the fall of Satan and of the nocturnal predominance

[27] Draft 6 (BM Add MS. 47483, p. 117).

of Jaun's brother Shem. As the Mulligan-like Jaun knows, his satanic twin is the possessor of the "proud lightning of the intellect" (*Ulysses*, p. 51).

"... ~~while~~ ~~when~~ till I'd followed with my nephewscope" evidences already some consistency in Joyce's preference for the vague "till," though the versatility of this chameleon word becomes apparent only when it is examined in the light of the three "till's" employed in the final version of the sentence. In the present context, "while," with its simple evocation of continuity, lacks the dual or "timeless" inference of a word which suggests continuous action but with an added note of finality, a note that is too strong in "when." Other aspects of this clause, such as the kinship suggested by "nephew," are far less clear. Perhaps, if, as some cultures do, we see the moon to be the brother of the female night or the male sun, the child born of the conjunction of the day with the night is the moon's nephew. When we recall that the sentence is illumined by the setting sun, we are tempted to consider the satellite in a ritual context. The bloodshed caused by its struggle with the clouds identifies it with the sacramental bread immersed in wine, symbolic of Jaun's destiny as a Christ figure. Christ-Jaun, the illegitimate son of the Holy Ghost,[28] might then be the nephew (nephew being the son of a priest) of God, the savior whose return will be signaled by the "bark of the day."

In keeping with the above, the allusion to "cope" introduces an element of the ecclesiastical garb, and the "nephew's cope" becomes the badge of office of a celebrant following the host in a procession. Since the cope was originally worn as a protection against inclement weather, Jaun will be protected both by his cloak and by his religious function from the ravages of the coming storm-catastrophe. In all events the "nephew-scope," as part of the hero's accouterment, gives its possessor special rights and privileges and a clearer view of the proceedings which will lead to the great event. Though the expression "followed with my nephewscope" suggests the action of watching from a safe distance with a telescope, the allusion to "nephoscope," a meteorological instrument for measuring the distance and velocity of clouds, suggests the reasons for Jaun's concern. It will permit him to judge the weather from a distance, to spot the approach

[28] See Joyce's application of this theme in *Ulysses:* "My mother's a jew, my father's a bird" (p. 20).

of a storm that could signal the new epoch and perhaps his own ruin.

Appropriately inserted into the lunar phrase, "cumuliously" describes the nature of the moon's action as it rolls toward the seated or floating figure of our hero. The "rugaby moon" is fighting its way through cumulous clouds (suggestive of a coming storm), gaining in size like a snowball rolled through the snow. Its approach is like that of a conquering hero, a Julius Caesar—that is, Iullii, or a god or god surrogate, a pathfinder. Clearly, such a deity can only be male, but in affirming this, Joyce weakened the nocturnal predominance of the female so evident in the last draft. No longer does a *female* moon[29] roll across the sky to watch the female goose prepare the new day which will be female or a "she egg" until the day hatches, breaking the subjective shell of night. By introducing an imposing male force, Joyce has created a new polarity for his sentence.

In relation to the secondary levels, "himself," "sheep's," and "lightning" all suggest magical qualities. Taking these elements one at a time, we find first that the moon is male in several important religions. It is outstandingly so in the Egyptian where the god Thoth, "bearing on his narrow ibis head the cusped moon,"[30] is the scribe who invented letters, the judge of the dead, the possessor of dark knowledge (Hermes Trismegistus was his medieval cognomen).[31] According to myth, Thoth was installed as vice-gerent taking the sun's place at night.[32] In *Finnegans Wake* he is reincarnated in Shem-the-pen, HCE's dark son, who is responsible for "lettruce invrention" (p. 424/20). Shem, like Thoth, is a *wandervogl* (p. 419/14); he too possesses infinite knowledge of the dark powers. As the moon, he shares with Jaun-the-shadow-sun the reflected light of the vanished Helios. Jaun calls him "Dave the Dancekerl," the "mightiest penumbrella I ever flourished on behond the shadow of a post!" (p. 462/21–22). He is, then, the modern equivalent of the nocturnal eye of Horus.[33] Jaun, as Osiris, sees in him both a continuator and

[29] ALP is elsewhere called "Mrs. Moonan" (p. 157/15).

[30] *A Portrait of the Artist*, p. 264.

[31] See also William Y. Tindall's article, "James Joyce and the Hermetic Tradition," *JHI*, XI (Jan. 1954), 23–39.

[32] Max Müller, *Egyptian*, in *The Mythology of all Races*, XII (Boston, 1918), 34.

[33] In Iliii, which recounts the conquest of the sun, HCE is variously named "ahorace" (p. 325), "horces" (p. 322), "Horuse" (p. 328).

an enemy, both a wanderer, whose journey must be followed by the new day, and a Cain (or diabolic Typhon-Set) who wittingly destroys his brother by goring him with a phallic tusk.

The newly introduced Christian liturgical motif ("cope") and the Buddhist parallel may both be interpreted in a similar way. Thus the moon represents the all too substantial Mara, god of sensual lust, who appears as an ambiguous enemy of the spiritual light throughout *Finnegans Wake*.[34] The evil principle is here pictured as leading his marshaled host across the night sky in an effort to intimidate the sedentary Buddha. Meanwhile, as the principle of spiritual light, enemy of sensuous clouds or temptations, the moon is the Vedic "destroyer of foes" or Buddha's active spirit striving for total illumination (*Lost Language*, I, 108). For the Christian, also, Shem's moon, the bright possessor of dark truth, personifies two mutually contradictory existences. He is Dave, the paraclete, Shaun's own shadow, who will continue the existence of Christ and pursue his ends till the dawn. Paradoxically, he is also Lucifer, the lightning of the intellect, the once bright god become an enemy and relegated to the night. Consequently, Shaun, who is often identified with Michael, is shepherd of God as opposed to Shem's Nick, the devil horrifying the innocent sheep after the defeat of the hero.[35]

Jaun's function as the youthful Christ places him in a primitive Christian context as the "Good Shepherd," an Abel figure awaiting Cain-the-tiller's blow.[36] Like the Good Shepherd, Jaun wishes to remain with his flock. Like Him also, his excuse for leaving is a *wholly* plausible one: he must prepare the coming era of salvation—he must fulfill the hero's duty. In such a setting the moon is the physical reflection of the dead, the proof of the existence of the godhead. Like the sheet lightning, his action is

[34] On p. 122 we witness the comic battle between God and O'Mara, while on p. 460 "Mrs. A'Mara makes up" with "Mrs. O'Morum." See also p. 407, "Mara O'Mario."

[35] A positive interpretation of Lucifer's role is also possible. Lucifer is the moral garbage collector who makes Christ's work possible. Bayley explains brother killing as the murder of love by learning. After cataloguing the pairs of opposites he states that "probably LUCIFER, the fallen angel was originally the twin brother of his opponent MICHAEL . . . subsequently one revolted against the other . . ." (*Lost Language*, II, 28). In mystic lore, love and learning are the 2 sons of wisdom (see ALP) (ibid., I, 272).

[36] See also the myth of Orpheus, reenforced later by the introduction of "wireless harps."

full of portent but heatless: *fearful*[37] for the wicked or impure, but *sublime* for the pure.

All things considered, the hero's moment of inaction has been altered but slightly by Jaun's statement of function. Even the sentence's rich possibilities, the elements that I have discussed in connection with this draft, have yet to be affirmed symbolically by later developments. In its stark economy the passage still lacks the sensual aspects which would make it more portentous, more human.

Nevertheless, in the next draft, Joyce did no more than apply a superficial gloss:

> laughing *lazy* at the sheep's lightning,
> my *old* nephewscope
> rolling himself west*asleep*
> golden sheeg for *me*.[38]

Adding another static nuance to Jaun's position, "lazy" suggests a semiprone attitude ("layzy"), that of the insomniac. In choosing this word, as in selecting the next addition, "old," Joyce was influenced by the tonal quality of his context. Through his reference to the age of the "nephewscope," the author evokes, first, the stability of Jaun as an institution capable of acquiring and conserving possessions and, second, the hero's place in the future era, which will provide him with a new cope. The next element, "asleep," gives added emphasis to the nursery-rhyme quality of the phrase without detracting from its more ominous aspects. The sleeping moon rocking through the little clouds is closely linked to the triumphant Rugby-ball moon beating its way to the west, slipping "westasleep" through the clouds toward his resting place.[39] Meanwhile, Shaun's relationship to

---

[37] A citation taken from *A Portrait of the Artist* illustrates the fact that Joyce has woven his own terror into the fabric of this sentence. "I fear many things," says the demonic Stephen Dedalus, "dogs, horses, firearms, the sea, thunderstorms, machinery, the country roads at night" (p. 287). Earlier, in reference to his aesthetic, Stephen said, "Terror is the feeling which arrests the mind in the presence of whatsoever is grave and constant in human sufferings and unites it with the secret cause" (p. 239). Seeing himself as the mirror of the human "constants," the artist has bestowed fresh life upon his youthful theory.

[38] Draft 7, clean copy of 1st typescript (BM Add MS. 47483, pp. 144–45).

[39] Stuart Gilbert, *Our Exagmination Round his Factification for Incamination of Work in Progress* (Paris, 1929), p. 70, sees in "westasleep" a reference to the revolutionary song "the West's Asleep."

the new sun is further defined by "for me." The new egg is his in at least four ways: he will be hatched from it; he will be rejuvenated by it; he will be saved by it; he will be enriched by it.

The polishing process continues in Drafts 4 and 5, which may be treated as a unit, the material in the fifth draft providing us with final developments of two puns begun in the fourth:

> till I'd followed ~~with~~ *through* my ~~old~~ *upfielded* nephewscope the rugaby moon cumuliously *goa*rolling himself westasleep ~~through~~ *amuckst* the ~~scrummages~~ ~~skyscrums~~ CLOUSCRUMS—[40]

> cumuliously godrolling himself westasleep amuckst the cloud-scrums[41]

The corrections and revisions in these two drafts all tend to point up the already existing sport-bloodshed motifs while complicating the pun structure of the sentence. After exchanging the *poor* words "with" and "old" for the rich ones "through" and "upfielded," Joyce found it necessary to replace a second "through" in order to avoid a weak repetition. These changes also affect the interpretation of "cope" elaborated in my discussion of the preceding draft. In the religious context, "followed through" might be interpreted as "followed through the grace of" or "by means of." The "field" in "upfielded" is then the decorated part of the priestly vestment.

"Followed through" expresses more clearly the action of observing with the aid of a telescope or in the mirror of a nephoscope. Simultaneously, it calls to mind Jaun's position as he gazes up from the bottom of a floating barrel, subject to the vicissitudes of the life liquid, which it no longer contains but which will not be denied. HCE's shadow form links the eternal Yin-Yang pair. His Guinness barrel once contained the stout "made from Liffey river water." Whereas the fluid stout is the blood of Jaun's father, the river of life is his mother. This wooden husk, this shell, is what remains of a man after his demise: his reputation, his life's work, his "bark." Clinging to lifeless modes and empty credos, Jaun's decadent spirit is symbolized by the hollowness of his barrel. The river of life, true to her function, will eventually wash such light material out to sea, where, once

[40] Draft 8 (BM Add MS. 47483, p. 173).

[41] Draft 11, April 1928—1st *transition* magazine proof sheets (BM Add MS. 47483, p. 188).

again full of vital liquid, it may regain its former validity as a male force. (A similar relationship may be posited if we see Jaun as the yellow sun ball sinking into the west and rising out of the sea to the east.) Colored by this promise of rejuvenescence, both "followed through" and "upfielded" suggest aspiration and achievement, active participation; both share in the combative aura of sports. There is innate in these expressions a vivacity which evokes hoards of images whose turbulence conflicts sharply with the startling quiescence of their context and of the age. The achieved effect is best described in terms of an action-still photograph.

The prefix "goa," which might well have been a slip of the pen, (and which for some reason appears as "god" in the next draft) adds little more than a slight Western tang to the sentence. In its final form, however, "god-rolling" reinforces the above-mentioned aspects of the moon as god surrogate. The familiar dualistic note is struck by the combination of the awesome aspect of the raging god with the clownish aspect of the moon who goes "drolling."

"Amuckst," the word Joyce chose as a replacement for "through," throws the suggestive balance of the cloud passage towards blatancy. Its colorful sensual connotations outweigh the simple social meanings, 'among' or 'amidst,' by their inference of grime ("muck"), bloodshed ("amuck"), and by the suggested picture of evening clouds dyed with the blood of the setting sun, an orgiastic scene. This situation is aggravated by the suggestive element of "moon madness" (i.e., to run amuck), which adds to the dangers of the night. To balance these nuances, the author crossed out "scrummages" with its brutal denotation, substituting for it the more childish and hence more indirect "sky-scrums." Shortly thereafter, he must have found this pun on clouds as the crumbs scattered in the sky singularly nonevocative. As a unit it has no substantial meaning; when broken down, its elements ("sky's crums" or "sky scrums") fail to jell in the reader's mind. Indeed, even the inference of "scrummages" is somewhat smothered by the abbreviation. Chosen for clarity's sake (Joyce has too often been accused of not wishing to communicate), the two final variants emphasize the nursery-rhyme effect while directing the reader's attention towards "crumbs" and "scrums" or the dramatic depiction of the havoc wrought by the moon as he progressively scatters his cumulous enemy. The final variant "cloudscrums" ensures the static emotional balance of the pun cluster, "westasleep," "amuckst," "cloudscrums."

The second of the above-treated drafts dates from April 1928. During the four years that had elapsed since 1924, nine revisions had been made. Joyce was already working from *transition* magazine page proofs. At that stage the sentence placed Shaun in conjunction with the larger natural phenomena: the solar and lunar cycles, the cloud formations, and the lightning. His drama, like that of Max Müller's solar heroes of mythology, was basically an astral one. Draft 12 marks the beginning of a trend toward greater integration, the introduction of the themes and patterns already established for the paragraph and for the book.

> I could sit on one side till the bark of the day *for hoopoe's hours*, laughing lazy at the sheep's lightning and crekking jugs at the grenoulls, ~~and~~ *leaving tea for the trout* AND ~~BELEEKS~~ BEL-LEEKS FOR THE WARY, till I'd followed through my up-fielded nephewscope the rugaby moon cumuliously godrolling himself westasleep amuckst the cloudscrums for to watch how carefully my nocturnal goosemother would lay her new golden sheegg for me down under in the shy orient.[42]

Due perhaps to the brevity of the 1924–26 sentence, as well as to a lack of detachment, Joyce had heretofore neglected to incorporate the background motifs, the rich bird, fish, and animal references which had long been present in the surrounding sentences. Functionally, these references replace conventional description, contributing to the passage a rich Garden of Eden backdrop which helps situate the action on several planes while providing no positive clues for the identification of locale or epoch. Furthermore, they contribute to the evocation of certain specific attitudes and analogies. For example, the three types of creatures abounding in Jaun's garden are suggestive of three locations: the heavens or "birds' lodging" (p. 449/17–18), the earth or "upon this earthlight" (p. 449/7), and the water world implicit in the phrase "flashing down the swansway, leaps ahead of the swift MacEels . . ." (p. 450/5–6). For each of these we find a symbolic manifestation of the hero: earth/the landbound postman, water/the barrel, air/the false sun—echoes all of the mystic

---

[42] Draft 12, 16 May 1928—2nd *transition* proof sheets, many changes (BM Add MS. 47483, p. 198). Third-level additions are indicated by boldface.

trinities. Again we may equate these elements with three realities being portrayed simultaneously: the temporal (i.e., Shaun-the-post, Tristan, Tom Sawyer), the priestly (i.e., liturgy and ritual), and the godly (i.e., Osiris, Christ, Buddha). More generally, by suggesting a Garden of Eden and making of our hero a childlike Adam, successor to his father in a recreated world, this "pastoral" setting amplifies the paradox already visible in earlier drafts. We may assume that Jaun is not a true Adam; as a child of decadence, he is preparing himself intellectually for the new era, "going primitive." In the coming age he will be, or hopes to be, the reincarnation of the original father, living the life of the romantics' "happy savage." Indeed, perhaps the passage's rich esoteric symbolism was included for a similar reason, the portrayal of man's debile search for lost truths and occult secrets as characterized by such late mystical beliefs as Theosophy, Rosicrucianism, or Gnosticism. As if to reenforce the negative and absurd quality, Joyce introduced references to two of Aristophanes' comedies: *The Birds* in which a molting and stinking hoopoe is king, and *The Frogs* in which a cowardly Dionysus makes his trip to Hades.

The pre-Fall atmosphere is also consonant with the sentence's ominous dual aspects: God-the-Avenger is present in the lightning, the bark, and the moon. The scene thus set is Phoenix Park where the wonderful sun bird dies and is reborn, where HCE sins and falls, where the youth prepares to assume the rights of manhood. It is the locale of the sacrificial death of the Nature god, of Buddha's denial of the flesh, that is, the garden of sensual delights or Buddha's second watch. By the sheer weight of this imagery we are brought to feel the nature of the loss sustained by the hero on denying, on being banished from or on leaving this world.

Letters as well as words become for Joyce applicable at once as sounds, shapes, and symbols. The nature of the resulting effects, available only after close study, is best illustrated in our sentence by the cluster, "for hoopoe's hours." Prolonging the cyclical aspect both audibly and visibly, "hoop" and "oe's" are both circle words; the sound "hours," like the clock face which it brings to mind, may be conceived of as being *rou*nd. The existence of a hidden pun on the French word *oripeau* ("'or hoopoe's"), that is, something that has a false brilliance, is substantiated by the more accessible "for who pose." Jaun-the-setting-sun would like to sit still till his hour returns; he would like his refracted glow to last the night through. In James Frazer's *Golden Bough* we read that the Swabians believe in the hoopoe's power to find the magical spring wort, supposed by them to bloom only on the night of the summer solstice.[43] The renewal element implied here gains force when we recall that this bird, whose nest is notoriously malodorous, is said to have an affinity for excrement (see also "sheegg"). An even stronger affirmation of the return theme is found in the predominant role played here by the shape and meaning of the letter *O*, the circle that will return us to the past while bringing us to the future. As a unit containing exactly five of these circles, "fOr hOOpOe's hOurs" may have a special and perhaps a mystical signification. For the Pythagoreans the number "five" typified light, and we are told that five circles were the Mayan and Egyptian symbols for "daylight and splendour."[44] In this connection we note that Joyce, who had at one time studied the mystical texts, was quite conscious of the esoteric associations implicit in letters. He appreciated the mystic value of the *E*, regarded as the symbol of light sacred to Apollo by dint perhaps of its five points and its position as "fifth character in the Egyptian, Phoenician, Greek and Latin alphabets . . ." (*Lost Language*, I, 291). Thus on page 454 of *Finnegans Wake* Jaun intones, "Shunt us! shunt us! shunt us! . . . Sacred ease there!" "Alpha and omega" are evoked in reverse order when, in her ritual address to the dying god, the priestess Issy speaks of "oval owes and artless awes" (p. 458/36). Again, in the majestic opening of ALP's chapter, the *O* synthesizes woman's unity in function:

O
tell me all about
Anna Livia! I want to hear all. [p. 196]

Although I do not believe that Joyce ever went to the extremes of a Rimbaud or a René Ghil in establishing color or

---

[43] London, 1914–17, XI, 70, n. 2.

[44] *Lost Language*, I, 267. Bayley also states that the "*khu* or intelligent portion of the Egyptian soul was figured as a crested bird [or Phoenix], perhaps the crested bird known nowadays as a *hoopoo* or *pupu*; Khu was the God of Light, and in ordinary use the word *khu* meant *glorious* or *shining*" (II, p. 117).

tonal values for the letters of the alphabet, I am convinced that he was acutely aware of the effects that can be achieved by means of the careful manipulation of significant sounds and shapes. Perhaps we may discount as early experimentation the letter experiences described in *A Portrait of the Artist as a Young Man* and in *Ulysses*,[45] but we are forced to affirm that the "Professor's" analysis of the letters used in ALP's "Mamafesto" is more than a satirical "leg-pull." When he speaks of a "bullsfooted bee" (p. 120/7), of "those throne open doubleyous . . . seated with such floprightdown determination and reminding uus ineluctably of nature at her naturalest" (p. 120/28–33), or of "that strange exotic serpentine, since so properly banished from our scripture" (p. 121/20–21), or again of the "trim trite truth letter" (p. 120/3–4), the author is no more nonsensical than when in that very same passage he mentions the sentence "to be nuzzled over a full trillion times for ever and a night till his noodle sink or swim by that ideal reader suffering from an ideal insomnia" (p. 120/12–14). ALP's letter is after all just another aspect of Joyce's gest book, and Joyce was never so serious as when he jested.

"*. . . leaving tea for the trout*" continues the alliterative mode, the jingle tone so well fitted to the gentle dullness of a Jaun. In order to kill time during the night, the postman is picnicking alongside the river. Tea, the first of the elements that he will leave behind him, is the fortuneteller's medium of knowing the future. But these leavings are more than presages, they signify the past; like the excavated detritus of dead cities, they illuminate stages of civilization. Jaun wishes to continue the developmental process begun by his father, leaving a further stratum of history. In the hope of gaining a measure of immortality, he is doing his bit to maintain the stream of life. Furthermore, the *T* or *T*au, as the mark of Thoth and the "truth letter," is equivalent to the word of God, symbolized also by the pages or "leaves" of the Bible or by the cross of Christ. "Tea" is then another variant for ALP's letter of life: the *word* as transcribed by Shem-the-pen, the garbled message brought to light by the culture-hero, Jaun, who has received it from the dark powers.

Significantly, in Iv we learn that a mysterious tea stain served

---

[45] See *Portrait of the Artist*, pp. 193, 274, 187, 255, 262, etc.; for *Ulysses* see Tindall, *James Joyce: His Way of Interpreting the Modern World* (New York, 1950), p. 10.

as a signature for the letter of ALP (p. 111/20–24),[46] whose symbol is the "trout."[47] In IIIi, the narrator (Shem?), after completing an account of Shaun's symbolic repast (the postman is feeding on the legacy or flesh of the father), addresses a prayer to ALP in the role of the matriarchal goddess of tea: "Ever of thee, Anne Lynch, he's deeply draiming: Houseanna. Tea is the Highest! For auld lang Ayternitay" (p. 406/27–28). The last word in this citation combines most of the nuances already treated with the associations *a-t-t-a:* the "first and the last, the last and the first"[48] (letters of the Hebrew alphabet or the Greek *a-o*).

By implication, Jaun's tea offering is also a "ritual of aversion"[49] directed towards ALP as the force which has imprisoned the male light. It is characteristic of all such gifts that the giver does not *bestow* but *leaves* or even *throws* his offering to the hated and feared god. Then, like Orpheus, turning his back towards the dread spot (see Jaun, "I'd followed through my upfielded nephewscope"), he quits the shrine. Jaun's "tealeaves," "jugs,"[50] and "bel-leaks" are appropriately base, as are the three forms of the deity, "frogs," "trout," and "the wary."

". . . *and belleeks for the wary*," with its reference to Belleek ware (the Irish porcelain), completes the tea imagery and provides the archeologist with a shard of modern man. Joyce's alteration of the spelling to "beleek" may have been a simple error, but more likely it was a first effort to imitate the shrieks of the two girls surprised by HCE while they were urinating in Phoenix Park. "Bel eeks" now becomes even more appropriately "belle-eeks" or "belle-leeks." Also implicated in that crime are the "wary" or those who are capable of profiting by the lessons

[46] We are told that the "*signa tau* or *signature*" is the "mark of enlightenment mentioned in Ezekiel as being branded on the foreheads of the elect" (*Lost Language*, I, 293).

[47] Joyce establishes this association in one of his notebooks. See Peter Spielberg's *James Joyce's Manuscripts and Letters at the University of Buffalo: A Catalogue* (Buffalo, 1962).

[48] "The expression 'last' is generally misunderstood in this connection, the truer implication being the end of the last days and the dawn of the new era or beginning" (*Lost Language*, I, 73).

[49] See Jane Harrison, *Prolegomena to the Study of Greek Religion* (New York, 1955), pp. 8–9.

[50] Traditionally *thrown* to Hecate "at the meeting of three ways" (ibid., p. 38).

of the past, the three soldiers or warriors ("war-y"), that is, the trinity, or a configuration of treacherous demigods who spied on HCE and published his crime. Perhaps, Jaun, whose function in life is to deliver the letter, will use his power to prevent others from falling as his father fell. Here we may read an aspect of Jaun's heroic function: he will deposit the word that will save us or he will take upon himself the onus of the crime, leaving holy shrines, sacred or vestigial fires dedicated to the solar god Baal or Bel.[51] On the other hand, Jaun's decadent character is revealed by the interpretation "I will leave the girls to the soldiers; I will leave revelation to those who are strong."

A third lazy occupation, *"crekking jugs at the grenoulls,"* takes us back to the garden where the first man was confronted with amphibious life and where Jaun awaits the sunrise. There is more than a hint of the primordial in the appearance of a frog (*grenouill*). According to the Egyptian creation tale cited above, frogs were on the hill which stood alone above the floodwaters of the earth. (Also on that hill was the goose egg containing the solar goose, which, once hatched, flew across the sky to make earthly life possible.)[52] This early flood myth is vaguely reminiscent of our own Genesis. When the flood, like the sunset, was at once a sign of God's wrath and His love. Jaun, sitting beside the crematory pyre of the sun bird,[53] reaffirms his desire to survive the catastrophe with its annihilation of values in order to participate in the slow reconstruction. This is signified by his "tossing jugs," that is, the shards, or "cracking jokes" at the frogs, symbols of new life ("grenoull," "renoull," renewal). The lighthearted tone of this phrase is, however, balanced by the overtones of brutality and by Jaun's own fear. The hero's *genoux* are "knocking" or "crekking" together (Gilbert, p. 70).

[51] See Belleek as a Baalbec or shrine to Baal, the sun (*Lost Language*, I, 150). The "belleeks," like the "tea," have both light and dark significations. Joyce refers to Baal or Bel several times and mentions Baalfires on p. 13/36 and p. 52/19.

[52] Adolph Erdman, *La religion des Egyptiens*, trans. Henri Wild (Paris, 1937), p. 86.

[53] In the larger context of the paragraph Jaun repeatedly associates himself with birds. Thus he *is* the hoopoe; he exchanges nightingale calls with the frogs; he lodges with the "pheasant." Later we see that he *is* the "phaynix"; "Shoot up on that, bright Bennu bird!" (473/17). The pun "phaynix" plays upon the French *fainéant* or do-nothing, an apt description of Jaun.

From Finnegans Wake: *A Sentence in Progress*

A further aspect of the destruction-renewal theme is found in the sounds "jug" and "brékkek." T. S. Eliot uses the Elizabethan "jug jug" of the nightingale in his *Wasteland* to signify sordid love. Again, in "Sweeney Among the Nightingales," he compares his hero to a gory Agamemnon sung over by that bird. In spite of its role as a harbinger of the spring, the nightingale is traditionally associated with the night, lovers, sadness, and loss, all predominantly female associations belonging to the low ebb of male existence. Joyce gave point to all of these interpretations when, to the next draft of another sentence in this paragraph he added the reference, "naughtingerls juckjucking benighth me"[54] which yields the interpretation, "naughty girls-nightingales joking-singing beneath me[55] in the night in their effort to benight me."

Jaun's "crekking" recalls the Aristophanian frog sounds figuring in a Joycian description of the beginnings of life after the Fall: "What clashes here of wills gen wonts . . . Brékkek Kékkek Kékkek Kékkek Kóax Kóax Kóax!" (p. 4/2). A few pages later Joyce amplifies this theme by linking it directly to the sunrise and the breakfast egg: "there'll be iggs for the brekkers come to mournhim, sunny side up with care."[56] Like so many others, this passage probably owes its development to a reciprocal interchange. Thus, the author waited four revisions and two years after writing the frog noises in Chapter Ii before he inserted the postdiluvian nuance in our sentence, completing the association "eggs," "frogs," "morning," "sunrise," "care."

As the major elements in the phrases added by this draft have strong sexual connotations, we may detect a note of hypocrisy even in Jaun's gift giving. The two feminine receptacles, the jug and the cup, are both discarded by the sterile publicist, who leaves them and the tea to the fertile trout and frogs and the omnipresent trio. Symbolically, Jaun-Buddha is renouncing the meager pleasures of the flesh, but as the shadow or mime hero, the follower of ritual, Jaun can only invoke the shadows of deeds. As the vestige, he is refusing a right he does not possess, the right to create. Though he glories in and associates himself with the heroic past, his is but a tentative existence. His picnic litter

[54] Draft 14 (BM Add MS. 47483, p. 217).

[55] Jaun is referring to his physical position as the sunset.

[56] Added July 1926 (BM Add MS. 47472, p. 15), *FW*, p. 12/14–15.

is indeed a mere approximation of the barrowful of rubbish left his heirs by that fallen Titan, the true Hero (p. 26).

In adding the pretty details, "cracking jokes with the frogs," "leaving my picnic litter," Joyce took care to maintain the original balance of mood. The next three *transition* proof sheets (two dated 5 June and one 13 June 1928), perfect the balance between earthly and cosmic realities.[57]

the bark of the [sic] ~~day~~ *Saint Grouse's*

I could sit on one side till the bark of the day for hoopoe's hours, laughing lazy at the sheep's lightning, *hearing the mails across the nightrives (peepet! peepet!) and whippoorwilly in the woody (moor park! moor park!), as peacefed as a philopotamus,* and crekking jugs at the grenoulls, leaving tea for the trout . . .[58]

I could sit on ~~one~~ *safe* side till the bark of ~~the day~~ *Saint Grousers* for hoopoe's hours . . . and whippoor willy in the woody . . . my upfielded ne~~ph~~viewscope . . . [59]

If the elements added by Draft 12 are, superficially at least, life aspects to be rejected by Jaun, the better part of those of this draft are passively accepted through his hearing. They are the prophetical noises, equivalents of the primitive "bark of the sun." Appropriately, Joyce began by eliminating the direct sun reference in favor of contradictory elements concealed in "Saint Grouse's." Besides its more evident bird signification, "grouse" means 'complain.' (It also suggests the sound of church bells.) The holy one who *rouses* us with his bark, *complaining* of our misdeeds, is the angel of the reckoning or the Christ or the hound of heaven. The variant "grousers" gives point to the hound nuance by adding a hunting element through which Joyce represents at once the hunted and the hunter. In *Finnegans Wake*, John Peel, the fabulous sportsman, is a sunrise symbol while

[57] Two of these drafts are complementary parts of a single revision of the corrected proofs. The 3rd, however, is composed mainly of corrections for a poorly set final *transition* proof sheet.

[58] Draft 13, 5 June 1928—3rd *transition* proof sheets, many revisions (BM Add MS. 47483, pp. 209, 217).

[59] Draft 14, 13 June 1928—4th *transition* proof sheets, obviously reset, numerous omissions (BM Add MS. 47483, p. 225). An accident of placement ("whippoor" falls at the end of a line of type) and an absent hyphen may have turned one word into two.

Humpty Dumpty is a symbol of the sunset or fall. Peel, with his barking hounds and his "halloo," was capable of waking the dead. But these barking hounds are perhaps conterparts of the devils and angels who will ferret out sinners on the day of judgment or who will lead the rejoicing righteous to the pearly gates. Joyce must have had this in mind when, later in 1928, he included in his fable, "The Ondt and the Gracehoper," the expression "grousious me."[60] He who damns us can also save. He who awakens us raises us and bestows upon us the joy of living.

While making Jaun's neutral position all the more clear by adding a further note of repose, the new version of "I could sit on one side"—"I could sit on safe side"—also contributes to the dualism of the sentence: Jaun's "on safe" is also "unsafe." Joyce, who considered the *S* a serpentine letter, was addicted to the use of the liturgical triple form as in Sanctus Sanctus Sanctus: "Sandhyas! Sandhyas! Sandhyas!" (p. 593/1), "She, she, she!" (p. 570/24), and so on. Both good and bad serpents, the Satan of the garden and the king serpent of the protecting Bodhi tree[61] are invoked by this alliterative group as is the doomed Sidon, "sit-on," the powerful *democratic* citadel of the prosperous Phoenicians.

By changing "nephew" to "neview" Joyce indicated that Jaun's vision is limited by the nature of his being. Incorrigibly sterile, he lacks both foresight and insight. Just as his "follow through" is a useless act as compared with the trail blazing of the hero, his "neviewscope" is but one of many examples of how Jaun practices the fine art of self-deception. Paradoxically, but on a mystic level, the "neviewscope," by denying the visual, may force the hero to discover more excellent truths while following the mystic leader.

First of the direct auditory evocations, "hearing the mails across the nightrives" recalls Jaun's function as postman while introducing the brother battle of the "males" or that of knights in armor ("mail"), the quarrel between the two banks of the river of life. This last aspect is developed by Joyce in the "Anna Livia Plurabelle" chapter (Iviii): "Reeve Gootch was right and

[60] Draft 1 (BM Add MS. 47483, p. 83), *FW*, p. 415: "Grouscious me and scarab my sohul!" says the Ondt linking the Grouse to the solar scarab of Egypt.

[61] J. Campbell, *The Hero with a Thousand Faces* (New York, 1956), pp. 31–33.

Reeve Droched was wrong."[62] The nocturnal reversal of roles evident in the sex of the sun or "sheegg" is also expressed here by the fact that the left bank or Shem was right and the right or Shaun was wrong (or left). Jaun's euphoric mood would not necessarily be disturbed by these sounds; he would continue to be a bystander. However, the ominous overtones and the call to duty are not calculated to put his mind at ease, especially since the mails are no doubt transmitting news of the catastrophe, marshaling forces for the recovery. The battle allusion is considerably enriched by two references; the first, from Plutarch, may well have been in the back of Joyce's mind at this point: "It is an observation, also, that extraordinary rains pretty generally fall after great battles, whether it be that some divine power thus washes and cleanses the polluted earth with showers from above. . . ."[63] After that fabulous brother battle fought by the Mooks (Shaun) and the Gripes (Shem), that is, the fox and the grapes, across the banks of the Liffey, we read of a similar rain:

> Ah dew! Ah dew! It was so dusk that the tears of night began to fall, first by ones and twos, then by threes and fours, at last by five sixes of sevens, for the tired ones were wecking, as we weep now with them. *O! O! O! Par la pluie!* [p. 158][64]

In "*(peepet! peepet!) and whippoorwilly in the woody (moor park! moor park!)*" the bird sounds made by the "mails" are full of portent. Both of the parenthetical expressions, which belong to the tonal backdrop of this passage, are reminiscent of Dean Swift's amours with his Stella and Vanessa.[65] The same elements reinforce the semi-incestuous infantilism of HCE's crime. "Peepet," a variant of Stella's pet name for Swift, is linked to "peacefed" and "belle leeks" by its urination associations, while by its defecation nuance *pet* (French) recalls the "sheegg," clearly linking HCE's crime with his creative act.

"*. . . as peacefed as a philopotamus*" reminds us once more of the river in which Jaun is floating and of Jaun's amphibious state. It also recalls the Eliot poem Joyce preferred, "The Hippopota-

[62] Added to the galley proofs for *Anna Livia Plurabelle* (New York, 1928) (BM Add MS. 47474, p. 259). See *FW*, p. 197, for a final version.

[63] *Plutarch's Lives*, Modern Library ed. (New York, n.d.), p. 507.

[64] The major portion of this was already present in fair copy dated 27 Aug. 1928 (BM Add MS. 47473, p. 231).

[65] Cf. J. Campbell and Henry M. Robinson, *A Skeleton Key to Finnegans Wake* (New York, 1944).

mus," a poem very much in the spirit of this passage. More than ever, the setting with its combined forest-river elements recalls those two Alpha and Omega events, the creation and the flood. As a "river-lover" or "philopotamus," Jaun associates himself with the prototypic crime and with the criminal, HCE, who loves the river Liffey. Furthermore, the slothful, overstuffed, piglike hippo is the image of Shaun's unproductive gluttony. Before leaving his picnic litter he will stuff himself full of food. Characteristically ungenerous, he will leave only waste, "tea leaves and leaks." Not all of the "philopotamus'" associations are distasteful, however. The "peaceful" river lover is also an Egyptian river god, an ascetic devotee of the life forces or a mangled Osiris. He symbolizes the nature of and the reason for the hero's sacrifice. Such a "peace" is a hard-earned victory in whose benefits we all share. Consequently, Joyce salutes the departing Jaun with a parenthetic listing of words for peace in many languages: "Frida! Freda! Paza! Paisy!" (pp. 470–71). These words accompany him as he floats down the Liffey, which is perhaps the river of peace and renewal prophesied by Isaiah for the faithful: "For thus saith the Lord, Behold I will extend peace to her like a river . . . then shall ye suck . . ." (LXVI.12).

The sixteenth draft, completed in 1936, is the end product of several minor revisions undertaken over a period of seven years. Consequently, these *transition* pages are generously annotated in a variety of Joycean scripts. (Joyce's handwriting varied with the state of his eyesight.)

> I could sit on safe side till the bark of Saint Grousers for hoopoe's hours, laughing lazy at the sheep's lightning, hearing *the wireless harps of sweet* **DEAR** *old Aerial and* the mails across the nightrives (peepet! peepet!) . . .[66]

The abortive shift from "sweet" to "dear" is another sign of the workings of Joyce's mind. Neither word adds a great deal to the context, but "sweet" carries, in addition to its pleasant emotional denotation, an overtone of sensation which reinforces the food aspects of the sentence. Joyce sacrificed the rhyme effect (a poor one) "hear"–"dear"–"Aer" for these added nuances.

The author's reference to Aerial's instrument evokes the pleas-

[66] Draft 16, completed 1936 (BM Add MS. 47486a, p. 88—*transition* pages annotated in the margins in ink at different periods, the annotator's handwriting varying from addition to addition.

ing tones, the refined music of the Aeolian harp or of the sprightly Ariel as opposed to the "tempest" aspect of Shakespeare's spirit being and the dark implications of the news that the "wireless harps" transmit. Perhaps Jaun's harps carry the thunder presaged by the lightning. There is some indication that we have to deal with those wind instruments commonly known as "bull roarers," by means of which primitive races throughout the world imitate the divine wind calling for heroic sacrifice—the death into rebirth of the initiation ritual.[67] For the super-civilized Buddha these sounds are Mara's threats and blandishments which the hero must ignore (transcend); but they are also the half sounds of his detached world or the true peace. For the ordinary hero they are a challenge which he must at all costs answer, but which he strives vainly to ignore. They assure us that Jaun's static desires will be thwarted by his kinetic function; for, like the rabbit in *Alice in Wonderland*, the postman is a victim of his own time complex; he is obliged to fulfill a duty. These intuited terrors, darker for their invisible nature, will be richly elaborated in succeeding drafts. The time interval has been filled. Now the drama must be underlined:

> I could sit on safe side till the bark of Saint ~~Grousers~~ *Grouseus* for hoopoe's hours, laughing lazy at the sheep's lightning, *and turn widamost ear* ~~dreamily~~ *Dreamily* [sic] *to the drummling of snipers,* hearing the wireless harps of sweet old Aerial and the mails across the nightrives . . .[68]

Though it weakened the hunting nuance and perhaps obliged Joyce to add a new phrase, "Grouseus" or "grace-us," by deepening the last-judgment aspect, which now permeates the first part of the sentence, gives new force to the image of the frightened "sheep's lightning." Here is the holy personage who will give the signal for the separation of the sheep from the goats; here is the two-sided, love-and-hate-bestowing Father, a god or his god surrogate for whose existence Jaun finds affirmation in the noises of the night.

[67] *Lost Language*, I, 87–88; Campbell, *The Hero with a Thousand Faces*, pp. 138–139.

[68] Draft 17, *transition* pages and typed correction sheets (BM Add MS. 47486b, pp. 325, 391). Joyce, in an effort to make his changes clear to the printers of *Finnegans Wake*, listed on separate sheets all the revisions included in Draft 16; but a final rereading seems to have lead to further corrections both on the separate sheets and on the *transition* page proofs.

From Finnegans Wake: *A Sentence in Progress*

While indicating the nature of one of these sounds, the insertion "and turn a widamost ear dreamily to the drummling of snipers" does yeoman's service, linking several of the ideational strands. Through it Joyce introduces a new bird name which compensates for the lack of animal elements in the "Aerial" phrase. Then using "widamost ear," he links the visual elements with the auditory: one "opens wide his eyes" although one may "keep his ears open." There is also something visual in the possible interpretations—'moist tear' for "wide-a—most ear" and 'witness' for "widamost." The total context would confirm our belief that Shaun is only feigning to be relaxed and disinterested (see also "neviewscope"). The "drummling of snipers" compensates for the lost hunting nuance in "grousers" and, by its war implications, reinforces both the soldier aspect of "mails" and the element of the soldier spies in "trout" and "wary." "Drummling" refers to the drumming sound made by the snipe's wings, and to the noise made by the hunters' or soldiers' (i.e., snipers') guns. Perhaps it is also a reference to a "drummlin" or an oval hill which would correspond to the barrow of the giant Finn-HCE. This would be the ideal location for the war or hunt or even the place where the devils have chased their victims.[69] Once dead, the hero becomes part of the landscape. His mound becomes the abode of the hidden forces which correspond to the world's evil, the ancestral demons.

With the inclusion of Joyce's additions to the second galley proofs of *Finnegans Wake*, our passage lacked but one syllable ("leaves") of the published sentence. Consequently, for the sake of brevity and clarity, I shall indicate below the variants from the two drafts within the formal unity of the printed version.

I could sit on safe side till the bark of Saint Grouseus for hoopoe's hours, *till heoll's ~~hazerisings~~ hoerrisings*, laughing lazy at the sheep's lightning and turn a widamost ear dreamily to the drummling of snipers, hearing the wireless harps of sweet old Aerial and the mails across the nightrives (peepet! peepet!) and whippoorwilly in the woody (moor park! moor park!) as peacefed as a philopotamus, and crekking jugs at the grenoulls, leaving tea*leaves* for the trout and belleeks for the wary, till I'd followed through my upfielded neviewscope the rugaby moon cumuliously godrolling himself westasleep amuckst the cloud-

---

[69] By adding a reference to *Hell* to his next draft, Joyce gave weight to this interpretation.

scrums for to watch how carefully my nocturnal goosemother would lay her new golden sheegg for me down under in the shy orient.[70]

Characteristically, Joyce's last changes lean heavily upon poetic devices. Both the rhythmic and the visual patterns are improved by the addition of the echoing "leaves," while the double *l* in "till" finds its reflection in "heoll's" and "hoerrisings." Of more consequence is the fact that the *o* and *e* in "hoop*oe*'s" gain in symbolic portent when combined with those in "heoll's hoerrisings" to form the first of an alternating departure-return series, *oe, eo, oe*. Throughout his sentence Joyce opposes *e*'s and especially double *e*'s to *o*'s and double *o*'s but only here does he associate them in this manner, employing them as rising and falling vitalities.[71] Man's unity in diversity is then symbolized by a digraph.

Jaun is stating his desire to remain beside the sun's or Hell's horizon until the dawn when *all* arise or until Christ, the hound, will come to harrow, that is, "till," Hell, or until Sheol-Hell rises up (forever or till the millenium). More poignant is the adolescent hero's willingness to await Aeolus' (Eol's) arising or the sound of the bullroarers which will summon him to the test. Here, as though to demonstrate the debased state of the heroic currency, Joyce links the awesome voice of God to the clamor of newspaper and radio, that is "Aerial" and the "mails." Perhaps the noise of the wind at dawn is vaguely present in "for hoopoe's hours, till heoll's hoerrisings," while the note of horror (and hoarfrost) is intended to imply Jaun's mood.[72] Such effects predominate in this last insertion, a penultimate piece of virtuosity. I believe that an identical love of effects motivated the late

[70] BM Add MS. 47487, p. 170b; all but *leaves* which is to be found in *FW*, p. 449.

[71] Though we may suppose that these clusters are not the only ones devised by Joyce for this pattern, I will content myself with these few tentative observations designed to illustrate the thoroughgoing nature of Joyce's organization, his manner of underlining desired effects. It may be noted in passing that these letter aspects belong to Joyce's later innovations, that they are consistently and deliberately emphasized by the author, that their function is pre-eminently reiterative. In this connection see also the use of a, o, e in the portrait of the dreamer quoted at the end of this article (where "hoell" becomes "hoel").

[72] The early "hazerisings," suggesting the morning mists, was replaced by "hoer"-hour to reenforce the chill that "would perish the Dane."

addition of "leaves" by which Joyce dotted a final *i*, applying a light touch of birdness ("teal"), a fortune-teller nuance, and a final rhyme. For indeed he had long since completed this subdivision of his mighty structure, leaving little to chance or to the reader's innocent whim.

To sum up the case before us now, the story of a sentence's evolution is the tale of the gradual mobilization by the artist of the tools available to him. Built, literally constructed, within a tactile framework of the established mysteries, myths, and symbols, the finished piece revolves like a carved bead about the central axis or universally accepted situation. While maintaining a static-kinetic balance through thirteen successive changes, while placing all movement in the future, while making it all tentative and equivocal, Joyce nevertheless suggests variety of actions and provides for delicate variations in mood. Working under self-imposed restrictions, he produces skillfully manipulated paradoxes from which arise the synthetic experience of the reader. Here, the crucified Christ and the abstracted Buddha mix their respective roles and remain intact;[73] terror is akin to peace; the sublime meets and occasionally submits to the inroads of the ridiculous; yet the finished product makes lively sense.

By approaching several levels of this sentence simultaneously, I have attempted to show how Joyce reconciled a variety of seemingly contradictory accounts of the mock- or shadow-hero's approach to the brink of the abyss, how he chose or formed words and even arranged letters to fit his evolving pattern. I have tried to indicate how Joyce managed to integrate a great mass of esoteric knowledge into an experiential mold. The three aspects of James Joyce's style best highlighted by this study are: the degree to which this knowledge is organized and controlled, the essentially poetic nature of the means, and finally the end which these means were intended to serve.

Joyce's new language demanded an even more rigid control than did the stylistic quirks and symbolism of *Ulysses*. Even if we neglect the series of parallels imposed by the author upon his

---

[73] Joyce has succeeded in making the ritual contemporaneous with the act and both contemporaneous with the reader's perception of them. "Only in its twofold unity of then and now does a myth fulfill its true essence. The cult is its present form, the re-enactment of an archetypal event, situated in the past but in essence eternal" (W. F. Otto, "The Meaning of the Eleusinian Mysteries" in *The Mysteries*, New York, 1955, p. 29).

chapter, section, and book, our sentence remains an example of the extremes to which planning can go. When he composed the first draft of his sentence, Joyce established a frame of reference vague enough to support elaboration. At that point the aspects fundamental to the action were present, but instead of splitting this unit in order to make of it his armature, Joyce preferred to safeguard its primitive integrity while elaborating by repetition the two final elements, "till" (or the duration) and "the bark of the day" (or the objective). Thus, two drafts later, three basically ambivalent thought units enjoyed equal emphasis: Jaun's rest, the moon's journey (i.e., the nature of duration), and the Sun's rebirth (i.e., the protagonist's motivation). In 1928, when Joyce became aware of the need for further coordination, he recognized also the all inclusive nature of his primary element. Thereafter, he concentrated on the elaboration of Jaun's nocturnal activities, which he modulated by means of strong interior references to the other two aspects. As the expanding sentence demanded new organizing principles, Joyce systematically developed such devices as the sensory climate of the sedentary decadent. An analysis of the completed sentence reveals that Jaun's sense of touch is evoked in the passages concerned with physical aspects of his lazy nocturnal activities; his ears are treated to a variety of sounds; his taste buds are titillated by the prospect of his picnic, of being "peacefed," of eating the "she-egg"; his eyes are pleased by the gentle prospects of the heavens and of the hunt; and his nostrils are filled by the odor of corruption so pleasing to his age—the stench of the hoopoe's nest, of "sheegg," and of the Father's crime, his overcultivated and abandoned heritage.

Meanwhile, Joyce tied Jaun to the soil of the book, elaborated and skillfully joined together the major motifs. Gradually, he superimposed upon the original triple division a four-part series of balanced opposites, a résumé of *Finnegans Wake*'s book structure. Even though the last of these parts to be developed stands first in the order of the sentence, there is every indication that Joyce had in mind a minutely organized progression of ideas. Thus, the complex rise-fall, heaven-hell evocations, whose generalized impersonality recalls the larger revolutions of the cycle, blend smoothly into overtones of the heroic crime, the creative-destructive act of the Father. This last is followed by the black-white, good-evil structure of the brother battle with its lunar aspects. Finally, in Part IV of the sentence as in Part IV of the book, Joyce briefly elaborates the maternal echo of the Father's act as the female sows the seed of her own dissolution.

The elaboration of the paragraph follows roughly the same pattern as does the development of the sentence. Coordination works two ways: echoes of the last-judgment motif are added to the sentence before ours in the course of the heavy revision of draft six, "breezes . . . do be devils to flirt." The fox-hunting motif with its John Peel elements is supported first by the addition, "I'll nose a blue fonx" (Draft 14), and later by "the fox! has broken at the coward sight . . ." (Draft 18). Sooner or later all the themes and background elements are held in common by the sentence and the paragraph. If, as I mentioned above, the germ of our sentence follows the essential movement of the germ paragraph, the completed sentence is virtually a microcosm of the paragraph as it now stands.

The movement of the preceding sentence parallels that of our own, consisting first of a statement of Jaun's desire to stay put, "leaning on my cubits," which is followed by a description of how he plans to pass the first five or six hours of the night (until "twoohoo the hour") gathering in the natural riches ("pinching stapandgo jewels" and "catching dimtop brilliants"). It concludes, as does the paragraph, on an ambiguous note of terror and peril: he fears the owl's cry "twoohoo" and the breezes that "do be devils to play flirt." The sentence we have been studying prolongs Jaun's projected stay till daybreak at which time the predicted sunrise will bring material or spiritual success or the "golden sheegg." Joyce begins our sentence on the same suppressed note of terror which punctuated the preceding one, but here he reverses the emotional progression, ending on a series of pleasant associations, that is, the sunrise as glory. Jaun's fears are sufficiently sublimated by this to permit him to expatiate in the second part of the paragraph on his future success.

Joyce's interest in narration is so secondary that, once the narrative content of a passage or of a chapter has been mapped out, he deliberately covers up the marks of his artistic act, turning his attention to the thickening of effects, and to the rarefaction of nuances by means of subtle transitionary devices, shifts of interior mood and psychology. Here perhaps we have a major key to the essential novelty of Joyce's sentence.

In the conventional narrative the sentence tends to be a linear construction. The reader lets his eyes follow its development and draws from it material capable of preparing him for what is to come. In our sentence, however, Joyce is dealing with a moment of doubt, a pause, which can hardly be isolated from all other such moments in man's history. Jaun's hesitation can be considered only in conjunction with the mass of experience that went into the epiphany of its revelation: the total being, a semimystical combination of Brahman-Atman, the self-nonself of man. Joyce's sentence, therefore, as I have tried to demonstrate, does not in any real sense advance the action or the argument of the paragraph. His "action" is essentially static, an embroidery about a theme or an instant. His book is broken up into sentences very much like the one we have examined. These, in the last analysis, resemble views of a cross section of some organism seen under varying lighting conditions and from a variety of different angles. The sentence, therefore, tends to atomize *the* meaning in favor of the *many possible* meanings rendering an *impression* to which all *ideas* are secondary. In spite of its total union with its context, the minor organism has a life of its own. The reader approaches it well supplied with images and impressions gathered from his experience with other parts of the book, but he is obliged to isolate this element, to subject it to a searching scrutiny before he can safely replace it in its context.

Toward the end of the last century, Mallarmé, who was himself writing an "omnibus" work for humanity, *Un coup de dés*, sanctified poetic obscurity: "La contemplation des objets, l'image s'envolant des rêveries suscitées par eux, sont le chant . . . [The poet must not deny] aux espirits cette joie délicieuse de croire qu'ils créent."[74] Indeed, the most obvious result of a technique such as Joyce's is to oblige the reader to retrace the steps of the artist's creative process in order to garner not only the intellectual but also the emotional wealth, the *song* or "*chant.*" Joyce's sentence is a construction built about a central armature and composed of parallel entities linked together by association and applicable on several levels simultaneously. These "entities" we have already examined closely. They are the thought subdivisions of the sentence, the phrases that Joyce attached to his armature from which they draw deeper life. Like musical overtones, they are designed to blend with and enrich the whole, but like our sentence, they assert their individual rights until they have been at least emotionally comprehended. Each of these units, as we have seen, tends to reinforce some elements in its fellows; therefore the total meaning is gradually revealed, if not

74 *Œuvres complètes* (Paris, 1945), p. 869.

as fact plainly stated, at least as the play of light so aptly described in another of Mallarmé's statements: "[words] . . . s'allument de reflets réciproques comme une virtuelle traînée de feux sur des pierreries . . ." (*Œuvres*, p. 366). To link these elements and to achieve his effects, Joyce used letter significations, alliteration, rhyme, and onomatopoeia. In an effort to explore all the surfaces of his subject he invented words, changed syntax, used puns; to keep the sentence intact he availed himself of these devious means to reiterate basic themes. Thus, through "tea," "sheegg," "belleek," "hoopoe" scintillates the "light" that one desires, that of the living Father, which is symptomatic of eternal good, enlightenment or wisdom.

The "ideal reader" of such a structure will discover first the imposed rhythm (Joyce's germ sentence is a metered statement of Shaun's attitude), then the armature, which is readily available as the grammatical core of the sentence. This armature, being sufficiently elastic to permit several interpretations, leads the reader past the background effects, which aid in establishing the climate, and along each of the parallel subdivisions. As he follows these strands of associations, he will notice antennae of possible meanings which are subject to justification by associations latent in other subdivisions. He will relate these meanings to different levels of the narrative until, finally, he begins to achieve insight into the total thematic effect. Step by step he will recreate the poem.

In its nature, this cognition differs radically from the logical apprehension of technical and didactic language. Even after reaching the point of "complete comprehension," even after understanding thoroughly in all its particulars the variegated structure, the reader would carry away an impression rather than an image or a concept, an experiential reference which may be highly personal. Joyce has ensured this effect by establishing interior conflict or tension within even the smallest units of his sentence, by employing vague words in eternally expansible contexts. The sensibility has absorbed a multitude of complex images, mostly self-contradictory, which, by their interaction, defy "comprehension." Logic tells us that the human mind, like the human eye, perceives only a limited number of images simultaneously. To achieve a synthesis, it must neglect the particular and the contradictions inherent in any juxtaposition of particulars. A synthesis then is far from being the true view towards which Joyce aimed when constructing his sentence. That the reader of *Finnegans Wake* never arrives at such a static overview is a tribute to rather than a criticism of Joyce's method. Knowledge of the existence of further reaches is as important as perception of intellectual content. Thus the *content* of our sentence —glossed superficially by my analysis, could be elaborated ad infinitum. Its consequences are boundless.

If we set aside *Finnegans Wake*'s formal aspects, we may conclude that the book, like our sentence, differs from other poems only in its scope, which Joyce widens to provide a greater area for contact. The interior world was for James Joyce what the exterior world was for the impressionists, "an ensemble of colored vibrations which vary constantly." Joyce permits all the possibilities of a given situation to interact. The reader is exposed to a new way of feeling, of perceiving. He encounters levels not only of meaning but also of sensation, attacking simultaneously or individually the various strata of consciousness. The perceptive reader need hardly perform exegeses or catalogue sensations. His personal receptors will receive and retail the positive emotional weight of the phrase. He need only read and reread at intervals to receive a kaleidoscopic or prismatic series of views, all incomplete but all provocative, the same that any man might see when in the process of self examination:

> Now, to be on anew and basking again in the panaroma of all flores of speech, if a human being duly fatigued by his dayety in the sooty, . . . were at this auctual futule preteriting unstant, in the states of suspensive exanimation, accorded, . . . with an earsighted view of old hopeinhaven with all the . . . ways to which in the . . . course of his tory will have been having recourses, the reverberration of knotcracking awes, the reconjungation of nodebinding ayes, the redissolusingness of mindmouldered ease and the thereby hang of the Hoel of it, could such a none, whiles even led comesilencers to comeliewithhers and till intempestuous Nox should catch the gallicry and spot lucan's dawn, byhold at ones what is main and why tis twain, how one once meet melts in tother wants poignings, the sap rising, the foles falling, the nimb now nihilant round the girlyhead so becoming, the wrestless in the womb, all the rivals to allsea, skakeagain, O disaster! shakealose, Ah how starring! but Heng's got a bit of Horsa's nose and Jeff's got the signs of Ham round his mouth . . . then *what* would that fargazer seem to seemself to seem seeming of, dimm it all?
>   Answer: A collideorscape! [*FW*, p. 143]

XVI

RUSSELL K. ALSPACH

Some Textual Problems in Yeats

This paper is based on the Variorum edition of Yeats's poems that Peter Allt, late professor of Anglo-Irish literature at the University of Groningen, and I have been preparing jointly for some ten years. Because of Peter Allt's untimely death in an accident in London two years ago the finishing of the work fell to me. His death was a severe personal blow, and it was a great loss to Yeats' scholarship.

In our work, we confined ourselves to versions of Yeat's poems published by him in magazine or book. We included no manuscript versions—they are quite numerous and widely scattered, and comparatively few are available for study. (And no manuscript version has the final polishing of proofreading by Yeats.) Nor did we include versions of his poems quoted by other writers, e.g. Katharine Tynan[1] and Dorothy Wellesley.[2] At best these are secondhand. As our standard text we used the two-volume limited and signed edition of *The Poems of W. B. Yeats* published by Macmillan of London in 1949. The publisher's brochure that accompanied this edition reads in part:

> For some time before his death, W. B. Yeats was engaged in revising the text of this edition of his poems, of which he had corrected the proofs and for which he had signed the special page to appear at the beginning of Volume I. The outbreak of the Second World War, however, came at a crucial stage in the production of the work, and Messrs. Macmillan & Co. Ltd. had to consider the effect of austere conditions on a publication which had been projected on a lavish scale and which, after the untimely death of this great writer, would have formed

Read before the English Institute on 7 September 1955. Reprinted from *Studies in Bibliography* IX (1957), 51–67, by permission of the author and the Bibliographical Society of the University of Virginia.

[1] *Twenty-five Years: Reminiscences* (1913), and *The Middle Years* (1916).

[2] *Letters on Poetry from W. B. Yeats to Dorothy Wellesley* (1940).

a worthy monument of him. It was finally decided that production should be discontinued until after the war, and it is only now, a decade later, that it has become possible to offer the work as it was originally planned.

With this definitive edition at hand it is possible to trace the evolution of a Yeats poem from its first published version through all its revisions to its final form and to see how in the process Yeats's concept of what he wanted the poem to say developed.

Under revisions I include all changes, even those in punctuation. Perhaps this is dangerous ground; much has been said about Yeats's carelessness in, and lack of knowledge of, punctuation. But the testimony varies. We know, for instance, that he wrote to Robert Bridges in 1915 that "I chiefly remember that you asked me about stops and commas. Do what you will. I do not understand stops. I write so completely for the ear that I feel helpless when I have to measure pauses by stops and commas."[3] But Mrs. Yeats told me in the summer of 1954 that she believed shifts in punctuation were very much a problem in any textual study of her husband's work, that W. B. was careful about "stops and commas," and that several times he had become quite irate with a publisher who had taken it upon himself to change the poet's punctuation. It took me a long time to convince my colleague on the variorum that punctuation must be noted. His point of view originally, and the point of view of others, was that it should be noted only where the meaning or rhythm is affected. But who is to judge where the meaning or rhythm is affected? Certainly not the textual critic or scholar who is working in the realm of facts and not of aesthetics. And in the case of Yeats the conflicting testimony about his knowledge of punctuation must be kept in mind. I believe further that a close study of the punctuational changes in his verse will convince others, as it has me, that these changes were in the main deliberate and not accidental.

That Yeats was an inveterate revisor soon became apparent to discriminating readers of his poetry during the years in which it was being published. He continued to revise until the end; he was never content. He comments often about his revisions. The best-known of these comments is the quatrain he wrote for the second volume of *The Collected Works* of 1908:

> The friends that have it I do wrong
> Whenever I remake a song,

[3] Allan Wade, *The Letters of W. B. Yeats* (1954), p. 598.

> Must know what issue is at stake:
> It is myself that I remake.[4]

Not so well known, but pertinent to this study, is his statement in the preface written in 1927 for the thirteenth reprinting and revision of *Poems* (1895): "This volume contains what is, I hope, the final text of the poems of my youth; and yet it may not be, ... One is always cutting out the dead woods."[5] We can, I think, profitably examine the last words of this statement, "One is always cutting out the dead wood," and the implications that arise from it.

In any textual study of Yeats's poems no edition, printing, impression, or reissue can be ignored. For example, the volume *Later Poems* was published in London in 1922 and reprinted there the same year. These printings are identical. In February 1924 it was reprinted again; this time there are a number of changes. In April 1924 it was published in New York, and this printing differed from the London printings of 1922 and February 1924. In 1926 and 1931 there were further reprintings in London: these printings differ from all previous printings and from each other. (A New York reprint of 1928 is identical to the first New York printing, that of 1924.) A second example is the trade edition of *The Wild Swans at Coole*, published in London and New York in 1919. These are identical. But a London reprint of 1920 has several changes. It is here, for instance, that we have for the first time the final form of "An Irish Airman Foresees His Death." A third example is the *Selected Poems* of 1929, published only in London. (Parenthetically, this is usually ignored by Yeats's textual critics, but textually it is very important. Many of the changes ascribed to *Collected Poems* (1933)[6] actually appeared first here.) *Selected Poems* was reprinted in 1930, 1932, 1936, 1938, 1951, and 1952—the last two in the Golden Treasury series. The printings of 1929, 1930, and 1932 are identical; but there are changes for the 1936 printing. From then on the printings are the same.

Nor can it be assumed that simultaneous periodical publication in Britain and America meant identity of form. In her admirable

[4] *The Collected Works in Verse and Prose of William Butler Yeats,* 8 vols. (Stratford-on-Avon, 1908), II [viii].

[5] (London).

[6] *The Collected Poems of W. B. Yeats* (London; New York: 1933).

study of Yeats's revisions of his later poems, Professor Witt[7] has discussed a case in point: that of "Among Schoolchildren" published first in both *The Dial* and *The London Mercury* for August 1927. Other examples are numerous. "The Two Kings" appeared in *Poetry* and *The British Review* in October 1913. In th 252 lines of these first printings there are over fifty changes, great and small, between the two. In "Upon a Dying Lady," in *The Little Review*, August 1917, and *The New Statesman*, 11 August 1917, there are some twenty changes in the seventy-three lines. And between the versions of "The Second Coming" in *The Dial*, November 1920, and the London *Nation*, 6 November 1920, there is a startling change. Line 19 reads in *The Dial*, "That thirty centuries of stony sleep," and in *The Nation* "That twenty centuries of stony sleep." Even with Yeats's handwriting it's a little difficult to make "thirty" out of "twenty."

So far in these examples I have been pointing up the truth of Yeats's assertion about "always cutting out the dead wood," an assertion that would have led one to believe that if he had the latest-dated Yeats volume he had the latest versions of its contents. But there are curious exceptions, exceptions where "dead wood" persisted beside "live wood." One of these is *The Wind Among the Reeds*, published in London and New York in 1899, and reprinted in both places a number of times. The last printing was London, 1911, called the "sixth edition."[8] All printings are identical. But in the meantime *The Wind Among the Reeds* was revised for the first volume of the 1906 *Poetical Works* published only in America,[9] and again revised for the first volume of the 1908 *Collected Works* published only in England. In 1908, therefore, we have in print three versions of the poems in *The Wind Among the Reeds*: the original version, the version in *The Poetical Works* I (1906), and the version in *The Collected Works* I (1908). To add to the mixup, *The Poetical Works* I (1906) was reprinted nine times, with no changes, to 1922. The same anomaly happens with the 1931 printing of *Later*

---

[7] Marion Witt, "A Competition for Eternity: Yeat's Revision of His Later Poems," *PMLA, LXIV* (1949), 40–58.

[8] A correspondent has informed me that he has seen a sixth edition with an American imprint on the verso of the title page. I have seen only the London edition.

[9] *The Poetical Works of William B. Yeats*, 2 vols. (New York, 1906). Vol. I, Lyrical Poems; vol. II, Dramatical Poems.

Poems that, while it has revisions, does not have all the revisions made for the 1929 *Selected Poems*. And the 1936 revised printing of *Selected Poems* does not have all the revisions of the 1933 *Collected Poems*. An accurate study of the development of a Yeats poem demands, it seems to me, the ability to work one's way through this maze in order to recognize the "dead wood" and the "live wood."

Closely allied to the "dead wood" and the "live wood" textual problem is the problem of the "early" Yeats and the "later" Yeats. Any one even faintly familiar with Yeats is aware of this much-discussed division of his work. The difficulty is the wide variance of opinion about where "early" stops and "later" begins. One critic dates the "early" Yeats from 1889 to 1901, another from 1889 to 1910, and another from 1889 to 1914. Perhaps we cannot do better than take the poet's own dates in definition of "early" and "later."

He first uses the words "Early Poems" in 1906 as a subheading in *The Poetical Works* I. Under "Early Poems" he includes the long narrative poem "The Wanderings of Oisin" and certain of the ballads and lyrics from his first two published volumes: *The Wanderings of Oisin and Other Poems* (London, 1889) and *The Countess Kathleen and Various Legends and Lyrics* (London; Boston and London, 1892). He uses the same subheading with almost the same inclusions in 1908 in *The Collected Works* I. In 1913 in the Tauchnitz edition of *A Selection from the Poetry of W.B. Yeats* (Leipzig) he modifies the subheading to "Early Poems (1885–1892)" and includes under it thirteen lyrics from the 1889 and 1892 volumes; later in the same year in *A Selection from the Love Poetry of William Butler Yeats* (The Cuala Press, Dundrum, Ireland) the subheading is again modified, this time to "Early Poems 1890–1892": the contents are four lyrics from the 1892 volume. In 1921 in *Selected Poems* (New York) the heading and the number of poems are the same as in the Tauchnitz edition but with some variation in the selection. In 1925, in the title of the volume *Early Poems and Stories* (London; New York), he uses the words for the last time; there is a slight shift in the inclusions but they are practically the same as in *The Poetical Work* I (1906). From here to the definitive edition of 1949 these early poems with the exception of "The Wanderings of Oisin" are called "Crossways" and "The Rose," descriptive titles Yeats had originally used when he took the shorter poems from the volumes of 1889 and 1892 and published them in *Poems* (1895). Apparently, then, Yeats thought of his early poetry as that written up to 1892. For he could, in 1906, have included *The Wind Among the Reeds* (1899) and *In the Seven Woods* (The Dun Emer Press, Dundrum, Ireland, 1903) among his "early" poems. And although by 1925 critical opinion was already dividing his work at this date or that date, Yeats stuck to his own division.

The term "later poems" he uses, and by using defines, just once: as the title of the 1922 *Later Poems*, that includes verse from the following volumes: *The Wind Among the Reeds* (1899), *In the Seven Woods* (1903), *Poems 1899–1905* (London and Dublin, 1906), *The Green Helmet and Other Poems* (New York and London, 1912), *Responsibilities* (London; New York, 1916), *The Wild Swans at Coole* (London; New York, 1919), and *Michael Robartes and the Dancer* (Cuala Press, Dundrum, 1921). The line of demarcation seems clear.

But having decided the dates of "early," the textual critic must next determine just what an early Yeats poem is: i.e., is it an early poem through all its revisions, or is it an early poem through only some of its revisions, or is it an early poem in only its first printing? Of the forty early poems, including "The Wanderings of Oisin," in the definitive edition there is not one that was not revised in greater or less degree. Eleven got their final polishing for the definitive edition of 1949, seventeen for *Collected Poems* (1933), four for *Selected Poems* (1929), three for the 1927 revision of *Poems* (1895), two for *Early Poems and Stories* (1925), one for the 1912 revision of *Poems* (1895), and two for the first edition of *Poems* (1895). Thirty-two of the forty were revised finally, then, from 1929 to 1939: the last ten years of Yeats's life. And, as a rule, the later the final polishing the heavier the revisions throughout. The problem becomes more complicated when we study an early poem like "The Ballad of the Foxhunter," published first in the magazine *East and West* for November 1889, then in *United Ireland* for 28 May 1892, then in *The Countess Kathleen*, etc. (September 1892), then in *Poems* (1895), and so on. In discussing this poem, one critic speaks blithely of "the early version" and then proceeds to quote the first four stanzas of the version in *Poems* (1895). But this is the fourth version. He ignores the three earlier versions. Here are lines 5–8 as they appear in each of the versions up to 1895.

In the first, that in *East and West* (November 1889) they read:

> And of my servants some one go,
> Bring my brown hunter near,
> And lead him slowly to and fro,
> My Lollard old and dear.

In the second version (*United Ireland*, 28 May 1892) these become

> And some one from the stable bring
> My Dermot dear and brown,
> And lead him gently in a ring,
> And slowly up and down.

The third version (*The Countess Kathleen*, etc., September 1892) is identical with the second; the fourth (*Poems*, 1895) changes from the third:

> And some one from the stables bring
> My Dermot dear and brown,
> And lead him gently in a ring
> And gently up and down.

It will be noted that in line 5 "stable" has become "stables" and in line 8 "slowly" has become "gently." One wonders by what magic this last version, differing so markedly from the first version and in degree from the second and third versions, becomes "the early version."

The same difficulty is present in "The Madness of King Goll" that likewise has several early versions: the first in *The Leisure Hour* for September 1887, the second in *Poems and Ballads of Young Ireland* (Dublin, 1888), the third in *The Wanderings of Oisin*, etc. (1889), and the fourth, and except for minor changes the final version, in *Poems* (1895). Each of the first three is extensively revised, yet we have a critic saying that "The Madness of King Goll" was revised so thoroughly that the 1895 version is practically a new poem, the implication of the context being that there was but one earlier version. Another critic of Yeats's revisions, in commenting on the line "And every mumbling old man said" from the second version of the poem, remarks that the metre exacts "an unnatural emphasis [on the word "old"]" and that Yeats improved the metre for *Poems* (1895) by changing the line to "And every ancient Ollave said." But in the first version this line has a metre similar to the final metre: "And every whispering Druid said."

There are other examples at hand, but these illustrate sufficiently something of the problem inherent in the term "early poem" and likewise the possible errors inherent in a study of "the early version" of a poem. To come back to my question, "What is an 'early Yeats poem'?", I should answer it by saying that it is a poem written originally before 1892. And immediately I should add that in any discussion of such a poem the details of its early publication must be given and the exact printing date of any quotation.

Revisions of the early poems continued, as I said, right up to the end. It is not until the definitive edition, for example, that we can clear up the vexing question of whether line 39 in "The Song of the Happy Shepherd" should be "Rewarding in melodious guile" or "Rewording in melodious guile." The textual history of the line is curious and provocative. In the first printing, in *The Dublin University Review* for October 1885, and in successive printings up to the 1901 revision of *Poems* (1895), it was "Rewording." In the 1904 revision of *Poems* (1895) it became "Rewarding." In *The Poetical Works* I (1906) and *The Collected Works* I (1908) it is "Rewording." But in the 1908 revision of *Poems* (1895) and in all subsequent printings through *Collected Poems* (1933) it is "Rewarding." In the definitive edition it becomes "Rewording"—a reversion to the original word and concept. (I am aware that what sometimes seem to be reversions in an author's work are nothing more in fact than the careless use of an earlier edition as copy for a later edition, but the reversions discussed in this paper were, I believe, purposely made by Yeats and represent a rejection of his own revisions.) Another revision in the same edition is a punctuational change—again a reversion—in line 7 of "Ephemera," "When the poor tired child, Passion, falls asleep." In the first printing, *The Wanderings of Oisin*, etc. (1889), the terminal punctuation was a period; but in the next printing, *Poems* (1895), the period was replaced by a colon that remained through *Collected Poems* (1933). The colon shifts the implication of the next two lines: "How far away the stars seem, and how far / Is our first kiss, and ah, how old my heart!" In the definitive edition the period reappears.

He even revised, in the definitive edition, his spelling of certain

Gaelic names. In "The Wanderings of Oisin," for instance, "Aed" becomes "Aedh," and "Blanid" becomes "Blanaid" (although the trade editions of 1950 and 1951 do not have the latter change[10]). He makes several slight punctuational revisions in the same poem; an example is the deletion of the terminal commas of lines 405 and 406, Book I. Here are lines 404–7 as they appear in all printings from *Poems* (1895) through *Collected Poems* (1950–51) except the definitive edition:

> He hears the storm in the chimney above,
> And bends to the fire and shakes with the cold,
> While his heart still dreams of battle and love,
> And the cry of the hounds on the hills of old.

And here they are in the definitive edition:

> He hears the storm in the chimney above,
> And bends to the fire and shakes with the cold
> While his heart still dreams of battle and love
> And the cry of the hounds on the hills of old.

Apparently Yeats felt that the elision of the commas after "cold" and "love" make the last three lines more clearly modify, rather than be in apposition with, the first line.

Collected Poems (1933), given frequently by textual critics as the source of numerous revisions, has actually not very many and they are not very extensive. Among them are the insertion of a comma after "last" in line 33 of "The Rose of Battle": "And when at last, defeated in His wars"; the hyphenation of "bean-rows" and "honey-bee" in line 3 of "The Lake Isle of Innisfree"; the final changing of "will" to "with" in "When You Are Old": "And loved your beauty with love false or true" [the printings oscillate between "with" and "will," the first "will,"[11] that displaces the original "with," being perhaps due to a misprint]; the substitution of "fear" for "fears" in line 6 of "Who Goes with Fergus?": "And brood on hopes and fear no more"—

10 *The Collected Poems of W. B. Yeats* (London, 1950), p. 437; (New York, 1951), p. 374.

11 In the 1912 revision of *Poems* (1895). The "will" remains in the 1913, 1919, 1920, 1922(2), 1923, and 1924 reprintings of *Poems* (1895); in *Early Poems and Stories* (1925); in the first two printings of *The Augustan Books of English Poetry/W. B. Yeats* (London, 1927, 1928); and in the first three printings of *Selected Poems* (London, 1929, 1930, 1932). But in *A Selection from the Love Poetry*, etc. (1913) and in *Selected Poems* (1921) it is "with."

it had been "fears" from the first printing in 1892; and a change in the punctuation in line 13 of "The Two Trees": "There the Loves a circle go." This line, that Yeats first used in *Selected Poems* (1929), he originally punctuated "There the Loves—a circle—go." In 1933 he eliminated the dashes. In line 18, Book I, of "The Wanderings of Oisin," "Where passionate Maeve is stony-still;", that makes dubious sense without a hyphen between "stony" and "still," he hyphenates the phrase—another reversion, for it had been hyphenated in the first printing; and, also in "The Wanderings of Oisin," he changes the spellings of some of the Gaelic names. One of those changed is "Conhor" that becomes "Conchubar" and necessitates a rewording of line 80, Book III, from "And the names of the demons whose hammers made armour for Conhor of old" to "And the name of the demon whose hammer made Conchubar's sword-blade of old."

Selected Poems (1929) includes thirteen of the shorter early poems and "The Wanderings of Oisin." Of the thirteen shorter poems, six are revised slightly. Two have major revisions, "The Man Who Dreamed of Faeryland" and "The Two Trees," revisions often credited to *Collected Poems* (1933). One critic strides in thus: "Yet in rewriting the poem ["The Man Who Dreamed of Faeryland"] for the 1933 *Collected Poems* . . . ." Our critic buttresses this surprising statement by boldly assigning the following versions of lines 41 and 42 to the 1901 revision of *Poems* (1895):

> Were not the worms that spired about his bones
> Proclaiming with a low and reedy cry . . .

and then says they were revised in 1933 to

> Did not the worms that spired about his bones
> Proclaim with that unwearied, reedy cry . . . .

He is almost right about line 41, but quite mixed up about line 42. In the original printing in *The National Observer* for 7 February 1891 the lines read:

> Were not the worms that spired about his bones
> A-telling with their low and reedy cry.

Line 41 stayed unchanged until *Selected Poems* (1929) when it was revised to "Did not the worms that spired about his bones": its final form. Line 42, however, went through several changes.

The first was for its second printing, *The Book of the Rhymer's Club* (London, 1892), where it had a terminal comma added. It kept this form until *Early Poems and Stories* (1925) where it became "Proclaiming with a low and reedy cry," that was changed finally in *Selected Poems* to "Proclaim with that unwearied, reedy cry." The remaining revisions in the poem are likewise incorrectly assigned to 1933. We have lost four years in a poet's development. (Incidentally, no comment is made on one of the most striking 1929 revisions: "That if a dancer stayed his hungry foot / It seemed the sun and moon were in the fruit" that replace "A Danaan fruitage makes a shower of moons, / And as it falls awakens leafy tunes.")

The extensive revisions in "The Two Trees" for *Selected Poems* are exemplified by the changes in lines 13-20. The original version of these lines that except for two unimportant punctuational changes lasted from its first printing in *The Countess Kathleen*, etc. (1892) through the final reprinting in 1929 of *Poems* (1895), reads,

> There, through bewildered branches, go
> Winged Loves borne on in gentle strife,
> Tossing and tossing to and fro
> The flaming circle of our life.
> When looking on their shaken hair,
> And dreaming how they dance and dart,
> Thine eyes grow full of tender care:
> Beloved, gaze in thine own heart.

Here is the revision for *Selected Poems:*

> There the Loves—a circle—go,
> The flaming circle of our days,
> Gyring, spiring to and fro
> In those great ignorant leafy ways;
> Remembering all that shaken hair
> And how the wingèd sandals dart,
> Thine eyes grow full of tender care:
> Beloved, gaze in thine own heart.

becoming, I think, a clearer statement of the desirability-of-innocence theme so superbly expressed ten years earlier in "A Prayer for My Daughter."

For "The Wanderings of Oisin" there are fifty-two changes, forty-two of which are punctuational with seven of the forty-two changes being reversions. The remaining ten changes are word and phrase revisions, with five "maidens" becoming "ladies." One wonders whether to ascribe this to the years or better diction.

Revisions for *Early Poems and Stories* (1925) and for the 1927 edition of *Poems* (1895) are considerable, among others being "Fergus and the Druid," "A Cradle Song," "The Sorrow of Love," "The Lamentation of the Old Pensioner," and "To Ireland in the Coming Times" for the 1925 volume; "The Ballad of the Foxhunter" and "The Countess Cathleen in Paradise," for the 1927 volume. "The Dedication to a Book of Stories selected from the Irish Novelists" was revised originally for its publication in *The Irish Statesman* for 8 November 1924; it was printed in *Early Poems and Stories* in its revised form. "Cuchulain's Fight with the Sea" has numerous revisions for both volumes; we might glance at these revisions, in particular the revised ending and some criticisms of it.

For *Early Poems and Stories* Yeats changed the title from "The Death of Cuchulain," deleted seven lines, and redid forty-two of the remaining eighty-six lines. For the 1927 *Poems* he deleted one line and redid twenty-two—ten of which he had just finished revising in 1925. Probably the most striking of the changes is the new ending of the poem, done for *Early Poems and Stories*. Here is the ending[12] Yeats revised:

> In three days' time, Cuchulain with a moan
> Stood up, and came to the long sands alone:
> For four days warred he with the bitter tide;
> And the waves flowed above him, and he died.

and here the revision:

> Cuchulain stirred,
> Stared on the horses of the sea, and heard
> The cars of battle and his own name cried;
> And fought with the invulnerable tide.

Criticism of the old vs. the new ending varies widely. We have this from one critic: "The second [ending] is fine too, but has not the same sense of water flowing on and on that is heard in the other. "And the waves flowed above him and he died"

[12] Except for minor altering these lines had not been changed from their original form in *United Ireland*, 11 June 1892, until the major revision discussed here.

hold the invulnerability of the sea, and the majesty ... of death."
But another writes that the new ending "transformed a mediocre
poem into a work of quite extraordinary power." A third apparently thought both endings were the same: "The changes [in
the revision of the entire poem] do not, however, concern the
contents—apart from one small detail: the name Finmole has
disappeared, ..." A little textual reading, not studying, would
have helped number three. Incidentally, I agree with the second
critic—that the poem is transformed into a work of extraordinary
power.

"The Lamentation of the Old Pensioner" was made over for
the 1925 volume into an entirely new poem. This rewriting has
been discussed again and again; so far as I know, however, no
one has commented on the brilliantly bitter and savage satire in
the mere use of the word "transfigure."[13]

Numerous other revisions of the early poems occur in the
following volumes[14]—going back chronologically from 1925: the
1912 reprinting of *Poems* (1895), *The Collected Works* I
(1908), the 1901 reprinting of *Poems* (1895), the 1899 reprinting of the same volume, the 1895 *Poems* itself, *The Countess
Kathleen*, etc. (1892), and *The Wanderings of Oisin*, etc.
(1889). The last two are listed because of the many changes
Yeats made between initial periodical publication and publication in these first two volumes of his verse. There is, as I have
implied, a tendency either to ignore the earliest changes or to
be unaware of them and to assign the first revisions to *Poems*
(1895).

I have emphasized by mention or discussion a number of the
volumes for which the early poems were revised. A ranking of
these volumes based on the number of revisions would show, in
my opinion, *Poems* (1895) as easily the first, followed by *The
Countess Kathleen*, etc. (1892), *The Wanderings of Oisin*, etc.
(1889), the 1912 reprinting of *Poems* (1895), *Early Poems and
Stories* (1925), the 1899 reprinting of *Poems* (1895), *The Collected Works* I (1908), the 1901 and the 1927 reprintings of
Poems (1895) in that order, *Collected Poems* (1933), and *The*

---

[13] I refer, of course, to the last line of the three stanzas in the rewritten
version: "Ere Time transfigured me" at the end of the first stanza, and
"That has transfigured me" at the end of the second and third stanzas.

[14] There were revisions for all the volumes in which the early poems
were printed; those volumes I mention were the more extensively revised.

Poems of W. B. Yeats I (1949). A ranking based on the significance of the revisions would show *Poems* (1895) as again first,
followed by the 1925, 1912, 1908, 1892, 1899, 1901, 1927, 1889,
1933, and 1949 volumes. *Selected Poems* (1929), despite its importance, is not listed because it includes less than half the early
poems. I think my ranking of the order of significance would be
authenticated by a detailed study, a study that I believe would
likewise show that reversions in later printings of the early poems
most often go back to the 1889 and 1908 volumes.

Before leaving the early poems I'd like to call attention to some
of the lines that should have been revised. One example is lines
15 and 16 of "The Sad Shepherd": "But naught they heard, for
they are always listening, / The dewdrops, for the sound of
their own dropping."— almost unchanged in all printings; another is lines 5-8 in "The Falling of the Leaves," with its tongue-
twisting line 6:

> The hour of the waning of love has beset us,
> And weary and worn are our sad souls now;
> Let us part, ere the season of passion forget us,
> With a kiss and a tear on thy drooping brow.

the third is lines 32 and 33 in Book I of the "Wanderings of
Oisin," ' "Why do you wind no horn?" she said, / And every
hero droop his head?"—a hackneyed rhythm "reminiscent," as
Peter Allt once remarked to me, of " 'Shoot if you must this old
grey head, / But spare your country's flag," she said."; and, as
a last example, line 51 in the same book of the same poem,
"Through bitter tide on foam-wet feet?" Yeats had a deal of
trouble with this line. Finn is asking Niamh why she is paying
a visit to his country. In *The Wanderings of Oisin*, etc. (1889)
part of line 50 and line 51 read:

> Young maiden, what may bring
> Thy wandering steps across the sea?

In *Poems* (1895) this becomes

> What may bring
> To this dim shore those gentle feet?

In the 1899 revision of *Poems* (1895) 50 and 51 are

> What dream came with you that you came
> To this dim shore on foam wet feet?

Fifty remained the same, but fifty-one received its final form in
Early Poems and Stories (1925):

> Through bitter tide on foam-wet feet?

Part of Niamh's answer—lines 57-59, in the final form they got in
the 1912 revision of *Poems* (1895)—is perhaps even worse,

> . . . , these four feet [of her horse]
> Ran through the foam and ran to this
> That I might have your son to kiss.

The later poems, using Yeats's own division, include everything from *The Wind Among the Reeds* (1899) to *Last Poems
and Plays* (London; New York, 1940), a total of 346 poems. The
observations made and the conclusions reached about any textual
study of the early poems are likewise applicable to the later
poems. This is borne out by the incidental references I have
made so far to the texts of a few of the later poems.

Beginning in 1903 a new textual source, the Dun Emer press,
after 1907 called the Cuala press, comes into the picture. The
Dun Emer press was started by Yeats's sister Elizabeth. Yeats himself took an active part in its work and for some years chose and
edited the books it issued, as well as having most of his own
poems, beginning with *In the Seven Woods* (1903), printed by
it. As a matter of statistics, there are 308 poems in the definitive
edition that date from 1903 to January 1939; of these, 264 are in
Dun Emer-Cuala books and of that number 94 are first printings.

Because of Yeats's close supervision of the Cuala press books,
one might be led to believe that here is a textual source more important than others, and that here if anywhere would be a
finality not found in other printings. But not so; the Cuala press
printing of a poem is not on that account likely to show more
permanence than any other printing of the poem.

But apparently the magic of the words "Cuala Press" indicated
to at least one critic that if a Yeats poem was printed in a Cuala
press edition the poem would never again be changed. So in
discussing "Broken Dreams" and "The Second Coming" from
"the 1918 and the 1920 volumes, . . . *The Wild Swans at Coole*
and *Michael Robartes and the Dancer*," he gives these two Cuala
press volumes as the sources for his quotations from the two
poems. But in both cases he quotes 1933 versions. This is not too
serious for "Broken Dreams" where the changes are minor, but it

is rather disastrous for "The Second Coming." The version of that poem in *Michael Robartes and the Dancer* has, as lines 13 and 17,

> Troubles my sight: a waste of desert sand; . . .
> Wind shadows of the indignant desert birds.

Whereas we are told they read

> Troubles my sight: somewhere in sands of the desert . . .
> Reel shadows of the indignant desert birds.

Hence by an assumption of the inviolability of a Cuala press printing the chance of commenting on two of Yeats's most brilliant changes is lost: of pointing out, for instance, how "somewhere in sands of the desert" brings into the poem a sense of the vastness and desolation of "the lone and level sands" stretching "far away"; and how "Reel" for "Wind" expresses far more effectively the bewildered terror of the desert birds. These revisions in "The Second Coming" were actually made for *Later Poems* (1922) and were retained to the end, but because when he quotes the poem our critic italicizes "Spiritus Mundi" in line 12 it is evident that he used the 1933 version where the italicization first appears. (Incidentally, there was no "1918" *Wild Swans at Coole*; the Cuala edition was 1917 and the trade edition 1919. The colophon in the Cuala edition of *Michael Robartes and the Dancer* says it was finished on All Soul's Day, 1920, the title page reads 1921.)

I have indicated that just as we are in trouble with careless use of the phrase "early poem," so with the phrase "later poem." Here, for example, we have one of Yeats's biographers talking about the poems in *In the Seven Woods* (1903) and saying that "The first, and perhaps the finest poem in the new "middle-aged" group, was 'The Folly of Being Comforted.' " and he then cites lines 7-14 of, presumably, the 1903 version of that poem, but actually of the 1933 version that except for one minor change made for the definitive edition is the final version. Now textually, he could hardly have picked a more difficult poem than "The Folly of Being Comforted." From its publication in *The Speaker* for 11 January 1902, down through the definitive edition, there are 36 changes in the published versions and a complete shift of meaning in lines 8-11,—a shift that appears first in the Tauchnitz *A Selection from the Poetry of W. B. Yeats*

(1913) and is completed in *Collected Poems* (1933). Lines 8-11, in the 1903 Dun Emer and trade editions of *In the Seven Woods*, were

> Time can but make her beauty over again
> Because of that great nobleness of hers;
> The fire that stirs about her, when she stirs
> Burns but more clearly;

The terminal semi-colon at line 9 makes that line modify line 8; the comma after "her" in line 10 makes the remainder of that line and line 11 modify the first part of line 10. In 1913, after some intermediate and relatively unimportant changes, the punctuation was changed significantly:

> Time can but make her beauty over again;
> Because of that great nobleness of hers
> The fire that stirs about her, when she stirs
> Burns but more clearly;

Now line 8 stands by itself, line 9 modifies lines 10 and 11, and there is a specific meaning in lines 10 and 11. The next significant change was for *Later Poems* (1922) where a colon replaces the semi-colon in line 8; the last was for the 1933 printing where a terminal comma after "stirs," in line 10, finally gave Yeats, it would seem, the meaning or meanings he wanted. It is this 1933 version that we are presented with as the 1903 version: proof that when a "later" as well as an "early" Yeats poem is discussed and quoted the exact printing date of the quotation must be given and pertinent facts from the poem's printing history.

The more important revision volumes for the later poems are *The Wind Among the Reeds* (1899)—on the basis of the many revisions from initial magazine printings; *Poems 1899-1905* (1906); *The Green Helmet and Other Poems* (1912); *Responsibilities* (1916); *Later Poems* (1922); *The Tower* (London; New York, 1928); *The Winding Stair and Other Poems* (London; New York, 1933); *Collected Poems* (1933); and *A Full Moon in March* (London, 1935). It would be misleading to list these volumes in an order based either on number or significance of revisions, for in only two of them, *Later Poems* and *Collected Poems*, are more than a handful of the later poems printed or reprinted. As a matter of fact, the later poems in their entirety appear only in the definitive edition of 1949 and the trade editions of 1950 and 1951.

These, then, are some of the textual facts and problems the student of Yeats must deal with. There are others: for instance, the existence of one version of a poem in the prose works and another version in the poetry volumes, examples being "The Moods," "Into the Twilight," and "The Happy Townland";[15] or the scores of title changes Yeats made;[16] or the changes made for, apparently, the sake of the rhythm only: "They'd mauled and bitten the night through" to "They mauled and bit the whole night through";[17] or "They'll cough in the ink to the world's end," to "All shuffle there; all cough in ink."[18]

[15] "The Moods." Originally in *The Bookman* (August 1893). With minor changes, and no title, reprinted in *The Celtic Twilight* (London, December 1893; New York, 1894), in the revised *The Celtic Twilight* (London; New York: 1902; rptd. London and Stratford-upon-Avon, 1911), and in *The Collected Works* V (1908). But for *The Wind Among the Reeds* (1899) the title was restored, marked changes were made in several lines, and in this form it was printed in *The Poetical Works* I (1906), *The Collected Works* I (1908), and so on through the definitive edition. "Into the Twilight." Originally in *The National Observer* (29 July 1893) entitled "The Celtic Twilight." With a new title "Into the Twilight" and minor changes reprinted in *The Celtic Twlight* (1893, 1894), in the revised *The Celtic Twilight* (1902, rptd 1911), in *The Collected Works* V (1908), and in *Early Poems and Stories* (1925). In the course of these printings a few additional changes were made. But for *The Wind Among the Reeds* (1899) marked changes were made . . . . [The remainder of this note is the same as that for "The Moods."]

"The Happy Townland." Originally in *The Weekly Critical Review*, June 1903; then with a new title "The Rider from the North" in *In the Seven Woods* (1903); with the original title restored, in *Poems, 1899–1905* (1906), and so on through the definitive edition. But for *The Collected Works* V (1908), *Stories of Red Hanrahan* (London and Stratford-upon-Avon; New York: 1913), *Early Poems and Stories* (1925), and *Stories of Red Hanrahan* (London, 1927) lines 1–12, much changed, are in the story "The Twisting of the Rope," and lines 1–32 and 41–60, with the same changes in lines 1–12 but the other lines unchanged, are in the story "Hanrahan's Vision."

[16] See Witt, "Competition for Eternity," for a brief discussion of title changes in the later poems.

[17] From "The Three Beggars." The earlier version of the line is in the first three printings: *Harper's Weekly* (15 November 1931), *Responsibilities* (Cuala Press, 1914), and *Responsibilities* (London; New York, 1916); the later and final version begins with the fourth printing: *Later Poems* (1922).

[18] From "The Scholars." The original version of lines 7–10 that lasted from their first printing in the *Catholic Anthology* (1914–1915) (London, 1915) through the 1926 revision of *Later Poems* (1922) are

Finally, two amusing revisions, the second probably a misprint. In the first printing of the poem "Lullaby" in *The New Keepsake* (London, 1931) lines 3–6 read

> What are all the world's alarms?
> What were they when Paris found
> Sleep upon a golden bed
> That first dawn in Helen's arms?

As revised for its next printing in *Words for Music Perhaps and Other Poems* (Cuala Press, Dublin, 1932) they become

> What were all the world's alarms
> To mighty Paris when he found
> Sleep upon a golden bed
> That first night in Helen's arms?

In the succeeding printing, *The Winding Stair and Other Poems* (1933), line six reverts to

> That first dawn in Helen's arms?

and remains so.

The second, the probable misprint, concerns line 36 of "Adam's Curse": "To love you in the old high way of love." In three of the printings, *The Gael* (February 1903),[19] *The Poetical Works* I (1906), and *Selected Poems* (1921) the words "high" and "way" have been joined, and the line reads "To love you in the old highway of love."

I give these two revisions to the Freudians "for free."

> They'll cough in the ink to the world's end;
> Wear out the carpet with their shoes
> Earning respect; have no strange friend;
> If they have sinned nobody knows:

The revised version, first in *Selected Poems* (1929), is

> All shuffle there; all cough in ink;
> All wear the carpet with their shoes;
> All think what other people think;
> All know the man their neighbour knows.

[19] A magazine published in New York 1881–1904 and October 1923–May 1924.

XVII

JAMES B. MERIWETHER

The Text of Ernest Hemingway

It is an interesting and in some ways challenging task to attempt to assess the present situation in the bibliographical and textual study of such a novelist as Hemingway. The last few years have seen a revolution in the methods and standards of textual bibliography, and the application to more recent literature of the techniques developed in the field of Renaissance drama by such scholars as McKerrow, Greg, and Bowers has demonstrated the urgency of our need to remake our bibliographies and our editions even of authors who lived in the era of machine-printed books. When the Centennial Edition of Hawthorne was begun at Ohio State recently under the textual supervision of Professor Bowers, it was found that virtually the entire editorial task had to be undertaken from the very beginning, though it might have been assumed that Hawthorne scholars had paid a considerable amount of attention to textual problems in his published work in the century since his death. With Hemingway, it is not so much a matter of having to do over again a task inadequately performed before, but of doing most of it for the first time. During the four decades of his mature literary career Hemingway published much, and at his death two years ago he left a considerable amount of unpublished work in manuscript. Throughout his career, too, he was a stylist, a perfectionist who lavished great care upon the polishing and revision of his novels and stories, as extant manuscript material (including typescripts and proofsheets within the definition) attests.

No full-scale bibliographical and textual study of Heming-

Revised from a paper read before the meeting of the Bibliographical Society of America on 14 July 1963, at the Newberry Library. In addition to the specific debts acknowledged in the footnotes, I wish to thank Professor Carlos Baker, Mrs. Louis Henry Cohn, and Mr. Thomas L. Mc-Haney for their assistance and suggestions. Reprinted with revisions from the *Papers of the Bibliographical Society of America*, vol. LVII (1963), by permission of the author and the Council for the Bibliographical Society of America.

way is underway at the present time, as far as I am aware. If such a study were undertaken, it would face all the problems of dealing with a body of work which is extensive, which is of great literary importance, and which is often textually complex—that is, which often exists in several versions, whether complete or fragmentary, that must be carefully collated and analyzed to recover the author's intentions from the conflicting evidence presented by house-styling, printer's errors, and editorial emendation. And these problems must be faced at a time when textual studies in general must measure up to new standards and make use of new techniques.

Although the first step in such a study, the basic one of discovering and listing the first publications of Hemingway's works, was taken by Louis Henry Cohn quite early in Hemingway's career,[1] and Audre Hanneman has brought Cohn's listing up to date,[2] we are still awaiting for Hemingway (as we are for so many of our writers) any further steps along bibliographical and textual lines. Indeed, so far as I know this paper represents the first attempt to examine any of the larger problems of the Hemingway text in the light of present-day bibliographical scholarship. As a result, it is necessary to emphasize here what needs to be done, rather than what has been done. The textual study of Hemingway is interesting not because of its achievements but because of its opportunities. My purpose here is therefore to call attention to some of the main obligations that exist in this area of Hemingway scholarship; to supply a few specific examples of the problems involved; and to draw some general conclusions, several of them rather tentative, about the relevance of the situation in the Hemingway text to that whole field, which we have seen so rapidly opened up in the past few years, of the application of the new bibliography to the literature, especially the fiction, written in English in this century.

Let me begin by recapitulating briefly Hemingway's career as a writer. We can date its beginning around 1923-24, when his first two books, the little pamphlet-sized limited editions of *Three Stories & Ten Poems* and the first *in our time* were pub-

[1] Cohn, *A Bibliography of the Works of Ernest Hemingway* (New York: Random House, 1931).

[2] Hanneman, *Ernest Hemingway: A Comprehensive Bibliography* (Princeton University Press, 1967).

lished in France. Preceding these were the usual juvenilia and ephemera—contributions to the student newspaper and literary magazine at Oak Park High School, dispatches and features in the newspapers he worked for, here and abroad, and so on. His first full-size book was the 1925 *In Our Time*, a volume of stories published in New York by Boni and Liveright. His first true novel was *The Sun Also Rises*, which was brought out in 1926 by Scribner after Hemingway had broken with Liveright over their failure to publish *The Torrents of Spring*, a short novel which parodied Sherwood Anderson, then Liveright's best-selling author. From 1926 onward all Hemingway's books were with Scribner: *A Farewell to Arms* in 1929, several collections of stories, the nonfiction *Death in the Afternoon* (1932) and *Green Hills of Africa* (1935), the novels *For Whom the Bell Tolls* (1940) and *Across the River and into the Trees* (1950), and the long story *The Old Man and the Sea* (1952). There is much uncollected work of importance buried in periodicals, particularly from the decade of the 1930's, and there is apparently a substantial body of late work, finished and unfinished, left in manuscript at his death.

Let us now imagine that a scholarly edition of Hemingway is to be prepared, one of the scope and standards which we find in the Ohio State Hawthorne. I do not know when such an edition can be undertaken, but obviously for a writer of Hemingway's stature we need it as soon as possible, though problems of copyright, among others, may long delay it. Before we have this edition, whenever it is done, we must have a bibliography; a real bibliography; what we might call a *textual* bibliography in order to distinguish it from those useful compilations of data, designed primarily for dealer and collector, that are concerned basically with the outsides of books rather than their insides, their bindings rather than their texts.

Towards such a bibliography an important step was taken in 1931 by Cohn. His was primarily a collector's and dealer's bibliography, of course, but of its kind it was superb, and it remains useful to the serious student of Hemingway. Subsequent listings by Lee Samuels[3] and Carlos Baker[4] are now entirely super-

---

[3] Samuels, *A Hemingway Check List* (New York: Scribner, 1951).

[4] Baker, "A Working Check-List of Hemingway's Prose, Poetry, and Journalism . . ." in *Hemingway: The Writer as Artist* (Princeton University Press, 1952; revised editions, 1956, 1963).

seded by the Hanneman bibliography, which in scope is more
akin to the Cohn. It contains unusually full data on the various
editions, impressions, and issues of the books, but only occasionally, where the information was already available, does it mention
textual changes.

A writer as prolific and as widely traveled as Hemingway
presents special problems in the solution of the basic bibliographical task of identifying and locating individual published works,
and I assume that the chances are good that despite the researches
of Hanneman, for a long time to come ephemeral Hemingway
items, previously unknown, will turn up in various places, some
of them perhaps in languages other than English. The possibility
is greatly increased by Hemingway's long service as a journalist.
Cohn, explaining in 1931 his reluctance to become involved in
the whole question of Hemingway's newspaper contributions,
quoted a letter that explained Hemingway's opposition to such
investigation and indicates the magnitude of the problem:

> It is the height of silliness [wrote Hemingway] to go into
> newspaper stuff I have written, which has nothing to do with
> the other writing which is entirely apart and starts with the
> first IN OUR TIME. Have written thousands of columns in
> newspapers. Also sent much in condensed cable-ese to be re-
> written in U. S. and Canada. This has nothing to do with signed
> and published writing in books or magazines and it is a hell of a
> trick on a man to dig it up and confuse the matter of judging
> the work he has published. . . . If you have made your living
> as a newspaperman, learning your trade, writing against dead-
> lines, writing to make stuff timely rather than permanent, no
> one has any right to dig this stuff up and use it against the stuff
> you have written to write the best you can.[5]

We can fully sympathize with Hemingway's point here without
agreeing that his journalism will be held against his mature fiction, and without abandoning the principle that for full understanding of a man's best work we need to know as much as we
can about his whole career including his most ephemeral productions. In the long run, no serious student of literary history
can gainsay the desirability of having, as soon as possible, the sort
of study of an important author's formative years that Charles

[5] Cohn, p. 112. As printed there the text of the letter appears entirely in
italics.

Fenton gave us in *The Apprenticeship of Ernest Hemingway*.[6] Error breeds error; to understand the man we must know the boy. I have no doubt that a great deal of the nonsense written in recent years about the mature career and work of William Faulkner, for one example, could have been avoided if we had had available half so good a study of his literary apprenticeship as Fenton's of Hemingway.

Despite all due sympathy for the views Hemingway expressed to Cohn, and with the reservation that the evidence of such material needs to be considered with a greater sense of literary proportion than is always the case, we still need, then, more exploration of the ephemeral and journalistic bread-and-butter products of Hemingway's pen before the first task of a full-scale bibliography will be accomplished.

The second major problem of the bibliographer, once he has his list of what the author wrote, is to trace the history of the text, unpublished and published. Which versions of the text of a work are the same, which different? If different, are the changes due an authorial or to an editorial hand? There was a special 1942 Limited Editions Club edition of *For Whom the Bell Tolls* —did Hemingway have anything to do with the text? We can assume that there was a certain amount of minor textual corruption in the new Scribner edition of *A Farewell to Arms* (1948)—a few changes in punctuation and spelling, possibly the omission or change of a word or two. Are there any authorial corrections or revisions of the original text present too, or can we forget the 1948 and base our critical studies entirely upon the 1929 edition? If we cleave to the first edition, do we need to know about corrections, made by changes in the plates, in later printings? Cohn tells us that by 1931 "various plate corrections" had been made in the 1926 Scribner *The Sun Also Rises*.[7] What were they? Were any further ones made? When the 1954 Scribner edition was set, was it set from a copy from the printing that incorporated *all* the plate corrections? A spot collation, for instance, of a few pages of the original (1926) edition of *The Sun Also Rises* with the first impression of the new (1954) Scribner edition reveals two minor changes, both presumably

[6] New York: Farrar, Straus & Young, 1954.

[7] Cohn, p. 27.

though not certainly errors.[8] Only the full collation of the relevant editions and impressions will reveal exactly what changes have taken place in the printed text during the author's lifetime, and so make it possible to decide whether the changes are printer's errors or author's revisions.

The history of the printed text, of course, cannot be fully traced until a manuscript census has been made. What manuscripts, typescripts, proofsheets exist, and where are they located? Presumably the full collation of all relevant manuscript and printed versions of Hemingway's writings and the establishment of the text will await the time when it is done in connection with a scholarly edition. But in the meantime the bibliographer should perform us the service of making a preliminary examination of the text and publishing his findings. In practice, if not in principle, the bibliographer must be aware of the distinction between his function and that of the editor of a scholarly edition of his author, but it is obvious that to a certain extent the value of his bibliography will be directly proportional to the amount of editorial burden which he is willing to assume. The bibliographer working without the pressure of specifically editorial obligations may well decide to stop short of investigating publishers' and agents' records and editorial correspondence, for instance, yet these may be indispensable to establishing the text, and the sooner they are investigated the better. Records are apt to be dispersed or destroyed, memories to fade, while the bibliography is being compiled but before the edition can be undertaken.

If such a bibliography as I am calling for seems unreasonably ambitious in scope, despite its supreme usefulness to the study of an important writer, what is being done in the bibliographical study of other twentieth-century novelists should be recalled. Work such as that done in recent years on Joyce by Herbert Cahoon; on Fitzgerald by Matthew Bruccoli; and on Conrad by Bruce Harkness, to give but three examples, has shown how valuable such textual study can be, and has set the standards by which future bibliographies in this area will be judged.

The function of the bibliographer often cannot be distin-

___

[8] The changes are: 1926 ed. 131.3 into [1954 ed. 127.9 *into;* 1926 ed. 134.24 custom [1954 ed. 130.24 customs.

guished from that of the editor; bibliographical and editorial problems, if not identical, are inseparable. The remainder of this paper will be devoted to textual problems more properly pertaining to the province of the editor, or associated with an edition of an author's works, but it must be emphasized once more that these are matters that *can* be settled before we have that edition, and some of them perhaps should be. If the scholarly edition must await a future when copyright limitations have expired, then so much the greater need for a good bibliography in the meantime to guide us in assessing the reliability of the text that is available.

One immediately striking aspect of the textual situation in Hemingway concerns his work that has not yet appeared in book form. When we examine the record of his serial publication in Hanneman, it is surprising to see how much of worth, even importance, Hemingway never collected between the covers of a book. It is, among other things, a remarkable tribute to his standards that he never did so. But clearly we need, and eventually will have, collections which will bring together such pieces as the series of twenty-five articles on big-game hunting and deep-sea fishing he contributed to *Esquire* between 1933 and 1936; the five short stories from *Cosmopolitan* and *Esquire*, 1938–39, which appeared too late for inclusion in the 1938 collected stories; the thirteen articles in *Ken*, 1938–39; and so on. There are important early pieces, like the appreciation of Conrad that appeared in the *transatlantic review* in 1924; late war dispatches like the 1944 series in *Collier's*; and the 1954 hunting pieces in *Look* which describe his near-fatal African safari of that year. I do not know how many of these pieces exist in manuscript or typescript versions, but taking into account the circumstances of magazine publication in this country, in recent years, we may doubt that in many cases Hemingway saw proofs for these, their only published appearances, and we may assume a much greater degree of editorial tampering and printer's errors than is true of the books. If they are collected in essentially unedited form—that is, if the magazine texts are used, without reference to manuscript or typescript—it will be a pity, and Hemingway will have been done an injustice. In the meantime we need especially to track down the author's manuscripts and typescripts of these pieces—and if they were sent to the periodical through an agent, we need to know if the agent had them retyped. It is not difficult to confuse a typescript which an agent has had retyped with one supplied by an author, and yet there may be serious differences between them.

The textual problems in the already published books tend to be more complex, if not so serious as those in unpublished or uncollected work. I give four examples which have come to my attention of the sort of difficulties which exist in the text of Hemingway's books, and which will have to be resolved before we have an edition of his writings commensurate with his importance.

The simplest of the examples is taken from *Death in the Afternoon*, that remarkable treatise on bull-fighting which was first published, with lavish illustrations, in 1932. The corrected galley proofs, fortunately still extant, reveal that the book underwent extensive revision in proof. At one point, Hemingway inserted a new sentence in mid-paragraph in the galley, and the resultant necessity for resetting the lines of the paragraph below the insertion produced what appears to have been a printer's or editor's error, the addition of commas around a short phrase.[9] A small matter, of course, but when we consider how sparing of commas Hemingway was, it is not insignificant, and barring the unlikely appearance of evidence to the contrary—editorial correspondence or corrected page proofs which show the change to be the author's—the editor of our future scholarly edition of Hemingway will leave those commas out. The point is that for such works as *Death in the Afternoon* where we have other substantive forms of the text—a typescript, or corrected proofs—we face eventually the necessity of full collation in process of re-editing to remove errors, and in the meantime it is vital that the bibliographer record the existence of such material.

This material will include English editions, of course, as well as American. Did Hemingway's English publishers afford him the opportunity for proof correction that may have produced substantive changes that never found their way into the American editions? For at least one of Hemingway's American contemporaries, James Gould Cozzens, this occurred.[10] And for one

[9] These galleys are in the collection of Mrs. Louis Henry Cohn, to whom I am indebted for permitting me to examine them. The long sentence on lines 6–10 of p. 37 of the 1932 Scribner edition of the book was added to the proofs, and the commas were added in line 12 around the phrase "and probably through."

[10] See James B. Meriwether, "The English Editions of James Gould Cozzens," *Studies in Bibliography* XV (1962), 207-17.

Hemingway novel we shall have to consider a translation. Maxwell Perkins, Hemingway's editor at Scribner's for two decades, stated in a letter in 1933 that "no genuine writer will allow a publisher to exercise this kind of censorship over him"—i.e., to strike out certain words from the text of a book which will be offensive to certain readers, and he upheld the right of writers, and publishers, to "the greatest freedom in respect to literary expression."[11] Yet a few years earlier, according to Hemingway, Perkins had insisted upon the deletion from the typescript of *A Farewell to Arms* of a number of the standard Anglo-Saxon four-letter obscenities. When Maurice Coindreau undertook the translation of this novel, about 1930, Hemingway wrote him that these editorial deletions or changes had been made over his strong protest, and he would like them restored in the French translation. So he took Coindreau's copy of the first edition of the book and carefully inserted all the obscenities again. I do not know if the original typescript survives, with original obscenities and editorial markings, but in its absence I take it that for those passages, Coindreau's copy of the novel should supply the text for the definitive edition of Hemingway.[12]

More complex is the case of *The Sun Also Rises*. The typescript setting copy has been preserved,[13] and spot-collation with the published book reveals a great many changes, most of them presumably editorial, but some as apt to be printer's errors as editor's revisions. Hemingway's hyphens are removed; new hyphens are inserted; some French words are anglicized (e.g. terrasse [terraces]); and many commas are added. One example will suffice: the conclusion of the novel, as published, gives Jake Barnes's final bitter and ironic commentary: " 'Yes,' I said. 'Isn't it pretty to think so?' " The comma after the "Yes" is not present in the typescript; nor is there a question mark at the end, but simply a period. This typescript gives evidence of somewhat

[11] *Editor to Author: The Letters of Maxwell E. Perkins*, ed. John Hall Wheelock (New York: Scribner, 1950), pp. 81–82. From the date and certain internal evidence it might be guessed that the work referred to was Hemingway's recently published *Death in the Afternoon*, which contained a sprinkling of four-letter vulgarities.

[12] Interview with M. Coindreau, October 1962. Further information on this point is provided in James B. Meriwether, "The Dashes in Hemingway's *A Farewell to Arms*," *Papers of the Bibliographical Society of America*, vol. LVIII (1964).

[13] In the collection of Mrs. Cohn.

hasty, careless typing, and called for a real job of copy-editing, but it is by no means certain that this is what Perkins gave it. The editorial correspondence and a careful collation of the typescript and the published book may solve all problems here, but it seems possible that a carefully edited text of the novel would present real difficulties. If an editor decided, very reasonably, to return to the typescript in removing a great deal of extraneous punctuation present in the printed book, and in restoring a number of Gallicisms that were Englished, what about the occurrence in the typescript, on several occasions, of the name "Duff" instead of the "Brett" of the published novel? Ever since its publication *The Sun Also Rises* has been known as a *roman à clef*, and the real identities of its major characters are no longer a secret.[14] A scholarly edition of the novel would eliminate the mixture of real and fictional names in the typescript, of course, but would identifications be called for in introduction or notes? Or, if a scholarly edition of *A Farewell to Arms* calls for the incorporation of Hemingway's additions to Coindreau's copy of the book, perhaps what we need for *The Sun Also Rises* is the preliminary cast of characters that Hemingway supplied for Herbert Gorman, identifying Jake as Hemingway, Brett as Lady Twysden, Bill as Donald Ogden Stewart, Cohn as Harold Loeb, and Braddocks as Ford Madox Ford, as well as giving the originals of Prentice, Harvey Stone, Michael, and Frances.[15]

In Our Time has had a chequered career. Beginning as a 30-page collection of eighteen brief prose fiction sketches or miniatures (1924 version), it was expanded to full size in 1925 and reprinted, somewhat revised, in 1930. In 1938 its contents were included in Hemingway's collected stories. To follow the published career of one of the stories, "Mr. and Mrs. Elliot," is instructive. Originally published in *The Little Review* in the issue of Autumn-Winter 1924–25, it ran into trouble upon its inclusion in the 1925 Liveright *In Our Time*. Hemingway, writing Liveright from Paris May 22, 1925, said that he was returning the galley proof that day, and congratulated whoever had done the editing upon an intelligent job. He agreed with most of the changes of punctuation that had been made; those he disagreed with, he said, he was changing back to the original reading.

[14] See Harold Loeb, *The Way It Was* (New York: Criterion Books, 1959); Carlos Baker, ed. *Ernest Heminway: Critiques of Four Major Novels* (New York: Scribner, 1962), p. 8.

[15] Copy in the collection of Mrs. Cohn.

But he had been forced to revise "Mr. and Mrs. Elliot," he noted. He agreed with Liveright that it would be very silly to get the entire book suppressed because of one story, and he had therefore eliminated the phrase that had caused the difficulty, though where it was omitted he had, for the sake of rhythm, inserted other phrases.[16]

A collation of the text of the *Little Review* and the three book versions reveals that the phrase which was (then) so offensive is that Mr. and Mrs. Elliot repeatedly "tried to have a baby." It is not surprising that only five years later a different publisher, Scribner, plucked up their courage sufficiently to allow Hemingway to restore the phrase. But in that edition (and its successor, the 1938 collected stories) Hemingway made a point of omitting a number of the commas added by the Liveright editor in 1925— in spite of the fact that in 1925 he wrote Liveright he agreed to all the changes of punctuation he was not changing then. This is a point to be pondered by those who feel that in overseeing the publication of a book and correcting its proofs an author is consenting to any editorial changes he does not reject by changing them back to the original reading. Lacking the editions of 1930 and 1938, the evidence of the corrected proofs, even without the assurance of Hemingway's letter, by such a theory would have established as authoritative the changes made by Liveright's editor.

Liveright insisted that another story, "Up in Michigan," be omitted entirely from the 1925 *In Our Time*. (It had originally appeared in the 1923 *Three Stories & Ten Poems*.) Hemingway revised it for inclusion in the 1930 Scribner edition, changing several names and toning down the details of the sexual contacts between Jim and Liz in order to make it more acceptable. But at the last minute Scribner rejected it too.[17] When it was finally republished in the 1938 collected stories, it was the revised version of 1930 which appeared. But should we not return today to the original 1923 text, which is certainly tame enough by present publishing standards?

Let us now examine the unpublished work. And we might begin, unhappily enough, with work that will probably never

[16] Letter in the collection of Mrs. Cohn.

[17] The revised typescript is in Mrs. Cohn's collection. See also Cohn, *A Bibliography*, p. 16.

be published—the letters. According to Professor Baker, Hemingway forbade the publication of the letters in a "special document" executed in "May 1958," specifying *never*." In the official biography, Baker will paraphrase, never quoting directly from the letters.[18]

There is a precedent for this, of course. Willa Cather directed the executors of her estate, in her will, to refuse "publication in any form whatsoever, of the whole, or any part of any letter or letters written by me."[19] How long such an injunction can remain legally binding is not clear. Edward Taylor apparently directed his heirs not to publish any of his writings, but in 1937 the legal opinion was given that "there is no present legal force to such an instruction if it existed, and that if the University lawfully possesses these manuscripts the instruction does not legally interfere with their publication." The legal counsel concluded that "Personally I can see no moral obligations after such a lapse of time."[20] Miss Cather may have been recognizing this fact when in her will she added that realizing "the right to publish letters written by me, and other rights in said letters, may ultimately vest in my legatees . . . I earnestly request such of my legatees . . . as may acquire said rights" not to permit publication.[21] Baker notes that "I cannot speculate about the long future, but would regard chances of publication as extremely bleak for many reasons."[22]

No one who is familiar with Hemingway's letters, the best of them, can contemplate this decision of the author without the keenest regret. Baker has recently described the acquisition by Princeton of the highly important correspondence with Major General Charles T. Lanham, 600 pages of it covering the period between 1945 and 1961.[23] Also at Princeton is the long correspondence with the artist Henry Strater which began in 1923 and is rich in descriptions of Hemingway's Cuban fishing and

[18] Letter, Carlos Baker to James B. Meriwether, 4 July 1963.

[19] Norman Holmes Pearson, "Problems of Literary Executorship," *Studies in Bibliography* V (1952–53), 8.

[20] *Ibid.*, p. 6.

[21] *Ibid.*, p. 8.

[22] Baker, letter cited.

[23] Baker, "Letters from Hemingway," *PULC* XXIV (Winter 1963), 104. See also the references to the Princeton University Library's Hemingway materials in *Princeton Alumni Weekly* LXIII (16 Nov. 1962), 6–11, 15.

Western hunting adventures.[24] Even more to be regretted, perhaps, is the loss of the opportunity of making available Hemingway's side of the important correspondence with F. Scott Fitzgerald. Fitzgerald's letters can be published, are being published; when both sides of a literary correspondence are of approximately equal significance, the virtual loss of half of it is bound to have an irritating, cumulatively distorting effect upon the serious study of the two men involved.

A good many Hemingway letters have already been published, of course, at least in part. There is no legal, and I assume no moral, obligation for scholars not to continue to quote from these properly published sources in the future. Before the ban, Professor Baker was able to quote directly from important Hemingway letters in his 1952 critical study, and a valuable feature of Cohn's 1931 bibliography was his quotations from his own correspondence from Hemingway. The ban upon the further publication of letters will undoubtedly place an increased stress upon the tracking down of even small fragments of Hemingway letters that have appeared in print. Two recent exhibition catalogues contain very interesting quotations from letters, for instance,[25] and booksellers' catalogues often include quotations from letters offered for sale.

These latter categories raise the question of what sort of obligation, legal or moral, may restrain scholars from quoting letters which may have been published, in whole or in part, without authorization. A 1951 master's thesis, subsequently made available by microfilm and Xerox photocopies from University Microfilms, Inc., quoted twenty of Hemingway's letters to Fitzgerald, some of them extensively.[26] I do not know whether the availability of this thesis from University Microfilms constitutes publication, but it is entirely possible that scholars unaware of the ban will use this thesis and quote from the letters. Certainly the number of awkward situations likely to arise in the perfectly

[24] Baker, "Letters from Hemingway," p. 106.

[25] See *PULC* XVII (Summer 1956), 248; and the 8-page pamphlet, *Ernest Hemingway: . . . Guide to a Memorial Exhibition,* by William White (University of Detroit Library, 1961).

[26] Frank Ernest Mayer, "The Influence of F. Scott Fitzgerald on William Faulkner and Ernest Hemingway," a 1951 New York University master's thesis in English, pp. 164–73. I have examined a Xerox copy obtained by the University of Mississippi Library from University Microfilms, Inc.

normal course of events in the world of Hemingway scholarship is distressingly large. What of a letter written in 1950, for instance, and published in 1957, but published in Italian?[27] Presumably a scholar may quote the Italian text; presumably he may translate it; suppose in so doing he recovers the original English? That such questions are bound to arise, and do so frequently, may have an effect not envisaged by Hemingway when his understandable irritation at invasions of his privacy caused him to take such steps in 1958.

But fortunately the letters are far from being the most important unpublished Hemingway manuscript material. For a decade before his death, there were reports that he had in progress a long novel about the sea, or about "The Land, the Sea, and the Air."[28] In 1960 *Life* published three excerpts from *The Dangerous Summer,* an account of Hemingway's recent bull-fighting experiences.[29] And immediately after his death in Idaho in July 1961 there were reports of a completed book of "reminiscences of Paris in the 1920s," soon to appear,[30] and of "at least two unpublished novels and a bit of poetry" left as a literary legacy.[31] At least part of the explanation for the existence of important, completed, unpublished works, it appeared, was the tax situation: "He was never eager to publish," Mrs. Hemingway was quoted as saying. "Why should you make your income tax go from 75 to 95 per cent? In a sense, it [the unpublished work] was his bank account."[32] The decision what, and when, to publish had been left to Mrs. Hemingway by her husband,[33] and obviously a responsibility of such great literary and personal significance could not easily be discharged. In the following two years, however, while nothing has been published, there have been many

[27] The letter appears (in Italian) on p. 228 of *Il Cinquantennio Editoriale di Arnoldo Mondadori, 1907–1957* (Verona, 1957). It may, of course, have been originally written in that language, which would add to the confusion, though many of the letters in the volume were obviously translated.

[28] Baker, *Hemingway,* p. 295; "Hemingway," *Saturday Review* XLIV (29 July 1961), 12.

[29] *Life,* 49 (5 Sept., 12 Sept., 19 Sept. 1960).

[30] Baker, "Hemingway," p. 11.

[31] *New York Times,* 9 July 1961, p. 45 (quoting Mrs. Hemingway).

[32] *Ibid.* (The brackets appear in the newspaper text.)

[33] See Hemingway's will, quoted and reproduced in part, *New York Times,* 25 Aug. 1961, p. 27.

confusing and contradictory reports of what exists and may be brought out. As an interim report likely quite soon to be out-dated, I offer the following brief summary of the situation concerning these unpublished works.

The "big one all about the land, the sea and the air," which was reported by Mrs. Hemingway from Idaho on 8 July 1961 to be "in a Cuban bank,"[34] must unfortunately, according to later reports, be dismissed as having "never existed except in his [Hemingway's] imagination."[35]

The Sea Chase, a short novel completed about 1956, became known when at the White House dinner given for Nobel Prize winners in April 1962 Fredric March read to the guests its first chapter. After the reading, according to one reporter, Mrs. Hemingway told the audience that it had been finished six years before and laid away, for Hemingway "did not wish to publish it then because he didn't want to pay income tax on it. It will be published one day, but there is no hurry." Newspaper accounts of the dinner quoted the first sentence (one wonders how accurately) and supplied a synopsis, given by Mrs. Hemingway, of the whole work, which concerns the pursuit by an American artist in his own fishing boat of the crew of a sunken U-boat off the north coast of Cuba in 1942.[36]

The Dangerous Summer, Carlos Baker reported in 1961, might as a whole "look better than the published excerpts would prophesy,"[37] but he now surmises that it is "doubtful" that the book will appear "for some time."[38]

The book of Paris reminiscences, which Mrs. Hemingway reported in March 1962 as in the hands of the publishers, who liked it,[39] has been announced by Scribners for publication in early May 1964 under the title *A Movable Feast*.

The possibility still remains that other completed manuscripts exist and will eventually be published. Reference has been made to "a kind of 'fictional interpretation' of Africa," dating from 1954;[40] to "a series of connecting sketches of World War II

34 *New York Times*, 9 July 1961, p. 45.

35 Baker, letter cited.

36 *Washington Post*, 30 April 1962, Section B, p. 6.

37 Baker, "Hemingway," p. 11.

38 Baker, letter cited.

39 *New York Times*, 9 March 1962, p. 31.

40 *Ibid.*

battles in Europe";[41] to a "fairly lengthy" manuscript upon which he was working at the time of his death and which he kept "in an Idaho bank vault";[42] to a "three-part collection" of which *The Old Man and the Sea* had been the first part;[43] and to "dozens of stories and sketches" and "much poetry."[44] Obviously the bulk and worth of what remains may have been exaggerated in newspaper accounts and Mrs. Hemingway is being careful to avoid raising our hopes too high. But in the long run, it appears, we can look forward to considerable additions to the body of Hemingway's known prose, some of it possibly of high quality, unless his exacting standards, and his widow's sense of obligation towards them, result in that grievous loss to posterity, the destruction of these papers.

When it was reported, not long after Hemingway's death, that Mrs. Hemingway might feel bound to destroy unpublished manuscripts, Glenway Wescott wrote the *New York Times*[45] to state that it would be a major and unjustifiable loss to the literary world if this were to happen. "I feel impelled, almost honor-bound and duty-bound," wrote Wescott, "to express my sadness and dismay at the possibility at any such waste and loss." It is not necessary to agree wholly with Wescott's estimate of Hemingway's importance to agree with the stress he laid upon the importance of preserving for publication work which might somehow fall short of its author's highest standards. "In my opinion," he continued,

> [Hemingway] was the most important and influential writer of his generation in the world. Any and every piece of his work, even unfinished work, is to be valued. Indeed, as he was a perfectionist, some things that he was not able to express to his satisfaction may prove to be of greater interest (to future biographers and students of literature if not to the general reading public) than certain of his second-best stories already published. . . .
>
> In the general world-wide lament for Hemingway's death there has been a constant note of gratitude to Mrs. Heming-

---

[41] *Ibid.*

[42] *New York Times*, 9 July 1961, p. 45. According to Professor Baker, this was probably the Paris reminiscences.

[43] *Ibid.*

[44] *New York Times*, 9 March 1962, p. 31.

[45] *New York Times*, 9 Aug. 1961, p. 32.

way for her devotion and helpfulness which he so grandly acknowledged again and again, and at the compassion appropriate to the final fatal circumstance. I hope that I have not implied that her judgment of his literary art is less sure and less authoritative than anyone else's.

But the evaluation of posthumous literary material requires above all an objective mind or, better still, a number of objective minds. She ought not to expect objectivity of herself now. Let her not feel any anxiety about Hemingway's reputation.

All of his work may be confidently entrusted to the world for that general delight and edification which he intended and for which he labored, tiring himself to death.

Wescott's plea was properly addressed not only to Mrs. Hemingway, but, through the columns of the *New York Times,* to the entire literary world, and we would all do well to ponder its implications. The conclusion can hardly be avoided that we are likely to see further examples of writers whose reaction to the glare and intrusions of present-day publicity, the irresponsibilities of so much present-day literary criticism, is to withdraw not only themselves but also their works from inspection. I am not here proposing any solutions to this problem; but if solutions are to be found, we had better face the facts of the problem as soon as possible.

Even so cursory examination as this of the bibliographical and textual problems in the study of Hemingway reveals a situation of unusual interest. The published work appears to offer precisely the same needs, or opportunities, that we find in the work of his important contemporaries among novelists in the English language: the necessity for a collected edition that will make available, as soon as is possible, all his significant work, and which for the already published books will bring out newly edited texts, where there is manuscript authority, which will rectify changes made earlier by now unjustifiable editorial tampering, housestyling, and undetected printer's errors. In connection with such an edition, I should like to suggest that a major and so far quite neglected area of bibliographical investigation for an author of Hemingway's importance is the study of the relationship between editor and author. Recent investigation of the text of both Fitzgerald and Wolfe,[46] for instance, both Scribner authors ed-

[46] Bruce Harkness, "Bibliography and the Novelistic Fallacy," *Studies in Bibliography* XII (1959), especially pp. 67–73; Matthew Bruccoli, "A Collation of F. Scott Fitzgerald's *This Side of Paradise*," *Studies in Bibli-*

The Text of Ernest Hemingway

ited by Maxwell Perkins, supports the tentative conclusions indicated by this brief examination of several of the Hemingway books—that despite his quite remarkable qualities and undeniable brilliance in many aspects of the editor-author relationship, Perkins' work as editor leaves much to be desired from the standpoint of the scholar who is concerned with our having the best possible text of a book once it is finished.

The unpublished work appears to be extensive, some of it important, and its future status in doubt. It is obvious that no final conclusions can be drawn about Hemingway until we have seen more of his late work, and though it is unlikely that any major reappraisal will be in order, it is quite possible that we will eventually have to modify considerably many of our ideas about various aspects of Hemingway's art.

The literary scholar or bibliographer who cares nothing for Hemingway may still find the present situation regarding the unpublished Hemingway papers instructive in several ways. First there is the unfortunate repetition of Willa Cather's decision that the letters never be published, or even quoted in part. No literary scholar can afford not to deplore precedents so dangerous; each time it happens, we have lost an area of literary research that we

---

ography IX (1957), 263–65; Richard S. Kennedy, *The Window of Memory* (University of North Carolina Press, 1962), pp. 266–71. None of these three scholars blames Perkins specifically for the errors and inconsistencies which they note in the texts of these novels edited by Perkins, but it is clear from the evidence that Perkins was far from meticulous in eliminating, or seeing to it that someone else eliminated, flaws in the text of the typescripts his authors sent him, despite his most impressive accomplishments in larger editorial tasks. Elizabeth Nowell, in her biography of Wolfe ([New York, 1960], p. 137), concluded that "Certainly the work that Perkins did upon *Look Homeward, Angel* was entirely responsible for transforming it from an amateurish, too long, too inchoate, and virtually unpublishable novel into the great book that it basically was," but in a recent article, "The Editing of *Look Homeward, Angel*" (*Papers of the Bibliographical Society of America* LVII [First Quarter, 1963], 1–13), Francis E. Skipp, who collated a carbon of the unedited typescript with the published book, demonstrates that the shaping (as opposed to the cutting) done by Perkins has been exaggerated. (See Kennedy, *The Window of Memory*, p. 176.) *Of Time and the River* is another matter, of course, but even there it is interesting that it was not Perkins but another Scribner editor, John Hall Wheelock, who had the job of reading the proofs and of making a number of corrections necessitated by the change from first to third person and by Wolfe's failure to read and revise portions of the typescript before it went to press. (See Nowell, *Thomas Wolfe*, pp. 239–40.)

331

are used to depending upon, and in the long run that loss is bound to affect, perhaps somewhat to distort, our perception of the man and his career. But we must not stop at deploring the situation; we need to remind ourselves that if a writer of Hemingway's importance was driven to take such a step, we ourselves did our fair share of the driving. Perhaps it is impossible to do anything about the irresponsible scholarship which joins irresponsible journalism in invading the privacy of artists and creating that general situation against which Hemingway understandably reacted with his 1958 interdict. But we need to face the fact that this sort of thing has twice resulted in a very serious deprivation to the world of letters, and we need to consider what can be done about it if we don't like the idea of its happening again.

The matter of Hemingway's letters had a precedent in Willa Cather. But the apparently sizable bulk of his unpublished work raises some interesting questions indeed. If Hemingway completed but failed to publish any important works because of our present tax laws, it is we who are the losers; what do we intend to do about it? I know no more about the situation than the bare details that are presented in this paper, but this is what appears to be the case; there is every reason to expect it to happen again; and I do not think anyone can argue that it is anything but pernicious. Clearly our whole system of copyright, income tax, and death duties is here working to the detriment of important rights and traditions which our society seeks to preserve, if a major artist chooses to make the sacrifices and run the risks of refusing to publish finished work during his lifetime. For letters and other personal papers to be closed to the public for a period of years is a familiar literary situation and often quite justified. For a work of art to be lost to the world, possibly for a whole generation, can hardly be too much regretted, and it is up to the generation that is thus the loser to see what can be done about it.

POSTSCRIPT, MAY 1968

I am indebted to Mr. Charles W. Mann, who, with Professor Philip Young, is engaged in compiling an inventory of the Hemingway papers, for the following data which supplement and correct my remarks in this article.

Mrs. Hemingway in 1961 and 1962 collected her husband's papers, which were widely scattered. Eventually the entire archive, including correspondence, may be given to the John F. Kennedy Memorial Library in Cambridge, Massachusetts. In addition to manuscripts, typescripts, and proofsheets of pubblished works, there is a great deal of unpublished material, some of which will certainly be published, perhaps in the near future. "The Dangerous Summer" and "The Sea Chase" are already known. A novel, variously entitled "Bimini Piece" or "Sea Novel," exists in several drafts, with many revisions. A slightly fictionalized account of six weeks as a game warden in Africa in 1953 is substantial but unfinished. Less likely to see publication are an incomplete early novel, "Jimmy Breen," and a late one, tentatively entitled "Garden of Eden." Among a dozen unpublished short stories are three dealing with Nick Adams, at least one of which will be included in a forthcoming collection of the Nick Adams stories edited by Professor Young.

J. B. M.

BIBLIOGRAPHY

A complete bibliography of articles in this field is published annually in *Studies in Bibliography* (1948–). The following list, which does not include any item cited in the Introduction, is selective and representative of current research in bibliography and textual criticism of the eighteenth, nineteenth, and twentieth centuries. *Studies in Bibliography* and *Papers of the Bibliographical Society of America* are referred to as *SB* and *PBSA* respectively.

GENERAL

Alston, R. C. "Bibliography and Historical Linguistics," *Library*, 5th ser., 21 (1966): 181–91.

Bowers, Fredson. "Bibliography, Pure Bibliography, and Literary Studies," *PBSA* 46 (1952): 186–208.

———. "Purposes of Descriptive Bibliography, with Some Remarks on Methods," *Library*, 5th ser., 8 (1953): 1–22.

Dearing, Vinton A. *A Manual of Textual Analysis*. Berkeley, 1959.

———. "Some Routines for Textual Criticism," *Library*, 5th ser., 21 (1966): 309–17.

Foxon, David. "Modern Aids to Bibliographical Research," *Library Trends* 7 (1959): 574–81.

———. *Thomas J. Wise and the Pre-Restoration Drama: A Study in Theft and Sophistication*. London, 1959.

Foxon, David, and William B. Todd. "*Thomas J. Wise and the Pre-Restoration Drama*: A Supplement," *Library*, 5th ser., 16 (1961): 287–93.

Greg, W. W. *Collected Papers*, ed. J. C. Maxwell. Oxford, 1966.

Halsband, Robert. "Editing the Letters of Letter-Writers," *SB* 11 (1958): 25–37.

Hill, Archibald A. "Some Postulates for Distributional Study of Texts," *SB* 3 (1951): 63–95.

Hinman, C. J. K. "Mechanized Collation at the Houghton Library," *Harvard Library Bulletin* 9 (1955): 132–34.

Jackson, W. A. *Bibliography and Literary Studies*. Los Angeles, 1962.

Leary, Lewis. "Bibliographical and Textual Studies and American Literary History," *Texas Quarterly* 3 (1960): 160–66.

McKerrow, Ronald B. *An Introduction to Bibliography for Literary Students*. Oxford, 1927.

Ray, Gordon N. "The Importance of Original Editions," *Nineteenth-Century English Books*, ed. Gordon N. Ray, *et al.*, pp. 3–24. Urbana, 1952.

335

Statement of Editorial Principles: A Working Manual For Editing Nineteenth Century American Texts. Center for Editions of American Authors, Modern Language Association of America, July 1967.

Stevenson, A. H. Observations on Paper as Evidence. Lawrence, Kan., 1961.

————. "Papers as Bibliographical Evidence," Library, 5th ser., 17 (1962): 197–212.

EIGHTEENTH CENTURY

Battestin, Martin C. "Fielding's Revisions of Joseph Andrews," SB 16 (1963): 81–118.

Bentley, G. E., Jr. "The Date of Blake's Pickering Manuscript or the Way of a Poet with Paper," SB 19 (1966): 232–43.

————. "Blake's Protean Text," Editing Eighteenth-Century Texts, ed. D. I. B. Smith. Toronto, 1968.

Bond, D. F. "The First Printing of the Spectator," Modern Philology 47 (1950): 164–77.

————. "The Text of the Spectator," SB 5 (1952): 109–28.

Bond, Richmond P. "The Pirate and the Tatler," Library 5th ser., 18 (1963): 257–74.

Bowers, Fredson. "The Text of Johnson," Modern Philology 61 (1964): 298–309.

Copeland, Thomas W. "Edmund Burke's Friends and The Annual Register," Library, 5th ser., 18 (1963): 29–39.

Craddock, Patricia B. "Gibbon's Revision of the Decline and Fall," SB 21 (1968): 191–204.

Dawson, Giles E. "Warburton, Hanmer, and the 1745 Edition of Shakespeare," SB 2 (1950): 35–48.

Eaves, T. C. Duncan, and Ben D. Kimpel. "Richardson's Revisions of Pamela," SB 20 (1967): 61–88.

Eddy, Donald D. "Dodsley's Collection of Poems by Several Hands (Six Volumes), 1758 Index of Authors," PBSA 60 (1966): 9–30.

Fleeman, J. D. "Johnson's 'Journey' (1775), and Its Cancels," PBSA 58 (1964): 232–38.

————. "The Making of Johnson's Life of Savage, 1744," Library 5th ser., 22 (1967): 346–52.

Foxon, D. F. "The Printing of Lyrical Ballads, 1798," Library, 5th ser., 9 (1954): 221–41.

Gaskell, Philip. "Printing the Classics in the Eighteenth Century," Book Collector 1 (1952): 98–111.

————. "Notes on Eighteenth-Century British Paper," Library 5th ser., 12 (1957): 34–42.

Haig, Robert L. "New Light on the King's Printing Office, 1680–1730," SB 13 (1956): 157–67.

Bibliography

Hemlow, Joyce. "The Diaries and Journals of Mme. D'Arblay," *Editing Eighteenth-Century Texts*, ed. D. I. B. Smith. Toronto, 1968.

Hernlund, Patricia. "William Strahan's Ledgers: Standard Charges for Printing, 1738–1785," *SB* 20 (1967): 89–111.

———. "William Strahan's Ledgers, II: Charges for Papers, 1738–1785," *SB* 22 (1969): 179–95.

Jenkins, Clauston. "The Ford Changes and the Text of *Gulliver's Travels*," *PBSA* 62 (1968): 1–23.

Keast, W. R. "The Preface to *A Dictionary of the English Language*: Johnson's Revision and the Establishment of the Text," *SB* 5 (1953): 129–46.

Leed, Jacob. "Some Reprintings of the *Gentleman's Magazine*," *SB* 17 (1964): 210–14.

Mack, Maynard. "Two Variant Copies of Pope's Works . . . Volume II: Further Light on Some Problems of Authorship, Bibliography, and Text," *Library*, 5th ser., 12 (1957): 48–53.

McKenzie, D. F. "Press Figures: A Case History of 1701–1703," *Transactions, Cambridge Bibliographical Society* 3 (1959–1963): 32–46.

Miller, C. William. "Franklin's *Poor Richard Almanacs*: Their Printing and Publication," *SB* 14 (1961): 97–115.

Mossner, E. C., and Harry Ransom. "Hume and the 'Conspiracy of the Booksellers': The Publication and Early Fortunes of the *History of England*," *University of Texas Studies in English* 29 (1950): 162–82.

Povey, Kenneth. "On the Diagnosis of Half-sheet Impositions," *Library*, 5th ser., 11 (1956): 268–72.

———. "A Century of Press-Figures," *Library*, 5th ser., 14 (1959): 251–73.

———. "Working to Rule, 1600–1800: A Study of Pressmen's Practice," *Library*, 5th ser., 20 (1965): 13–54.

Povey, Kenneth, and I. J. C. Foster. "Turned Chain-lines," *Library*, 5th ser., 5 (1950): 184–200.

Stillinger, Jack. "Dwight's *Triumph of Infidelity*: Text and Interpretation," *SB* 15 (1962): 259–66.

Tanselle, G. Thomas. "Early American Fiction in England: The Case of *The Algerine Captive*," *PBSA* 59 (1965): 367–84.

Todd, William B. "The Early Issues of *The Monk*, with a Bibliography," *SB* 2 (1950): 3–24.

———. "Concurrent Printing: An Analysis of Dodsley's *Collections of Poems by Several Hands*," *PBSA* 46 (1952): 45–57.

———. "The Bibliographical History of Burke's *Reflections on the Revolution in France*," *Library*, 5th ser., 6 (1951): 100–108.

———. "Concealed Editions of Samuel Johnson," *Book Collector* 2 (1953): 59–65.

———. "Quadruple Imposition: An Account of Goldsmith's *Traveller*," *SB* 7 (1955): 103–11.

———. "The First Editions of *The Good Natur'd Man* and *She Stoops to Conquer*," *SB* 11 (1958): 133–42.

———. "A Bibliographical Account of *The Gentleman's Magazine*, 1731–1754," *SB* 18 (1965): 81 109

Vieth, D. M. "A Textual Paradox: Rochester's 'To a Lady in a Letter,'" *PBSA* 54 (1960): 147–62.

Wiles, Roy M. "Dates in English Imprints, 1700–52," *Library*, 5th ser., 12 (1957): 190–93.

NINETEENTH CENTURY

Adams, Raymond. "The Bibliographical History of Thoreau's *Week on the Concord and Merrimack Rivers*," *PBSA* 43 (1949): 39–47.

Altick, Richard D. "From Aldine to Everyman: Cheap Reprint Series of the English Classics 1830–1906," *SB* 11 (1958): 3–24.

———. "English Publishing and the Mass Audience in 1852," *SB* 6 (1954): 1–24.

Birch, Brian. "Henry James: Some Bibliographical and Textual Matters," *Library*, 5th ser., 20 (1965): 108–23.

Blair, Walter. "When Was *Huckleberry Finn* Written," *American Literature* 30 (1958): 1–25.

Bond, W. H. "The Publication of *Alice's Adventures in Wonderland*," *Harvard Library Bulletin* 10 (1956): 306–24.

Bowers, Fredson. "The Earliest Manuscript of Whitman's 'Passage to India' and its Notebook," *Bulletin of the New York Public Library* 61 (1957): 319–52.

Carter, Paul J., Jr. "Olivia Clemens Edits *Following the Equator*," *American Literature* 30 (1958): 192–209.

Cauthen, I. B., Jr. "Poe's *Alone*: Its Background, Source, and Manuscripts," *SB* 3 (1951): 284–91.

Charvat, William. "Melville and the Common Reader," *SB* 12 (1959): 41–57.

Coxe, Campbell R. "The Pre-Publication Printings of Tarkington's *Penrod*," *SB* 5 (1953): 153–57.

Edel, Leon. "The Text of *The Ambassadors*," *Harvard Library Bulletin* 14 (1960): 453–60.

Gettman, Royal A. "Colburn-Bentley and the March of Intellect," *SB* 9 (1957): 197–213.

Hill, Hamlin. "Toward A Critical Text of *The Gilded Age*," *PBSA* 59 (1965): 142–49.

Johnson, Thomas H. "Establishing a Text: The Emily Dickinson Papers," *SB* 5 (1953): 21–32.

Bibliography

Kramer, Dale. "Two 'New' Texts of Thomas Hardy's *The Wood-landers*," *SB* 20 (1967): 135–50.

Krause, Sidney J. "James's Revisions of the Style of *The Portrait of a Lady*," *American Literature* 30 (1958): 67–88.

Laurence, Dan H. "A Bibliographical Novitiate: In Search of Henry James," *PBSA* 52 (1958): 23–33.

Maurer, Oscar. " 'My Squeamish Public': Some Problems of Victorian Magazine Publishers and Editors," *SB* 12 (1959): 21–40.

Metzdorf, R. F. "The Publishing History of Richard Henry Dana's *Two Years Before the Mast*," *Harvard Library Bulletin* 7 (1953): 313–32.

Nowell-Smith, Simon. "Signatures in Some Nineteenth-Century Massachusetts Duodecimos: A Query," *Library*, 5th ser., 3 (1949): 58–62. Answer: William A. Jackson and A. T. Hazen, ibid., 3 (1949): 224–29.

———. "The Printing of George Meredith's *The amazing marriage*," *Library*, 5th ser., 21 (1966): 300–8.

Rosenbaum, S. P. "Emily Dickinson and the Machine," *SB* 18 (1965): 207–27.

Scott, A. L. "Mark Twain's Revisions of *The Innocents Abroad* for the British Edition of 1872," *American Literature* 25 (1953): 43–61.

Schweitzer, Joan. "The Chapter Numbering in *Oliver Twist*," *PBSA* 60 (1966): 337–43.

Shanley, J. L. *The Making of 'Walden' with the Text of the First Version*. Chicago, 1957.

Shannon, Edgar F., Jr. "The History of a Poem: Tennyson's *Ode on the Death of the Duke of Wellington*," *SB* 13 (1960): 149–77.

Steele, Oliver L. "On the Imposition of the First Edition of Hawthorne's *The Scarlet Letter*," *Library*, 5th ser., 17 (1962): 250–55.

Stevens, Joan. " 'Woodcuts dropped into the Text': the Illustrations in *The Old Curiosity Shop* and *Barnaby Rudge*," *SB* 20 (1967): 113–34.

Walts, Robert W. "William Dean Howells and His 'Library Edition,' " *PBSA* 52 (1958): 283–94.

Woof, R. S. "Wordsworth's Poetry and Stuart's Newspapers: 1797–1803," *SB* 15 (1962): 149–89.

Twentieth Century

Adams, Robert M. "Light on Joyce's *Exiles*? A New MS, a Curious Analogue, and Some Speculations," *SB* 17 (1964): 83–105.

Beaurline, L. A. "*The Glass Menagerie*: From Story to Play," *Modern Drama* 8 (1965): 142–49.

Bruccoli, Matthew J. "Textual Variants in Sinclair Lewis' *Babbitt*," *SB* 11 (1958): 263–68.

———. "A Mirror for Bibliographers: Duplicate Plates in Modern Printing," *PBSA* 54 (1960): 83–88.

Bruccoli, Matthew J. "Material for a Centenary Edition of *Tender is the Night*," *SB* 17 (1964): 177–93.

Bruccoli, Matthew J., and Charles A. Rheault, Jr. "Imposition Figures and Plate Gangs in [Conrad's] *The Rescue*," *SB* 14 (1961): 258–62.

Meriwether, James B. "The English Editions of James Gould Cozzens," *SB* 15 (1962): 207–17.

Meriwether, James B., et al. "Bibliographical and Textual Studies of Twentieth-Century Writers," *Approaches to the Study of Twentieth-Century Literature*, pp. 35–51. East Lansing, 1961.

Scholes, Robert E. "Some Observations on the Text of *Dubliners:* 'The Dead,'" *SB* 15 (1962): 191–205.

———. "Further Observations on the Text of *Dubliners*," *SB* 17 (1964): 107–22.

Skipp, Francis E. "The Editing of *Look Homeward, Angel*," *PBSA* 57 (1963): 1–13.

Steele, Oliver L. "Half-Sheet Imposition of Eight-Leaf Quires in Formes of Thirty-two and Sixty-four Pages," *SB* 15 (1962): 274–78.

———. "Evidence of Plate Damage As Applied to the First Impression of Ellen Glasgow's *The Wheel of Life* (1906)," *SB* 16 (1963): 223–31.

Tanselle, G. Thomas. "Ficke's *Sonnets of a Portrait-Painter:* Textual Problems in a Modern Poet," *Yale University Library Gazette* 36 (1961): 33–39.

White, William. "*A Shropshire Lad* in Process," *Library*, 5th ser., 9 (1954): 255–64.

Woodward, Daniel H. "Notes on the Publishing History and Text of *The Waste Land*," *PBSA* 58 (1964): 252–69.

Wyllie, John C. "The Forms of Twentieth-Century Cancels," *PBSA* 47 (1953): 95–112.

———. "Bledsoe's 'Is Davis A Traitor?' A Note on an Imprint Changed without Cancellation," *PBSA* 52 (1958): 220.

INDEX

Accidentals: in authoritative text, 195; in copy-text, 48; cumulative effect of, 245; definition of, 43; Greg's differentiation of, 60; in manuscripts, 44; reaction to by scribes, 43–44; in revisions, 65–72. *See also* Editing, treatment of accidentals

Advertisements. *See* Newspaper advertisements

Aesthetics: and literary artifacts, 106–9; objects defined, 105–6

Archetype, 41, 92–94. *See also* Editing

Audience, nature of, 129

Authoritative editions, 8

Authorship: composite nature of, 123–24; in plays, 117–19

"Best text." *See* Texts

Bibliographical method, 5

Bibliographical Society, The, 7–8

Bibliography, analytical, new evidence for, 9

Bibliography, descriptive, 156

Bibliography, textual, new techniques of, 12

Bond, Donald F., ed., *The Spectator*, 10

Bowers, Fredson, 14, 15, 19, 227; ed., *The Dramatic Works of Thomas Dekker*, 8

British editions of American novels, 20. *See also* Revision

Browne, Sir Thomas: *Religio Medici*, 130

Bruccoli, Matthew J., 19, 20, 34; "Twentieth Century Books," 10

Center for Editions of American Authors, 13

Clemens, Samuel L.: *The Adventures of Tom Sawyer*, 204; *Christian Science*, 204; *A Connecticut Yankee in King Arthur's Court*, 205; *The Gilded Age*, 204; *Innocents Abroad*, 204; *Joan of Arc*, 205; *The Prince and the Pauper*, 204; *Roughing It*, 205; *A Tramp Abroad*, 205

Collation, 196–97

—, methods of: Chamberlin, 85; frame device, 85; machine, 196, 199–200; Manly-Rickert, 87; typescript of copy-text, 84–85. *See also* Dryden, John, California edition of; Hinman, Charles

Compositor: errors of, in *White Jacket*, 26–28, 102, 109; reaction to substantives and accidentals, 43–44; role in revision, 69–71. *See also* Revision, non-authorial

Computer language, 96

Computers: in editorial procedure, 93–95; instruction in, 96–98; programming, 96–97; recording variants with, 73; in textual studies, 17

Concealed printing, 197; methods of discovering, 19, 173, 235–38

Conrad, Joseph, *The Nigger of the Narcissus*, 25

Copy-text: archetype as, 92; author's manuscript as, 198; choice of, 72; in classical and biblical texts, 41–42; first editions as, 55, 188–89; general theory of, 14–15, 24–25, 46–48, 51–53, 60–64, 83, 195, 227;